Effective Supervision in School Psychology

Virginia Smith Harvey, Ph.D.
University of Massachusetts Boston

Joan A. Struzziero, Ph.D.
University of Massachusetts Boston
Whitman-Hanson Regional Schools, Massachusetts

Bethesda, MD | National Association of School Psychologists | 2000

Copies may be ordered from
NASP Publications
4340 East West Highway, Suite 402
Bethesda, MD 20814
(301) 657-0270
(301) 657-0275, fax
e-mail: *publications@naspweb.org*
www.naspweb.org

ISBN 0-932955-94-0

Printed in the United States of America

First Printing, Spring 2000

10 9 8 7 6 5 4 3 2 1

From the NASP Publications Board Operations Manual
The content of this document reflects the ideas and positions of the authors. The responsibility lies solely with the authors and does not necessarily reflect the position or ideas of the National Association of School Psychologists.

Abstract

Effective Supervision in School Psychology is a comprehensive treatment of the supervision of school psychologists. It is useful for field supervisors of school psychology interns, school psychologists acting as supervising school psychologists, and graduate students enrolled in a supervision course. Because of the book's emphasis on human development, effective management strategies, case examples, and ethical dilemmas, it is particularly relevant to those new to the supervisory role. Case studies, exercises, supervisory protocols, and suggestions are provided to facilitate the development of supervisory expertise. In addition, examples of pertinent ethical dilemmas provide opportunities for exercises in supervisory problem solving.

Table of Contents

About the Authors

Virginia Smith Harvey, Ph.D., is Associate Professor, Associate Dean, and former Director of the School Psychology program at the University of Massachusetts Boston. She was a practicing school psychologist for 18 years, and supervised school psychology interns and school psychologists throughout those years. During her six years as a university professor she has supervised practicum, intern, and post-graduate students. She has researched the functioning of school psychologists, and has published articles on improving readability of psychological reports and providing a system of care for students through interagency collaboration. Dr. Harvey was co-chair of the ethics committee of the Massachusetts Association of School Psychologists from 1993 through 1998.

Joan A. Struzziero, Ph.D., is a Clinical Lecturer at the University of Massachusetts Boston and has been employed for ten years as a school psychologist in the Whitman-Hanson Regional Schools in Massachusetts. She has supervised school psychology interns as both a university and field supervisor, and has been a supervisor for the Global School Psychology Network. She also has recent experience receiving supervision as a doctoral intern and post-doctoral fellow. Dr. Struzziero is co-chair of the ethics committee of the Massachusetts Association of School Psychologists.

Acknowlegements and Dedication

We have many individuals to acknowledge and thank for direct and indirect contributions to this book. These include our supervisors and mentors, past and present, particularly Gail Barringer, Cynthia Chase, Richard Clark, Vin Cristiani, Lou Kruger, Stu Swenson, and Sam Toto. We also would like to thank our manuscript reviewers and editors, who provided invaluable comments and suggestions: Fred Grossman, Sawyer Hunley, Veronica Lewis, Gayle Macklem, Leslie Paige, Lesley Portnoy, and Bethany Riddle. In addition, we would like to thank our students and collegues at the University of Massachusetts Boston and in our respective school districts, all of whom unknowingly contributed to our professional growth.

We would like to dedicate this book to our families, without whose love, support, and encouragement our profesional lives would not have been possible. Ginny Harvey particularly thanks Karen Harvey, Anne Duncan, Mary Smith, Theresa Olinger, Bobby Smith, Paul Smith, and Cathy Strate. Joan Struzziero would like to particularly thank Richard Stuzziero, Rick Stuzziero, and Alison Stuzziero.

ix

Introduction

This book grew out of the authors' experiences supervising school psychologists, practicum students, and interns. School psychologists typically first think of themselves as supervisors when they supervise interns, or supervise others working toward licensure. In addition, many school psychologists assume broad supervisory activities when they are named as chief, lead, or supervising school psychologists when districts have more than one psychologist. In truth, all practicing school psychologists perform a supervisory function in that they monitor their successes and direct their own professional development.

This book was written to meet the needs of individuals in any of these positions, and has the underlying premise that the practice of school psychology would improve if supervisors were more systematically educated. As supervisors, and in preparing this book, we read and utilized clinical, business, and educational supervision materials as well as our own experiential learning.

Our profession is complex and difficult to practice when isolated from others. Therefore, school psychologists need regular feedback to ensure the services they provide are appropriate. Other similar professions, such as social work and clinical psychology, have long recognized the importance of ongoing clinical supervision to obtain such feedback.

However, school psychology differs from social work and clinical psychology in ways that render clinical supervision alone insufficient. School psychology is unique in at least two aspects:

1. School psychology is multifaceted, composed not only of direct interventions (such as therapy) but also indirect interventions (such as consultation), assessment, and program evaluation. The contemporary role is too complex for training programs to adequately address. Supervisors help school psychologists develop in all areas of professional practice, and ensure that supervisees constantly keep abreast of emerging knowledge, research, and skills.

2. School psychology takes place in the context of the schools, and this context renders supervision of school psychologists even more complex. The logo of the National Association of School Psychologists depicts two interlocking circles: one containing the Greek letter psi (for psychology), and the other containing the lamp of learning (for education). Given the strength of the relationship between school psychology and the disciplines of both psychology and education, effective supervision encompasses best supervisory practices in both fields.

Unfortunately, supervision of school psychologists is not mandated in most states and therefore frequently does not occur. Therefore, many supervisors have never experienced adequate supervision beyond the internship experience. Even in situations where supervision does occur, such as in the supervision of interns or in large districts with a designated supervisor, chances are high that the designated supervisor has not received training in supervision, much less supervision in supervision.

This volume is based upon three premises:

1. The supervision of school psychologists is important in all aspects of practice to

improve services and to prevent professional stagnation.

2. Effective supervision of school psychologists encompasses the best supervisory practices of both psychology and education.

3. Because supervision will lead to improved services, a model of school psychology supervision will benefit the profession of school psychology and consequently the children we serve.

AUTHORS' ORIENTATIONS

Given that the authors' ideas greatly affect material presented, the ideas that support this volume will be explicitly stated at this time.

Premise 1. School psychologists can profoundly influence the lives of children and adolescents. Effective and ethically sound training, evaluation, and supervision procedures are critical. As Bowser (1995) indicates, school psychologists encounter ethical challenges almost daily. Supervisors of school psychology are similarly ethically challenged on a regular basis. The many examples of ethical dilemmas posed in the following pages were all experienced by school psychology supervisors.

Ethical principles for supervisors of school psychologists reflect the same fundamental ethical principles as for all mental health professionals: (1) respect the client, (2) provide competent services, (3) maintain integrity, and (4) be responsible to the community and society (Jacob-Timm & Hart-shorne, 1998). Regarding the child as the primary client underlies all school psychology practice and so rightly underlies the supervision of school psychologists.

Premise 2. Decisions are best when data based. This extends, into the realm of supervision, the concept of school psychologists as "data based decision makers" who act as "scientists" of the school system. Although there is not a broad base of theoretical or research literature on the supervision of school psychology, substantial literature on supervision exists in counseling psychology, industrial/organizational psychology, and education. Therefore, the following chapters draw upon this literature. The orientation toward data based decisions is also evident in the emphasis on the development of research and program evaluation skills in supervisees, and in the extensive consideration of the evaluation of school psychologists and school psychology programs.

Premise 3. School psychologists progress through developmental stages in learning, self-knowledge, and skill acquisition. Various skills in school psychology, although related, are independently developed. Thus a school psychologist may be an "advanced beginner" in one area, such as crisis intervention counseling, and simultaneously "proficient" in another area, such as curriculum based measurement. A major responsibility of supervisors is to facilitate the professional development of their supervisees, and of themselves, in all areas.

Premise 4. Effective supervision of school psychologists depends equally upon three components: conceptual skills, interpersonal skills, and technical skills. Effective supervisors of school psychologists develop a broad based and systemic understanding of the broader context in which the school psychologists practice. They also maintain a systemic conceptual understanding of the role of their supervisees. Interpersonal skills required of a supervisor are based on the foundation of interpersonal skills used in consultation, assessment, and the provision of direct services as a school psychologist. In addition, effective supervisors of school psychologists develop additional interpersonal and communication skills specific to their supervisory role, such as teaching skills.

The technical skills required of school psychology supervisors are extensive. They must have a grasp of administrative supervision, yet also maintain exemplary technical skills in the major domains of school psychology: indirect interventions, direct interventions, assessment, and program evaluation/research.

Effective supervision of school psychologists is eclectic, as warranted by the needs of a situation, and addresses both administrative and professional practice issues. It is most effectively systemic and problem-solving in orientation. It considers supervisory issues of primary concern in both of the foundation fields: education and psychology. Thus the context in which school psychology is practiced, as well as the individual relationship between the supervisee and client, is considered.

School psychology and supervision are dynamic, as are all systems and systemic relationships. The choice of strategy takes into account internal and external strengths and weaknesses, which then alters the structure of supervision, professional development, and service delivery. The altered structure, in turn, modifies strengths and weaknesses and consequently changes the strategies of choice. This again affects structure. Thus effective supervisory practice considers the context in which it occurs, affects that context, and is subsequently revised within the changed context (Chandler, 1962). Each component feeds into and affects the next:

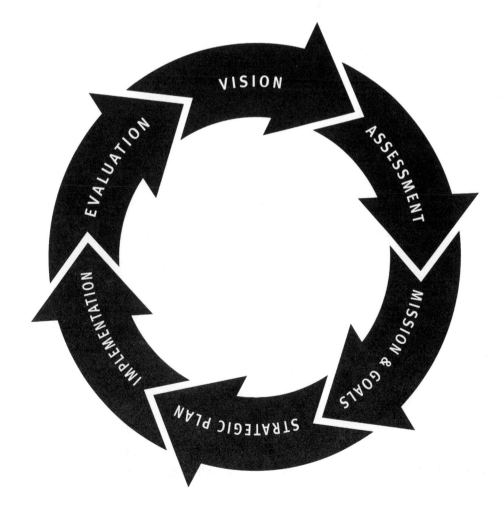

Organization of this Book

This book is organized into fifteen chapters. Throughout the book the reader is provided information on three levels: theories that undergird the topic, relevant policies such as ethical frameworks and integration of multicultural issues, and potential practices including concrete examples and ethical dilemmas that relate to the theories and practices.

Chapter 1 addresses general issues in the supervision of school psychologists: the definition and goals of supervision, and legal and ethical issues. Chapter 2 addresses communication and interpersonal skills required of supervisors, including those aspects of interpersonal skills affected by diversity. Chapter 3 discusses pertinent supervisory models, theories, and techniques. Chapters 4 through 8 address the technical skills required of administrative supervision: planning, personnel selection, individual evaluation, training and professional development, and promoting job satisfaction. Chapters 9 through 13 address the technical skills required in professional, or clinical, supervision of direct interventions, indirect interventions, assessment, research and program evaluation, and grant writing. Chapter 14 addresses the assessment and promotion of school psychological services, while Chapter 15 addresses supervisor development and evaluation. The appendix includes the NASP Standards: Training, Field Placement, and Credentialing and the NASP Professional Conduct Manual.

Ethical dilemma 1-1

You have been working as a school psychologist for ten years, and feel reasonably capable and competent in the position. One of your schools enters into an agreement with a nearby university to become a Professional Development School, which means that you are now expected to supervise interns. You feel that the supervision you received as an intern was excellent, but that was a long time ago. You are not sure your skills are completely up to date, you no longer have a supervisor, and you have neither had a course in supervision nor ever worked in a setting in which you received supervision, other than your internship. You feel that having interns would be exciting and enriching, but are concerned that you are being asked to practice in an area beyond your expertise. *What are the ethical issues? What steps should you take?*

The National Association of School Psychologists' Supervision Work Group (1998) defines the supervision of school psychology as "an ongoing, positive, systemic, collaborative process between a school psychologist and school psychology supervisor that focuses on promoting professional growth and exemplary professional practice leading to improved performance of all concerned--school psychologist, supervisor, students, and the entire school community" (p. 1). As this definition reveals, the supervision of school psychology is as complex and multifaceted as the field of school psychology itself. Supervision of school psychologists entails both administrative and professional supervision, all within the context of multiple systems.

The supervision of school psychologists can be thought of as having four primary goals. First, supervision provides leadership for the school psychology supervisees. Second, supervision improves the functioning of supervised school psychologists. Third, supervision protects the clients the school psychologists serve. Finally, supervision enhances the ability of each school psychologist to critically examine practice, make appropriate professional decisions independently, and learn to self-supervise (Knoff, 1986).

Supervisors help supervisees cope with the rapidly changing knowledge base and ever expanding technology essential to the responsible practice of school psychology. They serve as a link between school psychological services, the school administration, and constituent groups. Supervisors also help their supervisees sustain interpersonal skills and maintain objectivity in the face of potential bias and covert pressures (Knoff, 1986).

Supervisors of school psychologists share professional responsibility and accountability for the services provided by school psychologists under their supervision. Although supervision bears many similarities to consultation and training, it is unique in that it occurs over an extended time and includes an evaluative component (Bernard & Goodyear, 1998). As Crespi and Fischetti (1997) indicate, "supervision represents one of the critical ingredients in the training and development of mental health personnel" (p. 41).

STANDARDS FOR SUPERVISION

Standards for psychological supervision

The emphasis on supervision of therapists, including clinical psychologists, counselors, and

1

social workers, can be traced to the intensive supervision provided in the training of Freudian analysts. In general, therapists' supervision focuses on the relationship between the therapist and client. Supervision in social work, counseling, and clinical psychology has been extensively addressed in both journals and books (Bernard & Goodyear, 1998; Boylan, Malley, & Scott, 1995; Hess, 1980; Kadushin, 1985; Robiner & Schofield, 1990; Stoltenberg & Delworth, 1987; Stoltenberg, McNeill, & Delworth, 1998; Storm & Todd, 1997; Todd & Storm, 1997).

The American Counseling Association, the major counseling professional organization, has written and adopted standards for the provision of clinical supervision (Dye & Border, 1990). These standards delineate eleven core areas of knowledge and competence:

- training and supervised experience as a counselor;
- personal traits consistent with the role of a supervisor;
- mastery of the ethical, legal, and regulatory aspects of the profession;
- conceptual and applied knowledge of the supervisory relationship;
- knowledge of supervision methods and techniques;
- knowledge of the counselor development process;
- skills in case conceptualization and management;
- skills in client assessment and evaluation;
- oral and written reporting and recording skills;
- skills in the evaluation of counselors;
- knowledge about research in counseling and supervision.

The standards also recommend extensive supervised experience before sequenced training in supervision, ongoing continuing education, and participation in research on the effectiveness of supervision (Supervision Interest Network, 1990). The counseling supervision literature also includes extensive discussions regarding the ethics of supervision (Kessler, 1998; Pope & Vetter, 1992; Sherry, 1991; Storm & Haug, 1997; Vasquez, 1992).

Standards for educational supervision

The literature regarding educational supervision is even more long standing and voluminous than that of supervision in clinical and counseling psychology, for it stems from the mid-19th century (Firth & Pajak, 1994; Krajewski, 1996). A great deal of the literature in educational supervision is identified as both "administrative supervision" and "professional" or "clinical" supervision.

Much of educational supervision literature borrows from business management literature, which in turn incorporates industrial/organizational psychology research. Throughout the last 150 years the focus of educational supervision has moved, as has the focus of business management, from the "scientific management" approach, through "interactive," "cooperative," "curricular," "clinical," "peer supervision," "coaching/instructional," "collaborative," "outcome," and "effectiveness measurement" approaches (Krajewski, 1996; Noe, Hollenbeck, Gerhart, & Wright, 1996; Rue & Byars, 1997; Wise, 1994). The primary focus of educational supervision is on assessing and improving the skills of the educator within the context of the school setting, so that pupil growth and learning is improved. Sergiovanni and Starratt (1998) indicate that good educational supervision is:

- based on a philosophical and theoretical orientation and respects personality and individual differences;
- based on the assumption that supervisees are capable of growth;
- focused on leadership rather than authority;
- characterized by dynamic and data based problem solving approaches;

- marked by creativity rather than prescriptions; and,
- judged by the results it secures.

The "span of management" referred to in business literature is the number of supervisees a manager can effectively supervise. Urwick (1938) originally indicated that no one should attempt to supervise more than six individuals at a time. More recent literature suggests that this number is not absolute, but is reduced by the complexity and variety of jobs held by the supervisees and increased by physical proximity and high personnel quality (Rue & Byars, 1997). This figure is much lower than the number of supervisees typically supervised in school settings. For example, in a school of 500 children one principal probably attempts to supervise more than 30 individuals (20 teachers, a half dozen special service and support personnel, and several secretaries and custodians). Similarly, in a classroom a teacher is expected to supervise the learning of 25 children at a time. The level of supervision possible with ratios of 25:1 and 30:1 is reminiscent of industrial factories and is far below the level of supervision appropriate for complex settings.

Standards for school psychological supervision

Some standards for the provision of school psychology supervision have been promoted by the National Association of School Psychologists (1994, 1997) and the American Psychological Association (1981, 1992). Interestingly, the two organizations agree on some aspects and disagree on other aspects of supervision.

Regarding the frequency and duration of supervision, both NASP and APA standards and ethical guidelines assert the importance of regular, on-going supervision beyond the school psychology internship. Both organizations view supervision as a lifelong professional endeavor, although APA is more prescriptive than NASP.

NASP Standards (1994) recommend that school psychologists receive one to two hours of face-to-face supervision weekly for at least the first three years of practice and recommend that supervision should be available to all practitioners throughout their careers. APA indicates that non-doctoral school psychologists should receive weekly face-to-face sessions throughout their careers.

In addressing the qualifications of supervisors, both APA and NASP assert that it is imperative that supervision be provided by individuals qualified as school psychologists. NASP also asserts that the development, implementation, professional supervision, and evaluation of school psychological services be the responsibility of a school psychologist. The APA (1981) specialty guidelines indicate that doctoral level school psychologists should provide the supervision. The National Association of School Psychologists' Supervision Work Group (1998) suggests that a supervisor of school psychologists be a Nationally Certified School Psychologist, designated as a Supervisor or Lead Psychologist (except when restricted to supervising interns), hold a state school psychologist credential, and have at least three years of successful, documented, supervised experience as a school psychologist in settings appropriately relevant for those being supervised.

Both APA and NASP address the recommended ratio of supervisors to school psychologists. NASP indicates that one person should not supervise more than two interns or ten school psychologists simultaneously; APA indicates that one person should not supervise more than 15 supervisees at a time.

Despite generalized agreement on the importance of supervision in professional standards, multiple studies (Fischetti & Crespi, 1999; Ross & Goh, 1993; Welsh & Stout, 1993; Wenger & Pryzwansky, 1987; Zins, Murphy, & Wess, 1989) have found that school psychologists do not receive supervision. It is especially noteworthy

3

that the school psychology literature has relatively neglected the topic. Two state departments of education compiled handbooks for supervisors of school psychologists (Grimes & Happe, 1987; Wisconsin State Department of Instruction, 1989). Chapters in NASP's *Best Practices in School Psychology-III* contribute to the area (Conoley & Bahns, 1995; Fowler & Harrison, 1995; Franklin, 1995; Green, 1995; Talley, 1990; Thomas, 1995). Additionally, some journal articles (for example: Alessi, Lascurettes-Alessi, & Leyes, 1981; Beger, 1993; Bowser, 1981; Crespi & Fischetti, 1997; Curtis & Yager, 1987; Fischetti & Crespi, 1999; Knoff, 1986; Romans, Boswell, Carlozzi, & Ferguson, 1995; Sheridan, Salmon, Kratochwill, & Carrington Rotto, 1992; Zins, Murphy, & Wess, 1989) and dissertations (for example: Borden, 1992; Buehler, 1986; Haynes, 1993; Irvine, 1993; Rubenstein, 1993) have addressed the supervision of school psychologists. Yet, compared to the voluminous literature in counseling and clinical psychology as well as the literature in educational supervision, the material available regarding the supervision of school psychologists is sparse.

Besides focusing on administrative (evaluative) supervision, the supervisor of school psychologists must address professional components unique to the provision of school psychological services. These include the provision of indirect services, direct services, assessments, and program evaluations and research. This becomes problematic because individuals who are not credentialed as school psychologists frequently supervise school psychologists (Crespi & Fischetti, 1997).

Within the psychology supervision literature, there is no consensus about whether the same individual can provide both administrative and professional supervision. When one person takes both roles, it may result in dual relationships leading to supervisees' reluctance to reveal shortcomings to their evaluators (Bernard & Goodyear, 1998). On the other hand, as Mead (1990) points out, supervision invariably includes an evaluative

component, whether it results in the opportunity to continue in an academic program, to continue employment, or to receive a pay raise as a result of superior performance.

In truth, supervisors in all fields (including education) experience role conflict when acting as both evaluators and growth facilitators. Balancing both roles requires highly advanced interpersonal skills, acute ethical sensibilities, and vigilance in safeguarding client welfare.

Both Division 16 of APA and NASP indicate that both administrative (e.g. evaluative) and professional supervision should be provided by a qualified school psychologist. However, in a school system it is rarely possible to have two school psychologists acting as supervisors, one providing administrative supervision and another providing professional supervision. If the responsibilities are divided, it usually results in a non-school psychologist acting as the administrative supervisor, and consequently an individual insufficiently knowledgeable about professional practice and standards performing an evaluative function. Although a school administrator, such as a principal, may provide elements of administrative supervision, only an individual trained as a school psychologist can provide adequate professional, or clinical, supervision and evaluation.

Ethical dilemma 1-2

A school psychology department is co-supervised by a school psychologist and the director of special education. The director does not have training as a school psychologist, but did have some training in assessment. She is insisting that regardless of the presenting problem, the school psychologists use a standard battery of tests for all assessments: the Woodcock Johnson Cognitive and Achievement, and the BASC. *What are the ethical and legal dilemmas? What steps should be taken?*

It has been suggested that only individuals who are currently providing direct services themselves, and thus dealing with problems similar to those experienced by the staff, can provide effective professional supervision (Disenhouse, 1987). Individuals who have recently been practitioners, such as recently retired school psychologists, probably have fairly clear memories of practitioner issues, but those who have not practiced for a period of time probably do not. Whether administrative and professional supervision are provided by one individual (acting as administrative and professional supervisor), or by two individuals, efforts must be made to overcome the inevitable conflicts between professional standards and administrative directives (Pennington, 1989). The "unity of command" principle indicates that each supervisee should have only one immediate supervisor (Rue & Byars, 1997). But this is highly unlikely to occur in practice, because building principals almost always feel some right to supervise school psychologists assigned to their building.

BASIC SKILLS NEEDED FOR SUPERVISION

As mentioned previously, Katz (1955) identified three cardinal supervisory skills: technical skills (the ability to perform specific tasks using knowledge, methods, and techniques), interpersonal skills (the ability to work with people), and conceptual skills (the ability to take a systemic approach in viewing the broader context of the organization, culture, and environment). Each of these areas, as related to school psychology, will be described in greater detail.

"Supervisor development" is fostering attitudes and skills necessary to become an effective supervisor. Effective supervisor development is designed, conducted, and evaluated in accordance with professional standards and the school district's objectives. As indicated by Illback and Morrissey (1985), many professionals placed in supervisory roles have neither the training nor experience to provide effective supervision. Novice supervisors are often not experienced in budgeting, planning, evaluating, implementing programs, or managing personnel to promote effective programming for children.

Ross and Goh (1993) indicate that, although "a majority of school psychologists supervise other school psychologists at some point in their careers" (p. 71), a survey of supervising school psychologists revealed that only 25% received graduate training in supervision, and only 11% received this training within their school psychology programs. The demonstrated need for more widespread training (Ross & Goh, 1993) is reiterated in the curriculum analyses of Brown and Minke (1986), which found that few school psychology training programs provided training in supervision.

Professional standards in school psychology indicate that school psychologists should not provide services for which they have not had adequate training. Similarly, school psychology supervisors should only supervise areas in which they themselves are at least proficient. The lack of training in supervision typical for school psychologists is in direct contrast to the fields of family therapy, counseling psychology, clinical psychology, and school administration, all of which provide training in and have developed a body of literature about supervision. Furthermore, the lack of training in supervision directly contradicts the dictates of professional organizations.

Minimum qualifications

Present and future supervisors of school psychologists should assess their own levels of technical skills, find ways to increase their levels of proficiency in less developed areas, and seek support from more proficient professionals when appropriate. Supervisors could use the same tools used to evaluate supervisees to assess their technical skills in the major school psychology skill areas,

5

remembering to include newly developed techniques and instruments when conducting such self-assessments.

An important aspect of technical skills is keeping abreast of current knowledge in all domains relevant to the field. Relevant areas of psychology include school psychology, educational psychology, neuropsychology, and developmental psychology. In addition, school psychologists must remain current in general and special education, particularly the subspecialties of learning disabilities and behavior disorders. A current knowledge base is important not only to maintain skills, but also to maintain the referent and expert power necessary for successful leadership. Maintaining referent and expert power requires not only learning new assessment instruments and regularly reading the *School Psychology Review* and *Communiqué.* but also doing substantial additional reading in journals such as *American Psychologist, Exceptional Children, Educational Leadership*, the *Educational Psychologist, Learning Disabilities: Research and Practice, Behavioral Disorders, Psychology in the Schools*. This reading obviously takes real time. It is, however, time well spent.

Additional technical skills required of supervisors to a greater degree than staff school psychologists are skills specific to leadership positions. These include, but are not limited to, skills in advocating for the profession, developing and evaluating programs, writing and implementing grants, and dealing with change at the systems level.

The interpersonal skills required by supervisors of school psychologists include those needed by school psychologists as they consult with teachers and parents. Additionally, supervisors need interpersonal skills relevant to other aspects of school psychology. Necessary interpersonal skills relevant to administrative supervision are delegating, motivating, teaching, and evaluating. Necessary interpersonal skills relevant to therapy include learning how to deal with transference and counter transference experienced by the supervisee.

Supervisors need teaching skills such as the ability to identify learning needs, write learning goals, devise instructional strategies, present material didactically and/or experientially, evaluate learning, be comfortable in an authority role, and give constructive comments. Individual self-appraisal and feedback from supervisees can be used to assess supervisors' teaching skills and the results used to facilitate professional development.

Supervisors of school psychologists should also assess their knowledge and commitment to ethics. Supervisors demonstrate these traits in their knowledge of ethical standards by enhancing their own skills in applying ethical principles in complex situations, by fostering the ethical development of supervisees, and by ensuring that non-exploitative relationships are maintained between themselves and supervisees as well as between supervisees and clients (Conoley & Bahns, 1995). Within the supervisory process, supervisors of school psychologists must have the sophistication to make clear the subtle distinctions between administrative supervision, professional supervision, and case management, and between supervision and consultation (Pennington, 1989).

Conceptual skills required by supervisors of school psychologists include the following: the ability to view the broad environmental context of their supervisees, the ability to identify which supervisory model and theories are closest to their own, and skill to find methods to deal with ethical dilemmas common to the supervision of school psychologists. As Pennington (1989) discusses, supervisors of school psychologists must also have a thorough knowledge of professional standards and the functions and responsibilities of school psychologists. In addition, they need thorough knowledge of the organizational structure and policies in education and the delegation of duties and responsibilities for the school systems in which they work.

Combining their technical, interpersonal, and conceptual skills enables supervisors to accomplish complex tasks. These include assuming responsibility for supervisees' work; developing and implementing procedures for the resolution of disputes between administrators, teachers, and school psychologists; developing and implementing appropriate procedures for recruitment, supervision, discipline, and discharge; and, developing and implementing accurate, fair, and objective methods of conducting performance and program evaluations of school psychologists (Pennington, 1989).

SUPERVISION GOALS

As indicated previously, school psychology supervision can be thought of as having four primary goals: providing leadership, enhancing the functioning of the supervisees, fostering self-supervision, and protecting clients.

Providing leadership

Leadership is the key to the advancement of a profession, and school psychology needs leaders to translate theory into the realities of school psychological service provision in a way that meets the ever-changing needs of schools and society (Talley, 1990).

Enhancing functioning

Enhancing the functioning of school psychologists is an essential goal of supervision. To be effective practitioners, school psychologists must constantly keep abreast of the new knowledge, research, and skills that emerge during their professional careers (Knoff, 1986). Professional performance can deteriorate through either lack of practice or through carelessness, resulting from constant use without corrective comments (Franklin, Stillman, Burpeau, & Sabers, 1982). Wiley and Ray (1986) found that supervised experience influences the growth of a therapist, while unsupervised experience is unrelated to such growth. Therefore, professional supervision appears to be essential for both skill

development and maintenance throughout an individual's career. As indicated by Bernard and Goodyear (1998), often the most troublesome employees are those with extensive, unsupervised human service work experience.

To facilitate skill development and maintenance, supervisors evaluate the current developmental level of supervisees for knowledge, skill, confidence, objectivity, and interpersonal interactions and then systematically facilitate the professional development of supervisees in each of these areas (Knoff, 1986). We readily acknowledge that graduate training cannot provide all attitudes, knowledge, and skills necessary to function optimally as a school psychologist. Even if it did, effective school psychologists need an organizational framework for lifelong professional development (Rosenfield, 1985).

Fostering self-supervision

Supervisors foster the ability of supervisees to appropriately seek and respond to supervision with the ultimate goal of self-sufficiency or the ability to self-supervise (Knoff, 1986; Todd, 1997b). When they self-supervise, school psychologists protect the welfare of clients by monitoring and improving their own performance so that it more closely resembles a more experienced practitioner and/or ideal, best practices service delivery model (Todd, 1997b).

As self-supervisors, school psychologists monitor their skills by self-applying supervisory techniques normally required with novice supervisees. These include taping and analyzing counseling, consultation, and assessment sessions; obtaining evaluative information from clients, teachers, and administrators; and conducting evaluations of services.

As they achieve self-sufficiency, school psychologists improve their ability to know when to seek consultation or supervision. A self-supervising school psychologist thus fosters a network of experienced school psychologists, counselors, special educators, and social workers with whom to consult.

Self-supervising school psychologists compare their functioning with the functioning described as best practices. Many NASP publications provide models of the best practice of school psychology, including the *School Psychology: A Blueprint for Training and Practice II* (Ysseldyke, Dawson, Lehr, Reschly, Reynolds, & Telzrow, 1997), *Best Practices in School Psychology III* (Thomas & Grimes, 1995), and the *NASP Professional Conduct Manual* (1997).

To work toward eventual self-sufficiency in supervisees, Todd (1997b), indicates that supervisors:

1. Make self-sufficiency a clear goal of supervision, and develop a clear description of the behaviors shown by a competent and self-sufficient school psychologist.

2. Assess the supervisees' strengths and areas of relative weakness systematically and explicitly, and develop small and specific learning goals related to areas of relative weakness.

3. Explore supervisees' learning styles by providing a wide range of supervisory activities and observing those which are most effective with a given supervisee.

4. Help supervisees develop a theoretical framework in which to function so that they can "critique...sessions and look for behaviors that would be considered errors within that framework" (Todd, 1997b, p. 21).

5. Encourage supervisees to arrive at supervision sessions with clearly defined goals and questions for the session.

6. Encourage supervisees to choose the materials to bring to supervisory sessions.

7. Encourage supervisees to obtain feedback from children, parents, and teachers regarding the effectiveness of their practice, and then use this feedback to improve their performance. For example, one method is to routinely conduct six-month follow-up evaluations (Storm, 1995, as cited in Todd, 1997b).

8. Use supervision sessions to generate alternative hypotheses and collaboratively brainstorm rather than to give the supervisee "correct" answers.

9. Ask supervisees what they anticipate the supervisor will ask or recommend before either asking questions or making recommendations.

10. Encourage supervisees to develop skills in both generalizing from one case to another and differentiating one case from another. Ultimately, supervisees should be able to determine when it is appropriate for them to generalize and continue a particular form of service delivery and when they should differentiate from the form of service delivery promoted by their supervisor or any other source.

11. Obtain structured feedback on the supervisory process by taking a few minutes at the end and beginning of each session to discuss what aspects of the supervisory session were particularly helpful.

12. Encourage the supervisees to utilize additional forms of supervision, such as peer support groups.

Protecting clients

The fourth essential goal of supervision is to provide protection for the children and adolescents with whom the supervisees work. Supervisors monitor the welfare of the supervisee's clients (Knoff, 1986) and are legally responsible for the services provided by supervisees (Bernard & Goodyear, 1998). To adequately protect clients, supervisors master and apply a complex array of legal and ethical issues.

LEGAL AND ETHICAL ISSUES IN SUPERVISION

All legal and ethical issues pertinent to the practice of school psychology are also pertinent to the supervision of school psychologists. In addition, a number of ethical principles are specifically directed at the practice of supervision. Supervisors are ethically responsible on multiple levels: to clients, supervisees, the public, and the profession (Storm & Haug, 1997). Because supervisors' decisions have an ethical impact on clients, supervisees, the public, and the profession, supervisors must consider all of these elements as they resolve or help resolve ethical dilemmas.

General ethical responsibilities of supervisors include fostering the ability of supervisees to make appropriate ethical decisions, ensuring that supervisees practice legally and ethically, accepting ultimate responsible for services provided by supervisees, and continually learning about ethical and legal issues. A lack of knowledge of the ethical principles and laws does not exempt a supervisor from responsibility.

Supervisors should be thoroughly familiar with the following APA *Ethical Principles* (1992), Bersoff (1995), Bowser (1995), Fischer and Sorenson (1991), Jacob-Timm and Hartshorne (1998), Koocher and Keith-Spiegel (1998), the NASP *Professional Conduct Manual* (1997) which includes principles for professional ethics, and ethical dilemmas presented in the *Communiqué*. When choosing workshops and readings for their own professional development, supervisors should ensure that they attend at least one workshop focusing on ethical or legal issues annually.

In addition to adhering to ethical guidelines specific to supervision, supervisors are often responsible for fostering the ability of supervisees to make appropriate ethical decisions. Since school psychologists encounter ethical dilemmas almost daily, supervisors must be prepared to assist in resolving these dilemmas. As Bowser (1995) indicates, many ethical principles appear to be "common sense" that "sound easy enough in the abstract, from the comfort of one's favorite reading chair. But the real world is full of organizational pressures, conflicting regulations, and personal challenges that can very quickly make fuzzy and grey the sharp, black-and-white distinc-

tions found in a book" (p. 33). It the supervisor's responsibility to help supervisees deal with these organizational pressures, conflicting regulations, and personal challenges.

Ethical principles for supervisors of school psychologists incorporate and reflect the same fundamental ethical principles as for all mental health professionals: (1) respect individuals and protect the welfare of the client, (2) provide competent services, (3) maintain integrity in professional relationships, and (4) be responsible to the community and society (Jacob-Timm & Hartshorne, 1998).

Ethical dilemma 1-3

In a large district one of the psychologists observes that a number of colleagues do not follow NASP's *Best Practices III* recommended procedures. The school psychologist comes to you, as the supervising school psychologist, and insists that his colleagues be reported to NASP for ethical violations. *What should you do as supervising psychologist?*

Respecting individuals and protecting the welfare of clients

Adhering to this principle involves respecting the human rights of all individuals, including supervisees, children, teachers, and parents. The welfare of the child supersedes all else, but the rights of others must also be considered. This fundamental principle ensures that school psychologists and their supervisors protect individuals' rights to autonomy, confidentiality, due process, nondiscrimination, privacy, and self-determination. In a general sense, this means that supervisors do no harm, affirm supervisees' and clients' rights to make autonomous decisions (as long as they do not infringe upon the rights of others), ensure that supervisory actions benefit both supervisees and clients, treat supervisees and their clients fairly and equally, and act in a manner that is truthful, loyal, and reliable (Storm & Haug, 1997).

School psychologists and supervisors must respect individual differences and be sensitive to "physical, mental, emotional, political, economic, social, cultural, ethnic, racial, gender, sexual preference, and religious characteristics" of clients (NASP, 1994, 1997). In adhering to this principle, supervisors consider individual differences as they formulate supervisory recommendations. These cover a wide range of situations, for example, (1) recommending appropriate tools and techniques for supervisees' work with ethnic minority children, (2) ensuring that supervisees terminate treatment only when in the best interest of the child, and (3) selecting non-discriminatory methods in hiring and evaluating supervisees. These issues are more thoroughly addressed in Chapters 7 and 13, respectively.

Ethical dilemma 1-4

A new "high stakes" testing program has been mandated in your state. This program tests children in the 4th, 8th, and 10th grades. In your elementary school, many fourth grade students have been determined to have significant academic deficiencies in multiple areas. Due to concerns about adverse publicity, the principal has suggested that poorly performing, "at-risk" students be considered for retention in the 3rd grade. She feels that the extra year will boost scores and help the school avoid being adversely labeled. She has asked for your opinion as the supervising school psychologist. *What are the ethical issues? What steps should be taken?*

Obtaining informed consent is another essential characteristic of adhering to the fundamental principle of respecting the individual. Under this principle, supervisors ensure that supervisees obtain informed consent from the beginning of their relationship with clients, when they inform clients about the limits of confidentiality. These limits include the type, logistics, and limits of treatment; the potential risks of the treatment and alternative treatments available; the duty of the school psychologist to warn and intervene in dangerous situations; the limits of confidentiality; the possibility of consultation with colleagues and the supervisor; the possibility of tapes or observations by the supervisor; whether the psychologist is currently in training; and whether the client's communications with the school psychologist are privileged and protected from legal proceedings. To fail to obtain informed consent from clients, including parents of minor children, constitutes malpractice and leaves both school psychologists and supervisors open to liability. Since not all jurisdictions extend privilege, or the right to withhold confidential communications, to school psychologists, it is essential for supervisors of school psychologists to be knowledgeable regarding the laws of their jurisdiction and to consult with a lawyer to determine the same (Koocher & Keith-Spiegel, 1998).

This basic principle also applies to trainees, who must be fully informed of the parameters of their training and thus give informed consent before their entrance into the program. This implies that applicants to school psychology programs should know the evaluation methods used throughout the program and internship prior to matriculation, as well as whether they might be required to participate in individual or group counseling (Bernard & Goodyear, 1998).

Maintaining confidentiality is also essential, and supervisors must emphasize and re-emphasize this point in both individual and group supervision. To minimize the likelihood that inappropriate records will survive and be abused in the future, supervisors should also ensure that school psychologists develop a regular pattern of reviewing files, consolidating working notes, and culling obsolete material. State and local laws vary about the amount of time that psychologists must retain records (Koocher & Keith-Spiegel, 1998), and, again, supervisors must keep abreast of this information so that they can inform supervisees of the relevant laws and regulations. At minimum, the American Psychological Association (1993b) recommends retaining records for three years past the age of majority for minors. Additionally, local districts often formulate specific policy and practice standards for the retention of records.

Supervisors are also responsible for ensuring that confidentiality is maintained when student information is stored on computers. The American Psychological Association (1992) ethical guidelines indicate that encoding, encryption, and avoiding personal identifiers should occur when psychologists enter confidential information into databases or systems of records. Similar to paper records, electronic records should be reviewed and culled annually. If obsolete records are kept as a source of information about diagnostic and treatment strategies, identifiable information must be removed (Sturges, 1998).

Although school psychologists generally do not bill third party insurance companies, quite frequently they do share diagnostic and clinical information with independent practitioners, housed inside or outside the school walls, who in turn share it with third parties. Furthermore, in some states school psychological services are reimbursable to the school system as Medicaid services, and to obtain these reimbursements the school system must submit records. In each of these scenarios, the treatment plans and progress reports are reviewed by administrative personnel, computer technicians, and investigative government or legal entities who have never met the client in a professional capacity. School psychologists should advise clients that information about them is not completely safeguarded. In these cases, supervisors are responsible for ensuring that the formats used by the school district in reporting this information minimally infringes upon the confidentiality rights of children and

their parents and that their supervisees inform clients and parents of the limits of their privacy.

Further, supervisors should strive to educate school psychologists and school administrators about potential confidentiality violations in the use of computer related technologies such as e-mail messages, faxes, voice mail, and wireless or cellular phones. Unfortunately, others to whom the information was not addressed commonly receive these supposedly confidential communications and the sender has no control over who receives or intercepts messages. Faxes should not be used in the transmission of confidential information. In using these technologies even to confirm an appointment, client names should not be used (Harvey & Carlson, 1999).

Supervisors must carefully monitor the ethics of any supervisory techniques they employ. While direct observation of supervisees by supervisors greatly facilitates supervision (Rogers, 1965), issues of respect for the privacy of the client and confidentiality are still of paramount concern. Parents of minors, and clients themselves, should give informed consent before any audio or video recording of sessions with school psychologists. This informed consent must include information regarding the use and disposal of the tapes and the likelihood of supervisors viewing them.

Supervisors must also safeguard the confidentiality of supervisees. This means not only that they should not disclose personal information disclosed by supervisees in a supervisory relationship, but also that supervisors should make clear what information about supervisees they will share with others such as school district administrators and university supervisors.

Providing Competent Services

Supervisors are ethically responsible for the provision of competent services on four levels. First, they are responsible for monitoring and developing their own professional or clinical competence. As they provide direct supervision,

11

"supervisors must be more advanced than the trainee in all areas that the trainee is practicing" (Bernard & Goodyear, 1998, p. 193). If a supervisor is insufficiently experienced in a general (such as counseling individuals of a particular ethnic minority) or specific (such as eating disorders) area, he or she should consult another supervisor, an experienced school psychologist, or another appropriately qualified professional. If consultation is insufficient, another supervisor should be assigned to supervise the case.

Second, supervisors are responsible for developing their competence as supervisors. This should include participation in fundamental coursework and workshops, as well as ongoing collaboration with other supervisors. Supervisors should also document and track their supervision regarding the time expended, the supervisee's progress, and recommendations resulting from the supervision. Obtaining and reviewing raw data, such as taping and reviewing supervisory sessions, can also be extremely helpful to determine areas of strength and weakness in supervisory style.

Third, supervisors must respond to the basic principle of providing competent services in dealing with administrative pressure to sacrifice quality of services for expediency. Such pressure clearly must be resisted (Bowser, 1995). In addition to resisting pressure, the supervisor must use conceptual, conflict resolution/problem solving, and planning skills to satisfactorily analyze, address, and resolve the situation.

Fourth, supervisors are responsible for the services provided by their supervisees and thus are responsible for ensuring the competence of the supervisees and for meeting the great challenge of simultaneously attending to the needs of both the supervisee and the client (Bernard & Goodyear, 1998). To ensure that supervisees are competent, two approaches are critical. Supervisors must use direct observation and supervision: effective supervisors make use of

raw data, including tapes and observations of supervisees' practice, to obtain information regarding effectiveness. Also, supervisors and supervisees must work toward increasing the self-evaluation skills of supervisees (Knoff, 1986).

Ethical dilemma 1-5

The Director of Special Education in your district has recently consulted with you about whether or not to purchase a neuropsychological assessment battery for the school psychologists in the elementary schools. He expects that this will allow the district to avoid having to refer students to the local hospital learning disabilities clinic for expensive neuropsychological evaluations. *What are the ethical issues? What steps should be taken?*

In response to requests by parents and teachers, school psychologists should provide services that result in the improvement of the functioning of students, or "at the very least, they should do no harm" (Bowser, 1995, p. 34). Supervisors are responsible for helping supervisees determine which of their skills are sufficiently developed and which need further development before use. Further, supervisors are responsible for helping supervisees develop and acquire these necessary competencies. The emergence of technology has dramatically impacted both practice and supervision. For example, given the ubiquity and rapid development of computer related technology, it is essential that supervisors of school psychologists facilitate the professional development of their supervisees in the use of computers and related technology (Bardos, 1999).

Furthermore, supervisors are responsible for ensuring that school psychologists under their supervision use software test scoring and report writing programs appropriately and ethically. In

12

particular, supervisors must monitor whether or not supervisees use software programs to inappropriately practice beyond or outside their levels of expertise (Harvey & Carlson, 1999; Jacob-Timm & Hartshorne, 1998). As school psychology departments acquire computer software, supervisors must weigh the costs and benefits to make informed choices. Supervisors are responsible for ensuring that psychologists use computer applications to augment rather than replace clinical practice, and only within their areas of competence. The psychologist who recommends the use of software maintains legal responsibility for all treatment effects, including those that are inappropriate. The psychologist cannot attribute professional responsibility to the software manufacturer, the author of the treatment approach, or the computer programmer (Harvey & Carlson, 1999; Reynolds, McNamara, Marion, & Tobin, 1985).

Supervisors must also ensure that their supervisees are sensitive and responsive to the ethical issues in all areas of their professional practice. They must ensure that supervisees adhere to or establish principles of good testing practices, including writing reports that communicate meaningfully and convey results in a manner that takes into account contextual issues (Harvey, 1997b; Ownby, 1997).

When supervising consultation cases, supervisors must ensure that school psychologists monitor the results of their actions, work to offset harmful consequences, and terminate interventions when they do not achieve desired goals. Supervisors play a critical role in facilitating supervisees' progress through the consultation stages (entry, problem identification/clarification, intervention/problem solution, and evaluation) while adhering to the ethical principles of confidentiality and informed consent.

Ethical dilemma 1-6

A school psychologist in your district has 20 years experience and is well liked by both parents and teachers. It was recently discovered that consistent scoring errors on the WISC-R and WISC-III were made for many years. Specifically, the Digit Span and Symbol Search subtest scores were erroneously used in the computation of scores. Hence, students' Full Scale scores have been consistently inflated for many years. This error has resulted in a one-week suspension as well as a union grievance. The Superintendent would like to suspend the school psychologist immediately, for an indefinite period, but is asking for your opinion. *What are the ethical issues? What steps should be taken?*

Maintaining integrity in professional relationships

In adhering to this principle, supervisors openly address and resolve conflicts of interest. Many conflicts can be avoided by addressing common areas of difference before the onset of supervision. For example, it can be very helpful to have written contracts that delineate the responsibilities of the supervisor, supervisee, and other parties (i. e. principal, university supervisor).

Effective supervisors are also careful to avoid dual relationships (including friendships) with supervisees that may either impair their ability to judge and evaluate the supervisee accurately, or place the supervisee at risk of exploitation. A blatant example of an inappropriate dual relationship is a sexual relationship between a supervisor and supervisee. Research literature from the fields of clinical and counseling psychology indicates that between 6% and 16% of psychologists have had sexual relationships with supervisees. Although the majority thought these relationships were consensual at the time, in hindsight most supervisees felt some level of coercion (Bernard & Goodyear, 1998).

13

Pre-existing couples should not enter into supervisory relationships, and if any relationship emerges during supervision a new supervisor should be assigned. If this is not possible, the supervisor and supervisee should thoroughly document their work together and hire a second supervisor to evaluate the supervisee's work (Bernard & Goodyear, 1998).

While it is a responsibility of supervisors to help supervisees identify personal issues that interfere with their work, it is up to the supervisee to obtain appropriate help to resolve them. To avoid a dual relationship supervisors should be careful not act as a supervisee's therapist (Whiston & Emerson, 1989).

Supervisors must ensure that, whether conducted by themselves or their supervisees, research and program evaluations are conducted in an ethical manner. Relevant ethical guidelines include practicing within the realm of professional competence and responsibility, considering the welfare of the client, guaranteeing informed consent and maintenance of confidentiality, providing freedom from coercion and minimal risk, avoiding concealment and deception, and providing post-data collection debriefing and desensitization.

Ethical dilemma 1-7

You are providing supervision for a newly graduated school psychologist. A parent in your district recently requested help from this psychologist in obtaining a psychoeducational evaluation for her daughter as part of the admissions process for a local private high school. The parent has offered to pay for the evaluation and the intern would be happy to do it in order to earn extra money. *What are the ethical issues? What steps should be taken?*

Maintaining responsibility to the community and society

This broad principle has several implications for the supervisor of school psychologists. First, as an individual who is preparing and monitoring the growth of school psychologists, the supervisor has an ethical responsibility to safeguard the public from incompetent professionals. The supervisor has the challenge of balancing the needs of clients, supervisees, the public, and the profession.

Second, the supervisor has a responsibility to ensure that school psychologists uphold federal, state, and local laws relevant to the practice of school psychology. Supervisors frequently encounter situations in which individuals are uncomfortable or unsure of how to adhere to relevant laws. Ethical codes require that school psychologists know and adhere to current laws, statutes, administrative rulings, and local policies and procedures. As described by Prasse (1995), the legal influences on school psychology include not only those that influence psychology, but those that influence psychology and special education as well.

Ethical dilemma 1-8

A practicum student is enrolled in an individual intelligence testing course. He has sought volunteers for IQ test administration among friends and family. During the course of testing, serious concerns about his cousin's young son have emerged. There is a suspicion of child abuse. The student has come to you for guidance. *What are the ethical issues? What steps should be taken?*

Several laws are particularly relevant to the supervision of school psychologists. All supervisors of school psychologists should be thoroughly knowledgeable about the laws concerning:

1. Confidentiality and the duty to warn. The Tarasoff ruling (Tarasoff v. Regents of California, 1974), and resulting interpretations mandate that psychologists provide adequate warning to threatened individuals. In this case the supervisor was held vicariously responsibility for the lack of appropriate practice of the supervisee (Bernard & Goodyear, 1998). Super-visors must help supervisees determine when it is appropriate to break confidentiality and inform victims of intended harm (Munson, 1991).

2. Liability and malpractice (defined as providing services below acceptable standards and thereby causing harm). While unlikely to be accused of malpractice for supervision itself, supervisors may be named in a suit if supervisees are accused of malpractice (Bernard & Goodyear, 1998).

3. Direct and vicarious liability. An example of direct liability is providing inadequate supervision to a beginning or novice school psychologist. An example of indirect liability is being held liable for negligent acts of a supervisee (Bernard & Goodyear, 1998). The extent to which a supervisee's behavior falls within the scope of the supervisory relationship is determined by several factors including the supervisor's power over the supervisee, the supervisee's assigned duties, the time, place, purpose, and motivation of the behavior, and the likelihood of whether the supervisor would have been able to anticipate the supervisee's behavior (Disney & Stephens, 1994). To minimize the likelihood of being named as a co-defendant in a malpractice suit, supervisors should maintain open and trusting relationships with supervisees, keep up to date on ethical and legal issues, maintain liability insurance, consult with the school district's legal counsel, document all supervisory contacts, and invest adequate time and energy to supervision (Bernard & Goodyear, 1998).

4. Educational records and the student's right to privacy (Education of All Handicapped Children Act, 1975; Family Educational Rights and Privacy Act, 1976; Individuals with Disabilities Education Act, 1991).

5. Non-discriminatory laws, including the non-discriminatory testing of students (Civil Rights Act, 1871; Civil Rights Act, 1964; Education of All Handicapped Children Act, 1975; Individuals with Disabilities Education Act, 1991).

6. Federal, state, and local special education and disability laws and regulations including the IDEA (Individuals with Disabilities Education Act, 1991) and Section 504 of the Rehabilitation Act (Rehabilitation Act, 1973; Americans with Disabilities Act, 1990).

7. Laws relevant to behavior control, including laws regulating the use of corporal punishment and physical restraints, suspensions and expulsions, and due process for students (IDEA, 1991 and state specific laws).

8. Child abuse and neglect, particularly state laws mandating reporting by any individuals knowledgeable about child abuse or neglect.

9. Rights and statutes regarding civil rights including the Civil Rights Acts of 1964 and 1991, the Age Discrimination Act of 1967, the Americans with Disabilities Act of 1990, and the Family and Medical Leave Act of 1993.

10. Statutes regarding sexual harassment legislation as they pertain to both the education of children and employment practices.

11. The treatment and distribution of copyrighted materials including articles, test materials, and computer software (Copyright Law of the United States of America, 1996).

15

Ethical dilemma 1-9

The director of special education turns to you, as the supervising school psychologist, to set a policy regarding the sharing of test protocols. A local parent advocate has been recommending that her clients request copies of the inside pages of the WISC-III protocol to take to their children's private therapists. The state law mandates that parents have full access to all test results. *Are there ethical issues? What should the school psychologist do?*

At times laws conflict, and supervisors must keep abreast of current interpretations to be able to provide appropriate guidance. For example, a perennial question in school psychology is whether or not parents can be provided copies of test protocols. This question is perennial because there are two relevant but conflicting laws involved. The Family Educational Rights and Privacy Act (FERPA, 1974) permits individuals, and parents of minors, to review and inspect records. While personal notes not shown to another person are generally exempt from disclosure, the intent of the law is to render materials used to make decisions available to the individuals involved. This has led to the conclusion that test protocols are subject to disclosure and must be copied for parents if they are unable to view them in person. Yet photocopying test protocols clearly violates the copyright held by the publishers of such instruments, violates test security, and encourages inaccurate interpretation by untrained individuals. It is, therefore, illegal and unethical. Further, Supreme Court rulings (Detroit Edison Co. v. National Labor Relations Board, as cited in Koocher & Keith-Spiegel, 1998) have supported the right of a test developing company to retain test security.

Supervisees want to avoid being in a position where they are forced to break either of these conflicting laws. Supervisors can help them steer clear of this dilemma by ensuring that supervisees develop positive working relationships with parents, clearly interpret results, and provide parents with understandable reports. If necessary, under the direction of the supervisor, supervisees can send the data to a second psychologist trained in the interpretation of the instrument to obtain a second opinion about the interpretation of the results.

Ethical decision making

As is generally true for school psychologists, supervisors should cope with ethical issues by preparing in advance, by being constantly vigilant, and by seeking assistance from other professionals or professional associations. Discussing ethical dilemmas is an extremely valuable training technique and highly appropriate for group supervision sessions as well. Group discussion of ethical dilemmas both models and implements effective problem solving.

Supervisors of school psychologists should collaborate to find resolutions to ethical dilemmas that consider the needs of all parties involved. Consultation with others, and documentation of consultation and decisions, is essential in any case involving ethical or legal questions. It is very helpful to develop a consultative relationship with the school district or city/town attorney, to keep informed of new laws and statutes, and to have a knowledgeable person with whom to consult when difficulties arise. When unethical practice is suspected, the first course of action is to attempt to resolve the issue informally with the person about whom one is concerned. If this is not effective, both individuals can approach a colleague, state association, or national association for assistance and information. Only after these steps have been taken would the school psychologist file a complaint of an ethical violation with the licensing board or professional organization (Bowser, 1995).

In summary, professional standards mandate supervision of beginners and recommend that supervision continue throughout the professional career of school psychologists. Supervision has the general goals of providing leadership, enhancing functioning, protecting clients, and fostering self-supervision. A number of ethical and legal issues are pertinent to supervision, and supervisors additionally are responsible for supervisors helping supervisees negotiate myriad ethical and legal dilemmas as they practice school psychology. These demands make supervision an especially challenging professional activity that offers both personal and professional rewards.

18

Communication and interpersonal skills, along with conceptual and technical skills, are essential for effective supervision (Bernard & Goodyear, 1998; Ellis, 1991; Katz, 1955; Talley, 1990). This chapter reviews the communication and interpersonal skills essential to supervision, including those aspects of interpersonal skills relevant to issues of diversity.

COMMUNICATION

Communication skills, involving listening and asking as well as telling and informing, are as critical to supervision as they are to counseling, consultation, and assessment. Supervision requires many of the communication skills developed by school psychologists working with parents, children, and school personnel. These include attending to nonverbal cues, obtaining feedback regarding the accuracy of perceptions, listening actively, restating, active listening, and reviewing. These particular skills will not be addressed in detail, as we presume basic communication skills have already been mastered; instead, communication skills particularly challenged by supervision will be emphasized.

Activity 2-1

With your supervisee's permission, tape record supervisory sessions. Then transcribe the tape and analyze the tape and transcripts for process and content as you were taught in introductory counseling courses. What can you discern about your supervisory communication skills? Try to identify at what points you obtain feedback regarding the accuracy of perceptions, listen without evaluating, restate, actively listen, or review.

The fundamental purpose of communication is to share information, both verbal and nonverbal, so that the sender of the information is understood by the receiver and in turn understands the receiver's response. In supervision, communication failures are commonly a result of an attempt to communicate during periods of high emotion, erroneous perception of nonverbal cues, different understandings of word meanings, insufficient feedback, inaccurate assumptions, or inattentive listening (Rue & Byars, 1997). Research indicates that 48 hours after a ten minute oral presentation, only 25% of the information is retained, and less than 10% is retained after a period of a week (Ailes, 1988). In addition, supervisors of school psychologists are faced with the challenge of simultaneously responding to supervisee concerns and communicating district policies (Talley, 1990).

Strategy: Augment good communication skills. Supervisors can increase their communication skills by avoiding attempts to communicate during times of high emotion, listening effectively by focusing attention, and reinforcing oral communications with written notes. To minimize common communication failings, supervisors will find it helpful to seek verbal and nonverbal feedback regarding whether clarity has been achieved, and to check whether or not the supervisee shares assumptions and understandings of word meanings.

Supervisors should give instructions in a manner that is clear and results in task completion within the desired time frame. Necessary steps include considering the timing of the request, clearly communicating the reason for the request, and clearly and unambiguously delineating responsibilities, results expected, and method of reporting results, and checking to make sure that the task is progressing (some supervisors find it helpful to remind themselves to check progress by writing a note in their own appointment book), and evaluating both the process and the resultant product (Loen, 1994).

Activity 2-2

Review two situations in which you gave instructions a month previously, one written (perhaps a memo) and one oral (perhaps in a supervisory session, from supervisory session notes). Analyze them for how well you timed the request, communicated rationale, delineated responsibilities, described results expected and method for reporting them, set deadlines, checked to make sure that the task was progressing, and evaluated the result. Try and pinpoint the communication method that is most clear and effective.

Strategy: Delegate both responsibility and authority. On the part of supervisors, delegation involves assigning work, responsibility, power, and authority to supervisees. On the part of supervisees, delegation involves accepting responsibility for both task completion and the quality of the outcome. The "parity principle" dictates that in delegation, authority and responsibility coincide. That is, supervisors delegate enough authority so that supervisees are able to satisfactorily complete tasks, and supervisees accept responsibility for tasks only when they have sufficient authority to complete them (Rue & Byars, 1997).

One advantage to delegation is that supervisors are freed for other tasks. Additional advantages are that supervisees feel increased commitment and are better positioned to grow professionally. In general, supervisors should delegate routine tasks and spend their time and energy on exceptional situations. Effective

supervisors delegate to the maximum ability of supervisees (Rue & Byars, 1997).

However, in delegating, supervisors take the necessary risk of allowing supervisees to fail (Loen, 1994). Supervisors sometimes are reluctant to delegate tasks because they fear supervisees will not be successful. Additionally, supervisors may be reluctant to delegate because they believe it is easier or more comfortable to do tasks themselves or because they are unwilling to relinquish power or recognition (Rue & Byars, 1997).

In turn, supervisees may be resistant to accepting delegated tasks because they feel they have not yet attained sufficient skill proficiency. Supervisees may also resist because they feel overburdened, perceive that they lack the resources and/or information to do well, fear criticism, lack self confidence, feel a lack of incentives, or are not interested in taking responsibility for outcomes (Halloran, 1981).

Activity 2-3

With your supervisees, review specific situations in which you delegated responsibility. Identify situations in which they felt tasks were delegated to them prematurely or in which they not given adequate responsibility.

When determining whether to delegate a task, supervisors should consider the supervisee's training or ability to do the job, the adequacy of time and resources, and the reality of an open communication system. Most individuals are capable of and interested in carrying considerable responsibility, and it is up to supervisors to delegate effectively. It is important that assignments encourage the personal growth of the school psychologist. To delegate, a supervisor analyzes how he spends his time, decides which tasks can be delegated, determines which supervisees can handle the tasks, delegates authority, creates a sense of responsibility for the task, and controls and monitors the delegation.

A primary delegation responsibility for supervisors of school psychological services is assigning individual school psychologists to particular schools and programs within the district. In making assignments, the strengths of the individual school psychologist and the needs of each school or program should be matched as closely as possible. In addition, it is important that the assignments are equitable.

Ethical dilemma 2-1

As a supervising school psychologist, you are being pressured to assign school psychologists inequitably by the administration. Two elementary schools, both with populations of 1000, have heretofore had equitable school psychology service time. Effective pre-referral intervention strategies in one school, in which the school psychologist is heavily involved as a consultant and provider of direct services to children, have reduced the number of referrals for full psychological evaluations by 50%. The second school has neglected to implement a pre-referral process and thus continues to have a large number of referrals for traditional assessments. The central administration would like school psychology time to be reduced at the school with the pre-referral interventions and be assigned to the second school to "catch up" their referrals. *What are the ethical dilemmas? What steps should be taken?*

Beyond the internship level, few supervisors of school psychologists have difficulty delegating routine job tasks involving assessment, counseling, and consultation to capable supervisees. Sometimes, however, school administrators may have difficulty permitting task delegation to staff psychologists. For example, a direc-

tor of special education may be disinclined to give authority to the school psychologists in areas such as student placement.

Ethical dilemma 2-2

You, a supervising school psychologist, are finding that your supervisor, the Director of Special Education, tends to have difficulty fully delegating responsibility to school psychologists. The result is that you are expected to "take over" any case in the district that becomes "difficult." You feel this practice undermines your supervisees, prevents their professional growth, and needlessly assigns you to cases all over the district. *What are the ethical issues? What steps could be taken?*

Strategy: Use contracts. Communication within the supervisory process can be greatly facilitated by developing a formal supervisory agreement prior to the onset of supervision in the form of a written and signed supervisory contract (Storm, 1997a). Contracts clarify expectations, outline the responsibilities of each person, promote shared responsibility, provide direction when difficulties arise, maximize the fit between supervisee and supervisor, and provide a concrete method to measure the performance of both supervisees and supervisors. Well-written contracts include the following:

1. Credentialling, licensing, or professional organization (such as NCSP) requirements to be met by the supervision;
2. The logistics of supervision including frequency, time, place, length, and schedule of meetings; legal responsibility of supervisors; separation of responsibilities when more than one supervisor is involved; methods to deal with canceled supervision sessions; methods to deal with client notifica-

tion of supervision, and the supervisor's name and credentials;

3. Clarification of the supervisory process including theories and models espoused by the supervisor; willingness to explore additional ideas, methods, or styles; relationship power differentials; and methods to be used in conflict resolution;

4. Supervision goals.

5. Anticipated methods of supervision, such as audio or videotapes, collaborative work on cases, case presentations, and observations. (Sources of "raw" data such as observations and audiotapes are highly recommended, but must be conducted with full consideration of ethical implications);

6. Legal and liability issues, including the supervisor's responsibility for the supervisee's work, appropriate procedures when clients are a danger themselves or others, information needed by the supervisor to be able to intelligently consult about a case; and a method for the supervisor to review the supervisee's cases; and

7. Methods of individual performance evaluation, performance evaluation distribution procedures, the involvement of the supervisee in the evaluation process, and the method to be used to evaluate supervision itself.

Strategy: Develop a handbook. Developing a handbook for school psychologists can be an efficient method of ensuring that important communications are readily and repeatedly accessible. Handbooks are most effective when they are kept in a loose-leaf binder so individual pages are easily updated. Appropriate contents vary according to the orientation of the department, job descriptions of district personnel, available resources, and environmental factors.

Sample Contents of a District School Psychologists' Handbook

1. **SCHOOL PSYCHOLOGY SERVICES**
   Overview: Department mission, Vision, and Goals
   Brochure, Psychological Services
   Supervising School Psychologist, Job Description
   School Psychologist, Job Description
   Psychologists in the District
   School Psychologists' Schedule
   Provision of Group and Individual Supervision
   Individual Performance Evaluation Procedures
   Individual Performance Evaluation Form
   Personnel Policies
   Policies on Professional Development
   Methods of Stress Reduction
   Departmental Evaluation Policies and Schedule
   Psychology Department Goals

2. **DISTRICT PERSONNEL**
   District Personnel Organizational Chart
   Director of Special Education, Job Description
   Assistant Director of Special Ed, Job Description
   School Social Worker, Job Description
   Educational Examiners, Job Description
   Counselors, Job Description, Secondary
   Counselors, Job Description, Elementary
   District Team Leaders
   Team Leader Responsibilities

3. **DISTRICT FACILITIES AND SERVICES**
   School Calendar
   School times and telephone numbers
   Map of the District
   Non-special Support Services
       Counseling Department Services
       ESL Programs
       Alternative Classrooms
       Remedial Reading Programs
       Chapter 1 Programs
       District Vocational Education Programs
       Section 504 Services
   Special Education Programs
       Special Ed Department Goals
       Special Education Child Find Brochure
       Learning Disabilities Programs
       Resource Room Programs
       PreSchool Speech and Language Therapy
       PreSchool Special Needs Program
       Self-contained Program, Generic
       Self-contained Programs for students with EBD

23

Activity 2-4

Review the above table of contents, revise it to better match the needs of your setting, and compile a handbook.

Supervisee development

Considering the cognitive and professional developmental levels of supervisees is essential for effective communication within supervisory relationships. A number of models describe invariant stages through which individuals progress as they advance from novice to expert in a profession. Researchers have addressed, for example, the professional development of nurses (Benner, 1984), counselors (Bernard & Goodyear, 1998; Stoltenberg, McNeill, & Delworth, 1998), pilots, and chess players (Dreyfus & Dreyfus, 1991). Each stage is described as requiring different learning and/or supervisory strategies. Multiple research reviews support the significance of supervisees' experience level as an indicator of developmental level and consequent supervisory needs (Bernard & Goodyear, 1998).

Models of professional development differ in the number of stages described and the names attached, yet substantial similarities are present. For this discussion, we will use the terminology proposed by Dreyfus and Dreyfus (1991). This model has two advantages: it extends beyond the training and internship periods, and it uses intuitively understandable terminology.

Dreyfus and Dreyfus (1991) indicate that as individuals learn new skills, they pass through five levels of development: novice, advanced beginner, competent, proficient, and expert. During this progression, they shift from rule-based to intuitive behavior, change from an analytical to a holistic perspective, and evolve from "skill performing" to an "involved" self-image.

Novices have no previous experience. They rely on abstract principals, objective attributes, and "rules" to govern their behavior. Novices see situations as compilations of bits of information, tend to act as a detached observers, and "know about" rather than "know how to" (Benner, 1984). Their rule-governed behavior tends to be inflexible, which hinders actual performance because it interferes with the ability to respond to the entire context. Anxiety is normal for novices but can undermine self-confidence, self-efficacy, and performance (Friedlander, Keller, Peca-Baker, & Olk, 1986).

Most school psychology practicum students are at the novice level. However, students are not the only novices. All school psychologists are novices when they enter situations in which they have no previous experience, either in terms of the population with which they are working, or with regard to the procedures and/or tools used. Even more relevant to this discussion, all school psychology supervisors are novices in supervision at the onset of their supervisory role.

The stage of development at which an individual functions is context dependent. That is, the same school psychologist may be an expert diagnostician, a competent consultant, and a novice counselor. Therefore, a supervisor may need to call upon the supervisory and communication methods appropriate for work with novices, and those appropriate for work with experts, in the same supervision session with the same supervisee.

At the next level, advanced beginners demonstrate marginally acceptable performance and begin to take into account contextual aspects as well as objective attributes (Benner, 1984). Advanced beginners continue to have difficulty distinguishing the relative importance of client or contextual attributes. They need ongoing support and close supervision to set priorities. They continue to be concerned with learning and mastering technical aspects, leading to emotional disconnection. They also tend to hesitate to take responsibility and continue to rely on supervisors to help make decisions. Generally, school psychologists would be expected to be in this stage during the internship and first years of employment.

After two or three years of practice, hopefully a school psychologist has reached the level of competence and is better able to see relationships between situational components. At this stage, individuals attempt to limit the unexpected through planning and goal setting. A shift occurs from preoccupation with their own performance to a greater awareness of the client; they are oriented to both skills and people. The practitioner begins to feel increased responsibility for the outcome of interventions and for the performance of other team members. Because of this feeling of responsibility and frustration over unsuccessful outcomes, "competence" can be a difficult stage professionally and often results in individuals questioning their chosen career. It is also a stage of transition. To progress to the next stage requires a shift from a focus on analytical processes and technical issues to a focus on systemic issues. Many individuals never make this shift and remain at the competent level throughout their careers (Benner, 1984).

The fourth stage, the proficient level, can be reached in three to five years of practice. However, proficiency does not come from practice alone, but requires additional supervision that reinforces and requires reflective and integrative practice. Proficient practitioners tend to have an increased ability to recognize patterns and increased ability to see what is of primary importance. They tend to be attuned to, and engaged in, situations rather than detached from them. They move away from "figuring out" problems to recognizing familiar patterns. They also tend to be able to recognize when they can handle a situation and when they need help. Consequently, proficient practitioners tend to be fairly accurate in their self-assessment.

Finally, the expert relies on past experience to generate paradigms, sees situations as wholes, and acts as an involved performer. A person does not become an expert by simply adding more techniques: persons with expertise have transformed their thinking so that they have clinical grasps of entire situations, attend to context and environment, and base decisions on qualitative distinctions rather than on rules or multiple facts. The expert is at home in complex and rapidly changing situations.

The qualitative difference in the thinking of experts and novices/advanced beginners sometimes interferes with the ability of experts to teach beginners. That is, because experts no longer think in terms of rules, they have significant difficulty providing the "rules" sought by novices. They also have difficulty breaking down their grasps of total situations into the components needed by novices (Benner, 1984). Thus supervisors of school psychologists, hopefully at expert levels, may have difficulty communicating their thought processes to novice or advanced beginners. Hence, it is important to be both sensitive and responsive to the professional development of supervisees.

Activity 2-5

Develop a timeline of your own professional history with several different strands. At what point were you a novice, advanced beginner, competent, proficient, and expert in each of the following areas:

- consultation with teachers,
- consultation with parents,
- individual counseling with adolescents,
- individual counseling with children,
- group counseling,
- behavior management plan development,
- assessment of intelligence,
- assessment of achievement,
- assessment of personality and behavior,
- integration of assessment and intervention and/or,
- provision of in-service workshops for teachers?

25

Strategy: Foster a developmental model of supervision. As previously mentioned, models of skill development have been extended into developmental models of supervision. A significant body of research literature, summarized in Stoltenberg, McNeill, and Delworth (1998) supports this model. Table 2-1 summarizes the developmental and supervisory implications of the Dreyfus and Dreyfus (1991) and Benner (1984) and the Stoltenberg et al. (1998) models. As evident in this table, the models have substantial elements in common.

Table 2-1 Two Models of Developmental Skill Acquisition

Dreyfus & Dreyfus (1991) and Benner (1984)	Stoltenberg, McNeill, & Delworth (1998)
NOVICE	**LEVEL 1**
Supervisee characteristics: • Relies on abstract principles, objective attributes, "rules." • Sees situations as compilations of bits of information. • Gives extraneous information. • Incompletely grasps situations. • Is unlikely to look ahead. • Is unable to respond to context of situations. • Tends to be a detached observer rather than involved performer. • Is anxious. • Is self-doubting. • Is dependent on supervisor for direction in determining most important or relevant tasks to perform.	• Evaluates information against own experience. • Integrates schemata inaccurately or slowly. • Has simplistic understanding of complex constructs and processes. • If experienced in related field, reconceptualizes to fit prior experiences. • Focuses on skill acquisition. • Is highly motivated and anxious. • Has limited self-awareness. • Focuses on own anxiety and skills yet unaware of strengths and weaknesses. • Can allow anxiety to interfere with ability to empathize. • Is dependent upon supervisor for structure. • May uncritically accept supervisory suggestions without understanding, leading to dependency, inappropriate generalization, inadequate learning.
Supervisory considerations: • Provide very close supervision.	• Provide structure and positive feedback. • Assign clients with mild problems. • Use supervisory interventions that are facilitative (encouraging), prescriptive (suggest approaches, etc.), conceptual (tie theory to diagnosis and intervention). • Use supervisory techniques that result in raw data: video or live observation, role-playing, interpretation of dynamics, readings, and group supervision. • When providing feedback, address strengths first, then weaknesses. • Provide close client monitoring.
ADVANCED BEGINNER	**LEVEL 2**
Supervisee characteristics: • Focuses on mastery of technical aspects. • Begins to perceive recurring situations. • Still has difficulty taking in entire situation: spends energy remembering rules and procedures. • Begins to take context into account. • Has difficulty distinguishing the relative importance of various attributes. • Is emotionally disconnected from client due to focus on technique. • Needs help setting priorities. • Refrains from taking responsibility.	• Has increased confidence in ability to implement interventions, but understanding is limited in complexity. • Experiences decreased anxiety. • Has fluctuating motivation, sometimes highly confident but shaken by complexity, can lead to confusion, despair. • Has increased desire to personalize. • Focuses more on client: more understanding of client views. • May become enmeshed or confused: appropriate balance is an issue. • Begins to focus on self-reactions. • May desire more autonomy than warranted. • Dependency-autonomy conflict.

• Relies on supervisors to make decisions. • Demonstrates marginally acceptable performance.	• Can be assertive with own agenda. • Functions more independently.
Supervisory considerations: • Provide guidelines for recognizing recurring patterns. • Assist in formulating guidelines that dictate actions. • Continue to ensure client needs are met.	• Expose to complex (e.g., multicultural) issues. • Provide less structure and more autonomy. • Assign more difficult clients with more severe problems. • Use primarily facilitative supervisory interventions. • Use prescriptive supervisory interventions rarely. Also use confrontation, conceptual (introduce more alternative views), and catalytic supervision (process comments, highlight responses to client/supervisor). • Use video or live observation, role-playing, interpretation of dynamics, parallel process, and group supervision.
COMPETENT	**LEVEL 3**
Supervisee characteristics: • Is better able to see relationships. • Balances skills and empathy. • Perceives actions in terms of long term effects. • Develops plans that adjust to most important aspects. • Desires to limit the unexpected. • Engages in planning and goal setting. • Feels responsible for outcomes. • May feel responsible for entire team. • Questions chosen career. • Has greater awareness of the client. • Experiences decreased focus on self. • Feels sense of mastery. • Tends to be efficient and organized.	• Possesses sufficient skills so automatic performance can occur. • Has skills necessary to engage client, collect essential information, and facilitate functional behavior. • Is able to think ahead. • Matches patterns and makes insights that appear to be intuitive to novices. • Makes decisions quickly about which avenues to explore. • Develops schemata and links that activate related concepts. • Has stable motivation: has remaining, but not disabling, doubts. • Has total professional identity. • Accepts own strengths and weaknesses. • Is empathic and understanding. • Focuses on client, process, and self. • Uses therapeutic self in sessions. • Has firm belief in own autonomy. • Knows when to seek consultation. • Retains responsibility.
Supervisory considerations:	• Encourage trainee to provide supervisory structure. • Use facilitation, confrontation, conceptual, and catalytic supervisory interventions. • Use peer and group supervision. • Continue to use direct observation and tapes. • Work with administration to ensure that effective supervision is minimally constrained due to budgetary limitations.
PROFICIENT	
Supervisee characteristics: • Recognizes patterns and sees what is of primary importance. • Attunes to, and engages in, situations rather than detach self. • Moves away from analyzing problems toward recognizing familiar patterns. • Drops rules taught to novices. • Recognizes important aspects as relevant. • Sees situations as whole rather than as component parts. • Performance guided by nuances. • Perceives meaning of situations in terms of long term implications.	

27

• Knows what typical events to expect in given scenarios. • Recognizes when something doesn't "fit." • Makes decisions with less labor. • Hones in accurately on problem area: few options considered. • Frustrated if information is presented without a context. • Still needs indirect support/ supervision. • Recognizes when help is needed. • Might feel being required to analyze decisions is difficult and unnecessary. • Might feel theories are useless.	
Supervisory considerations: • Teach inductively through very complex case studies. • Analyze supervisee's case studies, both those with which they feel successful and those with which they were frustrated.	
EXPERT	**TRANSITION TO 3I**
Supervisee characteristics: • Relies on past concrete experiences to generate paradigms rather than rules. • Sees situations as wholes. • Bases decisions on qualitative distinctions rather than rules or multiple facts. • Feels at home in complex and rapidly changing situations. • No longer relies on analytical principles or rules, guidelines, or maxims. • Has an intuitive grasp of situations without wasteful consideration of large range of alternative diagnoses. • Experiences a transformation of skills so they are an extension of the self. • Acts as an involved performer rather than an observer. • Do not automatically reach this level: some remain competent or proficient many years.	• Efficiently assesses a number of factors that initially seem unrelated, moving quickly to assessment and treatment. • Integrates across domains of practice. • Strives for stable motivation across domains. • Personalizes understanding across relevant domains. • Moves conceptually and behaviorally across domains. • Professional identity solid across relevant domains.
Supervisory considerations: • Evaluate qualitatively as well as quantitatively. • Employ self-case analysis. • Use context in evaluation strategies.	

28

At the novice and advanced beginner levels, supervision is provided closely for every case. As such, practicum and intern supervision is collaboratively managed by field and university supervisors and employs strategies such as shadowing, co-practice, and frequent direct observation. Since self-report is notoriously inaccurate, observations, audio, and videotapes of novices and advanced beginners are essential.

It is challenging to provide supervisees with an atmosphere that permits them to feel comfortable while being observed. To minimize dis-

comfort experienced by most supervisees during observations, it helps to conduct frequent enough observations so they are routine, to avoid interruptions, negative facial expressions, and excessive note-taking, and to follow every observation with an immediate conference in which observation notes are shared in a collaborative and constructive analysis (Henry & Beasley, 1982).

At the competent level, supervision focuses on the discussion of cases that the supervisee finds particularly challenging, the development of specialized knowledge, and integration of the supervisee within the context of a complex organization. Supervision can be provided by a peer (another staff school psychologist who has sufficient expertise to provide supervision), an administratively appointed supervisor (whose job includes the supervision of school psychological services and staff implementing such services), or an external supervisor (with appropriate background but who is based in the community rather than the school system) (Knoff, 1986).

At the proficient level, the school psychologist assumes more autonomy. Supervision tends to be case related and is often at a higher level of conceptualization than at the earlier levels. School psychologists at the proficient and expert level continue to need supervision to help maintain subjectivity, deal with client resistance, appropriately choose methods of child advocacy, and continually upgrade skills.

Further, at the expert and proficient levels, the school psychologist is in a position to supervise school psychologists at levels of lesser expertise. Supervision of individuals at this level focuses on "metasupervision", or development of supervision. In particular, it addresses increasing the conceptual, interpersonal, and technical skills required in supervision (Knoff, 1986).

Ethical dilemma 2-3

As a supervisor of school psychologists, you hire a newly graduated certified school psychologist to provide a full spectrum of psychological services at the high school. This school psychologist has been trained as a reality therapist and appears to be an advanced beginner in this approach. While you recognize that reality therapy can be quite effective with adolescents, your own training and experience is in cognitive behavioral counseling. This advanced beginner psychologist clearly needs supervision in counseling cases, but you are not trained in this approach. *What are the ethical issues? What steps should be taken?*

INTERPERSONAL SKILLS

Poor interpersonal skills on the part of a supervisor can harm a supervisee, particularly since most supervisory relationships are involuntary and contain an evaluative component (Todd, 1997a). With or without intent, supervisors can neglect, harass, and provide demeaning or destructive supervision. Yet even in the most difficult situations, supervisees are unlikely to complain because they fear negative repercussions such as negative evaluations and have little faith that supervision will improve as a result of a complaint (Todd, 1997a).

Several aspects of interpersonal relationships within the supervisory relationship raise particular challenges for supervisors. First, supervisors must be cognizant of the implications of leadership. In addition, they must be sensitive to and willing to address issues related to rigidified supervisory patterns, dual relationships, and power differentials. In this increasingly evolving world, supervisors must address many types of diversity on multiple levels.

Leadership

Effective supervisors have highly developed abilities to work with people. These are not limited to basic interpersonal skills, but also include leadership, or the ability to initiate new structures and procedures to accomplish goals. Leaders (a) collaboratively set high and appropriate goals, (b) manage organizational elements to free supervisees to work up to their potential, (c) foster a democratic atmosphere which encourages individual participation, and (d) work continually to expand supervisees' self-direction. They provide opportunities for supervisees' personal growth, and they help individuals move from a dependent role with a limited repertoire and a short term perspective to a more mature, autonomous role with a varied repertoire and a long term perspective (Sergiovanni & Starratt, 1998).

29

Strategy: Consider yourself a leader.

Interpersonal influence flourishes in a climate of trust, respect, credibility, and shared purpose. In order for this climate to exist, staff must be provided with appropriate reinforcement, clear direction, consideration, and psychological support. Supervisees are most likely to comply with supervisors they trust and respect and with whom they can identify. Leadership by example is critical, as is an empathic understanding of the challenges of being an effective school psychologist. Leadership is enhanced by treating staff as you would like to be treated: as independent, mature, responsible professionals who have worked hard to attain their positions and are interested in performing well not only for themselves but in the service of the students.

Power

Another factor that impacts supervisors' effectiveness is level and type of power, or ability to influence decisions. French and Raven (1960) describe five bases for interpersonal power:

- reward power, or the ability to mediate rewards;
- coercive power, or the ability to mediate punishments;
- legitimate power, or the legal right and authority to prescribe behavior;
- referent power, or power based on supervisees' admiration and respect for and identification with the supervisor as a person; and
- expert power, or power based on a high level of knowledge, information, and skill.

Strategy: Foster expert and referent power.

Expert and referent power are most closely associated with high supervisee performance and satisfaction, whereas the use of coercive, legitimate, and reward power tends to be viewed quite negatively by supervisees and results in decreased performance and satisfaction (Sergiovanni & Starratt,

1998). Thus, supervising school psychologists are encouraged to focus their energy on fostering expert and referent power by making sure that their technical, conceptual, and interpersonal skills constantly improve.

Coercive power should be used only in extreme situations. However, supervisors can effectively use reward power. School psychology supervisors generally have limited ability to affect the pay of their supervisees but they do have other rewards at their disposal. For example, they can write letters of recognition and commendation, nominate individuals for local and state awards, obtain improved equipment, and assign work and schedules that meet the personal needs and professional strengths of individuals.

Power differentials

Supervisors have power over supervisees simply by virtue of their role. For example, the supervisor's theoretical orientation is more likely to drive supervision than the theoretical orientation of the supervisee (Putney, Worthington, & McCullough, 1992). This power differential is accentuated by the evaluative component, and is accentuated even more strongly by socially determined power differences such as race, ethnicity, class, gender, and sexual orientation.

Strategy: Overtly deal with power differences.

For supervision to be effective, it is essential that both supervisors and supervisees openly address the issues of race, class, gender, social, disabilities, sexual orientation, theoretical orientation, and religion in supervision (Bernard & Goodyear, 1998; Lappin & Hardy, 1997). Effective supervisors attend to complications in supervision that naturally arise from the intersection of axes of power, related both to the supervisory relationship and to issues of class, gender, race, religion, and sexual identity (Turner & Fine, 1997). Because persons of lower power are unlikely to voice feelings of injustice, it is incumbent upon

30

the supervisor to raise issues of power differences during supervision (Turner & Fine, 1997).

Dual relationships

Dual relationships, where supervisor and/or supervisee have more than a supervisory relationship, are "prevalent and inevitable in supervision, perhaps evolving naturally from the nature of the supervisory context. At the heart of supervision is the goal of assisting supervisees in becoming supervisors' peers" (Storm, Peterson, & Tomm, 1997, p. 253). The most common dual relationships between supervisor and supervisee are professional: mentor, teacher, collaborator, and co-worker. A second type combines casual personal or social connections. A third type, prohibited by professional ethics, includes sexual relationships with supervisees and/or supervisory relationships with family members. A fourth type, dual relationships engendered when supervisors act as a therapist with supervisees, is also prohibited by professional ethics (Storm, Peterson, & Tomm, 1997).

Dual relationships, even those permitted by professional ethics such as mentoring and casual social relationships, add complexity to supervisory relationships and increase the potential for supervisee exploitation. Some authors feel dual relationships are not all negative, since they may lead to a desired reduction of power differential, demystification, honesty, authenticity, and integrity. However, many feel that dual relationships have negative implications for both parties: supervisees are unable to freely consent to such a dual relationship and may be exploited, and supervisors may be unable to effectively complete evaluations (Tomm, 1991).

Strategy: Carefully consider dual relationships. When deciding to increase the complexity of a supervisory role by taking a mentoring or collaborative role, the supervisor should consider: benefits to the supervisee;

benefits to the supervisor; age, gender, and status differences; the supervisee's professional autonomy; established procedures for complaint registration; and access to consultation for both the supervisor and supervisee (Storm et al., 1997, p. 256).

Ethical dilemma 2-4

You have been recently promoted to supervising school psychologist, after working ten years as a practicing school psychologist in the same district. You consider several of the other six psychologists in the district among your closest and long-standing friends. You now will be in a position to complete evaluations on these friends. While you recognize this as a dual relationship and a potential conflict of interest, you also are loath to give up your friendships. *What can be done?*

Relationship patterns

As is true for any relationship, supervisory relationships can become ritualized. This occurs when complementary patterns are rigidified to the point that they interfere with growth and feedback (Kadushin, 1985; Todd, 1997a). In these patterns, supervisor and supervisee each consistently take complementary roles, and have difficulty taking any other role with each other.

Strategy: Remedy rigid patterns. Noticing and correcting rigidified patterns of interaction between supervisors and supervisees can be difficult. Critical examination of supervision notes or audiotapes of supervisory sessions can identify rigid patterns. After such identification, both supervisees and supervisors can work to reduce the pattern frequency.

31

Cultural variations

Individuals from different cultures communicate differently and have different expectations for interpersonal interactions. Counseling literature is replete with information regarding the implications of cross-cultural counseling and entire journals are devoted to such concerns (e.g., *Journal of Multicultural Counseling and Development, Journal of Non-white Concerns*). Clearly, cultural issues must be considered in the practice of school psychology (Mosley-Howard, 1995), and must be addressed by supervisors of school psychologists as well.

Culture is defined as patterns of attitudes, living, norms, traditions and values developed and influenced by parents and community (Mosley-Howard, 1995). While race and ethnicity are often reflected in culture, there are usually multiple cultures in any race or ethnic group. Culture involves the ever-changing values, traditions, social relationships, politics, and world-wide views created and shared by a group of people bound together by factors such as common history, geographic location, language, social class, and/or religion. It is expressed tangibly in foods, holidays, dress, and artistic expression and less tangibly in communication style, attitudes, values, and family relationships.

Hofstede (1993) determined dimensions along which cultures differ (quoted by Noe et al., 1996):

1. Individualism vs. collectivism indicates the degree to which persons act in individual interest;

2. Power distance describes the degree to which a culture attempts to reduce inequalities in power and wealth;

3. Uncertainty avoidance describes the degree to which cultures deal with the future's unpredictability by resorting to the structures of technology, law, and religion;

4. Masculinity-femininity describes the extent to which traditionally male (assertiveness, competitiveness, performance, and success) or female (care, service, and solidarity) traits are valued; and,

5. Long-term/short-term orientation describes the degree to which the culture focuses on and plans for the future over short-term gains.

It should be emphasized, however, that all individuals in the same culture are not identical. Culture is integral to the individual but affects every individual differently. Even when researched-based, taking generalizations about cultures from the group to the individual level can be misleading and damaging (Mosley-Howard, 1995).

Strategy: Foster respect for diversity. Supervisors of school psychologists must address cultural issues for several reasons. First, it is necessary for supervisors to ensure that their supervisees advance in their ability to work with children and adolescents whose race, ethnicity, or culture is different than their own. At this time, most school psychologists are middle class and white (Fagan & Wise, 1994, Thomas, 1999), but a significantly higher percentage of the general population are ethnic minorities, and an even higher percentage of culturally diverse children are identified as disabled under IDEA. Therefore, it can be surmised that middle class white school psychologists serve the vast majority of ethnic minority or working class children and adolescents.

As discussed in the previous chapter, ethical principles mandate that the rights of the client, including those from cultural minorities, supercede all other concerns. Fostering respect for diversity is a significant supervisory responsibility, and means integrating minority issues into supervision. This involves regularly and consciously including minority case studies and readings in supervisory sessions. Also, super-

32

visees should be asked to review role-plays and audiotapes for lack of sensitivity and language biases. Finally, supervisors should consciously build a department characterized by school psychologists from diverse backgrounds and facilitate their success.

Whether the cultural diversity is a result of race, ethnicity, class, religion, gender, or sexual orientation, supervisors can facilitate respect for diversity in themselves and their supervisees via specific steps:

1. Raise consciousness of issues through on-going reflections on gender expectations, and on the complex power dynamics related to class, gender, race, religion, and sexual identity (Turner & Fine, 1997);
2. Acquire knowledge and dispel stereotypes by becoming informed about perspectives on cultural similarities and differences, and increasing understanding of the complexity of cultural questions (Mosley-Howard, 1995, Okun, Fried, & Okun, 1999);
3. Examine critically personal beliefs and biases that were acquired in childhood and training and developing methods to reframe their own prejudices and those of the personnel with whom they work (Mosley-Howard, 1995);
4. Increase familiarity with the culture experiences, including class, gender, family system, acculturation, traditions, customs, and community of the children with whom they work by visits to families, communities, and community agencies (Mosley-Howard, 1995) or by shadowing children from another culture throughout a school day;
5. Involve family and community support systems in developing interventions;
6. Become familiar with assessment tools that address multifaceted aspects of ability, using tools that respect cultural and linguistic diversity, such as qualitative and authen-

tic assessment tools (American Psychological Association, 1993a; Henning-Stout, 1994; Mosley-Howard, 1995);

7. Increase contact with members of diverse groups;
8. Undergo supervised training with the diverse client populations; and
9. Check whether clients, particularly those from minority populations, feel respected. Relevant questions might include:
    a. Does your psychologist understand your situation?
    b. Is your psychologist missing anything?
    c. What is happening differently for you since you started seeing the psychologist?
    d. What would you like to see more different?
    e. Do you have any ideas on how to make that happen?
    f. Do you have any suggestions for the psychologist?
    g. Do you and/or your child experience your psychologist as sensitive to your loss of time, money, and privacy? (Adapted from Rambo and Shilts, 1997)

Thomas (1992) adds that school psychologists can help immigrant children in the United States by familiarizing themselves with the cultural practices and history of the children they serve, identifying ways schools can develop programs for helping students gain functional understanding of American educational and cultural practices, acting as liaisons with public programs outside of schools, conducting careful interviews with parents and observations of children in familiar settings, and actively educating school staff in both the educationally relevant issues faced by immigrants and the richness immigrant families bring to classrooms.

Race and ethnicity

Although a pivotal source of identity, issues of race and ethnicity are often marginalized, denied, ignored, and inappropriately left unspoken, particularly by members of the majority culture (Lappin & Hardy, 1997). As McIntosh (1989) describes, destructive racism is not only individual acts or statements of racism, but also the taking advantage of "white privilege" afforded on a daily basis. Many of these privileges are in the form of freedoms: of work, public accommodations, travel, residence, and choice of schooling.

Racism and discrimination are systemic manifestations of economic, political, and social power. Our society categorizes people according to visible and invisible traits, using such categorizations to deduce behavioral and mental traits, and applying policies and practices that jeopardize some while benefiting others. Such classification occurs with reference to race, ethnicity, gender, social class, and physical and social differences. As a result, gross exaggerations and stereotypes result. Both positive and negative stereotypes limit our perspective on an entire group of people and result in unjust resource allocation.

Supervisors have a mandate to address racism on multiple levels. First, to minimize the ill effects of racism, supervisors must develop their own awareness of these factors and encourage a similar awareness in supervisees. Second, supervisors of school psychologists are in a position to positively influence school policies that affect children from minority groups. When school personnel, including school psychologists, are "color blind" they are, in fact, refusing to accept differences. This truth is demonstrated by imagining school personnel being "disability blind," and refusing to accept differences resulting from disabilities. In fact, the Lau vs. Nichols Supreme Court case decision concluded that instruction of Chinese students in English was not providing an equal education-

al opportunity because students could not benefit from the instruction. In truth, accepting differences means making provisions for them. Hence, this becomes a major supervisory challenge.

As Nieto (1992) discusses, multiple structural factors in schools combine to render schools extremely hostile environments for students who are not Euro-American. These factors include

- tracking which discriminates on the basis of social class,
- testing which favors individuals from cultures favoring autonomy,
- curriculum content which ignores pluralism and favors Euro-American history and literature,
- teaching methods that do not favor multiple learning styles,
- disciplinary policies,
- negative attitudes toward students who speak languages other than English unless they are native English speakers studying a second language in school,
- the limited role of students,
- the limited role of teachers, and
- limited parent and community involvement.

Race, class, and gender affect school personnel's expectations of student achievement.

It is also important to examine issues pertinent to supervising school psychologists who are members of minority groups. Even in urban schools, a minority school psychologist may work almost entirely with majority culture teachers and administrators. This may affect his or her feelings of empowerment and efficacy when practicing consultation.

Finally, supervisors who are themselves members of racial or ethnic minority groups have additional issues to address . Dickens and Dickens (1991) indicate that minority supervisors' progress through four stages as they adjust to the supervisory role. A false sense of security, relief at the appointment, and a lack of personal goals characterize the entry phase. The second phase, adjusting, is characterized by dissatisfaction, frustration, testing of the organization, and anger. During the third phase, planned growth, the supervisor develops a concentrated and strategic effort to succeed. The fourth phase, success, is characterized by achieving confidence, reaching goals, and setting new goals for the future.

Strategy: Encourage supervisees to adopt methods found to be successful with ethnic and racial minority children. Recent work with white teachers who are successful in working with minority children has found that these teachers employ a number of strategies that separate them from teachers who are less successful with minority students. Successful teachers refuse to buy into myths such as meritocracy and cultural superiority, they emphasize the positive aspects of minority cultures and negative aspects of the majority culture, and they openly discuss cultural and language differences and politics with the children. Such an approach appears to empower the children to take responsibility for their learning and to acquire the level of English literacy required for academic success (Bartholeme, 1998). Similar adaptations in supervision appear appropriate.

Delpit (1995) argues that minority children need to be taught explicitly the written and spoken language for effective participation in the mainstream of American life. It is our responsibility not to eliminate students' home language but rather to add other voices to their repertoire.

Excellent books every supervisor and supervisee should read:

Nieto, S. (1992). *Affirming diversity: the sociopolitical context of multicultural education*. New York: Longman.

Okun, B., Fried, J., & Okun, M. L. (1999). *Understanding diversity*. Pacific Grove, CA: Brooks/Cole.

Barona, A., & Garcia, E. E. (1990). *Children at risk: Poverty, minority status, and other issues in educational equity*. Washington, DC: National Association of School Psychologists.

Kozol, J. (1991). *Savage inequalities: Children in America's schools*. New York: Harper.

Vargas, L. A., & Koss-Chioino (Eds.), (1992). *Working with culture: Psychotherapeutic interventions with ethnic minority children and adolescents*. San Francisco: Jossey-Bass.

Jones, R. L. (1988). *Psychoeducational assessment of minority group children: A casebook*. Berkeley, CA: Cobb & Henry.

35

Class

Class affects identity, feelings of loyalty, and expectations about education, life style, and many other variables. Classism is made more complex by our cultures' attribution of individual responsibility for class membership ("anyone can make it"). Class differences and classism may arise because of different backgrounds between the supervisor and supervisee. They most certainly will arise because of differences between supervisees and their clients, and have a profound impact on the practice of school psychology; inattention to class can result in "blaming the victim" (Lappin & Hardy, 1997). Finally, although many school personnel are not from middle class families, they have frequently adopted middle class values and stereotypes and may be intolerant of the values of other classes. This intolerance impacts the consultation strategies employed by school psychologists.

Strategy: Consider class. Because class is an important aspect of self-image and permeates interpersonal interactions, it is important for both supervisors and supervisees to become more aware of their attitudes toward class. The following exercise can be helpful.

Activity 2-6: Uncover your attitudes regarding class

- With what class did you identify as a child?
- As an adult?
- What have been your experiences with persons from a class other than your own?
- In what class are you raising your children?
- What do you believe happens when individuals from two different classes marry?
- Not infrequently after divorce one parent changes class. What is the experience of children living simultaneously in two different classes?
- What happens in a non college-educated family when one member receives a college scholarship?
- How would it change your family relationships if you suddenly had to immigrate to another country and live in the new country in a lower class?
- What does "your" class say about other classes?
- What do you think "other" classes say about yours?
- How do you judge to what class a person belongs? (Occupation? Level of education? Size or location of home?)
- At what age did your class of origin expect you to:
    - Finish with your education?
    - Be financially independent?
    - Get married?
    - Have children?

- Would you say your class expects individuals to:
    - Act in their own interest?
    - Share with less fortunate persons?
    - Rely on the structures of technology, law, and religion?
    - Value traditionally male traits of assertiveness, competition, performance, and success?
    - Value traditionally female traits of care, service, and solidarity?
    - Focus on and plan for the future over short-term gains?

(Adapted from Ross, 1995; Lappin & Hardy, 1997)

Strategy: Encourage supervisees to uncover cultural conflicts. Nieto (1992) explores complex interactions among personal, social, political, and educational factors that lead to the success or failure of children. Our education system was designed to tear down barriers of class and caste and provide all with equal education, yet our schools are unsuccessful with many students, particularly those from cultural minority, linguistically diverse, or poor families. Sometimes what is valued by a culture is devalued in schools, forcing a child to choose alienation from either school or family. For example, if a culture values cooperation and a child is in a school that values competition, a child may be forced to abandon the values of his culture to be successful in that competitive school. Therefore, frequently one of the prices of successful assimilation into our educational system is an abandonment of culture of origin, which is counterproductive and "an unnecessarily high price to pay for academic success and social acceptance" (Nieto, 1992).

In our schools very little bilingual education is provided, even though 14% of the population is in need. Political polemics notwithstanding, bilingual educators advocate students learning English. In fact, instruction in English as a Second Language (ESL) is always a component of a good bilingual program (Nieto, 1992). Bilingual education involves teaching content in both languages so that, for example, the child knows scientific terminology in both English and the native language. Bilingualism is seen as a threat because it is concerned with the relative power of groups, and because it challenges the American tradition that native language and culture need to be forgotten in order to be a successful student and a "real American." Yet research results reveal that bilingual education leads to success in school, improves communication with family members, and improves proficiency in English (Nieto, 1992). It takes children and adolescents five to seven years to become proficient in English, far too much time to postpone content instruction.

Successful minority students interviewed by Nieto (1992) discussed feeling unable to identify as both American and as part of their own cultural group. These feelings sometimes resulted in students "creating new cultures," or selecting from an array of values and behaviors. Most students are proud of their own culture and resist complete assimilation, but they are also aware that their culture may be devalued in school. For some students, the more they were involved in resisting assimilation while maintaining their culture and language, the more successful they were in school. In addition, success is almost inevitably associated with activities beyond academics such as hobbies, religious groups, and sports. These activities serve to focus the student, provide a shield against peer pressure, develop critical thinking and leadership skills, and provide a feeling of belonging. Supervisors should encourage school psychologists to consider these issues as they develop prevention programs and intervention plans for students.

Many successful bicultural or multicultural students speak of having teachers who showed they cared by preparing for classes, making classes interesting, having patience, and providing curriculum that affirmed their language, culture, or concerns (Nieto, 1992). Their parents were described as having a high regard for education and inclined to motivate their children by sacrificing for them and having high expectations. However, these parents often did not feel comfortable coming to the school or helping their children with homework.

Another example of conflicts between cultural values and schools is found in migrant families. The value placed on financially supporting the family, starting at ages 10-12, is so strong in migrant families that it interferes with school attendance, school completion, and community attachment. Additional challenges faced by migrant children include minimal health care despite considerable health risks, minimal income, multiple languages (English is often a third language, after Spanish and an indigenous language), and an extremely high rate of school transfers (Henning-Stout, 1996). School psychology supervisors can help effect needed supports such as increased communication, respect, a national curriculum, full inclusion and equal opportunity in school, and reliable transportation to and from school. Furthermore, supervisors working in agricultural areas employing migrant workers are challenged to help their schools develop specialized programs to meet the educational needs of migrant children.

37

Case study 2-1

A school psychologist working in a large Midwestern city noticed that a substantial number of parents, originally from Tennessee and Kentucky, did not return for second pupil personnel meetings to discuss their children. She decided that cultural issues were a concern and decided to learn more about the culture of these states. To do so, she read autobiographies, watched movies, and interviewed parents and teachers originally from the area. From this exploratory work, she developed several hypotheses that she checked with the aforementioned interviewees. She concluded that several factors were making the parents uncomfortable, and she made the following recommendations to the school pupil personnel team and principal:

1. Allow extra meeting time to permit polite socialization before going into the business part of the meeting.
2. To be respectful and avoid creating feelings of being "beholden" do not give clothing or other items as charity to children, but charge a nominal amount.
3. To respect the need for family solidarity, sometimes involve siblings when children are disciplined or participate in peer mediation.
4. Develop a school-wide policy against bullying and name-calling, and include "Hill Billy" and "Redneck" on the unacceptable list.

Harry, Allen, and McLaughlin (1996) described another example of a cultural conflict with education. They found that parents of African American pre-school children saw school as the root of success and defined the purposes of school as follows: to provide academics (reading, writing, and math), to teach the child social and personal behaviors needed for success in school and life (to share, sit down, pay attention), and to provide a safe haven. They were not concerned that the schools teach problem solving and practical skills, since those were thought to be learned at home or in the community. These parents perceived schools as "doing their job" when the children learned basic reading, writing, and arithmetic through explicit instruction, repeated drill, and practice. The parents had faith in phonics and perceived sight-reading as illogical. Parents also expected their children to receive explicit instruction in the dominant English dialect. A "good teacher" was described as having a sincere interest in the children, implementing firm classroom and behavior management, using structured teaching methods, and assigning and promptly grading regular homework. Evidence of the child's progress in basic skills was evidence of good teaching. "Pushing" by a teacher was seen as evidence of a teacher who cared.

A "good school" was defined as orderly and traditional, and as having firm discipline, a principal who wasn't afraid of the kids, and a focus on explicitly teaching children the behaviors that will make them more acceptable (and therefore safer) in mainstream society. Good schools were also expected to serve community needs and to provide a structured, sequenced environment in which the children made progress in reading, writing, and arithmetic (Harry et al., 1996). Schools and teachers that do not match parental definitions of "good" are likely to suffer from insufficient parental and community support.

Ethical dilemma 2-5

Your supervisee has been working in one particular school for several years. It is a school comprised of children from two distinct classes: children from the wealthy, gentrifying families and children from impoverished families. Your supervisee has noticed that one particular teacher invariably refers every boy from the impoverished families for psychological testing and is quite contemptuous toward the boys and their families. *What are the ethical concerns? What can be done?*

Strategy: Foster diversity among supervisees and supervisors. There are many advantages to counting bilingual and bicultural school psychologists among members of the school psychology department. There are clearly advantages for ethnic minority children and parents to have psychologists from their own ethnic group. In addition, diversity among department members can be a source of strength, creativity, and productivity. For this to occur between individuals of different cultures, there must be positive interdependence among members, a group identity based on a common set of values, personal relationships that encourage open discussions, and open clarification of common misunderstandings (Johnson & Johnson, 1994).

Dickens and Dickens (1991) suggest that minorities adopt a number of strategies to facilitate success. These suggestions may be helpful to ethnic minority school psychologists who work in schools with majority culture faculty. They would also be helpful to an ethnic minority supervisor. The suggestions include: prioritizing obtaining knowledge, clarifying expectations, finding areas of mutual interest, increasing comfort when you are the only minority in a meeting by reminding yourself that you are an integral part of the meetings, focusing on responsibilities and producing results, and cultivating two support networks, one with majority culture colleagues, the other (offsite if necessary) with members of your own minority group.

Gender

Counseling and family therapy literature reveals that gender issues affect supervision. Because of our culture's patriarchy, women's contributions, whether as supervisee or supervisor, are highly likely to be devalued (Bernard & Goodyear, 1998; Turner & Fine, 1997). This devaluing can occur in a wide variety of settings, from interactions with administrators to relationships with supervisees.

Strategy: Address gender as a supervisory issue. Supervisors can increase knowledge of supervisees and supervisors of both sexes regarding women and power equity issues. They can also ensure that male supervisors treat women supervisees appropriately, and be sensitive that women supervisors are accorded respect by male supervisees (Turner & Fine, 1997).

Ethical dilemma 2-6

A woman supervisor has a staff of eight school psychologists, six women and two men. All of them are capable school psychologists, approximately the same age, and married. The supervisor has become increasingly aware that she feels that the two men are inappropriately flirtatious toward her. They make casual sexual comments, touch her, and stand in close proximity. Relative to the women, they are casual about their work. For example, they are often late and not uncommonly leave group supervision meetings early. *What are the ethical issues? What should be done?*

Sexual orientation

Sexual orientation is relevant as a supervisory issue for two reasons. First, supervisees may be of a different sexual orientation than their supervisors, and it is important that supervisors create a safe environment for self-disclosure within the supervisory relationship. It is equally important to help supervisees with minority sexual orientations understand the implications and repercussions, if any, for self-disclosure to administrators and to others within the school district. Secondly, supervisees are very likely to encounter clients of different sexual orientations, and they will need to know how to create an environment for self-disclosure and support (Long, 1997).

39

Strategy: Address lesbian, gay, and bisexual issues. Once supervisees are aware of the importance of understanding persons of diverse sexual orientations, supervisors can help them increase their knowledge in several ways (Long, 1997; Powers & Ellis, 1995). For example, a supervisor can increase understanding of the heterosexual bias in theories and research of psychology, and the inappropriateness of application of heterosexuality as a source of normative standards. Supervisors can help supervisees acquire a greater understanding of the great psychological energy needed to maintain invisible relationships, of the "coming out" process in both the personal and professional spheres, of the gay rights movement and current social battles, and of the effects of homophobia, including the threat of physical harm or death. Through both individual and group supervision, supervisors can help supervisees relinquish homosexual stereotypes through knowledge of pertinent research findings. As reported in Long (1997), research has demonstrated that approximately 63% of lesbians and 50% of homosexuals are in steady relationships (Peplau & Cochran, 1990); that many gays and lesbians establish life-long partnerships (Blumstein & Schwartz, 1983; Bryant & Demian, 1994; McWhirter & Mattison, 1984); that relationship satisfaction of homosexual couples is comparable to satisfaction of heterosexual couples (Duffy & Rusbult, 1986; Kurdek & Schmitt, 1987; Peplau & Cochran, 1990); that no differences have been found between homosexuals and heterosexuals in effective parenting practices (Flaks, Ficher, Masterpasqua, & Joseph, 1995; Harris & Turner, 1985, 1986; Kirkpatrick, Smith, & Roy, 1981); that children of homosexuals do not experience sexual identity confusion, and are appropriately popular, socially adjusted, and socially competent (Golumbok, Spencer, & Rutter, 1983; Green, 1982; Kirkpatrick, Smith, & Roy, 1981; Patterson, 1994); and that children exposed to persons with minority sexual orientations are not more likely to be molested (Finkelhor, 1986; Riveria, 1987). Finally, supervisees can ensure that supervisees abide by ethical guidelines, refraining from trying to "convert" homosexuals to heterosexuality and referring them to other psychologists when the supervisee has insufficient knowledge, a conflict in values, or fears doing harm to the client.

Interpersonal conflict resolution

Interpersonal conflicts in supervision are sometimes overt. More often, they are covert wherein the supervisee and supervisor "collude" to ignore problems. The most common collusions are ignoring poor performance, permitting inadequate preparation for supervision, avoiding conflict, and ignoring areas of similarity or dissimilarity (Todd, 1997a).

Addressing conflicts and other interpersonal supervisory problems is an important aspect of a supervisor's interpersonal and communication skills. Such problem solving, including the identification and verification of the problem and the development, implementation, and confirmation of a solution, is, like consultation, best accomplished in conjunction with supervisees rather than in unilateral administrative actions (Loen, 1994).

Interpersonal problems in supervision can stem from two sources. First, they can involve the frustration of a goal, such as when a supervisee has a goal of increasing pre-referral intervention activities but the supervisor does not respect that process. Second, problems in supervision can involve unacceptable psychological distress on the part of either the supervisor or the supervisee. Supervisors may need to help supervisees resolve conflicts with other school personnel, such as dealing with administrators and teachers who demand inappropriate tests. As a leader of the school psychology department, the supervisor will probably both encounter and be in a position to help resolve conflict between various school personnel, whether due to negativity, questionable competence, or union politics. Finally, at times supervisors themselves are placed in two roles that can conflict, such as acting as both a school psychologist and a special education team leader.

Frequently, a supervisory problem involves more than one of these elements in that the frustration of a goal results in psychological distress. Poor job productivity, poor quality of service, and poor staff morale are all common symptoms of supervisory problems (McInerney, 1985). To resolve any of these conflicts the same basic strategies are employed.

Ethical dilemma 2-7

A supervisor of school psychologists believes that completing monthly reports on the status of services provided is a necessary and appropriate response to the long-term goal of complying with federal regulations. However, two individual school psychologists are neglecting to complete these reports, one because of inefficient time management and the other due to resentment. *What are the issues? What can be done?*

Strategy: Acquire conflict management strategies. Supervisors of school psychologists must not only be aware of effective methods to manage their own conflicts, but should also be prepared to guide their supervisees in the acquisition of conflict management skills. As Fleming, Fleming, Roach, and Oksman (1985) describe, school psychologists are likely to experience conflict within their jobs for a number of reasons. Examples of reasons include boundary-spanning roles across distinctly different subsystems with widely varied expectations, limited resources resulting in conflicts over the most appropriate interventions, rapidly advancing technology resulting in conflicts over appropriate assessment and interventions, and school organizations characterized by inadequate opportunities for communication.

Conflict should neither be perceived as "bad" nor ignored. Instead, conflict is best thought to signal a need to make remedial changes (Fleming, Fleming, Roach, & Oksman, 1985). A person's approach to handling conflict is characterized by the extent to which attempts are made to meet the interests of both partners in conflict (cooperating) as opposed to meeting one individual's needs (assertiveness) (Jamieson & Thomas, 1974). Conflict resolution focusing on assertively meeting one person's needs presumes that some issues are right, and that the use of persuasion, force, relationship endangering, and a win-lose strategy is appropriate. At the other extreme are supervisors who avoid conflict.

Collaborative conflict resolution can occur if a supervisor attempts to meet the needs of both sides. In this scenario, differences are seen as natural and appropriate. Resolution of conflict involves honest confrontation, objective problem solving, and the integration of both views into some common good (Sergiovanni & Starratt, 1998).

Conflict resolution takes place in three stages: exploration, discussion and communication, and resolution. During exploration, the objective is to identify the disputants and delineate the areas of conflict as specifically as possible (Maher, 1984).

During the discussion and communication phase, the disputants brainstorm a generous number of possible solutions without commentary. After a number of solutions are generated, the benefits and associated costs are discussed and one or more solutions are selected. During the resolution stage the plan is formalized, implemented, and evaluated. It is preferable to write the plan rather than simply present it orally. The plan should designate responsibility, time frames, and participation (Fleming et al., 1985). As is true for consultation, it is important that the results of the conflict resolution be evaluated through data collection.

In settings where school psychologists are unionized, the school psychologist may take an unresolved complaint to the union and file a grievance, which can progress up through the administration, involving increasing numbers of individuals at each level. To handle complaints and grievances well, it is important that supervisors treat them respectfully and with recognition so that the school psychologists feel they have merit. Respect is shown by listening carefully, discovering what is really of concern, remaining calm, getting all of the facts, asking him or her for his solution, explaining the reason for decisions, explaining how to appeal, and getting back to the person after the resolution for follow-up. To avoid grievances, the following steps are helpful (Halloran, 1981):

- communicate clear expectations;
- conduct frequent evaluations;
- give credit for good performances;
- give clear direction for needed areas of improvement;
- suggest policy changes to your own supervisor;
- enlist school psychologist participation in policy changes;
- make the best use of each school psychologist's strengths;
- encourage professional growth and responsibility; and,
- solicit problem solving from supervisees.

Ethical dilemma 2-8

In your district, school psychologists are not part of the teachers' bargaining unit. The teachers union has voted to "work to rule," which means that they arrive 15 minutes before the start of school and leave 15 minutes after the close. To show support for the teachers, and to avoid crossing picket lines and obliterate collegial and consultative relationships, school psychologists are also working to rule. Because at the high school team meetings are normally held after school hours, this has resulted in no team meetings being held. The Director of Special Education, your supervisor, is insisting that school psychologists cross the picket lines and meet with parents during after school hours. *What are the ethical issues? What can be done?*

Strategy: Assess and address conflict. To assess a supervision problem founded in interpersonal relations, the following steps are recommended by McInerney (1985):

1. Consciously observe actions and ask others to provide information about their feelings and thoughts. Look in particular for the presence of anger, persistent job dissatisfaction, limited expectations about the future, symptoms of depression, and self-defeating actions, feelings, or thoughts;

2. Assess whether overwork or underwork, either of which can lead to depression or job burnout, characterizes the situation;

3. Observe your own behavior as you exercise authority. Look for evidence that you avoid exercising authority, that you are unnecessarily authoritarian, sarcastic or hostile, that you are inconsistent or do not follow up on requests. If these traits are apparent, you may need to investigate your own feelings about the individuals involved as well as about the exercising of authority in general;

4. Brainstorm a number of potential solutions; and sort them into categories of minor (taking less than a month with available resources), moderate (under the control of the group, possible with available resources, and taking 3 to 6 months), and major (involving individuals not in the group, require additional resources, and/or taking more than a year) challenges;

5. Target one moderate goal per quarter, obtain help with major goals, and determine appropriate minor goals;

6. Plan and implement action plans with staff;

7. Evaluate the results; and

8. Repeat the process, since improvement should be ongoing.

Ethical dilemma 2-9

You are a supervising school psychologist in a large district. Because you are also assigned to three schools, you are only able to meet with your supervisees once a week for individual supervision and every other week for group supervision. Within a few weeks of the beginning of the school year numerous complaints surface from principals and parents about the new school psychologist in the district. These, along with your own observations, make it obvious that you made a serious hiring error. The new school psychologist is in need of substantial, daily supervision. He has a yearlong contract. *What are the ethical dilemmas? What should be done?*

Strategy: When appropriate, terminate a supervisory relationship. Situations do occur when a supervisory relationship needs to be terminated. At such a time, supervisors should summarize the progress made by the supervisee, discuss the supervisee's additional need for supervision and training, draw generalizations from the supervision, resolve interpersonal issues, review the written evaluation with the supervisee in a personal interview, and bring supervision to a closure (Mead, 1990; Todd, 1997a).

On rare occasions, supervisors may recommend that an intern not receive credit for an internship, or that a supervisee be advised to leave the profession of school psychology altogether due to clinical incompetence, academic status, ethical violations, or legal grounds. Clearly defined standards, evaluation methods, and procedures for dismissal, should be made available to supervisees at the beginning of a placement and/or job to adhere to ethical principles and to minimize objections and legal challenges (Todd, 1997a).

43

44

Theories provide practicing psychologists with structures and strategies to make sense of the multiple variables affecting the children and adults with whom they work. Theoretical orientation emerges as a result of both training and experience. An active awareness of the concepts and theories that underlie one's professional practice is essential for integrity in practicing school psychology and all of its components: assessment, consultation, counseling, and other direct interventions.

Just as psychological theories and concepts guide decisions made by practitioners, they similarly guide decisions made by supervisors. Supervisors' theoretical orientation and belief systems regarding assessment, consultation, and direct interventions profoundly affect their expectations of supervisees.

In addition to working from models and theories relevant to school psychology, supervisors of school psychologists work from a conscious or unconscious model of supervision. Although supervisory techniques are common across theoretical orientation (Mead, 1990), an active awareness of theories that underlie one's supervisory work is essential for effective supervision (Bernard & Goodyear, 1998; Conoley & Bahns, 1995). Counseling psychology, industrial/organizational psychology, and management literature propose an extremely large number of theories of supervision (Bernard & Goodyear, 1998; Noe et al., 1996; Rue & Byars, 1997; Todd & Storm, 1997). The following pages address a few of these models and theories and suggest their implications for school psychology supervision. The chapter concludes with a discussion of techniques of supervision, each more or less appropriate depending upon the theory of supervision and the developmental level of the supervisee.

Knowledge of these theories and models is essential to make informed decisions. However, supervisors of school psychologists should be wary of blindly adopting models without carefully considering their implications. As Sergiovanni (1995) indicates, school administrations should carefully consider the differences between schools and corporations before adopting management strategies. Furthermore, it should be noted that empirical research on the relative advantages and disadvantages of supervision models is scanty. It is particularly lacking in the field of school psychology (Pennington, 1989).

MODELS OF ADMINISTRATIVE SUPERVISION

Industrial psychology and business management literature discusses supervision from a number of perspectives, including supervision functions (such as planning, organizing, staffing, leading, and controlling), roles of supervision (for example, interpersonal roles, informational roles, and decisional roles), and supervision skills (conceptual, human relations, and technical) (Rue & Byars, 1997). Leadership behaviors have been categorized in several ways, including the following: planning and organizing, problem solving, clarifying, informing, monitoring, motivating, consulting, recognizing, supporting, managing conflict, team building, networking, delegating, developing and mentoring, and rewarding (Yukl, Wall, & Lepsinger, 1990).

Supervisory types
Sergiovanni and Starratt (1998) categorize supervisory practices into three different types. These types are the Traditional Management, Human Relations, and Human Resources approaches.

Traditional Management has an autocratic, product-based philosophy manifested by a focus on the following: controlling the supervisee, accounting to administrative goals, developing employee efficiency and competence, meeting performance objectives, and analyzing cost-benefits. This model was widely developed during and after the Industrial Revolution. In this model, the goals of administrators tend to take priority, leading to a "top-down" management style. Efficient production is the chief goal.

The Human Relations approach developed in reaction to the traditional management after World War I. This approach has an egalitarian, relationship-based philosophy and emphasizes creating satisfaction in staff, minimizing accountability, and responding to each individual's goals. In this model, the goals of supervisees take priority, leading to a "bottom-up" management style.

The Human Resources approach combines the product-based and relationship-based approaches and focuses on adopting shared decision-making practices. This approach leads to both increased effectiveness and employee satisfaction. In this model, the goals of the individual and the goals of the organization are integrated and simultaneously addressed. This model has become prevalent in many places of business. For example, in the "Search for Excellence" manifestation, high achieving companies were analyzed and found to have several common characteristics, including leadership and attention to both internal and external needs. This model has been adopted by some school districts, particularly those with "site based management." The "Total Quality Management" approach has been adopted by several school districts, and focuses on increasing the quality of products, meeting the needs of customers, coaching and empowering employees, and adopting collective and cross-

functional approaches (Noe, et al., 1996; Rue & Byars, 1997).

Traditional Management approaches can result in increased short-term effectiveness but decreased long-term effectiveness, due to decreased staff morale. In contrast, the Human Relations approach can result in increased staff morale, but compromises both short- and long-term effectiveness. The Human Resource perspective results in increased effectiveness both in the long- and short-term and increases staff morale as well (Sergiovanni & Starratt, 1998).

According to Sergiovanni and Starratt (1998), in each of these approaches, supervisors play a different role. In the Traditional Management approach, the supervisor translates the desires and objectives of the top administrator to the supervisees. In so doing, the supervisor acts as a buffer between administrators and those who provide direct services.

In the Human Relations approach, the supervisor is more peripheral; the supervisor is linked to both administration and supervisees, who in turn also have direct links to one another. The primary function of the supervisors is to support supervisees, to be sympathetic to their problems, and to attend to increasing overall satisfaction. In this scenario, a supervisor can become marginalized, excluded from important decisions, and reduced to impersonal activities associated with deskwork such as ordering materials.

In the Human Resources approach, supervisors are key members of the leadership team. They link top administration to supervisees but also link supervisees to top administration, taking an integrative rather than a buffering role. In this model, the supervisor of school psychologists has the best opportunity to assume a transformational leadership role.

The Human Resources model, with its emphasis on adopting shared decision-making practices, appears to be most appropriate for the

Table 3-1 Supervisory Styles

	Traditional	Human Relations	Human Resource
Short term effectivess	+	-	+
Long term effectiveness	-	-	+
Staff morale	-	+	+
Supervisor role between supervisees and administration	Buffer	Periphery	Key
Supervisee role with supervisor	Dependent	Independent	Inter-dependent

supervisor of school psychologists, since the ethical imperative for supervisors of school psychologists is to attend to the rights of supervisees, clients, the public, and the profession. However, while the Human Resource approach is generally the preferred approach in the supervision of professionals, individual differences in supervisees will lead to differences in the appropriate supervisory style. This approach is not appropriate for individuals in need of close supervision. For example, beginning school psychologists, or individuals who are not intrinsically motivated, may require a more traditional management style (Sergiovanni & Starratt, 1988). The differences among the three management styles are summarized in Table 3-1, above.

Leadership models of supervision

The literature on business management and educational supervision emphasizes the differentiation of leaders from non-leaders. As indicated by Hogan, Curphy, & Hogan (1994), leadership is one of the most thoroughly researched topics in applied psychology. A review of the literature by Bass (1990) found over 7,000 articles, books, and presentations. Unfortunately, effective leadership appears to be uncommon; between 50% and 70% of supervisees characterize their supervisors as incompetent, either unwilling to deal with problems and conflicts or

behaving tyrannically toward supervisees. Poor supervision can result in high turnover, insubordination, malingering, and even sabotage (Hogan et al., 1994). Because of the potential impact on children and adolescents, ineffective supervisors in school psychology can have inestimable negative consequences.

A person can hold a supervisory position without being a leader, but effective supervisors tend to be leaders who facilitate and integrate the needs of individuals within the goals of the organization (Mann, 1965). Both interpersonal and structural factors influence positive leadership outcomes. Interpersonal factors include trust, respect, warmth, and rapport resulting in an attachment between leaders and their subordinates. Structural factors include organizing, directing, defining group activities, and monitoring progress toward goals (Fleishman, 1967; Fleishman & Harris, 1962).

The leader's function is to keep the group oriented toward goals, to stabilize situations, to make decisions, to initiate change, and to mobilize people to face and attack difficult problems. Hogan et al. (1994) indicate that leadership involves "persuading other people to set aside for a period of time their individual concerns and to pursue a common goal that is important for the responsibilities and welfare of a group" (p. 493). Leaders do not dominate others, but

47

encourage others to adopt group goals as their own. They also build highly functional teams to achieve these goals. Effective educational leaders are characterized by vision, tenacity, self-evaluation and improvement, time commitment, and career dedication (Goldberg, 1995).

According to James MacGregor Burns (1978), leadership occurs when a person with motives and purposes mobilizes resources to arouse and satisfy the motives of his/her followers. Leadership can be either transactional or transformative.

Transactional leadership focuses on basic motives, fundamental needs, and extrinsic reinforcers. Leaders and followers barter needs and services to achieve different sets of objectives. Traditional Management scenarios often use this type of leadership.

Transformative leadership focuses on higher order needs and intrinsic reinforcers. Leaders and followers unite in the pursuit of common goals. Transformational leadership focuses on "building" or arousing potential, satisfying higher level needs, raising expectations, elevating shared goals into a covenant, and making improvement routine.

Supervisors are appointed by administrators, but leaders obtain their position from group consensus. Supervisors can be leaders if they are skillful and trustworthy, if they are well-respected, and if they listen to their supervisees. If a supervisor does not engage in or is incapable of effective leadership, the group chooses an informal leader within the group. Informal leaders are the individuals that the group perceives to be able to help the group achieve its objectives. Typically, informal leaders are skilled in communicating, setting objectives, and giving direction. Groups not infrequently choose two informal leaders: a task leader who pushes the group to accomplish objectives, and a social leader, who maintains harmony within the group (Rue & Byars, 1997).

A serious problem with such informal leadership is that the informal leader and the group frequently develop goals that conflict with the larger organization goals (Halloran, 1981). For example, in a school psychology department, this may occur when a subgroup develops a specialty interest and area of research not shared by the department supervisor or the rest of the department.

To ensure competence, traditional leadership emphasizes managing, manipulating, planning, giving directions, providing a monitoring system, using extrinsic motivators, and providing a congenial atmosphere. Value-added leadership moves beyond competence into excellence and is the type of leadership frequently found in highly successful businesses and schools (Sergiovanni, 1990). Value-added leadership involves extraordinary performance and emphasizes purpose, empowerment, preparation, guidance, accountability, intrinsic motivators, collegiality, and leadership with passion and focus.

Expressing and articulating a vision, or emphasizing purpose, is an essential aspect of leadership. The leader builds a covenant among administrators, parents, teachers, and students around shared values, commitments, and dreams. "The unique human response is one of spirit; and our spirit responds to values, beliefs, moral dimensions, and standards. Moral leadership taps the spirit" (Sergiovanni, 1990, p. 28).
In effective value-added leadership, the leader is credible, honest, forthright, and sincere. The leader models beliefs, exemplifies standards, and represents and symbolizes something of value to followers. Leadership is a grave moral responsibility because it unavoidably involves an unequal power relationship, and any relationship in which there is an unequal distribution of power raises moral questions (Sergiovanni, 1990). To avoid exploitation, value-added leaders take extra care when they and their supervisees have additional power differentials, such

as when the two individuals differ in age, ethnicity, gender, or race.

School leaders usually have goals to enhance student learning and functioning, to enhance the school's functioning, and to increase the competence, independence, and well-being of supervisees. "Leadership combines management know-how with values and ethics...questions of what is good, what makes sense, and what is worth doing deserve equal billing with questions of efficacy and effectiveness...leaders (are) known by the side they emphasize...moral considerations are the beginning and the end of value-added leadership" (Sergiovanni, 1990, p. 29).

Value added leaders find ways to make their supervisee's work intrinsically motivating. They are tough-minded when dealing with core values, and they expect adherence to the common values of the "vision." But they are also flexible and allow wide discretion in how individuals implement these values in day-to-day decisions. Tichy's (1997) model of leadership emphasizes the idea that leaders incorporate repeated change into their organization, have a clearly articulated vision that is reality- and experience-based, and teach this vision and corresponding values to all members of their organization. Tichy indicates that leaders repeatedly destroy and creatively remake their organizations in response to shifts in external factors such as economies, marketplaces, and societies. To do so, leaders must abandon old ideas and methods and "adopt new and better ones. They must also be able to help each and every employee generate the high levels of positive energy needed to do the same" (p. 24).

According to Tichy (1997), leaders generate ideas, instill values, create positive energy, and make difficult decisions. They assess current reality and deal with situations as they are, not as they were or as they would like them to be. After assessing reality, leaders decide on a response, determine what actions are needed,

mobilize appropriate resources, and ensure that desired actions are appropriately implemented.

Case study 3-1

A supervisor of school psychologists discovered that group testing scores revealed a curriculum weakness at the third grade level. In response, he initiated a "recovery" program, in which curriculum-based measurement and an exemplary reading program were implemented. A pilot program in one classroom proved a marked success. The school psychologist met with elementary level administrators to describe the program and its success. In turn, each administrator provided leadership in developing similar programs in their schools. The supervising school psychologist ensured that all district school psychologists were skilled in the measurement methods. The principals and assistant superintendent provided training for teachers in other classrooms and buildings and monitored the implementation of the program.

Leaders develop a teachable point of view composed of clearly articulated ideas and values based on knowledge and experience. When they articulate these views to others, they emphasize the importance of supervisees becoming leaders as well. The leaders' articulated ideas establish the framework for actions at all levels, provide a context for decision making, and motivate people toward a common goal. Through their own behavior, leaders exemplify their described values and model energy, focus, and determination.

Change

As mentioned above, encouraging change is an essential component in leadership. Change can be internal (within the department), external (within the district, community, or state), or technological (in the field); change is not only inevitable, but is institutionalized in effective organizations. Despite the need for change, individuals are naturally resistant to change when they are unsure of its effects or suspect that the change will not be in their best interest. Other typical reasons for resistance to change include a fear of the unknown, a fear of economic loss, a fear that current skills and expertise will be less valuable, a perceived threat to power, inconvenience, or a threat to pleasurable social interactions (Rue & Byars, 1997). To mitigate resistance, change is implemented in three steps: (a) breaking down forces that maintain the original procedure, (b) presenting a new alternative, and (c) establishing the new procedure by positively reinforcing change. In order to effectively move to the third step, supervisors need to build trust, discuss upcoming changes, involve supervisees, ensure that the changes are reasonable, avoid forcing the change, and follow a reasonable time schedule (Rue & Byars, 1997).

MODELS OF PSYCHOLOGICAL SUPERVISION

Models of supervision based on developmental theories

As described in the previous chapter, developmental models stem from the developmental theories of Dewey and Piaget who both suggested that an invariant sequence of cognitive development is characteristic of individuals as they learn. According to developmental models, individuals progress through distinct developmental stages as they learn a skill or a profession, each of which requires a unique supervisory approach (Cagnon & Russell, 1995; Dreyfus & Dreyfus, 1991; Stoltenberg & Delworth, 1987).

Models of supervision based on consultation theories

Business management (Brown, 1982), educational supervision (Hopkins & Moore, 1993),

mental health supervision (Wasik & Fishbein, 1982), and school psychology (Curtis & Yager, 1981, 1987) have all used a consultation/problem solving model in supervision. Supervision and consultation bear many similarities since they both involve collaborative problem solving. Supervisors, like consultants, attend to the stages of entry, problem identification and clarification, generation of alternative solutions, evaluation of alternative solutions, intervention application, and outcome evaluation.

A good interpersonal relationship between constituents is essential in both consultation and supervision. Both strive to improve the functioning of the consultee/supervisee so that future independent functioning is more likely. Consultation and supervision both focus on work-related problems rather than personal problems and avoid the complications of providing therapy (Knoff, 1986).

Supervisory relationships differ from consultative relationships in that the former involves authority and a power differential. The supervisory process is not voluntary and the supervisee is less able to reject recommended strategies. Furthermore, the supervisor shares responsibility for the client's welfare with the supervisee (Knoff, 1986). Supervisors and consultants also differ in terms of the evaluative component present in supervision. As noted by Bernard and Goodyear (1998), the evaluative nature of supervision differentiates it from both counseling and consultation.

As Curtis and Yager (1981, 1987) indicate, the supervisor of school psychologists takes the following steps in the application of the consultative model:

1. Establish a positive relationship with the supervisee;
2. Assess the supervisee's strengths and weaknesses;
3. Establish and reach a consensus with the supervisee regarding learning needs;

4. Determine the extent to which supervision should be process or content oriented;
5. Delineate the desired learning goals;
6. Implement interventions;
7. Evaluate progress; and,
8. Determine whether the goal has been met and either reach closure on that goal or continue to address the same problem through alternate interventions.

Models of supervision based on therapeutic theories

Psychodynamic orientations to supervision. As mentioned previously, the tradition of intense supervision of therapists began with the psychodynamic tradition (Greben & Ruskin, 1994). In this model, the supervisor focuses on developing a positive working relationship with the therapist, as well as fostering a therapeutic relationship between the client and therapist. It is presumed that the relationship between the supervisor and supervisee mirrors the dynamics of the relationship between the supervisee and the client. Just as clients are thought to relate to their therapists in the same style as they relate to others in their lives, especially parents, the supervisee is thought to relate to the supervisor in the same style as he or she relates to others, including clients. Issues of transference and counter-transference are emphasized. Supervisees' and supervisors' unresolved personal issues often emerge. However, it is important to note that supervision itself is distinct from therapy. When a supervisee has significant personal problems, the supervisor does not attempt to conduct therapy but instead refers the supervisee to another therapist (Neufeldt, Iversen, Juntunen, 1995).

While school psychology programs are rarely grounded in psychodynamic theory, many practicing school psychologists, and consequently supervisors, received their original training in the psychodynamic tradition. Regardless of their training, supervisors of school psychologists should be aware of the likelihood that supervisees' personal issues may interfere with their objectivity and practice. For example, school psychologists who are children of an alcoholics may find that they become either inappropriately over involved or distant when working with children of alcoholics themselves. While supervisors of school psychologists should not be providing therapy to supervisees, they should certainly be sensitive to recurring patterns of difficulty and should help develop problem solving strategies.

Ethical dilemma 3-1

You have been supervising a female school psychologist on a weekly basis for three years and have noticed a pattern where she almost invariably interprets the behavior of males–principals, teachers, other school psychologists, and parents–as sexually motivated. You suspect that these interpretations may not be accurate and that they are interfering with her ability to generate alternative hypotheses. *What are the ethical issues? What steps should you take?*

Client-centered approaches to supervision.

The client-centered approach to therapy, developed by Carl Rogers (1958), indicates that congruence, empathy, unconditional positive regard, and warmth are essential in therapy and in and of themselves lead to positive, individual psychological growth. Supervision from a client-centered approach relies on developing similar characteristics in the supervisor-supervisee relationship. It focuses on developing the supervisee's skills in fostering each of the above traits in client relationships through the use of audio tapes, live demonstrations, modeling, and role-

51

plays (Conoley & Bahns, 1995). The direct analysis of the content and process of sessions enables supervisees to recognize their tendency to inadvertently affect the progress of sessions.

Behavioral approaches to supervision. The behavioral approach to working with clients relies on modifying observable behaviors through immediate comments and positive reinforcement schedules (Krumboltz & Thorensen, 1969). The same principles hold for the behavioral approach to supervision (Neufeldt et al., 1995). In this model, supervisors and supervisees jointly assess skills and develop goals to remedy areas of weakness. The supervisor and supervisee generate and implement strategies to accomplish these goals, and the supervisor provides frequent feedback to shape the supervisee's behavior. The supervisor and supervisee conduct another assessment after intervention, and then reestablish goals based on the results. Benefits of this approach include clear communication, frequent feedback, and careful monitoring of supervisees (Conoley & Bahns, 1995).

Cognitive-behavioral orientation to supervision. The cognitive behaviorists focus on the interrelation of thinking, feelings, and actions of clients. Therapy addresses affect and the connections between thoughts and feelings; this approach addresses the processes of thinking through and practicing solutions to problems (Meichenbaum, 1977; Kendall & Braswell, 1985).

Similarly, a cognitive-behavioral approach to supervision of school psychologists focuses on changing observable behaviors by modifying cognitions, affect, and actions (Kratochwill, Bergan, & Mace, 1981). In this model, the following components are essential: behavioral feedback, behavior modification programs, didactic instruction, direct observation of the supervisees, program generalization, programmed instruction, modeling, and rehearsing or role-plays.

Models of supervision based on assessment theories

When school psychologists conduct assessments they adhere to models or theories regarding the interactions between the nature of intelligence, the meaning of achievement, the nature of personality, and the meaning of behavior. For many years, the typical school psychologist wrote reports determined by the Stanford-Binet or Wechsler definitions of intelligence, including utilitarian derived subscales as a means of analysis. In contrast, many currently trained school psychologists are using a cross-battery integrative approach to intelligence assessment (McGrew & Flanagan, 1996).

These are not the only possible models of intelligence. Others include Naglieri's PASS theory (Naglieri, 1997), the theory of multiple intelligences as promoted by Howard Gardner (1991), and Feuerstein's (1979) model of learning potential. Some models of assessment proceed as if the traditional definition of intelligence is irrelevant, and focus instead on discrete acquisition of academic skills as measured by Curriculum Based Measurement.

The model of assessment to which to which a supervisor adheres clearly impacts the expectations he or she has for those being supervised. Complications are minimal if both supervisor and supervisee adhere to the same model, but can be numerous and complicated if they differ.

Models of supervision based on systemic/ecological theories

The systems approach is another basic model of supervision used both in mental health work (Todd & Storm, 1997) and in business (Rue & Byars, 1997). Four basic principles drive systems theory:

1. the search for isomorphisms, or common rules stemming from similar causation, including communication, growth, and interactions of elements within their environment;

2. the arrangement of empirical facts hierarchically ordered on complexity, starting at the sim-

52

plest level and extending through the most complex;

3. the use of a holistic, non-reductionistic, *in toto* approach to elements, phenomena, and problems;

4. the simultaneous emphasis of both methodological theory and empirical investigation (Boulding, 1956; Sutherland, 1973; Von Bertalanffy, 1956).

The systems approach is applicable generally to the behavior sciences, education, and social sciences (Kaufman, 1972; Sarason, 1996; Sutherland, 1973) as well as to school psychology (Plas, 1986; Reschly & Ysseldyke, 1995). When using this perspective to support children and manage challenging behaviors, school psychologists assess and intervene at the systems (relational, family, school, and community) as well as the individual levels. The use of a holistic approach considers multiple factors, from the biological/neuropsychological elements and individual strengths and needs, to family, teacher, classroom, school, neighborhood, community, social, political, and cultural considerations. Studying the individual, or discrete aspects of the individual can be useful, but only if the psychologist feeds the "parts" back into the "whole" before the final analysis.

Considering all components of the system is an essential element of effective supervision of school psychologists. A school psychologist working from a systems approach looks beyond the comfortable boundaries of psychology and education into fields such as biology, social work, literature, art, and sociology. This requires abandoning defensive insularity and professional competition in favor of an integration of multiple perspectives and a collaboration with families and specialists from other fields. Ideally, unification of knowledge and disclosure of isomorphisms result. These in turn lead to effective communication, comprehensive treatment plans, and coordinated efforts.

In taking the systems approach, school psychologists shift from an emphasis on testing and categorization to an emphasis on supporting instruction in academic and social behaviors through direct and indirect interventions. During the past 20 years, school psychology as a profession has increasingly emphasized the importance of making a paradigm shift to the systems approach (Reschly & Ysseldyke, 1995; Talley & Short, 1995; Ysseldyke et al., 1997). Despite this emphasis, individual school psychologists do not all work from a systemic perspective. Effective supervision is essential to empower and enable school psychologists to make this paradigm shift.

Mead (1990) provides a systemic model of therapy supervision, called task-oriented supervision, which is designed to be independent of the theoretical model used by either supervisors or supervisees. This model focuses on changing the behavior of the therapist to increase its therapeutic impact "by arranging experiences or interventions that will change the therapist's responses to clients in clinical settings" (p. 19).

The task-oriented model considers three different systems: (1) the client, (2) the therapist, and (3) the supervisor. Mead considers these hierarchical; the client system, or level, is encompassed by the therapist system, and both the client and therapist systems are encompassed by the supervision system. Each system has six progressive stages: collecting data, setting goals, developing a plan, making observations, intervening, and determining progress.

In the client system, clients make observations about themselves, establish goals for therapy, and on some level evaluate the success of the therapy experience. At the therapist (supervisee) level, supervisees first make observations about themselves and prepare for clinical practice. Supervisees/therapists then make observations about the client, establish goals for therapy, and evaluate the success of the therapy. In turn, supervisors first make observations about their readiness for supervision, then assess the therapist's level of preparation. Supervisors then determine

53

supervision goals, develop assessment and observation procedures, develop a supervision plan, directly or indirectly observe the therapy, evaluate the success of the treatment, and then modify the assessment of the therapist accordingly. Finally, supervisors assess the success of the supervision.

Curtis and Yager (1981, 1987) describe a systemic approach to the supervision of school psychology. In this model, supervisors of school psychologists focus on the entire school system and its interactive parts, with overarching goals reflecting the progress of the school system and individuals within the system. Supervisors take the initiative to change the parts of the system that are most influential, which may be either at the individual psychologist's level or at the systemic (school or district) level. Regarding both systemic change and individual supervision, supervising school psychologists take the problem-solving steps described above.

A practical application of this approach is found in the strategic planning model found in business management literature (Noe et al., 1996; Rue & Byars, 1997). In this model the following steps are taken:

- Develop a vision.
- Conduct an assessment of:
  1. external opportunities and barriers, and
  2. internal strengths and weaknesses.
- Define a mission and articulate goals that address the vision and take into consideration the results of the assessment.
- Develop a strategic plan:
  1. list measurable objectives and major activities that support each goal,
  2. list action items for each objective which articulate responsibilities for the completion of each activity, deadlines, and budget, and also specify techniques for continual improvement of methods and procedures, and

3. obtain administrative approval.
- Implement the strategic plan.
- Evaluate the process and the results:
  1. conduct formative evaluation. Was the plan implemented as planned?
  2. conduct a summative evaluation. Were goals and objectives met?
- Feed the evaluation back into the vision and assessment.

"Building a home" is a helpful analogy for clarifying the strategic planning model:

Building a Home

- Develop a vision: *(Have a home and raise a family)*.
- Conduct an assessment of:
  1. external opportunities: *(Mortgage rates are low, good lot available in nice town, have a recommended builder)*; and barriers: *(Housing shortage, dream house too costly)*.
  2. internal strengths: *(Happy marriage, good jobs, pregnant)*; weaknesses: *(Live in a small apartment, insufficient cash)*.
- Define a mission and articulate goals that address the vision and take into consideration the results of the assessment: *(Build a house we can afford, within the time frame of low-rate loans, before the baby comes, "Victorian style" we like.)*.
- Develop a strategic plan and list measurable objectives and major activities that support each goal: *(Obtain building loan, hire architect and builder, develop blue print, etc.)*.
- Implement the strategic plan: *(Oversee building contractor, deal with details, make decisions: decor, etc.)*.
- Evaluate the process, the results, and determine whether the goals were met: *(Built as desired? Within budget? Within the time frame? Does it feel like a home?)*.

54

The model is most productively perceived as circular, in which each component feeds into and affects the next:

School psychologists will hopefully recognize this process as very similar to the development and implementation of an Individual Education Plan for a child, generalized to a larger process. It is an extremely effective model to use in the development of programs, including the development of school psychology delivery systems and supervision. It is also an effective model to use in the development of program subcomponents. The model can be applied to the development of the supervision of school psychologists in totality and can also be usefully applied to particular supervisory activities such as the selection of staff.

Models of Supervision Based on Eclectic and Integrative Approaches

When taking an eclectic approach, a psychologist selects among several theories, and when taking an integrative approach, a psychologist actually combines different theories. In integrating theories, psychologists "incorporate a wide repertoire of relational, conceptual, perceptual, and executive skills from discrete theories, therapies and techniques and know which skills to access to address the needs of clients" (Rigazio-DiGilio, 1997, p. 195).

Supervisors who take an integrative approach, or who have supervisees with such an orientation, introduce their supervisees to various theories and approaches and provide organizational structures to enable supervisees to coordinate various aspects of professional practice. They adapt supervision techniques to each particular situation.

Given the complexity of school psychology, it is almost inevitable that school psychologists will adopt eclectic or integrative approaches in their professional practice, which is actually an indication of becoming an advanced practitioner (Skovholt & Ronnestadt, 1992). Integrative models such as the systemic-cognitive-developmental therapy model and the integrative problem-centered therapy model have been developed in counseling psychology literature. As described by Rigazio-DiGilio (1997), these models have several core assumptions.

First, integrative models assume that psychologists must adopt a holistic perspective to understand the development and functioning of both humans and systems. Similarly, supervisors must adopt a holistic and recursive perspective to understand the development and functioning of supervisees.

Second, integrative models assume that non-adaptation by clients is not a result of a deficiency or pathology, but is instead a positive, "natural, and logical consequence of developmental and contextual history" (Rigazio-DiGilio, 1997, p. 196). Impasses in supervision are also natural and logical, and may reflect a mismatch between the needs of the supervisee and the context of supervision.

Third, the integrative models assume that the wide variety of issues presented by clients renders adherence to one theoretical approach insufficient. Flexibility is substantially increased by the opportunity to use multiple theories. Similarly, integrative approaches lend supervisors many strategies and thereby provide multi-

55

ple perspectives, multiple organizational schema, and opportunities for growth.

Norcross and Halgin (1997) have proposed principles of integrative supervision. They recommend developing contracts, adopting a coherent framework that matches the supervision method to the content of supervision, blending supervision methods and techniques, evaluating outcomes, and customizing supervision to match the developmental level, cognitive style, needs, and personal idiom of the supervisee.

However, many school psychologists are oblivious to their eclectic orientation and not uncommonly make professional decisions and recommendations based on multiple, and sometimes incompatible, theories. For example, a child may be diagnosed with a behavior disorder (medical model), placed on a behavior management plan (behaviorism), and referred to both individual (client-centered) and family (systemic) therapy, possibly resulting in contradictory strategies and foci.

SUPERVISION STRATEGIES

Supervision strategies cut across the school psychologist's service delivery; the same strategies can be used in counseling, conducting an assessment, and providing consultation. Furthermore, the same strategies are used with different styles and models of therapy although different models may be better suited to the use of particular techniques.

The most important supervisory strategy is the development of a written supervision plan. According to Mead (1990), an appropriate written supervision plan includes the following:

- A description of the supervisor's readiness for supervision, including the supervisor's education, theoretical orientations, and supervisory model;
- An assessment of the supervisee's readiness for practice, including clear and specific

delineation of areas of strength and weakness;

- The conditions of supervision, including general skills to be developed, the confidentiality (or lack thereof) of supervisory sessions, the type and number of clients to be seen by the supervisee, the frequency and duration of supervision sessions, steps the supervisee should take in emergencies, the manner and frequency of supervisory observations, and the method a supervisee takes to counteract a negative evaluation;
- Supervisory goals and objectives, based on the supervisor's skills, the supervisee's needs, and the conditions of supervision;
- Supervision techniques and procedures for both supervisees and supervisors. For example, if the supervisee is expected to prepare and analyze transcripts of audio-taped counseling sessions, this procedure and its anticipated frequency are designated. Techniques and procedures are determined by the supervisee's skills, the availability of equipment, and the intensity (degree of accuracy and likely need for immediate intervention) of supervision needed;
- Methods that will be used to assess the supervisee's progress and reasoning. Examples are Case Progress Notes and Post Session Analysis questions (see chapter's end);
- Evaluation methods, and their frequency, of the progress made toward the accomplishment of specific goals of supervisee, supervisor, and clients;
- Methods that will be used by the supervisor to intervene when the supervisees' actions need modification.

Assessing supervisor's and supervisee's skills

As described in Chapters 7 and 15, critical skills are determined and assessed by a variety of methods, including self-report and direct observation. The supervisee's skills and developmental level affect the appropriateness of different supervisory techniques (Stoltenberg, McNeill, & Delworth, 1998). Novices require very close supervision during which they receive frequent positive feedback and strengths are addressed before weaknesses. Techniques resulting in the accumulation of raw data (video or live observation) are essential. Role-playing, interpretation of dynamics, transcripts and their analysis, readings, and group supervision are also helpful.

Advanced beginners need guidelines to help them recognize recurring patterns, and prescriptive supervisory interventions should be used only occasionally. Supervisors should focus on increasing the supervisee's conceptualization skills by introducing alternative views and more complicated cases. Video or live observations, occasional role-playing, interpretation of dynamics, parallel process, and group supervision continue to be helpful.

When supervisees reach the competent level, they begin to provide the supervisory structure. The supervisor provides facilitative, confrontational, and conceptual supervisory interventions. Direct observation, video, and audiotapes continue to be helpful, although peer and group supervision begin to play a more prominent role.

The proficient and expert practitioners learn best through the presentation of very complex case studies, both their own and others'. Cases with which supervisees feel successful, as well as those with which they are frustrated, are fruitfully discussed and analyzed.

Setting supervision goals

One of the most important supervision strategies is the development of written supervision goals. "Just as it is good practice to have written treatment goals for therapy, it is good practice to have written supervision goals. Supervision practice will undoubtedly be improved by having specific and concrete goals clearly delineated" (Mead,

1990, p. 51). Written goals improve communication, are a crucial part of the supervision plan, help determine supervisory interventions, and facilitate the evaluation of both supervisees and supervisors.

In developing supervision goals, a general goal is first written in abstract language. Then, measurable and observable objectives are listed and reviewed to ensure that an observer could assess the completion of each goal. The objectives preferably focus on increasing positive behaviors, rather than decreasing negative behaviors. As is true for a child's education plan, supervision goals are useful only if they contain observable outcomes, specify action steps needed to reach the outcome, and specify evaluation procedures to be followed.

As described by Mead (1990), supervisors and supervisees often differ in their supervision goals, and it is important to reconcile these differences at the beginning of the supervisory relationship. Supervisees and supervisors may have different goals for supervision based on their respective positions. A supervisee's supervision goals may be to "learn a specific skill or technique,...evaluate therapy as a career, search for support and reinforcement, look for an answer to personal problems, seek personal growth and development, or to attempt to evaluate or validate a specific therapeutic model" (Mead, 1990, p. 59).

In contrast, a supervisor's overarching supervision goal is to improve a supervisee's skills so that he or she performs more like an experienced practitioner. Subsidiary goals may include learning how to conduct an initial interview, use a basic assessment technique, hypothesize about cases, develop effective treatment plans, and evaluate student progress (Mead, 1990). Experienced therapists build a positive relationship with each family member, structure sessions, use good therapeutic strategies, (Kniskern & Gurman, 1988), maintain an active role in sessions, and use a wide variety of techniques (Pinsoff, 1979). Therefore,

57

supervision goals logically strive to increase each of these behaviors. These findings can be generalized to the practice of school psychology: supervisees will learn to build positive, non-blaming relationships with each person (student, teacher, principal, and parent); will develop expertise in a wide variety of effective techniques; and will be an active participant in consultation sessions, counseling sessions, and assessment team meetings.

Furthermore, supervisors and supervisees may have different goals as a result of the supervisee's developmental level. A beginning practitioner is likely to seek help for a specific case, while supervisors prefer the supervisee develop skills "to deal with a class of problems, rather than finding a technique to fix a specific problem" (Mead, 1990, p. 57). With intermediate supervisees, supervisors are likely to push them more than they are comfortable to add new theories and techniques to their repertoire. Supervisors also may need to push advanced supervisees to articulate the theories and principles behind their work.

Techniques of supervision

Individual, group, and peer supervision. In both individual and group supervision, the supervisor takes an advisory and evaluative role. Peer supervision differs from individual and group supervision in that the relationship is generally collaborative, voluntary, occurs between professionals of equal status, and no evaluative component is present. The supervisee in peer supervision is free to reject recommended strategies and maintains responsibility for the client (Kruger & Struzziero, 1997). All three types of supervision are helpful to school psychologists at all levels of development, although beginning school psychologists should not be limited to peer supervision alone. Many supervising school psychologists find it helpful to schedule both individual and group supervision with each supervisee.

Supervisory interventions. Supervisory interventions can occur during a live session or during the conference following the session. As soon as possible after any session, the supervisor meets with the supervisee to hear the supervisee's observations and perceptions of the session, examine the supervisees' hypotheses, and facilitate plans for the case (Mead, 1990). The supervisees' observations and perceptions can be verified by the supervisor through the use of highly accurate observation technique such as direct observation or videotapes; otherwise, the supervisor will be dependent upon the supervisee's accuracy.

Questions helpful in discerning a supervisee's thinking are suggested in the **Post-Session Analysis Form** at the end of this chapter. The supervisor: takes notes on the supervisee's responses during the supervision session; determines whether the supervisees have identified all important variables, tasks, and theories; compares the supervisee's responses with behavior during the session for consistency; and contrasts the supervisee's reasoning and behavior with that of an expert school psychologist (Mead, 1990). The supervisor then determines which supervisory interventions to use.

Supervisory interventions can be verbal or non-verbal. Verbal interventions can be:

- facilitative and encouraging;
- prescriptive, in which approaches are suggested;
- conceptual, during which theory is tied to diagnosis and intervention, or alternative views are presented;
- confrontational, in which the supervisee's actions are questioned; and,
- catalytic, in which the supervisee's responses to the client or supervisor are highlighted.

Non-verbal interventions can include the modeling of appropriate behaviors by the supervisor,

58

or role-playing techniques in which supervisees act as either themselves or as clients.

Techniques. There are several reasons for the supervisor to observe supervisees' work directly. Observations enable supervisors to assess supervisees' skills, determine the effects of supervisees on clients, observe supervisees' ability to reason about their impact on clients, and use the results of their observations to help supervisees improve (Mead, 1990). A number of different techniques are available for providing supervision of counseling. Different techniques are often better suited to different types of counseling. The job of the effective supervisor is to be aware of what techniques are most practical with specific types of counseling and to choose accordingly. Both the supervisor and the clinician must be vigilant in assuring that techniques are used in a manner which is both appropriate and pragmatic. Some supervision techniques are less appropriate for schools. For example, techniques of "live supervision" found in the family therapy literature do not easily adapt to school settings where one way mirrors and observation rooms are scarce. Whereas school psychologists are in constant competition with other educational specialists for space, phones, and basic necessities, it is unlikely that this will change in the near future. Hence, different techniques must be used.

Methods for the supervision of counseling range from direct observation to indirect examination of process notes. For example, it is possible for supervisors to "sit in" on a group, listen to audiotapes of sessions, view videotapes, or talk to teachers and students. Ethics and considerations for client welfare must underlie all methods chosen. The least invasive way to oversee counseling is usually preferable.

Techniques which enhance supervision of mental health consultation include the use of process notes, the examination of parallel process issues, the examination of transference and countertransference, and the use of reflection. Audiotapes, videotapes, and process analysis are also helpful (Bernard & Goodyear, 1998).

As described by Mead (1990), each supervisory technique has advantages and disadvantages. Techniques vary in accuracy, the ability of the supervisor to intervene and quickly modify the supervisee's behavior, the reliance on technology, the amount of time required, the level of supervisee skill or development required, and the decrease of intrusiveness. Supervisory techniques are summarized in Table 3-1. They are arranged in order of the required level of supervisee skill. However, as Mead (1990) points out, the technique requiring the most supervisee skill (case presentation) is unfortunately utilized the most. This is also the case with school psychology interns, as Ward (1999) found that the percentage of supervision time spent in case presentation was 20%. The percentage of supervisory time spent in reviewing reports was 17%, direct supervisor modeling was 15%, direct observation of intern was 15%, sharing resources was 11%, planning and setting goals was 9%, and evaluation of performance was 9%. Less than 1% (.5%) of supervisory time was spent in activities with the highest accuracy, such as reviewing audio and videotapes of supervisees.

59

Table 3-1

Supervisory techniques, advantages and disadvantages

1. **Didactic instruction and assigned reading**
   - Information accuracy: *Not applicable.*
   - Supervisor's ability to intervene: *Not applicable.*
   - Reliance on technology: *Low.*
   - Supervisor time required: *Low.*
   - Supervisee skill level required: *Low.*
   - Intrusion on client: *Not applicable.*

2. **Modeling**
   - Information accuracy: *Not applicable.*
   - Supervisor's ability to intervene: *Not applicable.*
   - Reliance on technology: *Low.*
   - Supervisor time required: *Moderate.*
   - Supervisee skill level required: *Low.*
   - Intrusion on client: *Not applicable.*

3. **Role-playing**
   - Information accuracy: *Low; rarely completely reflects practice.*
   - Supervisor's ability to intervene: *High.*
   - Reliance on technology: *Low.*
   - Supervisor time required: *High.*
   - Supervisee skill level required: *Low.*
   - Intrusion on client: *Not applicable.*

4. **Direct observation in room**
   - Information accuracy: *High.*
   - Supervisor's ability to intervene: *High.*
   - Reliance on technology: *Low.*
   - Supervisor time required: *Very high: supervisor must be present, and meet before and after the session to plan and analyze.*
   - Supervisee skill level required: *Low.*
   - Intrusion on client: *High.*

5. **Direct observation through one-way mirror**
   - Information accuracy: *High.*
   - Supervisor's ability to intervene: *High, although it requires interrupting the session (unless a "bug-in-the-ear" receiver is used).*
   - Reliance on technology: *High, requires one-way mirror.*
   - Supervisor time required: *Very high; supervisor must be present, and meet before and after session to plan and analyze.*
   - Supervisee skill level required: *Low.*
   - Intrusion on client: *Moderate to high.*

6. **Collaborative work: Co-counseling, collaborative assessment, collaborative consultation**
   - Information accuracy: *High accuracy, but sessions affected by supervisor's presence.*
   - Supervisor's ability to intervene: *Too high; experienced psychologist finds it almost impossible not to take over session.*
   - Reliance on technology: *Low.*
   - Supervisor time required: *Very high; supervisor must be present, and must meet before and after the session to plan and analyze.*
   - Supervisee skill level required: *Low to moderate.*
   - Intrusion on client: *Usually low.*

7. **Audiotape of session with typed transcript and analysis**
   - Information accuracy: *High, although lack of non-verbal behaviors are a serious detriment. Typed transcript and analysis of the content and process of the session greatly facilitates supervisee observations.*
   - Supervisor's ability to intervene: *Low: delayed until at least the next session, if not longer.*
   - Reliance on technology: *Requires audiotaping equipment, the ability to type and analyze transcripts.*

60

- Supervisor time required: *High: supervisor must listen to tapes, supervisee must transcribe and analyze.*
- Supervisee skill level required: *Low to moderate.*
- Intrusion on client: *Moderate.*

8. **Audiotape of session**
   - Information accuracy: *High, although lack of non-verbal behaviors are a serious detriment.*
   - Supervisor's ability to intervene: *Low: delayed until next session.*
   - Reliance on technology: *Requires audiotaping equipment and the ability to type and analyze transcripts.*
   - Supervisor time required: *High: supervisor must listen to tapes.*
   - Supervisee skill level required: *Moderate.*
   - Intrusion on client: *Moderate.*

9. **Video tape of session**
   - Information accuracy: *High.*
   - Supervisor's ability to intervene: *Low: delayed until next session.*
   - Reliance on technology: *Requires videotaping equipment.*
   - Supervisor time required: *High: supervisor must watch tapes.*
   - Supervisee skill level required: *Moderate.*
   - Intrusion on client: *High.*

10. **Review of psychological reports**
    - Information accuracy: *Moderate: supervisor does not have access to raw data other than test protocols, but the text reveals the thought processes of the supervisee.*
    - Supervisor's ability to intervene: *Very low.*
    - Reliance on technology: *Low.*
    - Supervisor time required: *Low.*
    - Supervisee skill level required: *All levels.*
    - Intrusion on client: *Not applicable.*

11. **Case process notes, reviewed in individual supervision** To be effective, case process notes must be organized in a consistent format, systematically and routinely kept, and include specific, observable, and verifiable information. A **Case Process Note Form** is provided at this chapter's end.
    - Information accuracy: *Very low: Prone to supervisee's intentional or unintentional distortion; supervisor has neither verbal nor non-verbal client cues.*
    - Supervisor's ability to intervene: *Low: delayed until next session.*
    - Reliance on technology: *Low.*
    - Supervisor time required: *Low.*
    - Supervisee skill level required: *High.*
    - Intrusion on client: *Not applicable.*

12. **Case process notes, reviewed in peer supervision**
    - Information accuracy: *Very low: Prone to supervisee's distortion, peer supervisors have neither verbal nor non-verbal client cues.*
    - Supervisor's ability to intervene: *Low: case presentation often postponed; peer supervisors' intervention delayed to session following.*
    - Reliance on technology: *Low.*
    - Supervisor time required: *Low.*
    - Supervisee skill level required: *High.*
    - Intrusion on client: *Not applicable.*

Regardless of supervisory technique, maintaining accurate and complete records is important both to facilitate effective practice and to provide a method to guide supervision. Record-keeping in public schools is governed by federal law, state law, and local practice. Effective supervisors must adhere to the above dictates themselves and must insure that supervisees adhere to them in a way that simultaneously fosters clinical growth and client welfare. Invariably, the developmental needs of participants must be considered. For example, when supervising the application of a new intervention with a novice practitioner, more comprehensive records are necessary than when supervising a seasoned practitioner who has previously performed the clinical activity multiple times.

Effective supervisors must insure that their supervisees write up a treatment summary. It is helpful to develop a series of pre-prepared forms to guide the collection of information desired (e.g., students' developmental and academic history forms, parent consent forms, etc.). Establishing a protocol that determines what is to be kept in various student folders is also helpful. This promotes consistency of records over time and from one school psychologist to another. Furthermore, this allows for a continuity of care and service when cases are transferred and as children progress through the grades and schools. For example, in some school systems, interns and/or practicum students traditionally lead specific, focused groups and many of the same children participate from one year to the next. Good records make it more likely that appropriate continuity from one year to the next will occur. This also enables new interns to avoid repetitious activities and to sustain progress.

The use of process notes is a form of formalized record-keeping which can be extremely helpful in supervision. Process notes consist not only of what occurred during a counseling session, but also of the therapist's subjective reactions and plans for a future direction. Process notes remind the counselor of what has occurred previously, provide a developmental overview of the case, to assist a new counselor if a case is transferred, serve as a learning device, can be useful in evaluation and research, allow for multiple professionals working on the same case to learn from one another, and provide a protective function if legal or ethical issues arise (Goldberg, 1986; Pruitt, McColgan, Pugh, & Kiser, 1986).

Process notes are an especially invaluable tool in supervision because they foster the examination of affective tones as well as factual developments. Such examination is particularly important in the early stages of training. During supervision, a careful examination of the hypotheses and explanations that emerge in supervisees' process notes provides an objective way to examine underlying theories around factors that induce and support client change. The use of case summary notes provides a similar function. In general, to support both clinical and administrative supervision efforts, effective supervisors develop a standard of record-keeping to which all school psychologists in the district must adhere.

Case Process Notes

Student name _____   Date _____

School _____   Session number_____

School psychologist _____   Supervisor _____

Session notes

_____
_____
_____
_____
_____
_____
_____
_____
_____

Subjective status information (client's description) _____
_____
_____

    (theories and hypotheses) _____
_____

Objective status information (behavioral observations, intervention results, data collected by client, grades, etc.) _____
_____
_____

    (theories and hypotheses) _____
_____
_____

Observations of the therapist's words and behaviors _____
_____
_____

    (theories and hypotheses) _____
_____
_____

Plans, goals, and strategies (intervention homework, future session topics, etc.) _____
_____
_____

    (theories and hypotheses) _____
_____
_____

Post-Session Analysis

1. What were the desired outcomes of this session? _____
   _____
   _____

2. What information did you obtain during the session? _____
   _____
   _____

   a. What evidence do you have for this information? _____
      _____
      _____

   b. What theories organize your observations? _____
      _____
      _____

3. What client behaviors, affect, or expressed thoughts made you choose particular words or actions?
   _____
   _____

   a. How did your words and actions impact your client? _____
      _____
      _____

   b. What evidence do you have for these observations? _____
      _____
      _____

   c. What theories explain your impact on your client? _____
      _____
      _____

4. Which tasks are completed? Which have yet to be completed? _____
   _____
   _____

   a. What theories underlie your choice of tasks? _____
      _____
      _____

   b. What hypotheses have you developed? What will you do to test them? ___
      _____
      _____

Effective supervisors plan at both the detail and the systemic levels. At both levels, the leadership vision affects goals and objectives of individuals as well as those of the larger group. It is very helpful for supervisees, supervisors, and the administration to compare and discuss their opinions, orientations, philosophies, and vision of school psychological services. It is then helpful to compare these philosophies with the expressed and unexpressed philosophies of the school or school system. If the philosophies are widely divergent, the school psychologist will need to find some method of reconciliation (Sergiovanni & Starratt, 1998) in order to develop compatible general goals for the department.

Well-executed planning and implementation greatly facilitates service provision and reduces conflict and system failure. Poorly executed planning exacerbates individual and systemic weaknesses and has a substantially negative impact on service delivery. Strategic planning has six interactive, recursive components: Developing a Vision; Conducting an Assessment; Developing Mission and Goals; Designing a Strategic Plan; Implementing a Structure, and Conducting an Evaluation.

In effective supervision, after collaborating with staff school psychologists and school district administrators, the supervisor develops a vision and overall goals for the delivery of school psychological services. At the same time, the internal and external strengths and weaknesses of the district and staff are assessed. The results of this assessment are reflected in revisions of the vision and in the development of the "mission" and general goals. The supervisor, in collaboration with the administration and staff psychologists, then develops a strategic plan that integrates responsive policies, objectives, action steps, and resource allocation into a meaningful and cohesive whole. The strategic plan is implemented by developing an appropriate structure that incorporates job analysis, delegation of responsibilities, selecting staff, training, and evaluation of personnel and programs. After a period of implementation, the entire process is evaluated. The evaluation results are then integrated into subsequently revised vision, goals, strategic plan, and structure.

DEVELOPING A VISION

Effective supervisors of school psychologists are leaders with a clear vision of effective school psychological services. A quality vision statement: comes from the heart; is unique to the setting; is simple, dramatic, and compelling; conveys hope and idealism; and is moral (Block, 1987). Sergiovanni (1990) indicates that effective leaders have a vision that clarifies the present, leads to a commitment to the future, and reflects the dreams, interests, and values of all stakeholders. A vision is a "compass," giving direction and inducing enthusiasm so that stakeholders develop a joint strategic plan. "Planning represents the rungs on the ladder that must be climbed, but purposes speak to where the ladder leads" (Sergiovanni, 1990, p. 58). Visions are not static, they constantly change over time. As indicated by Houle (1984), professions have a constantly changing sense of mission which in turn has profound implications for training and professional development.

Belief systems: Human nature and the nature of change

The practice of school psychology is, at its most basic level, about helping children to function best, either by empowering the children to change themselves, or by changing something in their environment such as the curriculum or academic placement. Similarly, supervision is fundamentally about helping

65

supervisees function best, either by empowering the supervisees to change themselves, or by changing something in their environment.

To understand one's approach to these basic levels, one must have knowledge about one's basic understandings about human nature and the nature of change. A conscious understanding of one's beliefs about human nature and the nature of change is therefore the first step in developing a vision of the supervision of school psychology.

Assumptions regarding human nature color a supervisor's vision and style of supervision (Sergiovanni & Starratt, 1998). For example, a supervisor who believes that by nature the average person is lazy, works as little as possible, lacks ambition, prefers to be led, is self-centered, resists change, and is incompetent will have a markedly different supervisory style from another supervisor who believes that the average person is energetic, ethical, hard-working, self-starting, responsive to organizational needs, open to change, and capable. A person with the first set of assumptions would almost inevitably turn to a traditional, non-trusting management style. The person with the second set of assumptions would be more likely to adopt a human resources model of leadership.

Activity 4-1
Uncover your belief system about human nature. Ask:

To what extent are people (students and supervisees) inherently good, naturally inclined to develop affection, trust, compassion, and a sense of justice? (Rousseau)

To what extent are people inherently selfish and aggressive, needing extensive rules, regulations, and the surrendering of personal freedom for the common good? (Hobbes)

To what extent are people blank slates, passive recipients of information and experiences? (Locke)

Similarly, it is important to examine one's beliefs about change.

Activity 4-2
Uncover your belief system about change. Ask:

What do you believe causes a person to change?
What do you believe causes a person to learn?
What developmental or learning theories do these beliefs reflect?
Describe a personal situation in which you changed in some way or learned something new.
Does your description of your personal experience agree with or depart from your belief system?
(Adapted from Neufeldt et al., 1995)

Belief systems: Education

The next level to consider is one's belief systems about education in general. School psychologists, supervisors of school psychologists, and other educators differ in their fundamental belief systems about education on a number of dimensions. To develop a meaningful vision for the practice of school psychology, effective supervisors of school psychologists must determine their belief systems about education. Responding to the following questions and activity can help clarify your own belief system:

Activity 4-3
Uncover your belief system about education. Ask:

- What do you believe about how children learn?
- What are the main purposes of education?
- What type of teacher-student relationship is best?
- What type of school climate is best?
- What metaphor describes the ideal school?

- What metaphor describes your own school?
- What should students achieve during a school year?
- Are schools responsible for building character and morality, or is the school's primary responsibility the promotion of intellectual rigor in traditional academic disciplines?
- Is the function of schools to enable individual students to meet their individual potential, or is the primary function or schools to prepare students to become functioning members of society?
- Why do children display maladaptive behavior?
- Are individual differences of value, or detrimental?

One individual's "personal vision of a good school" will be provided as an example. According to Barth (1990), a good school is composed of a community of learners, where principals, teachers, and students all simultaneously learn and teach. It is characterized by positive and collegial relationships among administrators, teachers, students, and parents; students and adults alike feel safe and are encouraged to take risks. All adults are at the school by choice. Teachers, parents, students, and administrators accept and rejoice in diversity and individual differences.

Belief system: School psychology

A supervisor's personal vision, which influences the departmental vision, describes what the supervising school psychologist would like school psychological services to provide children, adolescents, school personnel, parents, and the community. While the vision should be responsive to both "external" and "internal" needs, it should also convey a sense of morality

and justice in which not only clients, but also school psychologists, are fairly, equitably, and ethically treated (Sergiovanni, 1990).

Your view of ideal services is your personal leadership vision. When tempered by strengths and weaknesses of the setting in which you work and of your staff school psychologists, it becomes your departmental vision. Although your personal vision may be seemingly (and actually) unattainable, it shapes your global direction as a supervisory leader. It is essential to develop the departmental vision in conjunction with the school administration so that the administrators are aware of school psychologists' concepts regarding best practices, leadership vision, reform efforts, and standards of practice (Talley, 1990).

Activity 4-4
Uncover your beliefs about school psychology. Ask:

- Within the educational context, what function does a school psychologist serve?
- How are we unique?
- What do we believe in?
- What are we trying to accomplish?
- How do we respond to the needs of the client?
- How do we know whether or not we are doing a good job?
- What would our services look like in an ideal world?
- If you were to receive an award for exemplary practice ten years from now, how would the award be worded?

(Adapted from Dawson, 1999; Sergiovanni, 1990)

67

Activity 4-5
Uncover a view of your department's ideal

Write a brochure that would convince your clients that your services are the ones to choose, assuming they have an alternative. First write this brochure describing your current services. Then, write one describing the services you would ideally be providing in five years.

(Adapted from Dawson, 1999; Sergiovanni, 1990)

In developing a leadership vision, the first step is to analyze personal attitudes, beliefs, and values regarding every aspect of school psychology. The training of psychologists is notoriously divergent, with various programs emphasizing psychotherapeutic, behavioral, integrative, systemic, or developmental approaches. To minimize communication errors and to maximize the effectiveness of supervision, supervisors must clarify their belief systems and communicate them to supervisees.

Reschly and Ysseldyke (1995) provide an example of a global vision of school psychological services. "Problem solving [is] the foundation for school psychological services with an outcome criterion used as the basis for determining the success of problem-solving efforts" (p. 17). This vision leads to the following goals:

- Replacing categorically-based placement practices of mildly disabled students with curriculum-based and behavioral assessment measures and interventions in natural settings;
- Implementing behavioral interventions at the systems level rather than focusing on identification of within-child disorders;
- Increasing the capacity of general education programs to identify and remedy learning and behavior problems rather than relying on special education placement;

- Transforming the school psychologist's role from a diagnostic role to a supportive role in which the school psychologist is involved in problem-solving consultation and direct interventions in general education classes; and
- Increasing working relationships with parents and teachers to facilitate implementation of interventions.

(Reschly & Ysseldyke, 1995, p. 22).

Another "vision" of school psychology is suggested by Franklin's (1995) analysis of six delivery programs. These effective programs had numerous commonalties:

- School psychologists were highly qualified practitioners;
- School psychologists with a wide range of expertise were included in the department;
- School psychology services were expansive, comprehensive, and met the needs of all students;
- School psychologists engaged in prereferral intervention and prevention activities;
- School psychologists participated in school-based collaborative consultation;
- Assessments were linked to instructional intervention rather than only classification;
- Successes of both individuals and the department were articulated;
- Individual school psychologists and the entire department gathered efficacy data to establish accountability;
- The department changed its focus in response to situational needs;
- The department emphasized ongoing professional development;
- The department was autonomous;
- Clinical supervision was provided to school psychologists;
- A supervising school psychologist conducted individual performance evaluations;
- District school psychologists were active consumers and conductors of research;

- Department members were involved in the training of future school psychologists.

CONDUCTING AN ASSESSMENT

Both before and after the vision and general goals have been developed, the supervisor, in collaboration with supervisees, conducts a comprehensive assessment of the environment (Noe et al., 1996). This involves (1) an assessment of external opportunities and barriers, and (2) an assessment of internal strengths and weaknesses of both individuals and the school psychology department. After assessing both internal and external factors the supervisor develops a strategic plan regarding the structure of school psychological services and facilitates movement toward the envisioned level of functioning. As the structure of school psychology services is modified in accord with the strategic plan, internal strengths and weaknesses and external barriers and opportunities change. The resulting changes are taken into account during the subsequent internal and external assessments, leading to a systemic, interactive series of events.

Assessing external opportunities and barriers.

Effective supervision is contextual and responsive to the environment in which it functions. School psychological services generally take place within the context of a school and community, both of which are complex systems. Plans for school psychological service delivery must consider external factors to a major extent. The following is a partial listing:

At the national level.

- What are the laws relevant to school psychological service delivery?
- Which services are truly mandated and in what situations? (For example, the IDEA of 1997 mandates functional behavioral assessments for all students with behavioral issues, even if those behaviors are as commonplace as lack of homework completion. On the other hand, the same law renders the completion of a comprehensive three-year re-evaluation neither required nor dismissed, but rather up to the discretion of the school team.)
- Are nationally based support systems such as NASP, the NASP Listserve, and the Global School Psychology Network being used? If so, are they being used effectively?
- Are opportunities for federal grants to facilitate the provision of school psychological services being pursued? If so, by whom?
- Does the practice of school psychology in your district reflect the standards promoted by the National Association of School Psychologists and the American Psychological Association?
- Would more of the school district's school psychology resources be appropriately spent working at the national level (for example, providing comments to legislators, or applying for federal grants)?

At the state level.

- What are the state laws relevant to school psychological service delivery?
- What services are truly mandated?
- What support exists at the state Department of Education for school psychological services and school psychologists? Is there a position at the state level that supports school psychology?
- Do district school psychologists belong to the state school psychology organization and use it as a resource? Do district school psychologists take advantage of other local school psychological supports, such as regional support groups?
- Would some of the school district's school psychology resources be more appropriately spent working at the state level (for example, providing comments to legislators on laws, working on certification revision committees,

69

or working with the state department as they develop methods of student evaluation, curriculum frameworks, or state policies)?

Case study 4-1

Differences between states significantly impact the practice of school psychology and illuminate the impact of external factors on supervisory issues. Massachusetts is one of the only states in the country that does not require disability categorization of special education students. While seemingly a child-centered approach, this has paradoxically had the result of a higher percentage of children being identified as eligible for special education services (18% as opposed to the national averages of 12%). This has the circular repercussions of (1) further increasing the amount of time that school psychologists' spend in assessment, team meetings, and re-evaluations, (2) further decreasing the availability of non-special education services available to the total school population, (3) thereby increasing the number of children identified as eligible for special education services, and so forth.

Massachusetts has a history of considering master's and specialist level psychologists as independent practitioners. While considering individuals as independent practitioners could be seen as conveying greater respect and autonomy, it can sometimes lead to isolation and professional stagnation.

At the community level.
- Are district school psychologists knowledgeable about the cultures of the members of the community?
- What are the strengths and resources of the community for children, parents, and families? For example, what community resources exist to facilitate translating for non-native English speakers? For supervised homework supervision? For emergency shelter for children and adolescents? For treatment of teenage alcohol and drug abuse? For the provision of individual and family therapy? For crisis intervention and suicide prevention?
- How effective are these services?
- What is the school psychologist's role in community services? Advocate? Community leader? Is it appropriate for school psychologists to be active in communities in which they work but do not reside?
- Has a community needs assessment been conducted? By whom? What are the capacities within the community for meeting the needs of children, parents, and families?
- How could school psychologists work more effectively with community services to improve the learning of children? For example, could the school psychologist work with the community center's after school program to improve behavior management and homework completion strategies?
- Could school psychologists serve on community boards, professional organizations, or in local government to obtain access to decision making processes (Talley, 1990)?

Ethical dilemma 4-1

You are a supervisor of school psychology working in a small city whose population has changed dramatically in the past ten years. The population, formerly primarily American-born blue-collar workers, has become 80% immigrant, primarily from the Caribbean and Southeast Asia. One of the school psychologists you supervise is only a few years from retirement. Although she is generally capable, she has not only neglected to become knowledgeable about the new populations, but frequently makes ethnic and racial slurs about the changing populations. She has not been responsive to your attempts at sensitization and education. *What are the ethical issues? What steps should you take?*

At the district level.

- What are the policies regarding the provision of school psychological services? Do these match state regulations, federal law, and professional standards?
- How does the administrative structure facilitate or hinder the provision of effective school psychology services?
- How do the school psychologists' job descriptions compare to national standards for the provision of services?
- What other positions in the district overlap with the school psychologist's position? For example, does the district have social workers who conduct parent interviews? Contracted psychologists who provide therapy?
- Are there district level committees on which school psychologists might effectively serve (Talley, 1990)?
- How are conflicts resolved at the district level?

Ethical dilemma 4-2

In reviewing federal and state regulations, you, a supervising school psychologist, realize that neither the federal nor state laws actually require a full assessment battery for three-year re-evaluations. The district, however, requires that school psychologists conduct three year re-evaluations identical to initial evaluations, with the following components: classroom observation, functional behavior assessment, parent interview, teacher interview, individual intelligence test, individual achievement test, and clinical interview.

Because 25% of the school-aged population is identified as eligible for special education services, these extensive re-evaluations consume an extremely high percentage of school psychologists' time. The members of the school psychology department feel that their time would be better spent providing direct services to children, parents, and teachers. *What are the ethical issues? What steps should you take?*

At the school level.

- What are each school's strengths and weaknesses?
- Which school personnel have strengths on which the school psychologists can draw?
- Which schools have personnel with weaknesses that could be balanced by strengths of a particular school psychologist?
- What are each school's student population's unique needs?
- What are the strengths, weaknesses, and personal style of each principal?
- What is the climate of each school? What strengths are needed by the school psychologist to improve the climate?
- What is the relationship of the school psychologist to the principal? (If school psychologists are evaluated by principals, even only administratively, it is more difficult for them to develop and maintain egalitarian consultative relationships. On the other hand, principals are often best positioned to observe a school psychologist's attendance, work ethic, organization, and interpersonal skills.)
- Is there a mechanism whereby the supervisor can help with conflicts between the school psychologist and the principal?

Ethical dilemma 4-3

You are a supervising school psychologist in a small district with three school psychologists. One of the psychologists is assigned to one small elementary school and is frequently expected to spend considerable time on activities not included in her job description. These include answering the office telephones, sending notifications of faculty meetings, and bus and recess duty. In addition, the school's guidance counselor refuses to retire (at age 78) yet has an antagonistic relationships with the children, so the school psychologist is in constant demand by both parents and children. *What are the ethical issues? What steps could you take?*

71

Assessing internal strengths and weaknesses

In this context, "internal" is defined as pertaining to the school psychology department as a whole and the individual school psychologists within the department. This designation is arbitrary; "internal" could be just as appropriately be defined at any level within the system, depending upon one's perspective.

Strengths and weaknesses of the school psychology department can be formally determined by combining the results of individual performance evaluations of school psychologists and/or conducting a program evaluation of the department, described in chapters 6, 14, and 15. Less formally, the supervisor and department members can discuss the following questions to determine the extent to which the department has the characteristics of a healthy organization as described by Miles (1965) and Likert (1967).

72

- Does the department have high performance goals that are clear to, and accepted by, the supervisees?
- Have the goals been prioritized, and does this prioritization fit with district priorities?
- Are the goals achievable with available resources?
- Are the goals appropriately congruent with the demands of the broader environment?
- Is there group decision making, accompanied by an equitable distribution of influence among members of the organization?
- Within the department, is there a focus on collaboration rather than coercion or competition?
- Are there structures that sense the inevitable problems within the department, develop possible solutions, and choose, implement, and evaluate the effectiveness of solutions?
- Is the departmental atmosphere perceived

as supportive, building and maintaining the member's sense of personal worth?
- Are personnel appropriately assigned tasks, neither overworked nor underworked?
- Is there a good fit between the individuals and the roles expected of them?
- Do group members display cohesiveness by showing a desire to stay an active member of the organization?
- Is there high morale, as shown by individual feelings of well being, satisfaction, and pleasure?
- Does the department have functional relationships with other groups, such as counselors, which allow for active responsiveness to the total environment?
- Does the department have the ability to restructure itself when environmental demands and organizational resources do not match?
- Is there distortion-free communication vertically and horizontally within the organization, as well as to those outside the organization?
- Is there a movement toward innovation, change, growth, and development, as manifested by movement toward new goals and procedures?

At the level of individual school psychologists, strengths and weaknesses can be formally determined through individual self-examinations and evaluations. Less rigorously, strengths and weaknesses can be assessed through informal discussions and brainstorming sessions with department members. Each person can indicate which tasks and activities he or she prefers or at which he or she feels most proficient, as well as which tasks and activities he or she feels weakest. The perceptions of the supervisor and other school psychologists also suggest areas of strength and weakness.

DEVELOPING MISSION AND GOALS

In effective planning, supervisors and supervisees mutually decide upon both long-term (5 year) and short-term (1 year) goals. These goals should be tied to the leadership vision and expectations of the district regarding the roles of school psychologists. Further, they should correspond to areas of determined need and highlight areas of determined strength.

Because goals selected have a major impact on the direction taken by school psychology departments, at this time we will consider decision-making strategies. However, the reader should remember that considerations regarding decision-making apply similarly to decisions made during all aspects of the strategic planning process.

Making decisions has three stages: intelligence, design, and choice (Simon, 1960). Making decisions can be based on hunches, intuition, tradition, or emotional attachments rather than facts. To avoid inappropriately basing decisions on intuition, supervisors should attend to facts, become aware of biases, and seek independent opinions from an individual (with appropriate attention to maintaining confidentiality) who does not have a vested interest in the decision (Rue & Byars, 1997).

"Rational" approaches to decision making have been advocated by management literature (Rue & Byars, 1997). These include the following steps:

- Identify the need for a decision;
- Establish and rank the criteria for the decision;
- Gather data and information;
- Identity alternatives;
- Evaluate each alternative relative to established criteria; and
- Select either the alternative that is "best" or that meets at least a minimum standard of satisfaction.

The environment of the school system impacts the supervisor's flexibility in making decisions, as do the backgrounds, expectations, and personality of both administrators and school psychologists for and with whom the supervisor works. The ability to make decisions depends greatly upon the supervisor's position within the school system. A supervisor with close working relationships with upper administration has greater decision making power.

The extent to which others are involved in helping to make decisions has a decided impact on both the choices which are made and their implementation. In general, the performance of a group surpasses the performance of individual members in isolation because the sum total of knowledge is greater, leading to a wider range of alternatives. Groups can also surpass individuals in the ability to develop creative and innovative problem solutions, in part because group decisions tend to be riskier and more extreme than decisions made in isolation. The final advantage to group decision-making is due to the fact that when members have understood the alternatives considered, they are more likely to accept the decision. There are some disadvantages to group decision-making; such decisions generally take longer, and they can be dominated by one or two individuals, social pressure, or competition (Rue & Byars, 1997).

Because of these advantages and disadvantages, no one method works for all decisions. Vroom and Yetton (1973) developed a model that takes into account factors in decision-making. According to this model, a supervisor would only make a decision on his or her if one choice is not likely to be more rational than another, if acceptance of the decision by subordinates is not critical to implementation, or if the supervisor has enough information to make a high-quality decision. If any of these factors are not the case, others, including subordinates, are brought into the decision-making process. Whether they are sim-

73

ply consulted or actually participate in a group-based decision depends on the extent to which supervisees' acceptance of the decision is critical, organization goals are shared, or there is conflict among subordinates in response to the preferred solutions.

Ethical dilemma 4-4

You, a supervising school psychologist, realize that the goals of the school system are contradictory. That is, the first stated goal of the school system is to improve the group test scores of the students in the district, while the second goal is to reduce dropout rates. You realize that, logically, as more low-achieving students stay in school and take standardized tests, scores will be likely to decrease. *What are the ethical issues? What steps should you take?*

DESIGNING A STRATEGIC PLAN

As described in the previous chapter, designing a strategic plan is similar to developing the overall plan for a house, including the blueprint and financial strategies. In developing the strategic plan, the supervisor defines specific measurable objectives, action steps, timelines, potential barriers, and potential resources for each annual goal. This strategic plan then leads logically to the implementation of structure. In supervising school psychology, strategic planning involves making decisions regarding issues both large and small, from the structure of the department to the methods for the selection and evaluation of staff. There are five important components in strategy management: organizational structure, information and decision processes, job analysis and design, selection and training of staff, and performance evaluation and reward systems (Noe et al., 1996).

Job analysis

Job analysis and design is so critical that it has been "called the building block of everything that personnel does" (Noe et al., 1996, p. 172). It affects selection of personnel, performance appraisal, training and development, individual performance evaluation, career planning, and work redesign. Job design involves specifying the work activities of staff school psychologists and school psychological services. When supervisors conduct a job design, they ask, "How is the job to be performed? Who is to perform the job, and where?" In school psychology, job design is made immensely complex because different individuals react differently to the same job due to varied levels of interest, training, experience, development, and skill. In addition, the same procedure in two different environments, or schools, results in markedly different outcomes. To effectively conduct a job analysis, one must understand the larger context, identify the desired outcomes, specify standards of quality for these outcomes, examine the processes used to generate outcomes (example: team meetings), and identify the inputs used in the development of the outcomes (human skills, equipment, and supplies).

After a job analysis is conducted, the job description is written. This lists the observable actions in response to the duties, responsibilities, and tasks required. A job specification further indicates the abilities, knowledge, and skills an individual should possess for success.

Information about job dimensions and tasks can be developed by holding a meeting in which the individuals identify four to eight groups of major, interrelated tasks. In school psychology, these can be derived from the *NASP Professional Conduct Manual* (1997), modified to fit the needs of the school district (assessment, direct interventions, etc.). The group then brainstorms the tasks which encompass each dimension and identifies the abilities, knowledge, and skills

74

necessary to perform the tasks effectively. The group then brainstorms the environmental and technological factors that are likely to change in the next five years that will affect the tasks or necessary abilities, knowledge, and skills; the group takes these changes into account when developing the job description.

Most often, school psychology job descriptions focus on generalists. Currently, there is some movement in the direction of specialists, such as a school psychologist with a specialization in working with children diagnosed with Pervasive Developmental Disorder.

In large departments, specialization has some benefits in terms of promoting specialized areas of competence. Dividing labor increases efficiency in each unit. As Franklin (1995) indicates, a needs assessment prior to hiring a new staff person may indicate a particular area of need, such as a specialist in early childhood. On the other hand, specialization can lead to a fragmentation of services. Further, if there are sub-groups of specialists and generalists within a department, it may have unintended side effects. Thus, the entire school psychology department may have one set of goals that conflict with the goals of a particular specialization subgroup (Sergiovanni & Starratt, 1998).

Resource allocation

Supervisors allocate resources by determining which tasks to complete, who should do each task, and how much time and money should be devoted to tasks in the following steps: delineating a strategy (goal) for each task, listing measurable objectives and major activities that support that goal, setting deadlines, drafting a budget, and obtaining administrative approval (Loen, 1994). Frequently in business, supervisors demonstrate the anticipated "dollar impact" for a task or a decision. Similar activities can be useful for supervisors of school psychologists. While supervisors of school psychologists may not be

as methodical as business managers, they do have goals and objectives, although perhaps not well specified. At this point we will discuss one aspect of the strategic plan for the provision of school psychological services that can have major impact on all other functions: the administrative structure.

Administrative structure

The administrative structure within a school system can facilitate or hinder the provision of effective school psychological services. As described by Talley (1990), the superior to whom school psychologists report has direct bearing on the provision of school psychological services. Each prototype appears to have its own advantages and disadvantages. If the supervisor of school psychologists reports directly to a superintendent, there are few levels of bureaucracy, yet there may also be fewer administrators in the system who feel directly benefited by school psychologists. If the supervisor of school psychology reports to the director of pupil personnel services or the director of special education, there may be presumptions and restrictions regarding the population with whom the school psychologist works. If the school psychologist reports to a regional service center that provides services to separate school districts, the psychologist most likely has increased autonomy but decreased networking ability within each district. Many school psychologists report directly to principals; positive effects include the ability to generalize the school psychologist's clientele to all students, while negative effects include the difficulties the school psychologist might have disagreeing with the principal.

Regardless of the type of administrative structure, school psychologists will need to educate their supervisors about the full range of school psychological services and advocate for their appropriate delivery. While supervisors of school psychologists may have little influence over their position in the school hierarchy, an awareness of the advantages and disadvantages of each structure provides useful ideas regarding potential steps to counteract the negative aspects of one's position. For example, supervisors reporting to a regional service center can counteract the decreased networking ability by assigning each school psychologist to particular schools on a regular schedule rather than assigning school psychologists to cases on an individual basis.

Because a healthy organizational climate is necessary for effective work, supervisors of school psychologists must attend to the development of a positive organizational climate within a school system. Frequently, school systems are bureaucratic organizations characterized by division of labor, hierarchies, written policies and regulation, and an impersonal environment. Although bureaucratic organizations can be efficient, they can also be rigid and impersonal to the point of becoming dysfunctional (Weber, 1946). Therefore, it is important for a supervisor of school psychologists to be sensitive not only to the bureaucracy in which they work, but to the level of bureaucracy they themselves contribute to the system by adding departmental policies, rules, and regulations.

Another aspect of administrative structure to which the supervisor of school psychologists must be responsive is the administrative structure of the psychological services unit. Although one person can theoretically supervise 12 to 21 individuals, a natural working group is 5 to 9 individuals and groups of 10 and larger tend to break into smaller groups, each with their own leader. To encourage these leaders to be formal rather than informal, supervisors of school psychologists with 10 or more supervisees should consider dividing their supervisees into smaller subgroups with designated leaders. These generally serve as peer support groups, peer supervision groups, or professional development

groups. However, supervisors must be careful to maintain a balance. Having only a few administrative levels in an organization decreases communication and reduce red tape, but it can result in each supervisor having too many supervisees. This results in difficulty managing training, communication, and quality control.

Supervision is effective only when it is backed by frequent contact. Novice and advanced beginner school psychologists need daily contact with their supervisors, preferably face-to-face, although telephone and email communication are successful methods to augment communication. School psychologists who have reached the competent level generally need at least weekly appointments with their supervisors. Even proficient and expert practitioners continue to need supervision, but will probably be comfortable with peer supervision and scheduling appointments as needed.

Excessively close supervision can reduce the effectiveness of supervisees for three reasons: supervisees spend too much time reporting to the supervisor, individuals tend to feel threatened by constant evaluation, and close supervision can imply incompetence. In general, supervisees want enough supervision to know they are completing their work correctly. The supervisor must determine the amount of supervision necessary to effect that goal (Halloran, 1981; Loen, 1994).

IMPLEMENTING A STRUCTURE

Implementing a structure is analogous to actually building a house under the supervision of a building contractor. It involves myriad decisions and attention to detail regarding a number of topics. An example of this function in the supervision of school psychology is process selection.

Process selection involves making decisions about processes to be used, the sequence of these processes, and the necessary tools (Rue &

Byars, 1997). Many of the processes and procedures used in school psychology are prescribed by professional standards. However, the supervisor of school psychologists is frequently in a position to make process selection decisions that have direct impact on the provision of school psychological services. The following examples are process decisions faced by one school psychology supervisor:

- When and how to convert to a revised version of an intelligence test;
- Whether and how to encourage school psychologists to use standard reporting forms and test descriptors;
- How to implement a newly mandated service; and
- Whether and how to modify an existing procedure, such as method of referral to the self-contained program for behaviorally disordered students.

In making such decisions, multiple factors must be taken into consideration. These include cost, availability of school psychologists, the amount of training required for school psychologists, availability of materials, potential for efficient record keeping, compatibility with existing procedures, and ethical and legal concerns.

On occasion, supervisors of school psychologists will be consulted regarding other aspects of operation planning, such as site selection and facilities layout. For example, one supervisor of school psychologists was consulted about the space needed for school psychological services in a new administration building and the most appropriate layout of space in a suite of rooms for a program for adolescents with behavioral disorders. As indicated by Rue and Byars (1997), all of these decisions must be based on a combination of factors, including a balance of space needs and an estimate of future demands.

CONDUCTING AN EVALUATION

The strategic plan incorporates techniques for continual improvement of methods and procedures. This is necessary not only because every service and method can improve, but also because organizations undergo constant, systemic change. It is therefore necessary to institutionalize methods for change at both the individual and departmental level. Supervisors are responsible for helping their supervisees understand the need for continual improvement (Loen, 1994). The evaluation of the results and process of planning is essential for effective supervision. These topics are treated in depth in subsequent chapters.

77

Filling staff vacancies with outstanding personnel is a critically important responsibility for school psychology supervisors. As suggested by Gile (1987), the method of selecting staff has an immediate bearing on the quality of staff. Good leaders are effective team builders, and hiring an outstanding team of school psychologists is pivotal to developing an outstanding department of psychological services. Furthermore, many supervisors of school psychologists are also responsible for supervising staff in addition to school psychologists. These may include social workers, teachers, counselors, clerical staff, and paraprofessionals. Although most of the examples given in this chapter address the selection of school psychologists, the same principles apply to the selection of staff regardless of the position.

Due to the importance of selecting staff, business management literature has extensive information addressing issues of reliability, validity, and legality in the selection process, pre-interview strategies, interview strategies, post-interview strategies, and considerations regarding promotion. This chapter summarizes this information and provides information specific to the supervision of school psychology.

Because supervisors of school psychologists are held accountable for the performance of those they oversee, they should play a major role in the selection of supervisees. Because staffing errors can have costly effects on children and on supervisors' resources including time, energy, and money, substantial energy and time should be spent to hire staff carefully. Expectations for school psychologists are high, and there is little room for mediocrity. Incompetent interns or school psychologists can harm children, undermine the work of other school psychologists, and take an extraordinary amount of supervisors' time. Thus minimizing the number of "hiring errors" is highly desirable.

STANDARDS IN SELECTION METHODS

Selecting and hiring a school psychologist requires assessment of his or her skills and potential relative to the job's requirements. As in any assessment process, methods used in personnel selection must meet standards of reliability, validity, generalizability, and legality. Methods must be relatively free of random error, associated with success on the job, and conformable to current law (Noe et al., 1996).

Unfortunately, many methods commonly used to discriminate one applicant from another do not meet standards of reliability or validity. Interviews are notoriously unreliable. Grade point averages, above a certain minimal level, have little ability to predict job success, and thus do not have predictive validity. References have become so universally positive that they are only minimally helpful.

Therefore, to avoid hiring errors, supervisors must combine multiple measures and methods of comparison, including multiple opportunities to see applicants "in action" (Mornell, 1998). To conform to current laws, supervisors must apply measures and methods uniformly to all candidates in a standardized hiring process.

A review of selected employment laws is relevant. These include the Equal Pay Act of 1963, the Civil Rights Act of 1964, the Age Discrimination Employment Act of 1967, the Rehabilitation Act of 1973, the Americans with Disabilities Act of 1990, and the Civil Rights Act of 1991. In sum, these laws proscribe any discrimination on the basis of race, color, sex, religion, national origin, and age (40 to 70) concerning hiring, compensation, and working conditions (Noe et al., 1996; Rue & Byars, 1997). It should be noted that "minorities" is a relative term. In school psychology, minorities include men as well as ethnic and racial minorities.

The Americans with Disabilities Act of 1991 protects individuals with a history of current physical or mental disabilities. This law requires employers to make "reasonable accommodations" for those who are "otherwise qualified" for the job. Reasonable accommodations have been interpreted to include activities such as modifying equipment or work schedules, providing readers, and restructuring jobs (Noe et al., 1996).

As a result of these laws, employers must be able to prove that the methods used in employee selection measure traits and behaviors essential to job success. While these laws specifically address hiring and firing practices, it is important to understand that discrimination also occurs and is similarly unacceptable in other areas essential to job success, such as communication, mentoring, networking, evaluation, and promotion (Rue & Byars, 1997).

If selection methods do not measure traits essential to job success, and discriminate in illegal variables such as race, color, sex, religion, national origin, disability, and/or age, the laws permit jury trials and the awarding of punitive damages. During the past 30 years, such trials have led to large monetary awards for those with successful lawsuits. Hence, supervisors must be vigilantly aware of potential litigation and liability.

These laws thus restrict questions that supervisors can ask applicants and forbid questions about an applicant's race, ethnicity, gender, religion, national origin, age, or disabilities. They also restrict discriminatory screening methods and measures. To make sure that a hiring process is legally sound, it is highly recommended that a standardized hiring process be devel-

oped and reviewed by the school district's personnel director and legal counsel. Before beginning the screening or interviewing process supervisors should determine and minimize biases regarding age, sex, ethnicity, and race. It is helpful to compose a team that is reflective of the composition of the school population to participate in each stage of the process.

To ensure compliance with legal anti-discrimination laws, the following are recommended:

1. Maintain a file of not-hired minority applicants (males and ethnic minorities), and contact them when an opening occurs (Rue & Byars, 1997);
2. Use males and ethnic minorities as recruiters, screeners, and interviewers;
3. Ensure that advertisements do not indicate sex, race, or age qualification for the job;
4. Advertise in media directed toward minorities;
5. Include the phrase "equal opportunity employer" in all advertisements; and
6. Encourage and mentor men and ethnic minorities to enter and complete school psychology programs.

Ethical dilemma 5-1

A supervisor hires a school psychologist who appears highly qualified. However, after she begins work it becomes immediately apparent that the school psychologist has great difficulty listening to others, including students, parents, teachers, and the supervisor. The supervisor raises this point with the school psychologist, who then discloses that she has ADD and deficits in auditory processing. The supervisor feels that listening skills constitute an essential aspect of school psychology practice. The school psychologist feels that job accommodations must be made to due to her disability. *What are the ethical dilemmas? What should be done?*

80

PRE-INTERVIEW STRATEGIES

Developing a comprehensive job description

Effective hiring begins with a job description that indicates desired education, experience, knowledge, and skills, as well as a list of the requirements and duties of the position. The accuracy of the job description has a direct relationship to the potential for success in the staffing process. The job description should be in agreement with the departmental vision of service provision and coordinated with individual performance evaluation tools and procedures. The supervisor writes the job description after the development of a job specification, a "written statement that identifies the abilities, skills, traits, or attributes necessary for successful performance in a particular job" (Rue & Byars, 1997, p. 236). In addition, at times individuals with very specialized skills are needed, and these requirements must be included in the posting.

Formal training and certification as a school psychologist are obviously prerequisites for a position as a school psychologist. However, formal training does not guarantee that any given candidate has the skills necessary for a particular opening. Many training programs do not provide training in specialty areas, such as crisis intervention, pre-school assessment, parent training, and personality assessment. Besides formal training, certain personal characteristics are essential to job success. Supervisors should hire on the basis of integrity, motivation, capacity, understanding, knowledge, and experience. "Without integrity, motivation is dangerous; without motivation, capacity is impotent; without capacity, understanding is limited; without understanding, knowledge is meaningless; without knowledge, experience is blind. Experience is easy to provide and quickly put to use with the other qualities" (Dee Hock, as quoted by Mornell, 1998, p. 168).

Many would agree that excellent school psychologists possess the skills described by Fagan and Wise (1994):

1. Listening skills;
2. Skills in oral expression;
3. Writing skills;
4. An ability to respond to constructive criticism professionally;
5. Overall emotional maturity;
6. An ability to work with children;
7. An ability to work with peers, parents, and school or agency personnel;
8. A willingness to go beyond basic requirements;
9. Flexibility in adapting to change;
10. Observance of protocol and rules;
11. Responsivity to professional ethics; and
12. A respect for individual and group differences.

A great challenge in hiring is to discriminate between qualified candidates on the basis of these characteristics, while using selection methods that are reliable, valid, and legal.

For several reasons, graduating from a reputable school psychology program unfortunately does not guarantee that individuals possess the above traits. University programs can and do make admissions errors, despite using references and interviews as well as standardized tests and grade point averages to screen candidates. Following admissions, programs monitor the professional skills of students and "counsel" students ill-suited for the profession into a more appropriate profession. However, university programs have little legal ground to eliminate students on the basis of mediocrity. Furthermore, some students who are ill-suited to the profession are excellent academically, and their academic skills overshadow weak application skills in many courses. Formal courses provide enough structure so those students who work well only

81

in structured settings do not surface as problematic until their internships. Although practica and internships serve as additional screening opportunities, a student's performance under close supervision is not necessarily predictive of his or her performance as a practitioner.

Ethical dilemma 5-2

You are working in the district school that houses the program for (signing) deaf children. The Director of Special Education inadvertently hired a teacher of the hearing impaired without realizing that her graduate program was oral/aural and she does not sign. You feel that the children are not being adequately serviced, but the Director indicates that the posting stipulated only that the person be qualified to teach the deaf, not that signing be used to do so. In addition, the administration indicates that the teacher was offered and signed a contract, and therefore must finish the school year. *What are the ethical issues? What can be done?*

Clearly enumerating job responsibilities and delineating expectations can greatly reduce the likelihood of unqualified and/or unsuitable candidates submitting job applications. This can result in significant timesaving. The supervising school psychologist and other relevant administrators should agree upon requirements, duties, education, experience, knowledge, and skills for successful candidates before the job is posted and advertised. It is also helpful if consumers, such as parents, teachers, and school board members, agree with the job description.

Components included in the job description should reflect district's expectations. The following two examples convey these expectations: (a) the school psychologists provide a broad range of psychological services, (b) they are able to demonstrate success, (c) supervision will be provided and, (d) the supervisor provides direct services as well as supervision.

Sample Job Description:

School Psychologist
POSITION TITLE: School Psychologist
REPORTS TO AND EVALUATED BY: Director of Special Education and Supervising School Psychologist (who also provides direct supervision and consultation).
SUPERVISES: None
COORDINATES WITH: Other Staff Psychologists and School Personnel

The School Psychologist provides student psychological services and recommends and implements appropriate programs and placements.

Principal Duties:
1. Provides effective psychological consultation services to school personnel and parents (e.g., observation, review of records, teacher conferences, parent conferences, student interviews, brief reports, staffing).
2. Conducts comprehensive psychological evaluations (e.g., including all of the above as well as the administration and interpretation of psychological instruments).
3. Prepares psychological reports on individual students.
4. Recommends and implements effective intervention strategies as required and appropriate.
5. Provides and assists in providing effective psychological therapy for individual students.
6. Provides facilitative psychological consultation to counselors and therapists for students with emotional or behavior disorders.
7. Participates effectively in building- and district-level team meetings.
8. Performs other duties within the general scope of the position which may be assigned by the Director of Special Education.

Subsidiary Activities:

1. Provides training for staff and parents.
2. Makes on-site visits to out-of-district placement locations and determines appropriateness.

Combination Tasks:

1. Makes programmatic recommendations for IEPs in coordination with placement team.
2. Exchanges information with external agencies for purposes of student assessment and programs.

Minimum Requirements: meets requirements for state certification as a School Psychologist and is qualified to assess emotional/behavioral disorders. Possesses knowledge of and willingness to implement statutes and ethical guidelines related to psychology and special education. Displays good communication and interpersonal skills.

Sample Job Description:

Supervising School Psychologist

POSITION TITLE: Supervising School Psychologist

REPORTS TO AND EVALUATED BY: Director of Special Education

SUPERVISES: School Psychologists, Counselors, Social Worker, and Educational Examiners

COORDINATES WITH: School Administrators and Personnel

The Supervising School Psychologist provides student psychological services and recommends appropriate programs and placements at designated programs. The Supervising School Psychologist also coordinates and supervises the provision of psychological services throughout the district.

Principal Duties:

1. Provides effective psychological consultation services to school personnel and parents (e.g., observation, review of records, teacher conferences, parent conferences, student interviews, brief reports, staffing).
2. Conducts comprehensive psychological evaluations (e.g., including all of the above as well as the administration and interpretation of psychological instruments).
3. Prepares psychological reports on individual students.
4. Recommends and implements effective intervention strategies as required and appropriate.
5. Provides and assists in providing effective psychological therapy for individual students.
6. Provides facilitative psychological consultation to counselors and therapists for students with emotional or behavioral disorders.
7. Participates effectively in building and district level team meetings.
8. Provides effective clinical supervision for staff School Psychologists via weekly individual and biweekly group meetings.
9. Holds bimonthly meetings with educational examiners that result in improved practice.
10. Provides clinical supervision and consultation to district social workers that results in improved practice.
11. Provides administrative supervision to staff school psychologists, educational examiners, and district social workers (e.g., hiring, evaluating, and planning) in an effective manner.
12. Performs other duties within the general scope of the position that may be assigned by the Director of Special Education.

Subsidiary Activities:

1. Provides training for staff and parents.
2. Makes onsite visits to out-of-district placement locations and determines appropriateness.

Combination Tasks:

1. Makes programmatic recommendations for

83

IEPs in coordination with placement team.

2 Exchanges information with external agencies for purposes of student assessment and programs.

Minimum Requirements:

Has attained certification as School Psychologist. Possesses knowledge of and a willingness to implement statutes and ethical guidelines related to psychology and special education. Displays good communication and interpersonal skills. Some training or experience in supervision preferred.

Determining hiring process

After agreement is reached on the job description, the supervisor and administrators determine the hiring process. For example, it must be decided who will make the selection of the final candidate, formally offer the job, and negotiate salary. In many situations the upper level administration is happy to take the recommendation of the supervising school psychologist in the selection of an intern or school psychologist, but retains the right to actually offer the job and negotiate salary. The supervisor and administrators address the following questions in developing the hiring process:

- Who formally hires the school psychologist and offers the job?
- How negotiable are the salary and benefits? If mandated by union contract, what factors determine the placement of the new hire in the salary schedule?
- What recruitment methods will be used?
- What information and work samples will applicants be asked to supply?
- Who will initially screen the applicants, and what criterion will be used?
- Who will telephone candidates to invite them in for interviews?
- What semi-structured interview questions or assignments will be asked of each candidate?
- What biases are the individuals conducting screenings and interviews likely to have, and how can the effect of these biases be minimized?
- What type of references will be contacted? Who will telephone them? What questions will be asked, and what criteria will be used to evaluate the responses?
- What will be the format of the interviews? Who will participate as interviewers? Will they be asked to provide an impromptu work sample, and if so, what?
- How will biographical information be verified?

To avoid the frustration of completing the hiring process only to have job offers refused, supervisors and administrators must consider factors that influence whether a candidate will accept a job. The following factors are often critical: promptness of job offers, pay level, challenge and responsibility, job security, advancement opportunities, geographic location, and employee benefits (Noe et al., 1996). Although employers attempt to minimize expenditures, often some negotiation must occur to successfully hire qualified applicants. For example, some administrators believe a school psychologist without experience as a contracted school district employee should start at the lowest pay level. However, a certified school psychologist with ten years experience working in a mental health clinic is unlikely to be willing to enter a school system at that pay level. If the applicant has worked for a number of years in a clinic setting, the supervising school psychologist may be able to successfully negotiate to have those years credited on the salary scale.

Recruitment

There are a number of methods of recruitment differentiated in management literature. Each method has its own benefits, drawbacks, and success rates. For example, newspaper advertising generates a large number of applicants, but often only a small percentage of those applicants are qualified. In contrast, a smaller number of applicants are generated through referrals by current employees or by university programs, and those candidates are very likely to be qualified. Generating a list of referred candidates may initially be time consuming but is less costly in the long run because the candidates are more likely to be qualified (Noe et al., 1996). Methods of recruitment discussed in the following pages include internal hiring, direct/referred applicants, college and university postings and recruitment, newspaper advertisement, professional newsletter advertisements, convention recruitment, and the Internet.

Internal hiring consists of selecting an individual who is already employed by the school system. The most common example of this in school psychology is hiring a person who obtained additional certification as a school psychologist, but who is currently a teacher or counselor in the district. These candidates have either obtained this certification on their own, or were encouraged to obtain certification by district school psychologists or administrators. The advantages to hiring internally are that the abilities of the applicant are already well known, the applicant is already familiar with the job parameters, the adjustment period of the new hire is decreased, and vacancies are filled more quickly and less expensively. Furthermore, it leads to the possibility of internal job changes and/or promotions, which increases general job satisfaction and improves morale. School districts often have job-posting rules that are determined by union contract and mandate internal posting prior to new recruitment of outside applicants.

The primary disadvantages to internal hiring are that there are often insufficient qualified internal applicants, and external hires bring new ideas and generate growth in the department. Relying entirely on internal hires may "result in a workforce whose members all think alike and who therefore may be poorly suited for innovation" (Noe et al., 1996, p. 293). Internal hiring can also lead to "political infighting" for positions and a decrease in morale for those who apply for positions and are not hired (Rue & Byars, 1997).

A second applicant category is *direct applicants and referrals*. Direct applicants are individuals who contact the school system to inquire about a position without being aware of an opening. Referrals are individuals who have been urged to apply by someone already working for the school system. The primary advantage of recruiting from both of these groups is that, at least to some extent, they have investigated the school system or job already and have drawn the conclusion that there is a "good fit" between themselves and the school system. In the case of referrals, they often know a fair amount about the school system because they have spoken with the person(s) who urged them to apply. Another advantage of direct applicants and referrals is that hiring them greatly reduces the cost of the recruitment process (Noe et al., 1996).

Networking to enlarge and enrich the referred applicant pool is also a recommended method. That is, the supervisor, other school psychologists in the district, and other school personnel contact potential candidates and invite them to apply. Sources of referrals might be school psychologists who may know of other interested school psychologists, university professors, special educators, general educators, administrators, or community agency personnel. Colleges and universities are also excellent sources of prospective applicants. Campus placement services (and often school psychology programs themselves) offer links to current students and graduates of school psychology programs. Many campuses have job fairs or group sessions with potential interns or job

85

applicants. In addition, some supervisors have found that a chief benefit of teaching a course for a local school psychology program is the opportunity to observe and recruit future job applicants.

Newspapers and professional periodical advertisements are a traditional method of recruitment. School systems are most familiar with newspaper advertisements. They have the advantage of reaching a large number of individuals in a given geographic area, of having a short lead-time, and of being relatively inexpensive. However, they can become quite expensive when they are long enough to contain sufficient information for readers to accurately assess their qualifications for the position. They often reach a large number of unqualified people, and are not read by individuals who are not actively job searching.

Advertisements in professional periodicals, such as state association newsletters and the *Communiqué*, are more efficient, because they reach only qualified individuals. In addition, the ads might attract the interest school psychologists not actively job searching. On the other hand, they create an additional expense and require substantial lead-time relative to the short time line under which school systems commonly operate. For example, a school system might obtain final approval for a September position in July, long past the *Communiqué* summer deadline.

The *Internet* is being used with increasing success to recruit job applicants. Various state Departments of Education, newspapers, and professional organizations are posting jobs. The NASP web page (www.naspweb.org/information/links/links_state_orgs.html), and a school psychology job employment service (www.onelist.com/subscribe/schpsy-jobs-only), are potential sources. Several additional sites are listed by Benner (1999) and search engines, such as Netscape and Yahoo, can be also be used to obtain additional opportunities.

Application requirements

When applicants respond to a recruitment effort they should be asked to submit the following as part of the application process:

1. Letter of application;
2. Résumé;
3. Undergraduate and graduate college and university transcripts;
4. At least three letters of reference, particularly from supervisors;
5. Relevant job evaluations, such as internship evaluations;
6. Evidence of school psychology certification;
7. A completed formal job application, which includes a signed release to telephone references; and
8. Work samples.

School psychologists often submit several reports as work samples, but to demonstrate a breadth of skills they should be strongly encouraged to submit other materials as well. They might send:

- In-service workshop materials they developed and presented,
- consultation progress notes,
- authentic or functional assessments,
- intervention plans and evaluations of the results,
- grant applications they wrote, or
- other materials that prove their ability to perform the professional practice of school psychology at a high level.

Applicants can be asked to include with their application copies of their most professional work with identifying information deleted.

Screening

After the applications have been reviewed for completeness, a team of three to five diverse individuals screens them. The screening eliminates applicants who are not qualified, for example, those who do not have school psychology certification, and determines which applicants to invite for interviews. At this stage, it is preferable to be generous rather than highly critical. It is important not to exclude all but the "top" candidates solely on the basis of a paper evaluation, as highly qualified candidates may be inadvertently excluded. For example, a candidate with a range of grades from B to A may be as good a school psychologist as one with all A's (although a candidate with close to failing grades, including C's at the graduate level, is obviously not a strong candidate).

The screening team should verify résumés against the transcripts and other information for consistency, since a large proportion of job applicants misrepresent or falsify information (Mornell, 1998). The applications should also be screened for issues that indicate problematic behaviors. Not uncommonly the manner in which individuals present themselves in their cover letter and résumé reveals essential characteristics such as literacy, integrity, and stability. A candidate might, for example, state one grade point average on a résumé while the transcript lists quite another. Submitting a reference letter written by a relative reveals a lack of understanding of the fundamental ethical principle of avoiding dual relationships. Since past behavior tends to indicate future behavior, attending to past patterns can be illuminating. For example, if candidates have skipped among fields or positions in the past, they may be likely to do so in the future.

PRE-INTERVIEW STRATEGIES

After the screening committee generates a list of applicants to be interviewed, the supervisor telephones to set up the initial interview. It is best if the supervisor makes these telephone calls, rather than a secretary, as this demonstrates a level of respect for the candidate and his or her responses can provide additional information.

During this telephone call, the applicant can be asked to complete a brief pre-interview assignment that reveals how the applicant carries out tasks. This task can be as simple as visiting the district's web page or city library to obtain information about district schools and then sharing impressions and observations during the interview (Mornell, 1998). The completion of the assignment before the interview indicates the tendency to follow through in general; the supervisor can also assess the accuracy and helpfulness of the observations.

Developing semi-structured interview questions

Although interviews are the most common hiring selection process, research indicates that they are frequently unreliable, invalid, biased, and subjective. To increase the likelihood that interviews will be reliable and legal, interviews should be "structured, standardized and focused on...(coming) out of each interview with quantitative ratings on a small number of dimensions that are observable (e.g., interpersonal style or ability to express oneself), and avoid ratings of abilities that may be better measured by tests (e.g., intelligence)" (Noe et al., 1996, pp. 320-321).

To comply with the Americans with Disabilities Act, the interviewer cannot ask any questions that would disclose a disability, including whether or not the candidate had or has a physical illness, mental disability, or issues with substance abuse. On the other hand, it is permissible to ask questions that reveal the candidate's ability to successfully perform. For example, if it is a job requirement for the school psychologists to be onsite during school hours, it is permissible to ask whether candidates would be able to arrive by the time school opened at 7:00 A.M.. These questions can be asked both of candidates themselves and of their references.

Additionally, a set of standardized questions that raise issues the candidate is likely to encounter as a school psychologist are helpful. These can be based on the interviewees' own experiences or may draw on future problem-solving capabilities. In a typical interview, a candidate can be asked to respond to four or five such questions.

Potential Experiential Interview Questions

- Describe a case about which you feel particular success.

- Describe a difficult case where you wished you had done something different. How would you approach a similar situation differently in the future?

- What would your former supervisor(s) say about your work, including both positive and negative aspects?

- What would you describe as your greatest professional strength? In what circumstances does that strength become a weakness? What do you do in those circumstances?

- What factor regarding your work would you most like to improve? How will you go about improving it?

- School psychology is a constantly changing field. Describe how you go about learning new techniques in consultation, counseling, and assessment. How do you decide which techniques to learn? How do you acquire the necessary skills?

- What methods have you developed to cope with the inevitable stress that results from being a school psychologist? How do you release tension?

- What would you like to be doing professionally in ten years?

- With what type of person do you find it most difficult to work? How do you deal with that difficulty?

- What metaphor would you use to describe the profession of school psychology? What metaphor would you use to describe schools?

- What three things would you change about your current/most recent job?

- Pretending you were your former supervisor, how would you structure your job differently?

- Which professional books have most profoundly affected your thinking and professional work?

- What led you to leave your last positions?

- What responsibilities as a school psychologist do you like least, and how do you deal with them? What responsibilities as a school psychologist do you like most, and why?

- What work environment is most likely to induce your best performance?

- How do you handle working with individuals whose language or class is different than yours?

- What do you think are the most important characteristics for a school psychologist to have? Which of these characteristics do you display?

These questions do not necessarily have correct or incorrect answers. The candidates' responses can be evaluated, nonetheless, on several dimensions mentioned previously as characteristics necessary for school psychologists, including oral expression, ability to respond to constructive criticism professionally, overall emotional maturity, ability to work with children, ability to work with peers, parents, and school or agency personnel, willingness to go beyond basic requirements, flexibility in adapting to change, observance of protocol and rules, ability to act in accord with professional ethics, and ability to respect individual and group differences.

Some individuals prefer to hand each candidate a typed list of four to six questions at the beginning of the interview. This gives candidates the opportunity to exhibit their organizational skill, and makes it much less likely that interviewers will dominate the conversation (Mornell, 1998).

Besides delineating the interview questions and methods to evaluate the responses, the supervisor lists the additional traits that are to be observed during the interview when determining the hiring process. Often, interviews give the supervisor the opportunity to observe intangible traits such as curiosity, general attitude, interpersonal skills, punctuality, energy, enthusiasm, and humor. Again, to comply with legal requirements, whatever traits the supervisor notes in the interview should be observed and noted for all candidates and must be relevant to the job.

Determining and minimizing biases

All of us have biases, prejudices, and personal features that color our perceptions and can adversely affect the hiring process. To minimize the effect of these issues, interviewers should first identify and then sensitize themselves to their own biases regarding age, sex, ethnicity, and race before screening or interviewing candidates (Halloran, 1981). Furthermore, more than one person should be involved at each stage of the process. Initial interviews generally occur with the supervisor and at least one other person. It is particularly helpful to reflect the composition of the school population and include minorities when choosing co-interviewers. To increase the number of persons involved in the screening process, some supervisors turn to teleconferencing or videotaping interviews, although permission from the candidates must be obtained before the tapes are viewed by others (Noe et al., 1996).

INTERVIEW STRATEGIES

Initial interviewing

The supervisor invites a pool of approximately a dozen candidates for initial interviews. Initial interviews are short but critical. As Mornell (1998) indicates, they eliminate "paper tigers who have great resumes but are less impressive in person" (p. 49). Interviews test "how well someone interviews" because "a good con artist can con you every time" (Mornell, 1998, p. 55). Although immediate personal chemistry, or likeability, can be important in a school psychologist, it certainly is not appropriate as a sole decision criterion. While candidates' responses to the questions posed are important, their behavior is also important. Inexplicable or inappropriate behavior may indicate significant issues such as alcoholism (Mornell, 1998).

During the interview it is important to stress the importance of past performance as described in the résumé, university transcripts, and telephone references. The following steps are helpful in conducting a successful interview during which one could accurately appraise the candidates' personality, motivation, and character (Halloran, 1981):

- Review the candidates' materials before the interview to find patterns of accomplishments, strengths and attributes to explore;
- Eliminate visual distractions, interruptions, and phone calls to present a professional atmosphere;
- Establish rapport;
- Avoid inducing additional stress; and,
- Have the candidate do 75% of the talking, using open-ended questions to enable the applicant to reveal feelings and ideas.

Remember that it is not legal to ask questions regarding age, religion, citizenship of parents or spouse, type of military discharge,

89

national origin or ancestry, whether the candidate has ever been arrested, marital status or number of dependents, or disabilities. During the interview, discuss with the candidate his or her work history and outside activities, and describe the organization to the candidate. Before the candidate leaves, discuss the next step in the hiring process and provide as much feedback as possible.

Checking references

Supervisors often find it difficult to obtain relevant and accurate information regarding applicants. According to management research, 30% of applicants falsely represent themselves on their applications (Mornell, 1998). Lies range from an exaggeration of educational background to hiding criminal records. In addition, references are wary of disclosing negative information about candidates for fear of reprisal. Many states do not require criminal record checks on certification applications, yet employers are legally and ethically responsible for an employee's behavior, including circumstances in which a candidate with a history of sexual misconduct is hired to work with children (Noe et al., 1996). Supervisors should consult with school system personnel and legal departments to develop hiring procedures that are legal, ethical, and in accordance with child protection laws.

Following the initial interviews, interviewers assess each candidate on previously agreed upon criteria. The references of candidates with the strongest applications are then telephoned. Each reference can asked about:

1. Technical competency as a school psychologist;
2. Intelligence;
3. Ability to display good interpersonal skills with children, teachers, parents, other school psychologists, administrators, and supervisors; and
4. Energy and motivation.

Finally, each reference should be asked, "Is there anything that I haven't asked?" (Mornell, 1998, p. 141). It is critical to listen carefully to the responses and to allow the reference to disclose freely. As an interviewer, you are still obligated to refrain from asking questions that might violate employment laws. You have every right, however, to ask questions about the individual's ability to perform the job.

Although checking references is essential, the results are not necessarily reliable indicators of future job performance. This stems from two sources. First, candidates only request references from those whom they expect will give good reports. Second, references are hesitant to give negative responses due to justifiable fear of lawsuits (Noe et al., 1996).

Two methods improve the credibility of information gathered about prospective employees. First, ask for a large number of references. Second, if your district follows this policy, use other sources to verify the biographical information provided on résumés. Verification sources can include driving records, criminal records, education verification, and employment verification. In some states, many of these are routinely checked by Personnel Departments, but supervisors should not presume that to be the case.

Second interviews

Interaction skills exhibited in second interviews, when a candidate is often less nervous, often offer more accurate indications of the candidate's general persona than the first interview. Approximately three individuals, whose references are the most positive, are invited for more lengthy second interviews. These interviews are structured to include more interviewers and more interview sessions. A one-to-one session with the supervisor, a session with potential colleagues (other school psychologists), and a session with administrators (including the director of special education and either a principal or assistant superintendent) are all appropriate.

As indicated during the discussion on initial interviews, questions to be asked are developed ahead of time. It is thoughtful and efficient to coordinate questions so that candidates are not asked by different interviewers to reply to the same questions repeatedly.

In academia and business, it is common to expect applicants to perform a task during the interview process. In academia, the task is commonly to teach a class or give a lecture. In business, the applicant may be given a "problem," "work sample," or "in-basket" to analyze. In school psychology, giving candidates a case study to read and discuss could be the task.

Sample case study

Tracy Phillips, aged 18, was referred for a three-year re-evaluation to determine whether or not she would continue to be eligible for special education services. She had been identified as educationally disabled due to serious emotional disturbance on the basis of severe depression demonstrated by withdrawn behavior, school failure, and near fatal suicide attempts.

Tracy has a history of emotional and sexual abuse perpetrated by a brother eight years older. At the time of the onset of the abuse, Tracy was 12 and the brother was 20. After one year, the abuse was discovered, and the brother was incarcerated. The onset of Tracy's depression coincided with the arrest and incarceration of her brother. He returned to the household when Tracy was 17. Although she is secretive about the details, Tracy described their relationship at that time as "very close." School personnel were concerned and suspected that the abusive relationship had resumed. Tracy did not have friends among her classmates and was not active in extracurricular activities. Her vocational plans were unknown.

At the time of the initial diagnosis, Tracy was placed in a substantially separate classroom. In addition to receiving her academics in that setting, she received individual counseling from the school psychologist and participated in group counseling sessions. She continued to see a psychiatrist at the local mental health clinic for both therapy and medication. Tracy received special education services for three years.

During the re-evaluation, test results indicated that Tracy was significantly less depressed as compared with three years prior and her suicidal tendencies had been reduced to the point that she was no longer considered a suicidal risk. Self-esteem improved and her anxiety, hypochondriasis, and obsessionalism also decreased. Because of the re-evaluation, Tracy was discharged from all special education services and placed in general education classes. She graduated from high school the following year.

Tracy is now 20 years old and has been unemployed since high school graduation. She has been diagnosed as severely depressed in conjunction with post traumatic stress disorder. Her lawyer recently contact the school district for compensatory post-secondary education, stating that she had been inappropriately discharged from special education.

Discuss the following:

1. *Had Tracy improved at the time of re-evaluation?*
2. *How do you perceive the current lawsuit?*
3. *What would you do differently? The same?*

At the end of the scheduled sessions, each candidate meets again with the supervisor and is provided a final opportunity to raise questions. Just before the end of the final session, the supervisor should indicate that the interview is almost over. Frequently, the questions raised at this time are the most important (Mornell, 1998). Finally, the candidate is asked for the names and telephone numbers of additional references,

91

including previous supervisors, school administrators, school psychologists, and teachers.

POST-INTERVIEW STRATEGIES

Checking reference

Additional references are telephoned subsequent to the second interviews. In some districts, references are telephoned by persons in comparable positions (special education administrators telephoning special education administrators, teachers calling teachers, school psychologists telephoning school psychologists, etc.).

Follow-up tasks

According to Mornell (1998), asking candidates to telephone "on Monday" to discuss any additional thoughts they have or to raise additional questions provides yet another opportunity to observe whether candidates act responsibly by following through with tasks. Mornell also suggests that candidates be assigned a post-interview project, such as analyzing a case, editing a report, or writing up the responses to a critical issue currently faced by the school district. The finished result can be analyzed for accuracy, timeliness, attention to detail, and problem analysis.

Sample post-interview projects

1. Describe what you believe should be included in a workshop for teachers on functional behavior assessment.
2. Describe how you would help a school develop and implement a crisis intervention plan.
3. Delineate a recommended set of procedures for the district in assessing bilingual children.

PROMOTION

Promoting an intern to the position of a school psychologist, or a school psychologist to the position of supervising school psychologist, requires the same attention to developing a job description, recruiting, screening, and following the selection process described above. It cannot be presumed that because an individual functions successfully at one level that he or she will succeed at the next level. In management lore, the "Peter Principle" suggests the opposite, that individuals are promoted to their level of incompetence (Rue & Byars, 1997).

In summary, supervisors of school psychologists are well advised to spend time and effort developing strategies for selecting staff. The effective selection of staff greatly contributes to the quality of school psychological services.

A supervisor has a fundamental obligation to promote the best possible school psychological services for the children, school personnel, and parents in the district. Individual performance evaluations can be helpful in achieving this goal. However, they are effective only within the context of an appropriate job analysis, performance feedback, and subsequent improvement. Just as no one method or tool of evaluation is appropriate for all children, no one method or tool of evaluation is appropriate for all school psychologists. Any responsible evaluation tool is both context responsive and specific.

An example of a systemic model that addresses the steps of Individual Performance Evaluation from Vision to Evaluation is presented in Case Study 6-1.

Case study 6-1 One District's Individual Performance Evaluation Vision and Plan

VISION
The school psychology department is comprised of a superior staff that continually improves, and individual evaluations are an integral part of the improvement process.

ASSESSMENT
Internal:
(Strength) The department has a clear vision regarding excellent school psychological services.

(Strength) The supervisor determines psychologists' assignments.

(Strength) Each school psychologist has a well-defined job description.

(Strength) The department staff is knowledgeable about program evaluation.

(Weakness) The process to evaluate the individual performance of school psychologists has not been developed.

External:
(Opportunity) The school system is open to refining the process of school psychologist performance evaluations.

(Opportunity) The schools have excellent counselors.

(Threat/Barrier) The staff development funds are insufficient.

(Threat/Barrier) Employees must work within union regulations.

MISSION/GOAL
The school psychologists' individual performance evaluations will be integrated with the hiring, professional development, and supervision processes. Individual performance evaluations will be ongoing, meaningful, and facilitative.

STRATEGIC PLAN

1. An evaluation format will be developed that uses management by objective (MBO), based on the NASP *Professional Conduct Manual*,

2. Measurable objectives reflecting the job description and the NASP *Blueprint for Change* (Ysseldyke et al., 1997) will be developed by the supervising school psychologist in collaboration with the staff school psychologists.

3. The objectives will be used in the hiring process.

4. The objectives will be used for formative evaluations, biweekly with new school psychologists, quarterly with veterans.

5. Formative evaluative results will be used to create a professional development plan for each school psychologist.

6. Each school psychologist's objectives will be used as the foundation for summative individual performance evaluations.

7. The entire process will be evaluated by a summative evaluation after 12 months of implementation.

Conducting individual performance evaluations requires competencies in which supervisors of school psychologists are hopefully skilled: observing, gathering and recording supportive evidence, discriminating between relevant and irrelevant information, collecting selective and representative work samples, and deciding measurable aspects of performance (Rice, 1985).

Performance evaluations serve three fundamental purposes. They assess and recognize quality of service, guide future professional development activities, and provide direction for future practice.

In assessing the quality of services, an individual performance evaluation determines whether or not a job is being completed satisfactorily and provides a basis for professional recognition (Johnson, 1998). The underlying question is whether a school psychologist is providing quality services that have a positive impact on the functioning of students and staff. Evaluations should also address whether the school psychologist's practice is in accord with professional standards and local, state, and federal guidelines (Maher & Brabrack, 1981). When they are evaluated positively, school psychologists can be recognized by a variety of methods, including letters of commendation in personnel files and nomination for awards by professional organizations.

Individual performance evaluations foster professional development by providing supervisors with ongoing information about areas in which supervisees need additional training. The evaluation process increases the supervisor's understanding of the school psychologist, clarifies expectations, and enables supervisors to recognize and address areas of weakness.

When the quality of service is less than desired, individual performance evaluations lead to professional development plans to improve performance (Johnson, 1998). Hopefully,

performance evaluations not only identify areas of weakness but also differentiate the cause of the weakness, such as skill deficiency or motivational problems, and thereby lead to suggestions for growth.

Finally, individual performance evaluations determine future behavior and performance in a number of ways. The very experience of being evaluated affects behavior by increasing the measured behaviors. For example, if an evaluation focuses on compliance with state special education regulations, future behavior is likely to be more closely linked to compliance with these regulations and less closely linked to other factors. Furthermore, for ancillary services such as school psychology, positive individual performance evaluations affect both administrative and fiscal support for positions.

MEASUREMENT CRITERIA

As is the case for any evaluation method, techniques used in individual performance evaluations should adhere to appropriate measurement criteria. That is, they should be reasonably:

- reliable, or consistent across raters and time;
- valid, measuring relevant aspects of performance with minimal contamination by elements outside the control of the individual;
- meaningful and acceptable to both supervisors and supervisees (often achieved through the involvement of both supervisors and supervisees in the development of the evaluation methods);
- useful and specific, imparting clear information to supervisees regarding expectations and the manner in which to achieve them;
- practical to implement;
- strategically congruent, that is, consistent with the goals, strategy, and culture of the

school system and school psychology department. When such goals change, the evaluation tools should correspondingly change.

Ethical dilemma 6-1

You have recently been named the supervising school psychologist in a district and are quite pleased with the work of six of your supervisees. One district school psychologist, however, has extremely deficient skills. When you attempt to address these deficiencies, she informs you that every previous evaluation has been extremely positive. After pulling her personnel file, you discover that is indeed the case. *What are the ethical dilemmas? What can be done?*

LEGAL ISSUES IN INDIVIDUAL PERFORMANCE EVALUATION

A number of legal issues regarding individual performance evaluations are discussed in management literature. The most commonly mentioned are discrimination, due process, and union issues.

Discrimination

The most frequently cited sources of discrimination are race and gender. A substantial body of research has found that both white and black evaluators rate members of their own racial group higher than members of other racial groups. In addition, research has found that minorities (whether by gender or race) tend to receive less favorable ratings than members of majority populations (Noe et al., 1996). In school psychology, this may result in men, as well as ethnic minority populations, receiving unfairly low evaluations. Supervisors of school psychologists are ethically bound to minimize these discriminatory effects as much as possible.

Due process

Protecting the due process rights of supervisees is a critical ethical issue in individual performance evaluation. Supervisees should not be given a negative final evaluation, dismissed from a training program, or dismissed from a job without having been given adequate notice of inadequate performance, specific criteria for improvement, and time to improve that performance (Bernard & Goodyear, 1998). To protect due process rights, supervisors should establish very specific guidelines for dealing with impaired supervisees.

Impairment can be manifested in the inability to acquire and integrate professional standards, the inability to achieve competence in professional skills, and/or the "inability to control personal stress, psychological dysfunction, or emotional reactions that may affect professional functioning" (Lamb, Cochran, & Jackson, 1991, p. 292). Regardless of the impairment source, due process procedures for both interns and employed school psychologists are as follows:

1. Identify the problematic behavior;
2. Determine its negative impact on service delivery and identify serious ethical or legal repercussions;
3. Give training, feedback, and time for modification;
4. Document the behaviors of concern and note any changes;
5. Include behaviors of concern in formal evaluations;
6. Provide specific methods of remediation;
7. Implement a probationary period; and
8. Ensure that the supervisee understands due process rights (Bernard & Goodyear, 1998).

Union issues

The majority of supervisors of school psychologists supervise individuals who are union members (Hunley et al., in press). At times, union con-

95

tracts legally bind supervisors to particular evaluation methods, such as teacher evaluation forms. These forms can be appropriately used when they are used in conjunction with other methods that directly address the attributes, behaviors, and outcomes necessary in the practice of effective school psychology.

Ethical dilemma 6-2

A supervisor of school psychologists finds herself in a situation where she is permitted to use only the teacher evaluation form. This has resulted in one supervisee neglecting professional development in areas pertinent to school psychology. *What are the ethical considerations? What can be done?*

Addressing barriers to effective and legal evaluations

There are a number of common barriers to effective, legal, and productive evaluations. These, along with methods to minimize them, follow:

1. *Error: Evaluations are not in synch with quality performance.* Minimize by developing performance evaluation procedures from a job analysis that appropriately identifies important aspects of job performance.
2. *Error: Evaluations are unreliable.* Minimize by basing individual performance evaluations on behaviors or outcomes, rather than solely on attributes.
3. *Error: Evaluations are ignored or are not incorporated into professional development plans.* Minimize by training supervisors in the systemic individual performance evaluation process and involving both supervisors and supervisees in setting goals and dates to review progress.
4. *Error: Evaluations have minimal impact because the results are kept secret.* Minimize

by having upper level administrators review all performance ratings.

5. *Error: Supervisees perceive the evaluation process as capricious and arbitrary.* Minimize by involving supervisees in the development and implementation of the evaluation system. Develop a system of appeal that is communicated to all employees.
6. *Error: Due process rights are ignored.* Minimize by providing supervision to help poor performers improve skills before dismissal.
7. *Error: Supervisors rate a supervisee's performance higher when the individual shares similar beliefs or characteristics such as background, gender, and race.* Minimize by developing vigilant self-awareness and consulting with a colleague when evaluating persons from backgrounds dissimilar to your own.
8. *Error: Evaluations are conducted by contrasting individuals rather than by comparing an individual to an objective standard, which results in average performers looking weak in the company of outstanding performers or outstanding in the company of poor performers.* Minimize by developing operational definitions of excellent, satisfactory, and unsatisfactory performance.
9. *Error: Evaluators fail to use the full ranges of the rating scale, which results in difficulty discriminating among supervisees and reduces inter-rater reliability.* Minimize by encouraging and reinforcing the use of the full range of the scale.
10. *Error: Evaluators fail to consider each category independently, resulting in the "halo effect." An individual who is superior (or inferior) in one area is presumed to be superior (or inferior) in other areas.* Minimize by considering each trait separately, considering quality as well as quantity of work, avoiding focus on isolated instances of accomplishment or failure, tying the behavior to

goal development, and basing the evaluation on records of performance maintained throughout the evaluation period.

11. *Error: Supervisors avoid completing evaluations that require evaluative statements (particularly negative) about school psychologists' work*. Minimize by accepting the responsibility for completing the evaluation, holding school psychologists accountable for their work, and reporting appraisals honestly even at the risk of receiving complaints in the future. As stated by Halloran (1981), "to change the fear of evaluating to success as a supervisor, you must be willing to hear any reaction to your evaluation" (p. 165). Supervisors must be willing and able to deal with the discomfort of confronting another individual with professional or personal weaknesses (Noe et al., 1996).

12. *Error: The supervisee is surprised by the evaluation*. Minimize by giving such frequent and honest feedback that supervisees already know the forthcoming results prior to the formal evaluation. Supervisees are more likely to improve performance when they are not surprised by evaluations, and it is the supervisor's ethical responsibility to provide feedback as soon as they are aware of deficiencies. Novices should receive feedback daily, and more advanced school psychologists should receive feedback weekly.

13. *Error: Only one method or modality is used to give feedback*. Minimize by raising concerns along a continuum and through a variety of modalities to respect varied learning styles. Voice a concern immediately upon becoming aware of it, and follow the verbal statement with written feedback that includes timelines and specific criteria for the measurement of improvement. By the time a negative evaluation occurs, the supervisee should have received multiple verbal and written communications.

14. *Error: Supervisees feel disconnected from the evaluation process*. Minimize by asking supervisees to rate their performance before the feedback session. Evaluations are much more effective when supervisees reflect on their performance, determine their deficiencies, and develop their own professional development strategies. Such a process encourages supervisees to fully participate in the feedback session and allows the time together to focus on areas in which the supervisor and supervisee disagree (Noe et al., 1996). The feedback session can then have a problem solving approach, where supervisor and supervisee work together to brainstorm solutions to problems in an atmosphere of mutual respect.

15. *Error: Deficiencies become the main focus of the evaluation*. Minimize by a "fair pair" approach, in which the supervisor focuses on strengths as much or more than weaknesses. Supervisors should minimize criticism, help the supervisee develop specific goals, and focus discussions on behavior and results rather than on personal attributes (Noe et al., 1996).

SOURCES OF INFORMATION

Supervisors are judged appropriate sources of evaluative information because they are knowledgeable about standards of performance and have opportunities to directly observe supervisees in action. Supervisors also gather indirect evaluative information during supervision sessions and when reviewing psychological reports. Yet because of the logistics of school systems, supervisors of school psychologists may not have sufficient opportunity to observe supervisee performance. The performance of school psychologists may not be typical during scheduled visits.

In addition, favoritism or a generalized negative relationship may unfairly color an evaluation

97

conducted only by one supervisor. Gathering information from others, including teachers, school administrators, parents, clients, and the school psychologist himself greatly enriches the evaluation process (Fairchild, 1985). Information can be gathered by asking individuals to respond verbally or in writing to the attributes, behaviors, or objectives being used in the evaluation process.

Peers, particularly in situations where supervisees work in teams, are excellent sources of evaluation information because they tend to be both honest and knowledgeable about job requirements. It is not recommended that peers be placed in the uncomfortable position of being asked to participate in summative or administrative evaluations that result in personnel decisions. However, they can make significant contributions to formative evaluations to foster recommendations for professional development (Correll, McElwain, & Iffert-Jacobson, 1986).

In business, clients are valuable sources of information for performance evaluations. Like peers, they are particularly valuable for formative evaluations and are of questionable value for summative evaluations leading to administrative decisions. Although school psychologists generally do not have subordinates, they do have a substantial number of "clients" who could provide feedback regarding performance. These include general education teachers, nurses, occupational therapists, parents, physical therapists, physicians, principals, psychologists in private practice, remedial teachers, school counselors, social workers, special education administrators, special education teachers, speech/language therapists, upper level administrators, and students.

Finally, supervisees themselves are a rich source of information. Although individuals might deflate or inflate their own performance, they often provide helpful information when responding to a well-developed scale (Beer,

1981). A common practice in business, for example, is to have the supervisee provide peers, clients, and subordinates with evaluation forms, gather the written responses, and cite these written responses in his or her own written self-evaluation. This self-evaluation, along with supporting documentation, is submitted to the supervisor prior to the evaluation session and is used by the supervisor to prepare the formal evaluation.

MODELS OF EVALUATION

Individual performance evaluations can focus on attributes of the supervisee, behaviors of the supervisee, results the supervisee obtains, or a combination thereof (Noe et al., 1996). Evaluations can be summative or formative. Evaluations that occur at the end of a time period and summarize effectiveness are summative evaluations. In contrast, ongoing clinical (face-to-face) supervision, during which the school psychologist is given guidance, can be an example of a formative evaluation. For both formative and summative evaluations, the supervisor and supervisee determine an indicator of effective performance for each critical area of performance, collect data and monitor effectiveness on an ongoing basis, make a report on effectiveness, and develop a plan and objective for the future.

Appropriate methods for the evaluation of school psychological services are lacking (Fagan & Wise, 1994). Although formative and summative evaluations have been recommended (Bennett, 1988; Maher, 1984; Mowder & Prasse, 1981; Patton, 1982; Tuckman, 1985), too often school psychologists are evaluated by administrators using teacher evaluation forms. Norton and Perlin (1989) reveal that administrators have difficulty using teacher evaluation forms for school psychologists due to the diverse roles of the psychologists, and recommend that other instruments be used.

98

Attribute evaluation

The attribute approach to individual performance evaluation focuses on whether or not the individual possesses desirable attributes. The evaluation of school psychologists, as well as teachers, often involves observing and rating them using a locally-developed list of attributes. Usually this evaluation is completed following an observation and conference, and the evaluation is filed in the school psychologist's personnel file. The results of the evaluation may be used to recommend, or not recommend, certification for interns and tenure for practicing school psychologists. However, the results generally do not impact the functioning of the school psychologist.

Graphic rating scales, in which desirable attributes are rated numerically, are extremely popular in both business management and education. A common example of a graphic rating scale uses a Likert-type scale. Graphic rating scales have the substantial advantage of being relatively "easy," and are often used in teacher evaluation forms. However, the validity of these scales is often low because they are not strategically congruent with the school's specific goals and objectives. In addition, they are prone to poor reliability because they are highly subjective. An example of a graphic rating scale that addresses desirable attributes contributing to school psychologists' "Professional Behavior" is given in Example 6-1.

Example 6-1 Rating of Professional Behavior

Please use the following scale to rate

5	4	3	2	1	NA
Excellent	Very good	Satisfactory	Fair	Poor	No basis

___ 1. Listens well (listens to others, listens with empathy).

___ 2. Expresses self well orally.

___ 3. Writes well.

___ 4. Follows constructive criticism objectively and professionally (accepts and incorporates feedback on papers, reports, and in group work).

___ 5. Is emotionally mature (is responsible, has appropriate interpersonal boundaries, is emotionally stable).

___ 6. Works with children well (easily builds rapport, adjusts behavior, and expectations to developmental level).

___ 7. Works with peers, parents, and school or agency personnel in a positive, non-threatening manner (is poised, tactful, easily builds rapport, shows insight and sensitivity).

___ 8. Goes beyond basic requirements (does "homework," takes initiative, is consistent, persevering, industrious, hardworking).

___ 9. Adapts to change flexibly (is able to balance diverse expectations, adapts to novel or unexpected situations).

___ 10. Observes protocol and rules (is punctual, has good attendance, notifies of absence, has professional appearance and dress, obtains parental permission, demonstrates respect for authority figures).

___ 11. Acts in accord with professional ethics (maintains confidentiality, does not overstep boundaries of training, presents data honestly, and demonstrates academic integrity).

___ 12. Shows respect regarding individual and group differences (does not discriminate on basis of disability, gender, language, race, religion, and socioeconomic status).

Please explain low scores with specific comments and examples on the reverse side:

Mixed standard scales are designed to make attribute scales less subjective. Raters are asked to link attributes with corresponding statements representing good, average, and poor performance. A mixed standard score is obtained through the construction of operational definitions of pertinent attributes. The process of constructing these operational definitions can be quite enlightening. An example of an attribute (e.g., self-initiative) in a mixed standard scale format is provided in Example 6-2.

Example 6-2 Self initiative

Expert			Novice
Independent on all aspects of task completion, including initiation and evaluation.	Requires supervision on final aspect (evaluation) of task completion, but initiates and carries out tasks on own.	Requires supervision initiating task and evaluating task completion: completes task independently.	Requires supervision for all aspects of task: from initiation to completion.

Behavior evaluation

When designing a *behaviorally anchored rating scale*, a formal job analysis is conducted to determine what behaviors constitute adequate and superior performance. Those behavioral descriptors are then used to define the ratings on the scale. This is similar to the mixed standard scale format, but is data based.

Advantages to this approach include decreased ambiguity and bias, and increased reliability and relevance. The main disadvantage to this method is the lengthy time it takes to complete the job analysis and develop the scale. Furthermore, the scales cannot be generalized because the behavior necessary for adequate behavior in one setting may not be the same in a different setting. Finally, it can be difficult to develop such scales for complex positions in which essential behaviors (for example, "rapport") are not easily defined.

One type of evaluation based on a behavioral model is the *critical incident approach*, in which supervisors keep records of effective and ineffective supervisee performance. Such an approach can be highly effective for the following reasons: it can link performance to strategic goals, it can be reliable, valid, and acceptable, and it can provide clear and specific guidelines for performance improvement. On the negative side, using the critical incident approach requires very close supervision of the behaviors, is highly time consuming, and is not well suited to complex jobs (Noe et al., 1996). An example of a critical incident approach is provided in Example 6-3.

Example 6-3

To ensure that the school psychologist conveys assessment results to parents in a meaningful manner, the supervisor both observes parent conferences directly and gathers information from the parents to determine the level of understanding attained by the parent.

Another example of the application of a behavioral method, quite common in school psychology, is the enumeration of discrete behaviors. For example, the number of evaluations, reports, and conferences may be tallied (Zins, 1984). The advantage to this approach is that the behaviors are observable and administrators have a high interest in such data. The disadvantages are that the enumeration of behaviors does not reflect all relevant aspects of the job, takes substantial time to maintain, and ignores quality of performance (Sandoval & Lambert, 1977; Zins, 1984). Examples of activities that can be enumerated are contained in Example 6-4.

Example 6-4

Indirect interventions

Number of referrals for pre-referral interventions,
Contacts with outside agencies and/or professionals,
Classroom observations conducted,
School records reviewed,
Teacher interviews,
Parent interviews and telephone calls, and
Teacher assistance team meetings attended.

Direct interventions

Number of intervention referrals received,
Number of children counseled individually,
Number of children counseled in groups,
Time per week spent providing direct services,
Parent conferences held,
Parent training workshops held,
Staff development/in-service workshops conducted,
Parent information sessions held, and
Newsletters and other information distributed.

Assessment activities

Number of referrals received for assessment,
Assessments completed,
Number of assessed children identified as disabled,
Number of assessed children placed in special education,
Post-assessment team meetings attended.

Program development and evaluation activities

Programs implemented, modified, or evaluated,
Yearly goals attained,
Number of children in these programs, and
Number of staff trained in in-service workshops.

Result evaluation

When using the result approach in rating an individual's performance, supervisors focus on the accomplishment of objectives and measurable aspects of the job. Steps in conducting evaluations by this method include:

1. Supervisee and supervisor agree upon measurable objectives;
2. Supervisee keeps record of activities completed toward goals and objectives;
3. Supervisor and supervisee conduct periodic, joint review of progress toward goals and objectives;
4. The supervisor completes the individual performance evaluation based on the supervisee's progress in meeting objectives (Rosenfield, 1985).

The objectives can focus on either the school psychologist or on the behavior and learning of the children and adolescents with whom the school psychologist works. Some examples of outcomes based on the behavior with which the school psychologist works are included in Example 6-5.

Example 6-5
Student Outcome Objectives

Students with whom the school psychologist has worked:

1. Attended 90% of assigned classes,
2. Demonstrated at least six months growth in achievement test scores,
3. Passed all subjects with grades of C or better,
4. Passed their grade and/or graduated from high school,
5. Obtained a decreased number of discipline reports,
6. Were suspended fewer times than the previous year, and
7. Exhibited less depression and anxiety on psychometric instruments.

Results oriented evaluations can also focus on the attainment of performance objectives by the school psychologist. Such a focus is commonly called *Management by Objective* (MBO). In this approach, the supervisor and school psychologist jointly develop goals, measurable objectives, and timelines at the beginning of the year. The evaluation at the end of the year is based upon how well the supervisee meets these expectations. Objectives should be compatible with the school district goals, sufficiently challenging, attainable and realistic, and measurable (Halloran, 1981; Noe et al., 1996).

In business, MBO has been found to significantly increase productivity (Noe et al., 1996). Because it relies on objective, quantifiable indicators of performance, it minimizes subjectivity. MBO is likely to be tied to the organization's strategic management plan and is therefore acceptable to both supervisees and supervisors. It also has the advantage of clearly defining the manner in which performance is to be measured. Because the supervisee writes the objectives,

they have substantial validity for the individual and can be customized to meet specific needs and interests. Furthermore, when done well, MBO greatly facilitates communication between supervisees and supervisors and empowers supervisees to be responsible for their own professional growth. Some objectives pertinent to the school psychologist are included in Example 6-6.

On the negative side, MBO can be significantly contaminated by elements beyond the supervisee's control. It is difficult to set reasonable goals well in advance because outside variables can have a marked influence. For example, a school psychologist may be unable to meet an objective specifying that "all evaluations are completed within the legally mandated time frame" if a student is truant. Furthermore, not all important aspects of a position (particularly positions as complicated as school psychology) can be quantified. Consequently, there may be an overemphasis on the aspects of the job that are easily measurable. When abused, MBO can result in excessive pressure by the supervisor on the supervisee to produce results (Halloran, 1981; Noe et al., 1996).

Example 6-6
Objectives for 2000-2001

1. The school psychologist implemented a pre-referral process in 100% of individual referrals throughout the school year.
2. The school psychologist initiated all evaluations within 5 days of the referral and completed them within 30 days.
3. The school psychologist completed a 2-day workshop in conflict resolution and effectively applied the acquired skills in at least six situations.

Combination methods

Combination methods include more than one method of evaluation; for example, the assessment of both attributes and outcomes, or attributes and behaviors. Two examples of combination methods will be summarized: Total Quality Management and the Comprehensive Method.

Total Quality Management (TQM). TQM has considerable popularity in both industry and education. TQM uses attribute and outcomes methods to emphasis "quality" results. Feedback focuses on personal qualities of the supervisee and work results. TQM emphasizes measuring only behaviors over which the supervisees have control to increase morale and minimize dysfunctional behavior such as falsifying results. In focusing on measurable behaviors, TQM provides supervisees with feedback about areas in which they can improve.

Information regarding personal qualities is obtained through feedback from managers, peers, customers, and supervisees themselves regarding desired attributes such as communication skills. The portion of the evaluation addressing personal qualities also includes a discussion of the individual's career plans. Information regarding work results is gathered through objectively measured data.

Comprehensive Method. In using a Comprehensive Method, supervisors again focus on the contextual measurement of objectives, but also review attributes and behaviors of the supervisee. In a "field review," the evaluation is conducted by a group of people. For example, individuals working with a school psychologist (supervisor, clients, peers, themselves) participate in the evaluation process. To use this method, supervisors take the following steps (Illback & Morrissey, 1985):

1. Review the job description and evaluation materials to ensure congruence;
2. Conduct individual interviews with each staff person to discuss job requirements relative to training, prior job experience, and personal strengths and weaknesses;
3. Observe the school psychologist at work in various settings (consulting, conducting an assessment, running a support group, meeting with a parent);
4. Review personnel files;
5. Speak with, and/or have evaluation forms completed by, other staff who work with the school psychologist, including principals, teachers, and parents;
6. Review samples of the psychologist's previous and current work;
7. Draft an evaluation based on steps one through six, and simultaneously have the school psychologist complete a self-evaluation using the evaluation materials;
8. Meet with the school psychologist to discuss your draft evaluation and compare it to the self-evaluation;
9. Develop individual goals and objectives in conjunction with the school psychologist;
10. Review progress regarding the completion of goals and objectives frequently through the examination of activities completed; and
11. Revisit the vision, assessment, goals, etc.

An example of a form that could be used as a source of information in a comprehensive method is found in Example 6-7, at the end of this chapter. This form was developed in conjunction with the job description found in Chapter 5, and also incorporates elements of the NASP *Professional Conduct Manual*. It assumes that a high frequency of positive attributes is appropriate and preferred.

TIMING EVALUATIONS

Formal, summative evaluations should be completed at least once a year, although every six months is preferable, and novice school psychol-

103

ogists should be evaluated continuously. Formative evaluations can be continuous, occurring during every supervisory session.

Continuous evaluation is a process, rather than a product, by which plans, procedures, alternatives, and implications are continuously evaluated. Following each evaluation, the supervisee formulates a profile that indicates areas of strength and weakness and generates a plan for the next time frame. In the process, the supervisee is taught to evaluate his own effectiveness accurately (Henry & Beasley, 1982). Continuous evaluations can use any model of evaluation (attribute, behavior, results, or combination). A familiar example of continuous evaluation used with children is Curriculum Based Measurement, and continuous evaluations of supervisees similarly provide weekly or daily feedback. Continuous feedback is very appropriate for beginners, including interns.

Effective continuous evaluations are objective, focus on skills and techniques essential for good practice of school psychology, provide the next steps for professional development, and furnish an objective description of ability and potential (Henry & Beasley, 1982). For continuous evaluations to be effective, the full range of practice is addressed and a climate of open communication maintained. Supervisors should:

- make suggestions as soon as possible after observations;
- emphasize activities rather than qualities of the person;
- state suggestions for improvement positively;
- ask questions rather than list strong and weak qualities;
- use a variety of evaluative procedures and techniques; and,
- use a valid list of criteria and specific evaluations (Henry & Beasley, 1982; Mead, 1990).

While the focus of continuous evaluations is on formative evaluation, it also includes summa-tive evaluations at specific points. This occurs at midterm and term end for interns, and annually for more advanced school psychologists. The summative evaluations result in a final performance report.

COMMUNICATING FEEDBACK

After the evaluation is conducted, the supervisor meets personally with the supervisee to discuss strong and weak points and to make plans to address areas of weakness. It is most effective to begin with a detailed discussion of strengths. After supportive information has been shared, weaknesses are simply, clearly, and explicitly addressed. Finally, positive and specific suggestions for improvement are discussed. During the course of a successful meeting, supervisors clearly make their points, supervisees express their feelings regarding the evaluation, and a plan of action is developed (Halloran, 1981). To keep the feedback session as effective as possible, the following are helpful:

1. Establish a climate of open communication and make the evaluation process as non-threatening as possible;
2. Make suggestions as soon as possible after observations;
3. Emphasize performance and activities rather than the person or personal issues;
4. Conduct feedback evaluations privately;
5. State suggestions for improvement positively;
6. Vary evaluative procedures and techniques;
7. In order to provide specific examples, keep ongoing records and ask your supervisee for examples of specific incidents in which their performance was adequate or inadequate (Rice, 1985);
8. Be specific in criticisms and provide the supervisee with specific examples for change;
9. Give written warnings: share a "preview review" before giving a negative review,

indicating "your review will say this if the following does not change";

10. Review your written evaluation with your supervisee in person, and empower him or her to react honestly;

11. Be honest, straightforward, and kind;

12. Encourage self-assessment;

13. When specific criteria for improvement have been given and improvement does not occur, explore the cause. Is there a lack of skill, drug or alcohol problem, or fear of success? A determined cause does not excuse lack of performance but it does help determine the appropriate course of action, including a referral to outside services;

14. Listen to your supervisee's perspective and use the feedback session to obtain information about how you might help them do their jobs better (Rice, 1985);

15. Conclude with a summary and plan for the future (Jordan, 1987).

NEXT STEPS

Reviewing the completed job analysis and assessment of job competencies tends to lead naturally into generating goals and objectives. As is true for a child's Individual Educational Plan, goals are broad and objectives are specific, manageable, and measurable subcomponents of those goals. Some goals may reflect the philosophy of the school district; others may empower the school psychologist to work more effectively with a specific population; still others may be a result of a school psychologist's specific interest.

Before finalizing objectives, barriers should be analyzed. Necessary funding may not be available, the district may not consider a given objective a priority, or the individual psychologist may have little motivation to complete an objective. After conducting the barrier analysis, the school psychologist and the supervisor will be in a good position to select appropriate long- and short-term goals and objectives for professional development (Rosenfield, 1985).

Example 6-7 Job Description-Based Individual Performance Evaluation Form

SCHOOL PSYCHOLOGIST INDIVIDUAL PERFORMANCE EVALUATION

1. The school psychologist SHOWS GOOD COMMUNICATION SKILLS BY...	
1a. Listening well and encouraging others to ask questions.	|____|____|____|____| Almost Always .... Almost Never
1b. Communicating in the client's language.	|____|____|____|____| Almost Always .... Almost Never
1c. Maintaining records of meetings regarding test results and program recommendations, and making them available to all concerned.	|____|____|____|____| Almost Always .... Almost Never
1d. Communicating a clear referral system to parents and school personnel.	|____|____|____|____| Almost Always .... Almost Never

1e. Giving parents all important information, telling them how it relates to decision- making, and involving them in decision-making.	|____|____|____|____| Almost　　　　　　　Almost Always　　　　　　　Never
1f. Obtaining written parental consent before testing or providing special programs.	|____|____|____|____| Almost　　　　　　　Almost Always　　　　　　　Never
1g. Inviting parents to inspect and review any personally identifiable data relating to their child which were collected, maintained, or used in an evaluation.	|____|____|____|____| Almost　　　　　　　Almost Always　　　　　　　Never
1h. Clearly interpreting school psychological records to non-psychologists.	|____|____|____|____| Almost　　　　　　　Almost Always　　　　　　　Never
1i. Maintaining a cooperative relationship with colleagues and co-workers.	|____|____|____|____| Almost　　　　　　　Almost Always　　　　　　　Never
1j. Writing psychological reports that are easy for non-psychologists to understand.	|____|____|____|____| Almost　　　　　　　Almost Always　　　　　　　Never

2. WHEN PROVIDING CONSULTATION, the school psychologist.....

2a. Effectively consults and collaborates with parents and teachers regarding mental health, behavioral, and educational concerns.	|____|____|____|____| Almost　　　　　　　Almost Almost　　　　　　　Never
2b. Works with counselors and therapists to help students with emotional or behavior disorders, or educational concerns.	|____|____|____|____| Almost　　　　　　　Almost Always　　　　　　　Never
2c. Provides comprehensive consultation services that include observation, review of records, teacher conferences, parent conferences, student interviews, brief reports, and team meetings.	|____|____|____|____| Almost　　　　　　　Almost Always　　　　　　　Never
2d. Participates effectively in building and district level team meetings.	|____|____|____|____| Almost　　　　　　　Almost Always　　　　　　　Never
2e. Collaborates with school professionals (such as nurses, ESL teachers) in prevention, assessment, and intervention efforts.	|____|____|____|____| Almost　　　　　　　Almost Always　　　　　　　Never

106

2f. Is knowledgeable about community agencies and resources.	|_____|_____|_____|_____| Almost Almost Always Never
2g. Exchanges information with external agencies for purposes of student assessment and programs, after procuring releases.	|_____|_____|_____|_____| Almost Almost Always Never
2h. Participates in community agency staffings, and invites community agency personnel to participate in school system conferences concerning clients (with school system and written parental permission).	|_____|_____|_____|_____| Almost Almost Always Never
2i. Provides consulting services to the larger community regarding psychological, mental health, and educational issues.	|_____|_____|_____|_____| Almost Almost Always Never

3. WHEN CONDUCTING ASSESSMENTS, the school psychologist....

3a. Uses a variety of instruments, procedures, and techniques, including interviews, observations, and behavioral evaluations.	|_____|_____|_____|_____| Almost Almost Always Never
3b. Considers personality, emotional status, adaptive behavior, functional behavior, social skills, and social adjustment.	|_____|_____|_____|_____| Almost Almost Always Never
3c. Considers intelligence and cognitive functioning, scholastic aptitude, language and communication skills.	|_____|_____|_____|_____| Almost Almost Always Never
3d. Considers academic knowledge, achievement, and educational setting.	|_____|_____|_____|_____| Almost Almost Always Never
3e. Considers family and environmental-cultural influences.	|_____|_____|_____|_____| Almost Almost Always Never
3f. Considers career and vocational development, aptitude, and interests.	|_____|_____|_____|_____| Almost Almost Always Never
3g. Considers and comments on students' abilities, strengths, and talents.	|_____|_____|_____|_____| Almost Almost Always Never

107

3h. Demonstrates explicit regard for the context and setting in which assessments take place and are used.	|____|____|____|____| Almost Always	Almost Never
3i. Demonstrates respect for the student's ethnic background by adhering to professional resolutions and ethical guidelines regarding non-biased assessment and programming for all students.	|____|____|____|____| Almost Always	Almost Never
3j. Provides information that helps student achievement and adjustment and results in practical and effective recommendations.	|____|____|____|____| Almost Always	Almost Never

4. WHEN RECOMMENDING AND PROVIDING DIRECT SERVICES, the school psychologist. . .

4a. Recommends and implements effective strategies that enhance cognitive, affective, social and vocational development.	|____|____|____|____| Almost Always	Almost Never
4b. Coordinates with the school team to design direct service programs.	|____|____|____|____| Almost Always	Almost Never
4c. Provides effective psychological counseling for individuals and groups of students.	|____|____|____|____| Almost Always	Almost Never
4d. Provides additional direct services to students, such as crisis intervention, study skills training, and behavior modification plan implementation.	|____|____|____|____| Almost Always	Almost Never

5. IN DEVELOPING PROGRAMS, the school psychologist...

5a. Involves clients in developing assessment, direct services, and program evaluation procedures.	|____|____|____|____| Almost Always	Almost Never
5b. Designs and develops school-based procedures to prevent disorders, promote mental health and learning, and improve educational systems.	|____|____|____|____| Almost Always	Almost Never
5c. Visits out-of-district placement locations to determine appropriateness.	|____|____|____|____| Almost Always	Almost Never
5d. Provides program planning and evaluation services to schools to assist in decision-making.	|____|____|____|____| Almost Always	Almost Never

108

5e. Serves on committees responsible for developing and planning educational and educationally related activities.	|_____|_____|_____|_____| Almost Almost Always Never
5f. Provides skill enhancement activities to school personnel, parents, and others in the community regarding issues of human learning, human development, and behavior.	|_____|_____|_____|_____| Almost Almost Always Never

6. TO MAINTAIN PROFESSIONAL SKILLS, the school psychologist...

6a. Engages in supervision and peer review.	|_____|_____|_____|_____| Almost Almost Always Never
6b. Maintains certification as a school psychologist by engaging in continuing professional development.	|_____|_____|_____|_____| Almost Almost Always Never
6c. Keeps informed of and develops skills in new intervention techniques, assessment procedures, computerized assistance, and other advances in the field.	|_____|_____|_____|_____| Almost Almost Always Never
6d. Is a skilled and active consumer and reviewer of research in psychology and education.	|_____|_____|_____|_____| Almost Almost Always Never
6e. Adheres to the best available and most appropriate standards of practice.	|_____|_____|_____|_____| Almost Almost Always Never
6f. Restricts practice to those areas in which they have received training and supervised experience.	|_____|_____|_____|_____| Almost Almost Always Never
6g. Maintains active membership in professional organizations, reads professional books and journals, and discusses professional issues with colleagues.	|_____|_____|_____|_____| Almost Almost Always Never
6h. Maintains knowledge of statutes related to psychology and special education.	|_____|_____|_____|_____| Almost Almost Always Never
6i. Adheres to professional ethical principles.	|_____|_____|_____|_____| Almost Almost Always Never

7. THE SCHOOL PSYCHOLOGIST DEMONSTRATES ACCOUNTABILITY BY...	
7a. Following district procedures in the provision of school psychological services.	|____|____|____|____| Almost Almost Always Never
7b. Providing school psychological services in a coordinated, organized fashion.	|____|____|____|____| Almost Almost Always Never
7c. Keeping records of efforts, including counseling and consultation process notes.	|____|____|____|____| Almost Almost Always Never
7d. Evaluating the effectiveness of intervention efforts, and other services provided.	|____|____|____|____| Almost Almost Always Never
7e. Using records and effectiveness information to modify practice.	|____|____|____|____| Almost Almost Always Never
7f. Making information about services available to consumers so they can initiate, terminate, continue, modify, and evaluate psychological services.	|____|____|____|____| Almost Almost Always Never
7g. Practicing in full accord with the NASP *Professional Conduct Manual*.	|____|____|____|____| Almost Almost Always Never

8. Do you have any comments?

9. Do you have any suggestions for improvement?

Facilitating professional development is a pivotal supervisory role. "The most important role that the supervisor of school psychology plays . . . is that of teacher, mentor, and catalyst for change and growth" (Smith, 1987, p. 39). If, as is said to be true for teachers, school psychologists "peak out" after five to seven years of practice, supervisors must pay intense attention to supervisee's professional development in order to maintain enthusiasm and the capacity for change (Smith, 1987).

Professional isolation, a diversified profession, a growing knowledge base and professional advances, social changes, and changing legislation all result in the need for continuing and effective in-service training for individual school psychologists (Sinclair, 1987; Smith, 1987). As stated by Harper and Wild (1989), "School psychologists are committed to continuing professional development by statute and by the standards established by professional associations...Few professionals would disagree with the need for professional development" (p. 29). Fowler and Harrison (1995) provide an overview of recommended practice in an individual psychologist's continuing professional development, which they define as "a dynamic process that flows from the intrinsic motivation, interest, learning history, and professional contact of the individual" (p. 81).

Ethical dilemma 7-1

When initially hired, a staff school psychologist indicated that his strengths were working with secondary students and he was placed full-time at a high school. During the first two years of his employment, you observed that he had excellent counseling skills with adolescents, but that his assessment and consultation skills were relatively weak. During the past two years he has not progressed satisfactorily in these areas, possibly because the high school climate is conducive to neither. Most recently, you have become concerned that even his counseling skills have deteriorated in the *laissez-faire* atmosphere of the high school. The school psychologist wants to stay at the high school, but you feel that he needs a different assignment for professional growth. *What are the ethical issues? What steps should be taken?*

Supervisors of school psychologists are responsible for training and professional development from several perspectives. They orient and train school psychologists new to the district, facilitate the ongoing professional development of veteran school psychologists, and maintain their own professional development. If the district has school psychology interns, the supervisor oversees the training provided the interns by the district's school psychologists. In large districts, they help develop additional supervisors of school psychologists. Finally, since effective school psychology departments provide professional development activities for school district teachers, administrators, and paraprofessionals (Green, 1995), supervisors of school psychologists often are in the position of either planning professional development programs themselves, or of supervising district school psychologists as they plan and provide them. A supervisor of school psychologists is likely to be involved in many of the above activities simultaneously, as exemplified in the following case study.

Case study 7-1

An increasing number of poorly handled crises in a school district leads a supervising school psychologist to believe that the school psychology department should become more active in crisis prevention and intervention. District school psychologists and administrators concur. A needs assessment is conducted at all levels (school district, departmental, individual school psychologist, and school personnel) and confirms the impression that the entire district needs development in this area.

The supervising school psychologist and district school psychologists first increase their own levels of expertise through individual and group activities: reading professional literature, attending professional seminars and workshops, taking mediation courses at the local university, obtaining certification as non-violent crisis intervention instructors, holding departmental seminars, receiving training from the local hotline, and consulting with specialists in crisis prevention. Subsequently, the school psychology department leads the pupil personnel department in developing a crisis management handbook for the district. The psychologists also conduct a series of workshops for teachers, paraprofessionals, counselors, and administrators in crisis prevention and non-violent crisis intervention. In subsequent years, these workshops continued to facilitate the training and professional development of new employees. The professional development activities are evaluated not only by feedback regarding individual sessions, but also by careful monitoring of student discipline reports.

ORIENTING NEW EMPLOYEES

Orientation involves the introduction of new school psychologists to the school system, their schools, and their jobs. Orientation is both formal and informal. Informal and unofficial orientations, particularly from colleagues and school personnel, can be misleading and inaccurate. In contrast, when planned and provided by supervisors, peers, and the school system, effective formal orientations facilitate adjustment to the work environment and can reduce the stress of new employees, start-up costs, turnover rates, and time taken by new employees to be integrated (Rue & Byars, 1997).

Often the school district personnel department conducts a formal orientation and presents topics of relevance and interest to all employees. Usually this orientation provides new employees with a packet of information including the school calendar, benefits and insurance information, school district regulations and work policies, and union information.

The supervisor of school psychologists typically conducts the departmental and job orientation. New school psychologists should be given copies of tools used for individual performance evaluations, of school district and departmental regulations, of the district administrative organizational chart, and of policy and procedure handbooks. Additional helpful information includes:

- information regarding the population served in the schools;
- the philosophy, objectives, and mission statement of the district;
- district characteristics, facilities, and services;
- the schedule of faculty meetings, and staff development days;
- discipline procedures and policies;
- student and faculty dress code, if applicable;
- available student activities;
- emergency procedures;
- general education forms, grades, and reports;

112

- pre-referral and special education procedures, forms, and timelines;
- availability and procedures regarding pupil records;
- class schedules, schedules for specials (art, music, physical education, library), and schedule deviations (schedule changes for early release days or delayed openings);
- school and staff directories;
- school and district handbooks;
- maps of the district and each school; and,
- school calendars.

School psychologists new to the district should also be given clear guidelines regarding work policies. For example, they should have a clear understanding of expected work hours, responsibilities, after-hour report writing and parent contacts, attendance during inclement weather days, methods of reporting absence, and report formats.

New employees also appreciate information regarding available facilities, audiovisual services and resources, procedures for reproducing materials, and procedures for obtaining supplies and assessment tools. Not infrequently, space is an issue. From the beginning, every school psychologist needs a desk and access to other office equipment such as telephones. Individual offices may be difficult to obtain, but all school psychologists and second semester interns should have individual space to facilitate autonomy. Issues regarding compensation, contracts, and insurance issues should also be clarified.

These policies should be reviewed orally and supplied in written form. As described in Chapter 2, a well-organized and comprehensive handbook is the most efficient manner in which to convey essential information.

Case study 7-2

Failing to orient the new school psychologist thoroughly can lead to unintentional breaches of protocol that can ultimately lead to bad feeling. One new school psychology intern was not informed about informal parking rules. While she carefully avoided parking in the spots marked "Principal" and "Nurse," she consistently parked in the (frequently empty) spot next to the front door. Only after several months did she realize that she had consistently taken the spot "belonging" to the Director of Pupil Personnel—who happened to be her line supervisor.

Orientation also involves helping school psychologists understand where they fit into the school system's organization and how the work of the school psychology department fits into the functioning and success of the school system. Orientation to formal structures is generally fairly straightforward and can be accomplished through organizational charts. The primary complication in formal structure is that it is not uncommon for school psychologists to have more than one person claiming ownership of the psychologist's time and loyalty. For example, the school psychologist may directly report to the supervising school psychologist who reports to the Assistant Superintendent, the Director of Pupil Personnel Services, or the Director of Special Education. However, principals in a school psychologist's assigned schools also frequently have supervisory responsibilities. As long as competing demands and role conflicts are clarified, reporting to multiple "bosses" can be managed.

Informal structures are primarily developed from social relationships and are the primary route for informal communication in a school district. Orienting new hires to informal structures is more difficult than orienting them to the

113

formal structure because informal structures tend to be unstable, complex, and unexposed. Many school personnel are originally from the area and have blood relatives, in-laws, former in-laws, long-standing friends and enemies, and/or casual acquaintances from years past working within the school district. These relationships result in informal communication channels that affect the work of the school psychologist to an extraordinary degree, particularly if they are insensitive to or unaware of the relationships.

Ethical dilemma 7-2

A school psychology intern was assigned to two different schools, one elementary and one secondary. After several months, she discovered that the social worker in one building was sister to the speech therapist in the other building, that the secretary in the elementary school was living with the assistant superintendent, and that the guidance counselor in the secondary school was the roommate of her administrative supervisor, the Director of Special Education. Her site supervisor, a school psychologist, had not advised her of any of the informal structures in the school system, and the intern felt that she may have said or done something inappropriate. *What are the ethical issues? What should the supervising school psychologist have done?*

In addition to formal policies, it is important to orient new school psychologists to the informal mores of the school district, including professional dress. While school psychologists typically do not dress as formally as principals do, they do typically dress similarly to assistant principals or department heads—considerably less casually than graduate students. Most beginning school psychologists are sensitive and responsive to these issues, but some are not.

Ethical dilemma 7-3

Your department's most recently hired school psychologist has changed her style of dress considerably. At the time of her interview, she dressed traditionally. After being hired, she began to wear various body, ear, nose, lip, and tongue piercings, dyed her hair maroon, and stopped shaving her legs and underarms. Some school administrators are indicating to you, the supervising school psychologist, that they would prefer she not be assigned to their schools because of her appearance. Your supervisee maintains that she has the freedom to express herself in her dress. *What are the ethical issues? What should be done?*

SUPERVISING INTERNS AND PRACTICA STUDENTS

Supervising the novice practitioner offers a challenging responsibility. Effective supervision of interns demands specialized skills which include proficient teaching abilities, expert clinical knowledge, and strong technical expertise. Perhaps no other component of professional training has a greater impact on a student's skills and potential. During this structured learning experience, a foundation for future ethical practice and professional knowledge development is established. As is true for student teachers (Henry & Beasley, 1982), the model of practice demonstrated by the supervising school psychologist often becomes the model followed by the intern. Thus internship supervision has perpetuity because professionals tend to supervise others in the manner in which they were supervised.

Regrettably, despite the intensely demanding nature of this supervisory role, most internship supervisors have received little or no formal academic training in supervision and do not receive supervision of their supervision (Knoff, 1986; Ward, 1999; Zins et al., 1989). This impor-

114

tant role is customarily undertaken with little knowledge and insufficient ongoing support.

Overview of practica and internships

Two distinct types of fieldwork experience are provided during school psychology training: practica and internships. High quality internships and practica experiences are both systematically supervised and evaluated, conform to current legal and ethical standards, occur with university involvement, are awarded university credit, and are of sufficient and appropriate length to achieve the training objectives specified (NASP, 1994).

The practicum precedes the internship and focuses on the development of discrete, professional skills with specific populations in specific settings (Alessi et al., 1981). The NASP *Standards: Training Programs, Field Placement Programs, and Credentialing Standards* (1994) indicate that practica include (1) orientation to the educational process; (2) assessment for intervention; (3) direct intervention (including counseling and behavior management); and (4) indirect intervention methods (including consultation). Practica are less comprehensive than internships, and the learner is protected from many of the daily strains and pressures facing practicing school psychologists (Alessi et al., 1981).

In contrast, the internship experience is more comprehensive and professionally demanding. It focuses on the development and application of multiple professional skills across different settings with different populations. The internship is an integrative experience that constitutes the capstone experience of the graduate training program. This professional "rite of passage" offers a unifying experience for all school psychologists (Ross & Sisenwein, 1990).

The function of an internship program is to gradually increase the intern's responsibilities until he or she is able to function somewhat autonomously and effectively, with skills similar to those of an expert school psychologist (Mead,

1990). For this to occur, the environment needs to be structured so that the intern immediately practices reflectively and develops patterns of improving skills that result in increased future success. During the internship year, the aspiring school psychologist makes the transition from the academic world of theory to the clinical world of practice. When theory first meets practice, the experience can be an exhilarating, confusing, and challenging time for all participants.

The three overarching goals of the internship are: to foster the integration of multiple, distinct skills into a comprehensive professional perspective; to support the intern's transition from identification as a student to identification as a professional; and to familiarize the intern with the organizational structures of schools (Ross & Sisenwein, 1990). In light of these goals, the requirements of the internship are detailed specifically. The NASP *Standards* (1994) indicate that internships must consist of 1200 hours of work in settings appropriate to the specific training objectives–at least 600 of which must occur in a school setting. The internship is guided by formal written plans, which provide a broad range of training experiences and result in academic credit. Site supervisors of interns are credentialed school psychologists who do not supervise more than two interns and who provide at least two hours of supervision weekly. The entire internship process must support current ethical and legal professional standards and be systematically evaluated. The process also involves an agreement between the training university and the field site that the district will provide release time for internship supervisors and make a commitment to the internship as a training experience.

NASP (1994) further recommends that interns be provided a written contractual agreement specifying the period of appointment and the terms of compensation, a schedule of consistent with that of employed school psychologists, opportunities for participation in continuing professional development activities, expense reimbursement consistent with policies pertaining to employed school psychologists, and an appropriate work environment which includes adequate supplies, materials, secretarial services, and office space.

Since the student must attain specific professional competencies, it is imperative that the internship include exposure and access to diverse populations, ages, and grades. Furthermore, a multiplicity of school-based experiences (e.g., assessment, counseling, and consultation) must be provided. Interns should not be regarded as a source of inexpensive labor: sites should provide appropriate space, materials, and other resources (Ross & Sisenwein, 1990).

Ethical dilemma 7-4

In the late spring, the director of special education noticed that district school psychologists were overloaded with re-evaluations. She called a local university and volunteered her school district to serve as a training site for school psychology interns in the fall. Practicing school psychologists were told that things would be easier the following fall because help would be available when the interns arrived. They were also told that they would share the services of the interns and share supervision responsibilities. In the fall, two interns floated from school to school on an as-needed basis to conduct re-evaluations. When the interns mentioned that they were not receiving any training in counseling and/or consultation, they were told that they had to do what needed to be done and if time were available at the end of the year, they could consult and counsel. During the budget presentation, district school psychologists requested that an additional position be funded because special education referrals continued to escalate. However, they were told that the following year the district would accept four interns instead of hiring additional positions. *What are the ethical dilemmas? What would you do?*

Site supervisors: Qualifications and obligations

NASP (1994) recommends that supervisors meet the NCSP credentialing requirements, have completed a minimum of three years supervised experience as a school psychologist, and have been employed as a school psychologist for at least one year. Ross and Sisenwein (1990) further suggest that supervising school psychologists be employed full-time in the district. Although more than one supervisor may supervise an intern, it is advantageous to assign primary supervisory responsibility to only one person (Alessi et al., 1981). Finally, because supervising an intern takes the equivalent of a day per week, it is important that supervisors have sufficient release time allocated (Ward, 1999).

In addition to these formal qualifications, internship supervision requires significant interpersonal skills. The success of the internship is contingent upon the relationship between the intern and site supervisor. Interns tend to be insecure and frequently feel vulnerable. It is essential that the supervisor understands, accepts, and positively responds to the intern's uncertainty. This is accomplished when the supervisor develops a positive emotional climate; accords the intern professional equality by encouraging, accepting, and implementing the intern's ideas; and treats the intern as a person of authority in the presence of children, school personnel, and parents.

At the same time, the site supervisor should become familiar with the basic ethical and legal responsibilities and requirements for the internship year. This includes being aware of the legal status of interns in the state in which the internship is occurring. The site supervisor also needs to read the university internship handbook before internship occurs.

Ethical dilemma 7-5

You are supervising an intern whose university has very specific expectations for the performance of its interns. The intern is expected to perform the full range of school psychological services including direct and indirect interventions, and assessment. While you were trained in direct interventions such as counseling, your job has been restricted, omitting many of these activities, so that you feel extremely rusty and incompetent. *What are the ethical dilemmas? What should be done?*

University supervisors: Obligations and perspectives

The overarching job of the university supervisor is to insure that university and state requirements are being met. This necessitates interpreting policy, explaining program requirements, orienting the student to academic requirements, making specific suggestions to enhance training, completing appropriate forms, suggesting desirable activities, helping to determine the intern's schedule, and trouble-shooting when necessary.

The university supervisor serves as a liaison between the training site and the university program. Either before or at the beginning of the internship, the university supervisor should develop a relationship with the site supervisor to consider the following:

- the basic rationale for the internship program;
- the philosophy of the training program and its congruence with the philosophy of the field site;
- objectives and requirements of the internship;
- number of hours of the internship, including consideration of vacations and holidays;
- the schedule of observations and conferences with the site supervisor and intern;
- competencies to be achieved by the intern;
- schedule and form of evaluations of the intern,

the field site, and the university program;
- the types of activities and training plan; and
- grading responsibilities.

The university supervisor monitors the appropriateness of the site, ensures that requirements are met, serves as a feedback loop between the university training program and the field site, and, by the end of the internship, ensures that the student is sufficiently competent to warrant certification.

Throughout the course of the year, the university supervisor usually conducts a seminar that provides interns from different sites with opportunities to compare notes, ask questions, and formulate conclusions through peer interaction. The seminar gives the university supervisor the opportunity to observe the intern in a different environment, answer questions, and guide the discussion into an analysis of problems where alternatives for practice are considered. It is most helpful if the university supervisor has had significant experience working in schools and has achieved at least a proficient level of practice. Both in the seminar and during site visits, the university supervisor serves as a model of good practice.

Additionally, throughout the internship year, the university supervisor makes site visits which include direct observations of the intern engaging in various professional activities such as counseling, consultation, and assessment. After such observations, the university supervisor provides feedback and assists the intern in self-evaluation, as described in Chapter 3. The university supervisor also meets individually with the field supervisor, solicits his or her impressions through a private conversation, reviews progress toward the fulfillment of university and state requirements, suggests additional experiences for the intern, and summarizes the intern's progress for both the intern and site supervisor from a different perspective. If an intern is having difficulty, whether in practice or in the relationship with the site supervisor, the university supervisor serves as both mediator and problem solver. A good university supervisor extends communication beyond the site supervisor and establishes relationships with others in the building who work with the intern, including the principal, teachers, and paraprofessionals. An exchange of views and ideas with these individuals can be beneficial and informative for all involved.

Preparation for the internship year

In preparing for an internship year a number of considerations must be addressed. An intern must be selected, the intern must be prepared for the school system, and the site must be prepared for the arrival of an intern.

A supervisor selects an intern through the same personnel selection process described in Chapter 5. An appropriate, ethical, and legal selection process must be followed. Because of the close working relationship between interns and site supervisors, personal compatibility is particularly important.

Preparing an intern for the school system involves familiarizing him or her with the myriad of mechanical details that underlie school functioning. These have been described earlier under the heading "Orienting New Employees."

Initial preparation activities also include informing staff members about the arrival of the intern. It is important to create a feeling of anticipation and acceptance. Sharing some personal details about the intern may help further this aim, as will informing the staff about known strengths of the intern. For example, if the intern has previously worked as a behavior management specialist and has particular expertise in developing behavior management plans, this fact should be shared with the staff. Working out the anticipated role of the intern with other staff is also helpful.

Because school faculty are often confused about whether and when requests for services should go directly to the intern, clarification of procedures is helpful. If the intern and supervisor have agreed that a particular activity for the intern is desirable (for example, running a group for children of divorce) this should be shared with the staff. Finally, school personnel should be informed of procedures for contacting the intern, and should be informed of the intern's schedule so they know which days he or she will be in the building.

Practicum and intern supervision: A collaborative effort. A successful internship year offers an opportunity for growth for all participants. The site supervisor teaches the intern, and the intern teaches the site supervisor and serves as a resource for topical ideas and new materials. Both the site supervisor and the intern inform the university supervisor and program of current issues in the field and of needed university program adjustments. All of these interactions afford a mutually beneficial professional development opportunity. To maximize the benefit of the internship experience to all participants, close cooperation and collaboration between the university supervisor, site supervisor, and intern is critically important.

Frequent communication is vitally important. Written communication, phone conversations and e-mail can be used to supplement the face-to-face meetings between site supervisors, university supervisors, and interns.

Daily communication between interns and site supervisors can be facilitated by the use of a notebook in which either party can pose a question or make an observation to which the other can respond. Another method is to use e-mail correspondence, as long as confidentiality is maintained by avoiding the use of names. The purpose of such communication is threefold: it facilitates reflective practice, it gives the intern a mechanism for almost immediate information, and it creates a permanent record of useful ideas, information, and responsibility clarification.

Ethical dilemma 7-6

You are a supervisor of school psychologists in a district with twenty school psychologists. One of the interns has voiced complaints to you that she has been asked to perform menial tasks by her supervisor—such as filing, typing, answering the telephone, making appointments, and even cleaning the office. She would like to change supervisors and work with another district psychologist. *What are the ethical issues? What do you recommend be done?*

One of the most important responsibilities of both the university and field supervisor is to collaborate with the intern in the development of a training plan. Within the parameters of professional and university dictates, this comprehensive training plan should be designed according to the needs of the individual student. Students enter the internship with vastly different interests, experiences, and competencies. Although mandatory competencies must be achieved by all, it is important to recognize that great variability will exist. The initiation and evolution of an individual training plan is a dynamic, interactive process that involves all participants. Completion of self-assessment by the intern regarding skills and competencies offers a logical starting point. Conoley and Bahns (1995) suggest the following areas be considered: (a) competence, (b) emotional awareness, (c) identity, (d) respect for individual differences, (e) purpose and direction, (f) autonomy, (g) ethics, and (h) motivation.

Models of intern supervision

As discussed in Chapter 3, there may well exist a mismatch between site supervisors and interns in their theoretical orientation or in their perceptions of the role of the school psychologist. When their differences are significant, it becomes necessary to mutually address such issues, preferably early in the internship.

Expectations for supervision, including the anticipated model, should be examined (Mead, 1990). A commonly used model of intern supervision is the Problem-solving model, to which 77% of intern supervisors ascribe in some form (Ward, 1999). In this model, the supervisor facilitates the intern's problem analysis skills and guides learning to address problems in a systematic fashion (Knoff, 1986).

As discussed in Chapter 1, developmental models of supervision have also been advanced (Loganbill, Hardy, & Delworth, 1982; Stoltenberg, 1981; Stoltenberg, McNeill, & Delworth; 1998). These are certainly applicable to internship supervision and are ascribed to, sometimes in combination with other models, by 83% of intern supervisors (Ward, 1999).

For effective supervision to occur, the needs of the trainee must be met in accordance with his or her developmental stage. The new trainee will profit from increased support, structure, and guidance during the initial stages of supervision whereas autonomy and independence should be fostered during the later stages (Mead, 1990; Netherton & Mullins, 1997). Hence, the supervisor must assess the relative competence of his or her supervisee across various domains. For example, an intern may arrive with fairly well-developed assessment skills, expert counseling skills, and poorly developed consultation skills. To foster skill growth, different types of supervisory style will be necessary for different areas.

Alessi et al., (1981) offers a model for intern supervision that has a sequence of goal-directed teaching activities divided into five stages the length of which varies with the skills of the intern and the demands of the setting. An adaptation follows:

Stage 1: Shadowing and modeling. During the initial phase of supervision, the intern physi-

119

cally shadows the supervisor to directly observe the performance of professional activities from a comfortable, non-threatening vantage point. The task of the supervisor is to demonstrate the task the supervisee is to observe. During this period, the intern is introduced to various school personnel, views different programs, becomes familiar with the physical facility, learns about the organizational structure of the school, seeks information about the demographic characteristics of the larger community, school system, and individual schools, and is exposed to some of the procedures (both formal and informal) which are used in the performance of school psychology tasks. It is helpful for the intern to observe other practitioners in addition to the field supervisor to gain exposure to different skills and techniques in a relatively short period of time. To acquire knowledge regarding the scope and sequence of instruction, interns should be scheduled to visit classrooms varying by age of pupils, type of classroom, subject matter, and school. Observations should be conducted in general education classes, special education classes, art/music/gym classes, recess, lunch, after school activities, and counseling groups. Both expert and novice teachers should be observed. All observations should be maximally active in that the intern critiques and analyzes the observations and discusses them with the site supervisor.

As a professional courtesy to those being observed, observations should be scheduled in advance. Observations are most fruitful when students enter them with specific questions in mind, have time to speak to those observed ahead of time, thank those observed and give constructive comments regarding what was seen, and analyze the observation with the supervisor. Observations should result in:

- increased knowledge regarding the facilitation of learning of children and adolescents;
- increased ability to analyze and evaluate practice;
- recognition of theoretical orientations and implications for practice;
- formulation of a valid concept of what constitutes effective teaching and school psychology;
- formulation of a comprehensive concept of the school's scope and sequence of curriculum and relationship of various content areas;
- formulation of a concept of education as an integrated whole.

Stage 2: Observation and assessment of professional skills. The supervisor closely observes the intern performing both direct (e.g., assessment, interviewing, and counseling) and indirect (e.g., consultation) services. The developmental levels of the intern are assessed and a specific plan to provide appropriate training experiences is mutually formulated and agreed upon. This training plan considers the individual requirements of the intern and the overarching requirements of the university training program. Before every activity, the intern should be able to indicate the purpose, goals and objectives, methods and techniques, timing and sequencing, and methods of evaluating the effectiveness of the activity, as described in Chapter 3.

The site supervisor should refrain from correcting the intern or interrupting during an observation because such an interruption can reduce confidence and deteriorate the respect of others; however, interruptions should certainly occur when damage is being done. A planning conference should be able to prevent most difficulties, and most other concerns can be discussed in a conference after the observation.

Stage 3: Guided independent practice. During this stage, interns independently perform specific tasks in which they have been determined competent through prior observation. For example, familiar cognitive tests might be administered for re-evaluations. Under direct supervision and/or observation, the intern continues to observe and/or perform activities in which more direction and experience are necessary. The training plan is reviewed and revised, and decisions mutually agreed upon.

Cooperative practice can be an effective method of internship supervision at this stage. This involves the collaboration of the supervisor and intern on cases. When done well, mutual goals, shared responsibility, and teamwork characterize cooperative practice. Many activities lend themselves naturally to this practice; interns and their supervisors can conduct different aspects of a student evaluation or co-lead a counseling group.

Interns should be encouraged to have both long-range and daily plans regarding each case or group with whom they are working. Long-range plans require the intern to organize and consider a whole design rather than a daily combination of segments. The plans should be written and submitted to the supervisor several days in advance to allow for necessary revisions. It is helpful for interns to have access to several model plans so that they may follow them as they write their own plans. These model plans should include resources used by the supervisor, library resources, audiovisual materials, available supplies and equipment, community resources, available funds, and publications.

Stage 4: Increasing independent practice.

As more experience is gained by the intern, the scope of professional activities increases. Independent practice is encouraged within the framework of regular supervision. At this stage, interns take more initiative and responsibility for professional activities and become increasingly less dependent upon the supervisor. During this stage, independent decisions are made by the intern and discussed in supervision.

When supervising interns, the site supervisor must allow freedom while still maintaining responsibility. Site supervisors should expect to spend 50% of their time with the intern during the first semester, more at the beginning of the semester than at the end. The most common error made is in allowing too much independence too soon, forcing the intern to learn from trial and error. On the other hand, it is important to "let go" as the skills of the intern increase, since excessive supervision can smother growth.

School psychologists who decide to supervise interns should do so with the knowledge that it takes considerable time. Ward (1999) found that the average intern supervisor weekly spent 4.7 hours in direct supervision and 4.4 hours in indirect supervision, the equivalent of more than a day per week.

Ethical dilemma 7-7

An intern who is quite enthusiastic and eager–and who looks very young–is under your supervision. The majority of teachers in your school are mature and close to retirement. They have seen many educational fads come and go and have little patience with young enthusiasm. After six months, you perceive that the teachers in the school consistently turn to you even regarding those cases handled entirely by the intern. *What are the ethical issues? What steps should be taken?*

Stage 5: Professional independence.

Supervisors should not expect that interns will function completely independently by the end of the internship. Long term plans for professional development and ongoing supervision should be established during the final stage.

Evaluation

Evaluation constitutes a major component of the intern supervision process and includes regular, systematic feedback concerning strengths and weaknesses along with ways to improve functioning (Ross & Sisenwein, 1990). Evaluation is cooperatively conducted by the university supervisor and the site supervisor who conjointly confirm that the student is competent.

In addition to personal problems discussed in Chapter 2 under "Advising," interns often commonly have problems specific to their role. These can include severe financial difficulties, feelings of inadequacy and insecurity, and difficulty transitioning to relating to pupils and teachers in an adult manner. For example, they may attempt to take the role of an instant expert, relate to students as peers, or dress inappropriately and convey that they do not have the skills, responsibility, and authority of other adults in the school. Overextended schedules can also be problematic. To prevent overextension, as much as possible, interns should be encouraged to refrain from taking additional course work or employment during the internship.

One serious issue that must be addressed is that some students are below the advanced beginner level and are subsequently unable to progress in their prepracticum, practicum, or internship placement. Often these students have progressed to an advanced level in graduate school because they are proficient academically, but their difficulties with attending to others, communicating, being culturally aware, expressing themselves, or relating interpersonally interfere seriously with their ability to practice. These difficulties may be the result of developmental delays, lack of motivation, or unresolved interpersonal or intrapersonal concerns such as early childhood abuse, unhappy adult relationships, or substance abuse of their own (Stoltenberg, McNeill, & Delworth, 1998). Such individuals should be referred for therapy of their own, and

occasionally it may be necessary to recommend entry into a different profession. Both the university and site supervisor must document an intern's poor performance through audio and video recordings and written records. Difficulties most frequently arise when site supervisors fail to identify the problem early enough for a remediation plan to be developed, fail to keep complete records, and/or fail to notify the university supervisor when incompetence is evident.

In addition to the evaluation of interns, supervisors and training sites should also be evaluated. Training sites must be prudently recruited, selected, monitored, and regularly evaluated by university training programs. It is helpful for university supervisors, site supervisors, and exiting interns to all participate in this evaluative process. Such ongoing evaluations can help to eliminate ineffective, problematic training sites and/or site supervisors. If, for example, a school district limits interns' experience to testing, the necessary experiences in indirect service delivery are missed (Conoley & Gutkin, 1986). Without modification, such a site is not an appropriate training site.

DEVELOPING EFFECTIVE STAFF DEVELOPMENT PROGRAMS

Training and professional development activities range from those that are directed by supervisors and administration to those that are chosen by the individual. Traditional management approaches to staff development, in which the supervisor initiates and coordinates the program, are most appropriate when the entire staff have deficits in knowledge or skills. For example, when new technology, strategies, and professional tools are developed, all departmental personnel will need training.

At the other extreme are professional development programs that do not involve the supervisor at all. In this scenario, a school psycholo-

122

gist plans a professional development program independent of the school systems' goals and objectives. It can take the form of informal exploration and discovery by the school psychologist, a group of school psychologists engaging in peer supervision, or participation in workshops sponsored by professional organizations.

An intermediate planning approach involves both the supervisor and supervisee. This approach complements the literature describing adult learners as self-directed and experiential yet needing encouragement to critically evaluate their assumptions, practices, and values (Green, 1995). It also coincides with the approach recommended in business management literature (Noe et al., 1996; Rue & Byars, 1997), which asserts that the most effective staff development programs are characterized by:

- different training for individuals, with each person choosing goals and activities;
- active planning and goal setting by participants;
- activities that require active involvement;
- activities not limited to "one shot" workshops;
- evaluations of participant change.

A number of benefits result when supervisors of school psychologists take some responsibility for the professional development of supervisees rather than leaving their professional growth to chance or intermittent workshop attendance. Knowledge of subordinates is increased, intradepartmental cooperation and respect are promoted, all group members are benefited by improved skills, and supervisors consequently spend less time in corrective activities.

The basic steps in the development and implementation of effective training programs are: (a) conducting a needs assessment; (b) ensuring the readiness of the employees for training; (c) creating a learning environment, including identifying goals and objectives; (d) selecting appropriate materials and methods; and (e) evaluating the training program's effectiveness (Green, 1995; Noe et al., 1996).

Conduct needs assessment

Probably the most common but perhaps the least important reason that training is undertaken by school personnel, including school psychologists, is the requirement for professional development hours to maintain certification and licensure. Important reasons for training include changes in technology, job redesign, new legislation, and changes in the demographics or needs of the school district population. Other reasons include emerging strategies and techniques, performance problems, deficiencies in basic skills, and complaints from or requests by school personnel or parents (Noe et al., 1996). Before initiating a professional development program, a systematic needs assessment is conducted regarding school district, departmental, and/or individual needs.

Assessing the appropriateness of a professional development program from the school district perspective takes into account several factors. Among those to consider are:

- the self-perceived needs of the staff;
- the compatibility of the training objectives with the objectives and values of the school district or department;
- the degree to which administrators support participation in the training activities;
- the resources (time, budget, and expertise) available to support the training and the potential to take time for the collaboration necessary for meaningful change;
- the effectiveness of the district's procedures, norms, and communication processes; and,
- the degree to which administrators and peers support applying newly learned skills and behaviors (Green, 1995; Noe et al., 1996; Schmuck & Runkel, 1994).

123

Areas in which individuals need additional training can be determined through annual performance appraisals, brainstorming, committee meetings, conferences, consultants, interviews, observations, surveys, and questionnaires. To assess the individual psychologist's continuing professional development needs, a supervisor collaborates with each school psychologist to:

1. Review each skill and knowledge area required in professional practice (Fowler and Harrison, 1995);
2. Rate the individual psychologist in each knowledge/skill area as "satisfactory," "questionable," or "needing improvement" by the individual, the supervisor, peers, and consumers such as teachers and administrators;
3. Determine the importance of each skill area relative to the current position and the position if expanded to include new activities; and
4. Assign priority weights to each continuing professional development goal (Fowler & Harrison, 1995).

In addition to development in professionally related fields, many individual school psychologists find it fruitful to seek training in related fields such as remedial reading, special education, speech and language therapy, school administration, program evaluation, mediation, or marriage and family therapy. On a voluntary basis, many school psychologists also feel they benefit from development in non-occupationally related subjects such as art, music, and philosophy. These activities are broadening, facilitate creativity, and provide intellectual stimulation to counterbalance "the boredom and routine often produced by professional practice. In too many cases, work dominates life, and what an individual does becomes a symbol for what he or she is...life comes to be viewed in the increasingly rigid framework of a single profession" (Houle, 1984, p. 49).

When a problem with a particular school psychologist is identified, the supervisor must determine whether or not the apparent need for training stems from a lack of knowledge, motivational issues, or personal issues. Regardless, seeking personal or professional growth should be viewed as an indication of strength and never be interpreted as a symptom of incompetence.

Ethical dilemma 7-8

A school psychologist and his supervisor determine that his training in assessment is obsolete and decide that he should enroll in an assessment class at a local university. The following year the building principal writes a negative comment in the school psychologist's evaluation, indicating that his need for training revealed incompetence. The school psychologist feels that the receipt of training should not be reflected in his evaluation unless he had been warned ahead of time that this might be the case. *What are the legal and ethical issues? What could be done?*

Ensure readiness for training

For training to be worth expenditure of resources, participants must be motivated to learn, believe that they can successfully learn the material, and be inclined and able to practice the new skills and behaviors. To achieve this readiness for training it is important to:

1. Reach agreement on the nature of the problem, goals and objectives to solve the problem, and the need for training (Green, 1995);
2. Prepare participants for the content before the training begins;
3. Give choices on participation in training programs; and,
4. Provide materials, time, and evaluative feedback so employees are likely to practice and apply the newly learned skills and behaviors (Noe et al., 1996).

Create a learning environment and establish objectives.

To create the "learning environment" necessary for effective training, a number of steps are taken: training objectives are developed, employees are given opportunities to observe others practicing the desired skills, training programs are coordinated and well organized, varied teaching strategies are used, trainees perform the new task several times under direction, trainees are given opportunities to practice the new skills independently, supervisors develop standards of performance and use those standards in formal evaluations, and employees are given feedback about their proficiency in the application of the new skills (Noe et al., 1996).

Well-written training objectives are clearly defined, measurable, and conducive to productive evaluation. They specify what is to be learned, who is to be taught, when training will occur, and the anticipated impact on the school system, department, and individual. The current emphasis placed on student outcomes suggests that the most important goals and objectives will address the delivery of services to children, and the subsequent increased ability of children to learn and function (Wise & Leibbrand, 1996).

Select methods of training

Instructional methods are selected to complement the training goals. Technology has had a major impact on training programs in industry, as multimedia presentations have become commonplace. Technology has the potential to similarly revolutionize the training of school psychologists, and may be particularly helpful in addressing individual learning styles. As suggested by Phillips (1989) computers could facilitate the acquisition of factual knowledge by supplementing or even replacing traditional lectures, and courses could be offered in a self-paced fashion on CD-ROM (Belar, 1998). A virtual reality component to augment teaching test administration could be extraordinarily efficient and reduce potential damage to human "guinea pigs." Technology can also reduce the cost of training, as the use of distance learning technology saves time and money formerly devoted to travel (Noe et al., 1996).

A number of instructional methods are effectively used in training and professional development, each with their own advantages and disadvantages (Noe et al., 1996; Rue & Byars, 1997). These are summarized in the following outline:

A. *Formal university coursework*
    Advantages
    1. Most effective when participants have little knowledge
    2. Provides supervision, active learning, and feedback

    Disadvantages
    1. Not always available in areas of interest
    2. Requires repeated travel
    3. Can be costly and time consuming

B. *Lecture supplemented by question and discussion (e.g. professional and in-service workshops)*
    Advantages
    1. Quickly gets information to large groups
    2. Inexpensive and least time-consuming

    Disadvantages
    1. Effectiveness depends on audience ability to listen
    2. Effectiveness depends on presenter's ability to present clearly, and effectively incorporate active participation, case studies, examples, and exercises.
    3. Ineffective when presented as "one shot" workshops without subsequent experiential components

C. *Simulated case study presentations: participants think through problems, propose solutions, choose among alternatives, and analyze consequence of the decision*
    Advantages
    1. Brings note of realism

125

2. Can be used in small or large groups

Disadvantages

1. Simulated cases are usually simpler than real-life cases

2. Because participants are not actually involved in the case, the presentation lacks the emotional involvement and complications common in practice

D. *Distance learning: two-way communication via audio-conferencing, videoconferencing, and document sharing.*

Advantages

1. Telephone links permit questions and comments among individuals who are geographically dispersed

2. Saves travel costs

Disadvantages

1. Potential lack of interaction

2. On-site facilitator needed to answer questions

3. Technology not yet universally available

E. *Audiovisual techniques such as overheads, slides, prepared videos, videotaping participants, and PowerPoint*

Advantages

1. Trainer can slow down or speed up presentation in response to audience need

2. Trainees are exposed to equipment, problems, and events not easily demonstrated or presented verbally

3. Instruction can be made consistent from one training session to another

4. When videotaping is used in conjunction with role-playing, permits participants to see their own performance

5. Usually of greater interest than lectures alone

Disadvantages

1. Time necessary to prepare materials can be considerable (an estimated time to edit a video is one hour of editing per one minute of finished video)

2. Equipment can be expensive and is not readily available in school districts

F. *Peer group which focuses on collaborative problem solving or practicing new skills with one another (Fowler & Harrison, (1995)*

Advantages

1. Increased morale

2. Increased networking

3. Increased familiarity with resources

4. Improvement of skills

5. Increased participation in professional organizations

Disadvantages

1. School psychologists practicing in isolation may have difficulty developing such a group

2. Time pressures and geographical distances may preclude scheduling meetings frequently enough to be effective

G. *Role-playing assigned roles in "realistic" situations*

Advantages

1. Encourages active learning and participation

2. When used in conjunction with videotaping, effectiveness is increased through review and critique

Disadvantages

1. Success depends upon willingness of individuals to role-play realistically

H. *Behavior modeling, where interpersonal skills such as communicating ideas is taught by:*

- giving the rationale behind the desired behaviors;

- showing a video tape of modeled behaviors;

- providing trainees practice opportunities in role play;

- requiring trainees to evaluate a models' performance;

- giving feedback regarding how closely the trainee's behaviors match those of the model; and,

- having trainees indicate how they plan to use the desired behaviors on the job

Advantages

1. Effective methods to learn interpersonal skills

2. Videotaping facilitates self-observation

Disadvantages

1. Relies on willingness of participants to role-play

2. Relies on availability of modeled behavior samples.

I. *Group Building Techniques through shared ideas and experiences, designed to build a group identity. Examples: adventure learning (developing team work though outdoor activities), and team training (coordinating the performance of individuals who work together to achieve common goals)*

Advantages

1. Increases understanding of interpersonal dynamics

2. Increases knowledge of ones own and of colleagues' personal strengths and weaknesses

Disadvantages

1. Success limited by team's ability to identify and resolve errors, coordinate decisions, and reinforce each other

J. *Enabling access to professional journals, monographs, books, manuals, and digests through a professional library, dissemination of articles, and book purchases*

Advantages

1. Readily available

2. Less expensive than alternatives

Disadvantages

1. Additional support is required for effective implementation, and moving from knowing "about" to knowing "how." (Smith, 1987)

2. Does not provide guided practice or feedback.

K. *Self-directed learning through readings, CD-ROM or personal computer instruction*

Advantages

1. Trainees can participate in accordance with their own schedules

2. Trainees have increased personal responsibility for their own training

3. Computer learning provides immediate feedback, multiple learning opportunities, and self-paced instruction

Disadvantages

1. Motivation must be high for the program completion.

L. *Simulations (including virtual reality simulations) which represent real-life situations where trainee's decisions have outcomes similar to those that would occur on the job*

Advantages

1. Allows trainees to see impact of performance in a risk free environment

2. Effective in teaching interpersonal skills

Disadvantages

1. Virtual reality technology is neither fully developed nor readily available

M. *On the Job Training*

Advantages

1. Novice has opportunity to observe proficient or expert practitioners, imitate them, and practice under direct supervision

2. Effective in giving experience in all job aspects

3. Training occurs in a realistic situation before responsibility is assumed

Disadvantages

1. Novice is likely to acquire poor as well as good practices demonstrated by trainer

2. Requires trainee to shadow trainer, which may be expensive and time consuming

3. Requires that the trainer take time to break down tasks into the following steps: obtain equipment and supplies, demonstrate the task, explain key points of behaviors involved, demonstrate a

127

second time, have the trainee perform the task in incremental steps, praise correct performance and provide corrective feedback, provide additional supervised practice until independent practice is appropriate

N. *Mentoring.*

Successful mentoring programs are voluntary for both the mentor and protégé, can be ended at any time, and do not preclude informal relationships with other experienced practitioners. The programs have clearly understood purposes, specified projects and activities, a specified duration, a minimum level of contact between the mentor and protégé, opportunities for protégés to contact one another to discuss problems and share successes, a formal evaluation process, and rewarded participation (Noe et al., 1996). Many of these characteristics are reflected in the NASP (1994) standards for internships.

Advantages

1. Novice develops his or her own approach while still under guidance of more proficient practitioner.

2. Formal mentoring programs are accessible to minorities and women, not just to those with previous "network" connections (unlike informal mentor programs).

3. Mentoring relationships benefit both parties: mentors have opportunities to develop interpersonal skills, increase feelings of self-worth, and gain knowledge about new developments.

4. Protégés are benefited by receipt of career, psychosocial, and emotional support.

Disadvantages

1. Bad practices can be passed on to the novice.

2. Mentor might neglect responsibilities.

3. Mentor may have difficulty understanding the protege's total situation when only verbal descriptions are available.

4. All novice practitioners do not seek informal mentoring.

5. Formal mentoring programs may result in attempts to develop relationships inadequately matched for interests, values, and mutual regard.

Ethical dilemma 7-9

A supervisor of school psychology would like to update a department on the cross-battery approach to intelligence test interpretation. Since this is a relatively new model, none of the school psychologists in the district have received university training in this approach. One of the school psychologists has become familiar with the cross-battery approach through reading professional literature and workshop attendance. The department would like to generalize this knowledge to all members, but to purchase individual books and send each department member to workshops would be quite expensive. The administration suggests that the newly trained psychologist duplicates the workshop for the other psychologists, and makes photocopies of the readings and workshop materials for all department members. *What are the ethical dilemmas? What steps should be taken?*

EVALUATING TRAINING ACTIVITIES

The evaluation of training and professional development activities is conducted through surveys, observations, focus groups, personnel records, or ratings by participants' supervisors or peers. The choice of method is determined by the training objectives. Results of training and professional development can occur in four areas (Noe et al., 1996):

1. Affect: What was the reaction of the participants to the program? Did the attitudes of the participants changed in areas such as tolerance

for diversity or motivation? Reactions and attitudes are commonly measured through the use of post-training evaluation forms or surveys.

2. Cognitive: What concepts, facts, and principles did the participants learn? These are typically measured by pencil and paper tests.

3. Skill-based: Did the participants' skills change as a result of the training? Skill acquisition can be assessed by observation either during the training session or on the job, and the completion of rating scales by supervisors, peers, or participants.

4. Results: Did the training result in reduced costs, reduced turnover, or other savings to the school district? For example, after training in conflict resolution, did administrators suspend fewer students?

Following the implementation of a staff development program, evaluations should be both summative (considering whether goals have been met) and formative (considering to what extent new practices are being implemented appropriately). Furthermore, these evaluations should not be discontinued as soon as the professional development program is discontinued, but should address continuing support for staff into and through the maintenance of the new skill (Green, 1995).

Sample Internship Portfolio Requirements

A portfolio is a collection of multiple work samples, collected over time, that demonstrate competence. Throughout the course of the internship, you will be asked to submit portions of your portfolio to your University Supervisor for review and feedback. At the end of the semester, two copies of a completed professional portfolio are to be formally submitted. The original shall be returned to you and the copy kept on file. The portfolio will be read by the University Supervisor and the Program Director. The portfolio may also be reviewed by state or national accreditation team personnel. You may also choose to share your personal copy of your portfolio with potential future employers during interviews. Because it is relatively public, the portfolio is not an appropriate place to express confidential statements and opinions. Portfolios should be typewritten and double spaced. Because portfolios must be read prior to grade submission, it is essential that you adhere to submission deadlines. Late submissions will receive lowered grades. Information contained in the portfolio should be as follows:

A. **Title page** with your name, placement site and location, and dates of the assignment.

B. **Statements of personal growth:** a compilation of personal statements written at the following milestones:

- as an applicant to the school psychology program,
- as a beginning student in Issues in School Psychology,
- as an advanced student prior to the internship,
- as a graduating student.

These statements should include information regarding future goals and perceived areas of strength and weakness. You are encouraged to use the evaluation forms included in this handbook as a guide for domains of knowledge. The statements summarize:

- the attitudes and perceptions that you held about school psychology prior to and after the internship;
- your perception of the role and function of a school psychologist;
- areas in which you feel you need additional training and support; and
- your understanding, knowledge, and ability to function as a school psychologist.

C. **A description of your internship placement** including the placement site and location, dates of the assignment, setting, characteristics of the student/client population, the range of existing problems, and treatment techniques utilized to resolve them. Describe:

- the larger context and community, including resources;
- the population served--ages, sex, socioeconomic status, etc.;
- professional personnel and their qualifications;
- funding sources as appropriate (i.e., grants, etc.);
- school psychological services program philosophy and goals;
- program emphases re: treatment techniques, diagnostic consultative methods, follow-up procedures employed, and transitional programs utilized;
- pertinent therapeutic and psychoeducational approaches utilized;
- the student/client/patient-to-staff ratio; and
- the enrollment capacity of the program.

If you complete your entire practica/internship in one location, it is not necessary to repeat the placement description both semesters.

D. Evidence of your skills in consultation
DO NOT INCLUDE NAME(S). Evidence might include:

- progress notes of at least three ongoing teacher consultation cases;
- progress notes of at least three ongoing parent consultation cases;
- consultation/authentic assessment re-ports;
- any other information you feel demonstrates your skills in this domain.

In order to demonstrate your growth you might choose to include consultation process notes you have saved from earlier courses.

E. Evidence of your skills in direct interventions
DO NOT INCLUDE NAME(S). Evidence might include:

- process notes and/or transcripts of at least three ongoing individual counseling cases;
- progress notes and session plans for at least two ongoing group counseling series;
- progress notes, contracts, and data for at least two ongoing behavior management plans;
- any other information you feel demonstrates your skills in this domain.

In order to demonstrate your growth you might choose to include process notes you have saved from earlier courses.

F. Evidence of your skills in assessment
DO NOT INCLUDE NAME(S). Evidence might include:

- at least three comprehensive case study reports, including recommendations and all test protocols; and
- any other information you feel demonstrates your skills in this domain.

In order to demonstrate growth you might choose to include additional reports you have saved from earlier courses.

G. Evidence of skills in training, research, and/or program evaluation, as available.
Evidence might include:

- presented handouts from a series of in-service workshops you developed and provided, and/or
- a formative program evaluation of a group or individual program .

H. Conclusion. A brief summary of your experience as an intern.

I. Appendix: includes material not written by you, but which you feel is necessary for the reader's understanding your portfolio. An example would be a brochure for a program where you worked with children with behavior disorders. Do not include information that would be universal for all interns, such as special education regulations.

131

132

Chapter 8 | Promoting Job Satisfaction

Job satisfaction results when an individual perceives that a job fulfills, or allows for the fulfillment of, important values (Noe et al., 1996). As conveyed by this definition, job satisfaction is determined by an individual's values and by the perception (which may or may not be based in reality) of congruence between one's job and values.

Promoting job satisfaction has been an area of interest in industrial psychology for several decades. Job satisfaction has been found to be associated with self-esteem, general life adjustment, and physical and mental health. It is also associated with professional attendance, attitudes, turnover, and job performance and productivity (Levinson, 1990; Levinson, Fetchkan, & Hohenshil, 1988). Dissatisfaction can lead to absenteeism, tardiness, reduced work effort, reduced customer satisfaction, theft, and violence. More than 150 studies have determined a link between job dissatisfaction and consequent physical or psychological job withdrawal (Noe et al., 1996).

When employees are dissatisfied, they first express that dissatisfaction by trying to change the conditions under which they work. This can take the form of confronting supervisors, forming a union, whistle blowing, and filing grievances against the employer. If these efforts to promote change are unsuccessful, employees are likely to physically or psychologically withdraw from the job. Transferring to another job, being absent, or being late manifests physical withdrawal. Psychological withdrawal is manifested through minimal job involvement, low organizational commitment, or physical or mental health problems (Noe et al., 1996).

Studies examining job dissatisfaction of school psychologists have found the percentage of dissatisfied to range between 35% (Solly & Hohenshil, 1986) and 14% (Anderson, Hohenshil,

& Brown, 1984). In general, sources of job dissatisfaction stem from the tasks or role of the job, an individual's personal characteristics, the physical environment, or the social environment. Sources of school psychologists' dissatisfaction have been identified as:

- excessive workload (Wright & Gutkin, 1981);
- excessive caseloads, insufficient time, and lack of appreciation (Reiner & Hartshorne, 1982);
- disagreement with school system policies and practices, lack of advancement opportunities, insufficient compensation, poor working conditions, and insufficient supervision (Solly & Hohenshil, 1986); and,
- high student-to-psychologist ratios, disagreement with school district policies and practices, or the lack of the opportunity for advancement (Anderson et al., 1984).

In contrast, school psychologists' job satisfaction has been found to correlate with age, experience, ratio of psychologist to students, diversity of roles, participation in research, and membership in professional organizations (Levinson et al., 1988). Restricting school psychologists' activities and roles to psychoeducational assessment has been found to be a source of dissatisfaction (Guidubaldi, 1981; Jerrell, 1984; Levinson, 1990; Smith, 1984), while role diversity and "boundary spanning functions" such as interdisciplinary work (Jerrell, 1984), as well as role function and perceived control (Levinson, 1990, 1991) were correlated with increased job satisfaction and decreased burn-out (Huberty & Huebner, 1988). School psychologists working in large districts tend to be more dissatisfied with school district policies and opportunities for advancement than school psychologists working for smaller districts (Levinson, 1991).

133

In general, school psychologists indicate a desire to spend more time counseling, consulting, and conducting research and less time in assessment and clerical activities. Thus roles defined by supervisors as they develop job descriptions, select staff, ensure sufficient clerical staff, provide supervision, and conduct evaluations can clearly have an impact on the satisfaction, longevity, and job satisfaction of supervisees.

Probably the most effective way for supervisors of school psychologists to determine whether supervisees are satisfied with their jobs is to ask them how they feel and what would improve their satisfaction. Additional sources of information include formal instruments designed to determine job satisfaction, and/or anonymous surveys designed to pinpoint "what can we learn," rather than "who can we blame." If a direct approach is not productive, it can be helpful to look at problem areas to determine issues. Supervisors should also have exit interviews with those who terminate employment and encourage them to speak freely regarding positive and negative aspects of the job.

Supervisors can support job satisfaction by providing the following, listed in order of importance (Littrell, Billingsley, & Cross, 1994):

1. Emotional support. This topic is addressed in this chapter;

2. Appraisal support, or the provision of constructive and frequent feedback regarding work and clear guidance regarding responsibilities and improvement. This topic has been addressed in Chapter 6;

3. Instrumental support, or help in conducting work-related tasks. This includes procurement of materials, space, and resources, help with managerial concerns, and appropriate scheduling that allows enough time for assigned tasks. This topic is addressed in this chapter and Chapter 14;

4. Informational support, which includes providing information, methods, and instruction needed to improve performance. This topic has been addressed in Chapter 7.

In the following pages we will discuss a number of specific strategies for promoting job satisfaction, including providing emotional support, fostering stress management, encouraging time management and organizational skills, promoting a positive physical environment, facilitating job enrichment, and considering characteristics of individual school psychologists.

PROVIDE EMOTIONAL SUPPORT

The amount of emotional support provided by supervisors was found to be the most significant variable in promoting job satisfaction and preventing burnout for educators (Littrell et al., 1994; Russell, Altmaier, & Van Velzen, 1987), factory workers (House, 1981), mental health workers (Ross, Altmaier, & Russell, 1989), and nurses (Constable & Russell, 1986). A significant source of emotional support stems from the social environment. The social environment is determined by positive relationships between supervisees and their peers, as well as between supervisee and supervisor, and is characterized by similar values and philosophy, social support, and support in clarifying pathways to desired outcomes (Noe et al., 1996).

A supervisor can facilitate a positive social environment by several methods. First, supervisors improve the social environment when they encourage supervisees to develop a network of support among themselves rather than relying solely on the supervisor for problem solving. Because of the isolation of school psychologists, this requires deliberate planning and team assignments. Basically, the supervisor seeks to form a department with lines of communication between every individual, rather than a department in which all communications are directed to the supervisor as though the supervisor is a hub in a spoke wheel.

In addition, the supervisor encourages school psychologists to develop positive and professional networks within their schools. School psychologists feel less isolated when they psychologically become members of schools. This requires that the supervisor assign department members to schools and programs on a predictable and continuous basis. The degree to which school psychologists have predictable schedules determines the degree to which they are able to take part in community building activities such as PTA meetings, potlucks, and faculty meetings.

Ethical dilemma 8-1

Two of your supervisees disagree about the appropriateness of social contacts with school personnel, and turn to you for advice. One school psychologist believes that participating in social events outside of school hours is helpful and appropriate in that it enables her to build friendships with colleagues that also facilitate her work in the school as a consultant. Therefore, she accepts invitations to dinners, parties, and after-hour socializing in bars. The other believes that participating in social events is an ethical violation that leads to dual relationships. *What are the ethical dilemmas? What should you advise?*

Finally, supervisors increase social support by encouraging participation in professional organizations. Such participation positively correlates with job satisfaction (Levinson et al., 1988), and school psychologists are more likely to become active members of local, state, and national school psychology associations with their supervisor's support and example. Encouraging supervisees' participation in inter-national associations and Internet Listserve and consultation groups also increases their sense of community (Kruger & Struzziero, under review).

Supervisors additionally foster emotional support when they both privately and publicly show esteem, maintain an open communication system, demonstrate appreciation, and consider the ideas of each supervisee. McInerney (1985) recommends the following methods to foster positive working relationships:

1. Address supervisees' concerns. If it is not possible to address the concerns, communicate them to higher authorities;
2. Keep staff informed and provide rationales for decisions;
3. Ask staff how they feel about what they are doing and give them opportunities to talk about their work;
4. Be physically and psychologically present for both formal meetings and informal discussions;
5. Informally observe staff in action;
6. Give direction clearly;
7. Make sure that time and resources necessary for success are allocated; and,
8. Provide reinforcers for good work including monetary rewards, personal thanks or praise, a positive memorandum to a higher authority, and/or opportunities for further training or recognition.

FOSTER STRESS MANAGEMENT

Working in schools appears to be a stress-producing job for general education teachers, special education teachers, and school psychologists alike (Forman & Cecil, 1985). Supervisors of school psychologists are typically in a highly stressful situation themselves, and are additionally responsible for helping their supervisees fulfill responsibilities in the face of pressing demands and emotional stress.

135

Stress results when an individual perceives environmental demands to be greater than his or her ability to meet such demands (Lazarus, 1966). Adverse reactions to stress can be behavioral, cognitive, emotional, or physical and can be manifested by anxiety, apathy, avoidance, burn-out, compulsivity, critical attitudes, dependence, deterioration of work performance, frustration, impatience, negative attitudes, procrastination, rejection, retaliation, somatic illnesses, and/or temper outbursts. In contrast, a positive reaction to stress is manifested by calmness, creative problem solving, objective listening and questioning, and a comprehensive and rational response (Noe et al., 1996).

In general, stress is caused by career problems, change, errors, excessive workloads, health problems, interpersonal conflict, personal criticism, personal problems, tight deadlines, and unpleasant tasks (Loen, 1994). For school psychologists, excessive caseload, insufficient support from school personnel and administrators, and poor role definition has been found to be significant sources of stress (Forman, 1981; Reiner & Hartshorn, 1982).

Case study 8-1

As one of their "support" activities, a group of school psychologists generated a list of stress reduction strategies they found effective:

At work

1. List everything you have to do, record the amount of time necessary to complete each task, and include each item in your schedule. Include letter writing, report writing, and consultations with counselors, principals, and teachers.

2. Develop parameters for the expectations of others. For example, let people know where they stand on your waiting list.

3. Free yourself for a day to write reports.

4. Find methods to be in control of your schedule and less at the mercy of other's demands.

5. Be realistic. For example, if someone refers a student to you for counseling, and you do not have consistent time in your schedule for regular counseling with that student, refer him or her to another professional.

6. Schedule time to check in with the school counselors and building team leaders at least weekly.

7. Let secretaries and clerks do their jobs of copying, filing, and scheduling meetings rather than doing it yourself.

8. Use a teacher planning book for scheduling.

9. Maintain a "to do" book with three separate categories:
   - Telephone calls to make (with numbers),
   - Things to write/do on the computer, and
   - Action items.
   Code each item with an empty circle (°) if it is to be done within two weeks, with a filled in circle (•) if it is to be done within a week. Write down every item in your calendar.

10. Make a master schedule of the whereabouts of the children with whom you are working.

11. Keep a running list of children who you believe are better off for having worked with you and whose lives were improved because of your efforts.

12. Allocate an hour per day for phone calls, emptying your in-box, and scheduling.

13. Build mini-vacations into your day (a change in lunch routine, taking short walks, etc.).

14. Learn to relax and build a relaxed time into each day.

15. Think of at least three long-term professional goals you have for yourself, write them down, and begin working on each of them in some way.

16. Develop short and long term objectives and schedule them into your calendar.

17. Seek patterns to improve predictability instead of reacting to a series of unending crises. For example, determine how often there are "emergency" psychological evaluations and then schedule them in advance. Determine which times during

the school year are predictably problematic (such as holidays, just after report cards are issued, when state reports are due, and when annual IEP's are written). Schedule extra time during those periods into your appointment book.

18. Invest in, or get the school system to invest in, time-saving aids. The most significant time-saver is a lap top computer. Others include calculators, copies of often-used manuals, and test scoring software. To persuade the school system to invest in these aides, calculate your hourly wage and determine how quickly the item "pays itself off" in saved time.

19. Stay late at work a couple of days per week rather than bring work home.

At home:

1. Don't work.
2. Participate in activities that have concrete results, such as building, painting, etc.
3. Listen to entertaining TV and radio programs.
4. Exercise on a regular basis.
5. Think of at least three long-term personal goals you have for yourself, write them down, and begin working on each of them in some way.
6. Quickly write down 20 things you like to do. Take time to do at least one of these on a daily basis.
7. Relax on a daily basis, either formally (transcendental meditation, relaxation exercises) or informally (being a couch potato).
8. When you find yourself worrying about work in the middle of the night, while driving, or doing household chores, you may be trying to hold too many "things to do" in your memory. Write them down on your list!

ENCOURAGE TIME MANAGEMENT AND ORGANIZATIONAL SKILLS

One of the greatest challenges faced by beginning school psychologists is the establishment of effective time management and organizational skills. The greatest assets of the job (high flexibility, varied activities, unstructured time, challenging expectations) are also the attributes that require a high degree of time management and organization. Time management has been shown to increase both the quantity and quality of time for school psychologists. A lack of effective time management can result in anxiety, stress, and ineffectual practice (Maher & Cook, 1985). A supervisor of school psychology will probably need to help novice school psychologists increase these skills.

The following are necessary for good time management: an appreciation of time as a scarce resource, a clear understanding of the job for the entire school year, flexibility, and a consideration of time management as an ongoing problem-solving process that should be integrated into the work routine (Maher & Cook, 1985). The following suggestions can help improve time management and organization for school psychologists:

1. Conduct an assessment. First, determine how time is spent by keeping a precise log. Determine how much time it actually takes to provide ongoing consultation for a case, implement a behavior management plan, conduct a psychological assessment, run a parent support group, conduct a program evaluation, implement an in-service training, or write a grant. Then consider these time requirements before taking on or assigning new tasks.

2. Determine when different tasks are completed most efficiently. For example, some school psychologists have observed that writing a report takes them half as much time if completed in the morning than if completed in the afternoon or evening. Similarly, many school psychologists observe that it takes much less time to write a report within a day of seeing the child than after an intervening week. Some find that

137

just after lunch is the most efficient time to return telephone calls. After determining the most efficient time for these tasks, schedule sufficient time in your appointment book for their completion.

3. Write non-appointments into calendars. Block out time for report writing, making and receiving telephone calls, consultations, observations, reading student files, reading journals, supervision meetings, and travel time.

4. Schedule follow-up meetings during initial meetings, including follow-ups for behavior management plans, consultations, and sharing assessment results with students and parents.

5. Schedule the unexpected. Block into daily calendars time for the unexpected drop-in counseling or consultation session, unexpected phone calls, etc.

6. Organize papers so that materials are easily found. Many find that taking a half-hour at the end of the day to organize materials is extremely helpful.

7. Draw up lists of specific tasks to be completed and then complete them in order of priority. Break down large tasks into smaller units with deadlines.

8. Avoid distracting yourself; when focusing on one task (such as writing a report) you may remember another task to complete (such a making a telephone call). Add it to your list of things to do rather than acting on it at the moment.

9. Obtain copies of items that greatly increase efficiency. Always have copies of a school's recess, lunch, and art/music/library/physical education schedules so you know when teachers are available. Obtain copies of students' schedules. Have an extra copy of the most utilized test manuals at your desk.

10. Develop a report template on your computer that prompts you to type the background information for a report into the computer report template as you review a cumulative file.

11. Avoid handling any piece of paper more than once.

12. Conduct a more in-depth assessment of recurring problems in time management. For example, some novice psychologists take an inordinate amount of time to write a psychological report. In-depth assessment may reveal deficiencies in a particular skill, such as interpretation of test results, which need strengthening through professional development activities.

PROMOTE A POSITIVE PHYSICAL ENVIRONMENT

Another major consideration in fostering job satisfaction is that of the physical environment. While schools are generally not thought to be harsh physical environments, supervisors of school psychologists are frequently in a position where they must attend to the physical work environment of their supervisees. Because of the overcrowded nature of schools and the itinerant nature of school psychology, it is common to hear "horror stories" of school psychologists who are asked to work under highly undesirable conditions–in hallways, storage closets, and locker rooms adjacent to noisy physical education classes.

Adverse physical conditions have been shown to have a negative impact on employees (Rue & Byars, 1997) and these can be reasonably expected to have similar negative impact on the children and adolescents with whom the school psychologist works. Work settings should provide adequate lighting, ventilation, humidity, and temperature. Exposure to adverse conditions should be of limited duration. These recommendations are reflected in the NASP *Standards and Professional Conduct Manual* (NASP, 1994, 1997).

Often school psychologists themselves feel unable to negotiate for adequate workspace and so supervisors must negotiate for them. Of course, in negotiating for appropriate space it is necessary to be reasonable about resource availability. To demand deluxe accommodations–a private office with a telephone and window in every school–would certainly adversely affect relationships between the school psychologist and other school personnel. Often reasonable space can be achieved by taking into account the schedules of other itinerant specialists when developing the schedules of school psychologists. For example, school psychologists and speech therapists can quite comfortably share an office if they are not scheduled in the same school during overlapping time periods aside from regularly scheduled team meetings.

Ethical dilemma 8-2

One of your supervisees works in a very crowded elementary school without a room designated for his work. Initially, the principal indicated that the school psychologist could work with the children in the hallway. When your supervisee indicated that confidentiality would be compromised, the principal indicated that the school psychologist could use the principal's office. The school psychologist expressed concern that the children would feel that they were "in trouble," but the principal insisted that all of the children in the school see him as "a friend." There is no vacant space in the entire school. *What are the ethical concerns? What can be done?*

FACILITATE JOB ENRICHMENT

Primary predictors of job satisfaction and stress are the characteristics of the tasks and roles of the job itself. In general, the more complex a job, the greater the job satisfaction. The greater the boredom and monotony of a job, the greater the

dissatisfaction (Noe et al., 1996). To counteract job dissatisfaction stemming from monotony, a supervisor can facilitate *job enrichment* by adding complexity and meaningfulness to a job, and *job rotation* by moving an individual from one position to another over a period of time. The supervisor of school psychologists easily accomplishes either of these. Job enrichment can be accomplished through careful analysis of the roles and responsibilities of the job and by advocating increased complexity, particularly greater involvement in cases prior to the stage of psychoeducational assessment and greater involvement in research. Job rotation can be accomplished by encouraging rotation of school and program assignments after a period of three to five years.

Ethical dilemma 8-3

One of your supervisees has been working as a school psychologist for 22 years. She confesses to you that she has become so bored with the WISC-III that she finds herself giving it "automatically," reaching the end of the test without remembering either administering the test or recording the results, similar to driving automatically along a familiar route. Even worse, she admits that she often falls asleep while administering the battery. *What are the ethical concerns? What can be done?*

In addition, it is important to analyze the role of the school psychologist when expectations are ambiguous, conflicted, or unreasonable. To conduct such a role analysis, the school psychology supervisor, school psychologist, administrators, and teachers write down their expectations for the school psychologist. In a group meeting, each person reads his or her list. Expectations are written and ambiguities and conflicts identified, resolved, and removed.

Ethical dilemma 8-4

After several years, you conclude that the expectations for the school psychologist in one building are quite different than the expectations held at the district office. The principal seems to feel that the primary responsibility of the school psychologist is to recommend that students be removed from his school and sent to a different school for special education placement. In contrast, the Director of Special Education perceives that a school psychologist's primary responsibility is to develop programs that will keep the children in their neighborhood schools. Your supervisee is tired of being "caught in the middle," and turns to you for help. *What are the ethical issues? What can be done?*

As mentioned previously, the job satisfaction of school psychologists increases with participation in research (Levinson et al., 1988). As described in Chapter 12, supervisors can play a significant role in facilitating supervisees' skills in research consumption, dissemination, and production.

CONSIDER CHARACTERISTICS OF INDIVIDUAL SUPERVISEES

Individual characteristics can also play a role in job dissatisfaction. Chronic negative affect, or the tendency to have high levels of aversive moods such as anger, contempt, disgust, guilt, fear, and nervousness, increases job dissatisfaction. Such individuals tend to focus on negative aspects of themselves and others across all contexts (Noe et al., 1996).

Motivating

Quality services for children are primarily dependent upon the existence of highly motivated staff who are responsive to new situations and who remain motivated to continually update skills (Sergiovanni & Starratt, 1998). Motivation

is best understood as a three-step process: a need experienced by an individual, an action taken by that individual, and the resolution of that need. Fundamental aspects of motivating others include providing a sense of empowerment, expecting quality performance, giving meaningful recognition, training and encouraging self-development, asking individuals about job expectations, and helping individuals to meet their own needs (Loen, 1994).

Just as needs are highly individualized, motivators are highly individualized. It is essential that supervisors attend to the supervisees' needs, rather than assuming that the supervisees' needs are largely similar to their own. Beginning practitioners are often motivated to acquire and demonstrate expertise.

For experienced school psychologists, even an exciting field can become boring, routine, dull, and monotonous. Thus the supervising school psychologist is challenged to increase the motivation of experienced school psychologists who have become bored. This can be accomplished to some extent by encouraging them to apply their talents to continually improving their practice. It can also be accomplished by encouraging advanced supervisees to accept the challenge of mentoring beginning practitioners as formal or informal supervisors.

Maslow's (1954) theory of motivation can be a useful framework to apply in supervision. The basic physiological and safety needs are generally met by steady employment as a school psychologist. However, in school districts where job security is threatened, the safety need will not be fulfilled. This results in dissatisfaction, expenditure of energy in job seeking, or a search for job security through union involvement.

The next level of needs, social needs, can be thwarted when the school psychologist feels isolated. This can result in resistance, antagonism, and lack of cooperation. To a certain extent, the supervising school psychologist can ameliorate this problem by the steps described previously: fostering group cohesion among the district's school psychologists, encouraging contact with other school psychologists, and encouraging the development of professional relationships with district school personnel other than school psychologists.

After the needs for safety and social contacts have been satisfied, the ego needs for self esteem (self-confidence, independence, achievement, competence, and knowledge) and regard (status, recognition, appreciation, and respect) predominate. Although supervisors of school psychologists often cannot affect salary, they can increase the feelings of regard through awarding independence and recognition.

Finally, the needs for self-fulfillment (realizing one's own potential, continued self-development and creativity) are expressed. To meet these higher order needs, it is necessary for school psychologists to meet and exceed the minimal requirements of their job descriptions. Whether school psychologists have the energy to attempt to meet these needs is largely dependent upon the climates of the school psychology department, school district, and state. At times, meeting higher order needs can be frustrated by job components. For example, being expected to complete a significant amount of clerical work can frustrate school psychologists.

Union contracts tend to target extrinsic rewards such as fringe benefits. However, industrial research indicates that these are not the most important motivators. Aspects of work that motivate employees were ranked in the following order: interesting work, sufficient help and equipment, sufficient information, enough authority, and good pay. Being appreciated, interesting work, opportunities for advancement, and achievement are frequently mentioned as factors that make work more enjoyable (Halloran, 1981). To meet these needs the following are helpful:

- delegate tasks along with the authority to carry them out;

- involve supervisees in group decision making;
- permit flexible work hours;
- restructure jobs to provide variety, interest, and challenge;
- rotate jobs;
- provide praise and recognition for improved performance; and,
- listen to employees (Halloran, 1981).

Ethical dilemma 8-5

The school psychology department under your supervision shares a secretary with another department, and you do not supervise this secretary. Many of your supervisees have expressed frustration because this secretary's skills are very poor. As a result, the school psychologists complete all of their own typing, filing, and copying. *What are the ethical dilemmas? What can be done?*

141

Advising

Although it is extremely important for a supervisor to avoid taking the role of therapist with supervisees, supervisors almost inevitably find themselves in situations where it is necessary for them to provide personal advising. It is important that this be provided in response to early warning signals, rather than only in crisis situations. As in any counseling or consultation situation, the basic steps include active and responsive listening followed by an exploration of alternatives and solutions.

At some point in their lives, almost everyone has a personal problem so great that it seriously impacts their ability to work. School psychologists are no different. When individuals experience severe personal problems they generally display signs of emotional distress such as exaggerated behavior, overly controlled behavior, irrational behavior, an inability to concentrate, agitation, lack of sleep, loss of weight, irritability, or crying.

Frequently a school psychologist with a personal problem will share this problem with his or her supervisor. The role of the supervisor is to listen carefully and provide support. The amount and duration of support necessary is highly individualized and not easily quantifiable. For example, it is a mistake to assume that a bereaved person should be "back to normal" in a specific amount of time, since a person's reaction to a loss depends on many variables.

On the other hand, individuals who experience long-term personal problems that are considered shameful often avoid talking about them with supervisors. For example, alcoholism, drug abuse, and mental illness are stigmatizing and frequently not disclosed. Unfortunately, these disorders are common, occurring in more than 10% of the population (American Psychiatric Association, 1994).

Regardless of a long-term diagnosis, an effective supervisor focuses on the ability of the individual to complete assigned tasks. If a supervisee is unable to complete assigned tasks over an extended period, the supervisor collects documentation regarding job performance and conducts a corrective interview. If performance does not improve after the corrective interview, the supervisor continues through additional corrective steps as delineated in school district policy.

From the perspective of employers, an alcoholic is defined as "any employee whose repeated overindulgence in alcoholic beverages sharply reduces his or her effectiveness and dependability in carrying out work tasks" (Halloran, 1981, p. 341). Although supervisors tend to view alcoholics as having severe personal problems, they are highly ambivalent about dealing with the problem directly. A referral to a treatment program is highly appropriate. If the supervisee is not sufficiently rehabilitated and job performance remains unsatisfactory, the supervisor must take the same steps as would be appropriate for dismissal for unsatisfactory job performance for any reason (Noe et al., 1996).

Similar steps are be appropriate for supervisees who abuse prescription or illegal drugs. Symptoms of drug abuse vary with the drug of choice but regardless, the supervisor approaches the problem from two perspectives: addressing the problem by obtaining support for the individual and setting clear job performance expectations. Taking these steps can be particularly difficult for the supervisor of school psychologists because of a general orientation toward positive support. Nonetheless, the welfare of the children served must be paramount.

An additional consideration for any site receiving federal funds is the necessity to comply with the "Drug Free Schools and Campuses" acts. These require that school districts develop an alcohol and drug awareness policy that includes:

- standards of conduct that prohibit the unlawful possession, use, or distribution of illicit drugs and alcohol on school property;
- a description of applicable legal and institutional sanctions and health risks associated with drug and alcohol use; and,
- a description of any available drug or alcohol counseling treatment, rehabilitation, or re-entry programs.

Ethical dilemma 8-6

You have become suspicious that your supervisee, a school psychologist in his mid-forties, is developing a habit of drinking on the job. He brings a thermos to work daily, and once when you visited him on site he quickly hid his cup. You have not noticed any change in his work, yet feel uncomfortable ignoring the issue. *What are the ethical concerns? What should be done?*

142

School psychologists conduct indirect interventions when they develop educational or other treatment programs on behalf of a referred child, but do not personally implement the programs. Supervising school-based indirect interventions, such as consultation, is an especially demanding professional endeavor. Whereas consultation is one of a school psychologist's major responsibilities, ongoing monitoring and evaluation is critical for successful implementation of appropriate interventions (Zins & Erchul, 1995).

To develop a framework for consultation supervision, a general definition of consultation will be provided along with a brief exploration of factors that have supported its recent exponential growth in the schools. Models of consultation commonly employed in schools will be considered in terms of their impact on the supervision process, since different supervisory techniques and practices appear to be better suited to different models of consultation. Finally, specific strategies useful in the supervision of indirect services will be described.

GENERAL CONSIDERATIONS

Growth of consultation

Consultation has emerged as an important component of school psychology practice and has dramatically increased in the past quarter century (Fuchs, Fuchs, Dulan, Roberts, & Fernstrom, 1992; Pryzwansky, 1986; Sheridan, Welch, & Orme, 1996). School psychologists have endorsed consultation as a preferred, important, professional service (Curtis & Zins, 1980; Gutkin & Curtis, 1982). Such growth clearly reflects the fact that it is particularly well suited to meet contemporary needs.

Multiple factors have converged to support the growth of consultation within the schools. As a result of educational reform efforts, there is a growing trend toward the utilization of alternative methods of service provision (Curtis & Meyers, 1989; Stainback & Stainback, 1989). Furthermore, both the promotion of inclusion practices and the demand for formalized pre-referral efforts have increased the need for indirect services. Both are heavily dependent upon consultation (Curtis & Meyers, 1989; Sheridan, Salmon, Kratochwill & Carrington Rotto, 1992).

As classroom populations become increasingly heterogeneous, providing instruction to pupils with different learning styles, emotional needs, and socioeconomic and cultural backgrounds can become increasingly difficult. It becomes essential for school psychologists to support the efforts of classroom teachers to meet increasing demands for teacher accountability and to utilize innovative methods to assess and enhance students' performance (Batsche & Knoff, 1995; Fuchs & Fuchs, 1989). Consultation effectively addresses such needs.

It must also be recognized that in an effort to contain spiraling special education costs, some systems have sought to eliminate staff positions or to increase the job demands of the school psychologist (Kruger, Wandle, & Watts, 1992). In the future, the provision of direct psychological services may be increasingly limited, and a responsive shift to the provision of indirect services may be necessary. Assuredly, the growth of consultation as a major professional function of school psychologists will continue as practitioners confront new and evolving educational demands.

The expansion of consultation necessitates that new trainees enter the field with well-developed consultation skills and that seasoned professionals constantly refine and develop their own consultation skills. Importantly, the ability

143

to adapt professionally to an indirect service delivery model may ensure continued systemic demands for school psychological services. Hence, the development of effective supervision practices of indirect services is essential.

Multiple roles and relationships

The multiplicity of roles and relationships that exist in the supervision of consultation make achieving the goals of supervision extremely complex. Both consultation and supervision usually occur within dyadic relationships. However, both are actually triadic in that they involve three distinct participants. Some participants customarily have direct, face-to-face contact with each other while others do not. In school-based consultation, participants usually include the (1) consultant, (2) consultee, and (3) client-student. In the supervision of counseling and assessment, participants are the (1) supervisor, (2) supervisee, and (3) the individual with whom the supervisee is working.

In contrast, the supervision of consultation minimally involves four people with multiple, fluid roles: (1) supervisor, (2) consultant/supervisee, (3) teacher/consultee, and (4) student/client. Some interpersonal interactions are direct and always include face-to-face contact, while others remain indirect and rarely include face-to-face contact. Because of the interaction of both process and content variables across these multiple relationships, the supervision of consultation profits from a structured framework to guide both practice and supervision.

Effective supervision of consultation demands an awareness of the similarities and differences between the two processes. Both are professional relationships that are triadic, confidential, and extend over time. In contrast to the typical egalitarian approach to consultation, however, the supervisory relationship tends to be hierarchical, evaluative, and involuntary. Furthermore, during supervision, the supervisor retains ultimate responsibility for the case. In contrast, during con-

sultation, responsibility for the case can either be shared or remain with the consultee.

It may be helpful to consider figure 9-1:

Relationships in the Supervision of Consultation

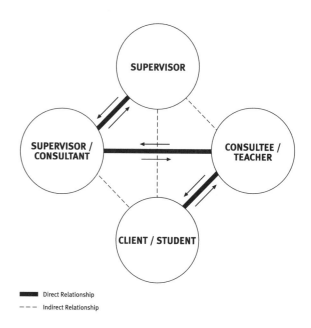

In contrast, during con-

Ethical issues

Ethical principles for supervisors of school psychologists practicing consultation incorporate and reflect the same fundamental ethical principles as for all mental health professionals. During the supervision of consultation, professional behavior is dictated by overarching ethical guidelines. Heron, Martz, and Margolis (1996) suggest that the inherent complexity of consultation and the intense emotions that often arise from dealing with complicated issues necessitate that consultants have a strong and clear ethical framework dictating their behavior. Furthermore, a concurrent awareness of cross-cultural issues is vital. Hence, one constant goal of the effective supervisor is to ensure that supervisees offer consultation services within an enduring framework of ethical and cultural sensitivity.

Strict maintenance of confidentiality is essential. In consulting, psychologists should not share confidential information leading to the identification of a client or other person or organization with whom they have a confidential relationship unless they have obtained the prior consent of the person, or disclosure cannot be avoided because the student is a danger to himself or another (American Psychological Association, 1992). Furthermore, psychologists share information only to the extent necessary to achieve the purposes of the consultation.

In summary, effective supervisors have a responsibility to simultaneously monitor and maximize the therapeutic benefits for the student(s), provide professional development and training for the supervisee, and ensure that ethical principals are constantly upheld.

Ethical dilemma 8-1

A new intern, anxious to demonstrate both her knowledge and good intentions, has offered to consult with a third grade teacher regarding a child with autism. The child, who is in an inclusive, regular education setting (adamantly demanded by his parents) is often disruptive and unruly in the classroom. Although previous teachers expressed some frustration and concerns in the past, the present teacher is truly enraged. She claims that in her thirty years of teaching, she has never encountered such a difficult child. She states that her whole class has been negatively impacted by this child's placement in her regular education class. She strongly feels that he needs a substantially separate placement. . .and soon! Day after day, her complaints have dominated the lunchroom conversation. Among other threats, she is stating that she is planning to file a grievance with the teachers' union. The staff is becoming extremely polarized regarding this issue.

The new intern, who is young, inexperienced, and eager, desperately wants to see if she can help alleviate the growing animosity. She has an autistic brother and feels like she has a handle on some of the emergent issues. *What are the ethical issues? What steps should be taken?*

MODELS OF CONSULTATION: IMPLICATIONS FOR SUPERVISION

Although numerous definitions have been advanced, the following definition reflects the general features of consultation: "Consultation is a collaborative problem solving process in which two or more persons (consultant and consultee) engage in efforts to benefit one or more other persons (client) for whom they bear some level of responsibility, within a context of reciprocal interactions" (Curtis & Meyers, 1989, p. 36).

The process of consultation has clear, well-defined goals, which reflect its prevention-oriented nature (Parsons & Meyers, 1984). Henning-Stout (1993) notes that the three interdependent, primary goals of school-based consultation are to assist in making appropriate psychological and educational services accessible to all children, to engage the consultees in this process of indirect service delivery, and to facilitate problem solving skills among all participants. Whereas similar goals direct the supervision process, it is essential to simultaneously consider the goals of the consultation within the framework of the supervision goals.

Various consultation models have been developed. They are founded upon distinct theoretical bases and are customarily adapted to the setting(s) in which they occur. The adoption of a particular consultation model is dependent upon one's theoretical orientation and past experiences and training. Theories, whether explicit or implicit, provide the structure from which one builds hypotheses, infers causes of behavior, and chooses interventions. One important supervisory task is to critically explore one's own beliefs about consultation. This is best accomplished by considering the various consultation models and by examining how tenets of each may be reflected in everyday practice.

Although distinct models of consultation have been delineated, Gutkin and Curtis (1982)

145

suggest that several defining characteristics are found across all models. Briefly, the commonalties are that:

- consultation is an indirect approach to service-delivery;
- the consultee and consultant share a coordinate status and the relationship is non-hierarchical;
- the consultee is actively involved in the consultation process at all times;
- consultees have the right to reject the advice and/or suggestions of the consultant;
- the relationship is voluntary;
- confidentiality is maintained;
- the focus is on professional problems in the work setting; and,
- the goals of consultation are to enhance the skills of the consultee as well as to assist the student (Gutkin & Curtis, 1982).

Behavioral consultation (Bergan & Kratochwill, 1990) and mental health consultation (Caplan, 1970) have emerged in school psychology as two major models. Recently, a hybrid model, the Integrated Model of School Consultation (Erchul & Martens, 1997) has been proposed. This model represents a melding of both behavioral consultation and mental health consultation.

Mental health consultation

Mental health consultation serves as the foundation for consultation in general (Erchul & Conoley, 1991; Erchul & Martens, 1997; Henning-Stout, 1993). Mental health consultation began fifty years ago when Gerald Caplan confronted the unmanageable task of providing mental health services to thousands of displaced, immigrant children in post-war Israel. Quickly recognizing that traditional models of service delivery were insufficient, he developed and refined an alternative model that reflected the newly emerging prevention movement. Mental health consultation is founded in psychodynamic theory and hypothesizes that the source of many student issues

that the teacher perceives as problematic actually reflect displacement and/or projection on the part of the teacher. The consultant's task is to avoid discussion of the teacher's unresolved conflict(s) while simultaneously trying to correct misperceptions about the client's problems.

School psychologists have raised two major objections to the practice of mental health consultation, both of which relate to its psychoanalytic foundation. First, school psychologists are uncomfortable with a perceived lack of honesty with the consultee, feeling that the model is manipulative. Second, school psychologists are uncomfortable believing that the teacher's theme interference is the primary source of student issues (Caplan, Caplan & Erchul, 1995). According to Caplan and Caplan (1993), these discomforts are because most school psychologists have not been trained in the psychodynamic model and because their practice is dominated by behaviorism and cognitive-behaviorism.

Due to these growing discomforts, the contemporary Caplanian model of mental health consultation gives minimal emphasis to theme interference. While mental health consultation remains firmly grounded in the psychodynamic/psychoanalytic tradition, it now focuses less on the therapeutic alteration of underlying perceptions and attitudes of consultees (Caplan & Caplan, 1993).

Four types of mental health consultation have been developed, differing in both foci and goals. Briefly, *client-centered case consultation* seeks to help a specific client/pupil. *Consultee-centered case consultation* has as a goal the development of generalized skills in the consultee. *Program centered administrative consultation* seeks to improve programs; *consultee centered administrative consultation* seeks to develop the skills of the consultee in dealing with problems of the organization.

The focus of supervision varies with the type of mental health consultation employed. Supervision of mental health consultation focuses on an awareness of relational issues, a strict maintenance of objectivity, and the utilization of an indirect, therapeutic approach. Techniques which enhance supervision of mental health consultation include the use of process notes, examination of parallel process issues (which assumes that supervisees unconsciously replicate client issues during supervision), examination of transference and counter-transference, and the use of reflection. The use of audiotape, videotape, and Interpersonal Process Recall (IRP) may also be helpful.

During the supervision of mental health consultation, strict interpersonal boundaries must be maintained so that the supervision does not become overtly therapeutic in nature. This type of supervision and consultation may be best suited for the more advanced practitioner and/or supervisor.

Behavioral consultation

The growth of behavioral consultation reflects the prevalent systemic, ecological viewpoint currently pervasive in the fields of psychology and education (Dougherty, 1995). Importantly, behavioral consultation may be particularly well suited to the needs of school psychologists practicing in an era that stresses accountability and research-based precepts. Martens (1993) has suggested that two specific aspects of behavioral consultation have largely contributed to its widespread acceptance: (a) it has been adequately operationalized so that standard techniques, instruments, and indices of effectiveness have been developed, and (b) its problem-solving objectives are founded on the well-accepted principles of applied behavioral analysis.

Like the mental health consultation model, behavioral consultation encourages the direct caregiver (e.g., the teacher, parent) to be the change-agent (Martens, 1993). It is also indirect, non-hierarchical, and triadic. However, unlike the mental health consultation model, the behavioral consultation model exclusively addresses the concrete, discrete, and observable behavior(s) of the client. Strongly rooted in applied behavioral analysis, behavioral consultation considers overt behavior to be more important than unconscious themes (Bergan, 1977).

In contrast to the mental health consultation model, the unconscious processes of the consultee are considered to be of little consequence.

Bergan (1977) offers a four stage, sequential problem-solving model of behavioral consultation that includes problem identification, problem analysis, plan implementation, and problem evaluation. The supervisee must define the targeted problem, isolate those variables which affect the problem, and devise a plan to manipulate the environment in such a way that continuation of the undesired behavior is not supported (Conoley & Conoley, 1988). It is essential that the consultant appropriately implement all four consultation stages.

Because success ultimately depends upon consistent, accurate delivery of agreed-upon interventions, no treatment can be successful without the full cooperation and active participation of the consultee. Treatment integrity, which refers to the "degree to which a consultation plan is implemented as intended" is largely dependent upon the consultee's acceptance of and investment in the chosen interventions (Gresham, 1989, p. 37). Hence, although supervising behavioral consultation may involve an emphasis on issues of technical adequacy, the impact of interpersonal relationships must also be considered.

The effective supervision of behavioral consultation will generally involve the design of appropriate behavioral intervention plans, application of functional behavioral analysis techniques, mutual examination of data obtained by the teacher and/or supervisee, and exploration of treatment effectiveness. Knowledge of operant conditioning, learning theory, and applied behavioral analysis provides the foundation for effective supervision.

Integrated model of consultation

In a concerted attempt to synthesize the most beneficial aspects of the behavioral consultation and mental health consultation models, Erchul and Martens (1997) have proposed an Integrated Model of Consultation. This model emphasizes problem-

147

solving orientation along with techniques of applied behavioral analysis. Concurrently, there is an explicit interest in the dynamic process of the consultation relationship. Erchul and Martens (1997) suggest that the conscious use of consultants' influence and power enhance effective consultation, and that successful school-based consultation involves "a combination of social influence and professional support within a problem-solving context...the model (integrates) two theoretically distinct approaches to consultation....mental health consultation...and behavioral consultation, as well as two general approaches to consultative practice (i.e., social influence and professional support) regarded by some as mutually exclusive" (p. 12).

Techniques of supervision which may be applicable to this model include those mentioned for both mental health consultation and behavioral consultation. That is, process notes, examination of parallel process issues, the use of reflection, audiotapes, videotapes, process recall and analysis, problem analysis, monitoring of behavioral intervention plans, mutual examination of data obtained by the teacher and/or supervisee, and explorations of treatment effectiveness may all be appropriate.

Ethical dilemma 9-2

A supervisor trained exclusively in the traditional Caplanian model of mental health consultation has been asked to provide supervision in reference to a very problematic child with autism in one of the district's elementary schools. The supervisee, who is very well trained and experienced in behavioral consultation, appears at the initial supervisory session armed with data sheets and behavior charts. The supervisor, who is unfamiliar with behavioral consultation, begins the session by asking about the consultee's possible resistance to intervention and suggests that parables be used. *What are the ethical issues?*

TECHNIQUES SPECIFIC TO SUPERVISION OF INDIRECT SERVICES

Supervision techniques that can be applied to direct services and assessment, as well as consultation, were discussed in Chapter 3. This section will discuss techniques specific to consultation.

Strategy: Develop a supervision plan

As is the case for all supervision, when directing consultation supervisors need to develop a supervision plan to monitor the results of their actions, offset harmful consequences, and terminate interventions when they do not achieve desired goals. Effectively guarding clients' welfare requires that the supervisor monitor the process and the content of the consultation as it impacts the consultee (teacher), the client (the child on whom the consultation is focused), and the supervisee/consultant. Additionally, professional standards require that the impact of the supervision on the entire system must be monitored (Mead, 1990). Thus the supervision and evaluation plan for consultation necessarily addresses the impact of consultation on all three consultation participants, as well as the impact of supervision on all three consultation participants and the supervisor.

In addition to overseeing interpersonal and relational issues, the effective supervisor is vigilant regarding the ethical and technical adequacy of chosen interventions. It may be helpful to consider the following questions when formulating a plan of supervision:

1. What previous experience do the participants have with the presenting problem?
2. How serious is the presenting problem? What might go wrong?
3. What level of monitoring and involvement is appropriate?
4. What is ethically appropriate?
5. Are potential cross-cultural issues considered?
6. How will the effectiveness of process and content variables be operationalized?

7. How often will progress be measured?
8. How will the consultation be terminated? By whom? When?

Strategy: Facilitate communication

In the supervision of consultation, well-developed communication and interpersonal skills are essential. Both effective supervision and effective consultation are founded upon communication and interpersonal skills: deficiencies in either area will render supervision of consultation impossible. In addition to helping supervisees develop verbal, para-verbal, and non-verbal skills, supervisors must simultaneously and constantly monitor themselves. Supervisors must be active listeners who elicit both qualitative and quantitative information.

Case discussions with supervisees during supervision sessions is the most common method used in supervising consultation. Many different techniques help reduce the subjectivity and bias inherent in self-reporting—process notes, audiotapes, videotapes, process recall, behavioral intervention plans, and behavioral intervention data are all useful. In addition, supervisees might choose to directly observe the supervisee in a consultation setting.

Supervisors can use similar techniques as they monitor their own supervision of indirect services. Maintaining supervision session process notes, reviewing audiotapes of sessions in which the supervision of consultation has occurred, and consulting with peers will enable supervisors to monitor and increase their own effectiveness.

Strategy: Interact directly with the client and consultee

One supervision task is determining whether direct interaction with the consultee is warranted. Because the welfare of the student is always of primary concern, the supervisor must first consider the student's needs in the context of the supervisee's developmental level and the nature of the presenting problem. With novice practitioners, face-to-face observation of the student who is the object of consultation is often advisable. In a Boston area group, school psychology practitioners were unanimous in stating that they favored direct contact with the client while supervising new interns. On the other hand, they felt that with more experienced practitioners, such contact may not necessarily be warranted.

Other variables that influence the supervisor's level of direct involvement include the communication and interpersonal skills of the supervisee, the nature and severity of the presenting problem, and the experience and expertise of the consultant/supervisee regarding the presenting problems.

As the professional knowledge gap between supervisor and supervisee diminishes, the need for intensive, direct monitoring and observation tends to decrease and supervision becomes increasingly consultative in nature. Peer supervision, for example, usually resembles consultation more than supervision. In such cases, direct contact with the student is much less likely to occur.

Strategy: Modify model to fit supervisee development

In addition to maintaining an awareness of theoretical models of consultation, the effective consultation supervisor considers the developmental stage of the supervisee and the nature of the presenting problem when deciding which model of consultation to recommend. For example, some models of consultation (e.g., behavioral consultation) may be more appropriate for novice practitioners or for particular presenting issues. Overall, the developmental stage of the supervisee, theoretical orientation of both the supervisor and supervisee, goals of the consultation, and goals of the supervision session guide both the techniques and specific models chosen in the supervision of consultation.

Strategy: Keep records

Because consultation involves multiple individuals and issues, good record-keeping is especially invaluable. An effective supervisor will encourage

149

the supervisee to vigilantly record both content and process variables that arise during consultation. Both supervisee and supervisor should keep written records of supervision sessions.

Strategy: Use computer-mediated consultation and supervision

Electronic mail (e-mail) offers a unique way to enhance both consultation and supervision efforts among school psychologists and educators. Using this technology, an electronic community of school psychologists was established in 1995. This Global School Psychology Network (GSPN) was initiated to enhance communication among school psychologists and other professionals (Kruger & Struzziero, 1997). International in scope, the GSPN has brought school psychologists together to tackle common professional problems and issues via electronic consultation. At the time of this writing, thousands of messages have been exchanged among school psychologists all over the world.

The GSPN uses e-mail to augment traditional, face-to-face communication and to provide a technologically innovative way to support consultation and supervision efforts among educators (Kruger & Struzziero, 1997; Struzziero, 1998). To adhere to appropriate ethical principles, the GSPN uses a closed computer network, pseudonyms, and avoids inclusion of identifying information. Informed consent is obtained before linking potential identifiers with consultation notes, and participants are formally trained in how to compose messages and minimize mistakes when using the system. Users must restrict the actual names of children, birth dates, test data, parent names, addresses, and all other information that might lead to the identification of the students.

However, no matter how secure a network appears, it is impossible to guarantee that any message will remain confidential. On the basis of experience with the GSPN, the following guidelines were developed for the ethical use of e-mail for consultation:

- Use e-mail to supplement, not replace, face-to-face consultation sessions;
- Receive appropriate training on ethical issues and using e-mail in consultation;
- Receive ongoing supervision or peer support in computer-mediated consultation;
- Use a highly secure computer network; and
- Avoid inclusion of identifying information when discussing consultees or clients.

Due to the rapidly expanding knowledge base in both education and psychology, it is often exceedingly difficult for the busy practitioner to stay abreast of current developments (Kruger & Struzziero, 1997). Therefore, this electronic network is also being utilized to provide professional development opportunities, training, and supervision of school psychologists, administrators, and teachers (Kruger, Cohen, Marca, & Matthews, 1996; Kruger & Struzziero, 1997; Struzziero, 1998).

It is evident that this communication method has the potential to revolutionize the way in which supervision occurs. Although it is not a replacement for face-to-face supervision, it has tremendous utility. It is expected that in the future, supervision will not be limited to a specific hour(s) of face-to-face contact, but will transcend the boundaries of time and place. Because developments and changes in cases can occur so rapidly, timely communication between professionals is essential.

The use of electronic communication in the training and supervision of school psychologists may be especially advantageous in some locations. For example, a training program in school psychology at Massey University in New Zealand uses electronic communication to provide supervision because distances are so great and students are seldom on campus. This "electronic supervision" supplements face-to-face meetings between students and professors.

Ethical dilemma 9-3

A school psychologist within your district is skillful on the computer and uses e-mail with teachers to facilitate consultation. This enables the psychologist opportunities for consultation follow-up that are highly effective. On the other hand, knowing that e-mail is not confidential for a number of reasons, you are concerned that confidentiality may not be maintained. *What are the ethical dilemmas? What should you do?*

As the use of e-mail continues to expand, it is important for the supervisors to be aware of potential obstacles and problems. One way to avoid problems is to be aware of the potential differences between computer-mediated communication and face-to-face communication. Although research is relatively sparse, it has been suggested that computer-mediated communication tends to support egalitarian relationships. Role and status, for example, have less importance than during face-to-face communication (Bordia, 1997; Sproull & Kiesler, 1991). Clearly, this has very significant implications for supervision. For instance, school psychologists using computers to mediate supervision must be sensitive to the lack of social cues and instructed in how to compose messages to convey these important cues. Whereas "the more anonymous nature of e-mail contributes to a sense of increased freedom in which traditional social rules and constraints become less consequential," supervisors must vigilantly monitor relationship issues (Kruger & Struzziero, 1999). Effective supervision mandates that a hierarchical relationship between supervisor and supervisee be vigilantly maintained. To accomplish this within the inherently democratic framework of e-mail communication will require that the effective supervisor be constantly attentive to potential problems.

Strategy: Encourage peer supervision

Independent peer support groups provide a viable means of obtaining ongoing supervision for proficient or expert school psychologists. Peer groups under the direction of a supervising school psychologist are also valuable for beginning school psychologists and should be encouraged by supervisors.

In the field of school psychology, peer support groups have emerged as an important professional development tool and provide a viable, important means to engage in career-long learning. Such groups have evolved in response to a distinct need for professional development and social support that was not being adequately met in other ways. As suggested by Zins, Maher, Murphy, and Wess (1988), changing professional demands obligate school psychologists to stay current with their field and to be able to implement new ideas. Peer support groups provide a logical, efficient way to accomplish this task.

Peer support groups are voluntary relationships among professionals with common interests (Kirschenbaum & Glaser, 1978) that facilitate professional development by means of the mutual sharing of advice, guidance, and social support. Peer support groups also offer a viable means by which professionals can respond to changing educational conditions and increasing demands for accountability.

Strategy: Support consultation with paraprofessionals

Although consultation and/or supervision with paraprofessionals may not constitute an "official" part of the school psychologist's professional responsibilities, in practice, such supervision and consultation often does occur both formally and informally. The multiple services performed by paraprofessionals in today's schools constitute a very important part of the school's ecology. When the collective impact of bus drivers, playground monitors, teacher aides, library assistants, custodi-

151

ans, lunchroom attendants, and clerical personnel is considered, it is obvious that paraprofessionals have an inestimable impact on the children they serve. Effective consultation with this group of adults, most of whom have had little formal training in education and/or psychology, can have a profoundly beneficial effect.

Supervision of consultation with paraprofessionals must enable the supervisee to consider the differences between consulting with paraprofessionals and with those who consider themselves professionals. During consultation with paraprofessionals, it is important to consider their role, abilities, openness to intervention, and the nature of the presenting problem. Perhaps most importantly, the level of intervention must be carefully chosen. The rights of the children must always take precedence.

Ethical dilemma 9-4

Mr. Smith has been a bus driver for the school system for almost twenty years. He recently approached the principal asking for an immediate transfer. He claims that he is angered and frustrated by the behavior of a sixth grade girl who rides his bus. She intermittently swears and incessantly picks at the padding of the bus seat. She has produced a large hole in her seat and will not respond to his repeated requests to stop. Her swearing, although usually whispered, offends nearby riders. This often leads to further confrontations. In general, the situation on the bus is unpleasant for all. Parents are beginning to complain as well. Your supervisee, the school psychologist, is called into a meeting for consultation. Your supervisee and the principal are aware of the fact that this child was recently diagnosed with Tourette's Disorder. The parents are extremely sensitive about maintaining strict confidentiality and do not want their daughter's condition disclosed-even to her teacher. *What are the ethical issues? What steps should be taken?*

EVALUATION

It is essential to determine a means to provide formative and summative evaluation of supervisees' consultation skills. Because supervisors have an ethical responsibility to inform their supervisees about the methods of evaluation which will be used to monitor progress (Pope & Vasquez, 1998), it is necessary to determine evaluation methods in the very early stages of the supervisory relationship.

One obvious way to evaluate the success of consultation efforts is to assess client change. Such measurement of progress is a part of the consultation process. However, it is far more difficult to determine change in the consultee or the system. Despite such inherent difficulty, it is possible to gather some objective and subjective data. The following questions might be investigated: (a) are the interventions being applied as agreed, resulting in treatment integrity? (b) are appointments regularly kept? (c) are consultation sessions active interchanges of ideas and information? Examination of such data as part of supervision is invaluable and can assist the supervisee in guiding the consultation and its supervision.

In addition, the evaluation of consultation supervision requires that the supervisee and supervisor assess the effectiveness of the supervision process. This requires that the supervisee and supervisor analyze the course of consultation relative to supervisory interventions on specific cases. It also requires that the supervisor and supervisee analyze the supervisee's progress in developing consultation skills over time.

In conclusion, the supervision of consultation offers an important and unique way to further the cause of students, teachers, and supervisees. Expansive in scope and demanding of considerable expertise, supervision of consultation is particularly rewarding on both personal and professional levels.

When school psychologists personally implement treatment programs they are conducting direct interventions. Examples of direct interventions include counseling (individual, group, crisis intervention), the implementation of behavioral management plans and functional behavior interventions, specific skill training (e.g. study skills, progressive relaxation), parent training and support groups, and prevention programs. Direct interventions may address specific identified issues (e.g., children dealing with divorce or chronic illness) or be prevention-oriented (e.g., "friendship groups" for students new to the school). Usually direct interventions are implemented in face-to-face meetings, but sometimes they are provided from a distance by using the telephone or Internet.

Types of direct interventions, along with their implications for supervision, will be reviewed in this chapter. To develop a framework, general supervisory considerations that affect all direct services will first be presented. Different models of direct service delivery commonly employed in schools will then be considered, and specific and useful supervision strategies described.

GENERAL CONSIDERATIONS

When deciding upon direct intervention strategies and developing appropriate supervision methods, a supervisor must consider the following factors:

- The nature of the referral question, problems addressed, and student characteristics including age, gender, ethnicity, and developmental level;
- Knowledge, experience, and theoretical orientation of both the supervisor and supervisee, as well as the level of supervision required, relative to the severity of the problem and the development of the supervisee;
- The prevailing resources and expectations of teachers, parents, administrators, and other professionals;
- Ethical considerations;
- Intervention plan development;
- Methods and frequency of evaluating progress; and
- Timing and process of termination.

Considering the nature of the referring problem

Summarizing the considerations relevant to all referral problems is far beyond the scope of this book. Fortunately, a number of references summarize research on effective treatment for various issues. These references, including *Best Practices in School Psychology III* (Thomas & Grimes, 1995), *Interventions for Achievement and Behavior Problems* (Stoner, Shinn, & Walker, 1991), *The Pre-referral Intervention Manual* (McCarney, 1988), and *Children's Needs II: Development, Problems, and Alternatives* (Bear, Minke, & Thomas, 1997), summarize an enormous amount of information regarding the treatment of many issues. Among others, covered topics include: ADHD, anger, biracial identity development, bullying, classroom management, depression, eating disorders, math difficulties, reading disorders, selective mutism, suicide, social skills, violence, and writing difficulties.

These references, and others, should be on the bookshelf of every school psychologist and referred to frequently. Supervisors should ensure that supervisees read relevant information before developing any treatment plan or attending supervisory sessions.

Considering the knowledge and experience of the supervisee

Because the developmental level of the supervisee necessarily determines supervisory methodology and techniques, effective supervisors must be competent in addressing skill levels ranging from novice to expert. Practicum students and interns, for example, require particular vigilance, and supervisors must have access to raw data such as audiotapes and direct observation. Supervision of direct interventions at this stage usually has an instructional, didactic focus (Ronnestad & Skovholt, 1993). Cases must be chosen carefully and the welfare of the student/client is always of paramount importance. Early career professionals should not be encouraged to engage in "high stakes" counseling activities (e.g., suicidal threats) without considerable support and monitoring.

Instead, consistent with the principles of developmentally-sensitive supervision, new practitioners may be more comfortable with activities requiring concrete, specific techniques for which didactic guidance is usually most appreciated. The assignment of professional activities that recognize these needs (e.g., facilitating "friendship groups" or dealing with less complex student adjustment issues) is appropriate. With experience, the emerging counselor "is less method bound and is concerned primarily with investing and using his/her own personality in the therapy work. Developing insight and differentiating personal reactions from client realities are recurring struggles in the learning process" (Scott, 1995, p. 4). With ever-increasing experience, the school psychologist is able to adopt a more egalitarian, non-hierarchical relationship with the supervisor until, finally, an independent level of functioning, and self-supervision, is achieved (Knoff, 1986; Scott, 1995).

Every supervisee should have reference books regarding intervention techniques. In addition to those mentioned previously, there are many references with detailed information regarding specific approaches to treatment. For example, Egan (1990) provides detailed information regarding cognitive-behaviorally based counseling, covering the entire process from developing the counseling relationship to helping clients construct the future, commit to agendas, develop strategies for action, formulate and choose plans, and put strategies to work. Cormier and Cormier (1985) discuss processes in cognitive behavioral counseling and also include chapters on techniques such as systematic desensitization, relaxation techniques, self-management strategies, and management of resistance. There are many sources that address the treatment of particular issues in greater depth, such as Stark's (1990) book on the treatment of childhood depression, Poland's (1989) book on suicide, and Nastasi and DeZoll's (1994) book on school based treatments for children of alcoholics. Even the most experienced supervisees will need to occasionally refresh their memories regarding effective procedures.

Considering the needs and expectations of the teacher, administrators, and school

The nature and extent of direct services are largely dictated by the settings in which they occur, and no single model of direct service delivery is appropriate. In addition to student needs, the effective supervisor must also assess and address the needs of the supervisee, teachers, parents, administrators, and school district. Furthermore, he or she must ensure that the staff school psychologists have skills that are congruent with the needs of the system. For example, a school psychologist extensively trained in long-term psychodynamic therapy may be a poor match for an elementary school wanting to establish time-limited parent groups.

The size of the school, the needs of the student population, the explicit job description, and the availability of other resources combine to dictate specific direct service needs. These variables similarly define the functional role of the school psychologist. For example, a school psychologist working in a large, suburban high school may share responsibilities for mental health services with counselors and social workers, whereas a geographically isolated, rural practitioner in a small elementary school may need to fulfill multiple, generalist roles. Supervisory roles are correspondingly diverse.

Supervising direct service delivery by school psychologists can be further complicated by the fact that mental health services in the schools are often offered by members of other related professions. For example, nurses offer health oriented prevention services, school adjustment counselors facilitate groups, and school social workers conduct family therapy. This has two consequences for supervisors of school psychologists. First, many supervisors also supervise non-school psychologists providing direct services such as counselors and social workers (Hunley et al., in press) and thus supervise individuals trained in disciplines and traditions other than school psychology. This requires that they become familiar with these disciplines and traditions and obtain peer supervision. Second, supervisees need supervisors' support in recognizing and dealing with complications ensuing from overlapping roles.

Ethical and legal issues

Supervisors must vigilantly keep abreast of district, state, and federal standards regarding the delivery of direct interventions. Despite diverse techniques and theoretical orientations, the same ethical guidelines govern the supervision of direct service delivery. When providing direct services, two specific ethical/legal issues are of particular importance: informed consent and confidentiality.

Informed consent. Both legally and ethically, parents of school-age children have a clearly defined right to determine whether their child participates in school-based psychological services (Jacob-Timm & Hartshorne, 1998). School psychologists must obtain parental consent for treatment and maintain a permanent, written record of such consent in the child's confidential records. Parents must be fully informed about the nature and intent of any direct interventions undertaken in the schools and the child should also be kept informed about treatment goals and methods. Although children are not legally autonomous in their right to initiate or deny psychological treatment, it is clinically and ethically sound to involve them and to obtain their assent for treatment.

Ethical Dilemma 10-1

A school psychologist has been hired through regular education funds to provide counseling and consultation services on a full-time basis at an elementary school. In order to overcome the delays and hassles associated with obtaining permission for service, he sent a letter to all parents indicating that individual and group counseling is now available to all students. He requested that parents notify him if they wished to discuss such services prior to any individual contact with their children. *Is this psychologist acting ethically? What should you, as his supervisor, do?*

Issues of parental permission can be quite complex with adolescents under the age of 18. For example, when high school students self-refer for counseling, they may do so with the specific request that their parents not be notified. Prudent practice dictates that the school psychologist interview the student initially to determine the severity and nature of the presenting problems. Decisions about how to proceed can then be made. The right of minors to seek treatment without parental consent varies

155

with local statutes and state laws, but is generally limited to specific medical concerns (Jacob-Timm & Hartshorne, 1998). Therefore, it is essential for supervisors to be knowledgeable about applicable laws and to ensure supervisees' adherence.

Ethical dilemma 10-2

One of your supervisees is assigned full time to the local high school. He is twenty years younger than the school's guidance counselors. The students consider him relatively "cool" and are self-referring for counseling in large numbers. Generally, he meets with a self-referred student once to assess the situation, and then has the student obtain written parental permission before continuing with additional sessions. In a recent supervision session he indicated that one self-referred student revealed serious personal problems which clearly require counseling either in or outside of school. However, she adamantly refuses to approach her parents for permission or to allow the school psychologist to call them. She does not appear to be a danger to herself or others, and, as far as the supervisee can determine, is not being abused. *What are the ethical issues? What should be done?*

Intern supervisors have an ethical obligation to inform parents when a trainee is providing direct services. Universities and agencies often provide specific disclosure forms for this purpose. As noted by Bernard and Goodyear (1998), "any attempt to obscure the status of a supervisee may expose both supervisee and supervisor to civil suits alleging fraud, misrepresentation, deceit, and lack of informed consent" (p. 185).

Confidentiality. Supervisors are also responsible for ensuring that supervisees explain the limits of confidentiality during the initial meetings

with parents and students in an open, clear manner (Jacob-Timm & Hartshorne, 1998). When considering the demands of law and ethics, it is important to remember that school psychologists are often viewed differently than licensed psychologists in their right to maintain student confidentiality (Jacob-Timm & Hartshorne, 1998).

Both parents and students should know that three situations may obligate the school psychologist to break confidentiality: (1) parental permission for release of information, (2) "duty to protect" provisions, such as danger to self or others, and, (3) mandated legal testimony (Jacob-Timm & Hartshorne, 1998). An essential component of orienting new school psychologists, including interns, is informing them of methods to handle these situations when they arise.

Ethical dilemma 10-3

Parents of a 16 year old boy signed permission for counseling sessions on a form that indicated that confidentiality would be maintained unless there was a danger to self or others. The father, however, feels that this restriction does not apply to him and calls your supervisee frequently to ask questions regarding the boy's progress. The boy is angry at his father regarding a number of issues, but does not want the school psychologist to discuss these issues with the father. Your supervisee is uncertain about what to say to the father, feeling conflicted between wanting to respect the boy's wishes and being open in an attempt to help the father and son resolve their conflicts. *What are the ethical dilemmas? What steps should be taken?*

In addition, when staff school psychologists are using supervisory techniques that are intrusive (such as videotapes, audiotapes, and direct observation), parents should be informed and written records of their permission obtained.

When obtaining such parental permission, it is important to clarify the nature and purpose of supervision so parents fully understand why and how information about their child will be shared. Effective supervisors ensure that this occurs by including the limits of confidentiality in the initial interview questionnaire and the standard permission form. As an example, a sample *Intern Permission Statement* is attached at the end of this chapter.

One of the most difficult situations concerning confidentiality arises when instances of child abuse, whether sexual, physical, and/or emotional, arises during counseling sessions. It is essential that supervisors of school psychologists be knowledgeable and vigilant in following both legal and ethical dictates. Statutes regarding the reporting of abuse must be honored within the appropriate time frames and with the appropriate written follow-up. Supervisors must assure that their supervisees are aware that law supercedes the maintenance of confidentiality and that in school-based counseling the right of "privileged communication" cannot be typically invoked.

Intervention plan development

As discussed in Chapter 3, conceptualizing the case and developing an appropriate treatment plan is essential. In developing a direct intervention treatment plan, the supervisee defines the problem, collects data, delineates strategies, generates hypotheses, and develops an implementation plan. The *Treatment Plan Development Form*, found at the end of this chapter, can be used to facilitate this process. This form can be used both to facilitate supervisory sessions and as a tool in assessing supervisee progress.

Methods and frequency of evaluating client and supervisee progress

The fundamental question in evaluating client progress is whether or not the goals and objectives of the treatment plan have been met.

Consequently, considerable supervision time should be spent helping supervisees develop an adequate treatment plan, including evaluative methods. Client progress can be measured by observable behaviors, self-report measures of internal states such as anxiety and depression, or student outcome measures such as school attendance, grades, and achievement test scores. In determining which evaluation methods to use, care should be taken to ensure that these methods are congruent with both the referring problem and the selected intervention strategies.

General methods to evaluate supervisee progress are delineated in Chapter 6. In addition, when supervisors evaluate the progress of supervisees providing direct interventions, they should evaluate progress in specific, discrete skills. For example, supervisors should review raw data provided in observations or tape recordings to assess the supervisee's skills in developing a counseling relationship, generating hypotheses, evaluating the process and content of sessions, developing treatment plans, and implementing interventions. In addition, they should assess the growth of supervisees across time by comparing a sequence of treatment plan development forms, case process notes, and written treatment plans.

Timing and process of termination

Methods of terminating direct interventions vary according to the type of intervention. Some direct interventions, such as parent training groups, have a termination date determined at the onset. Most direct interventions, however, have an indeterminate termination point, and termination occurs over a period of sessions in which the client's progress is reviewed. In the counseling literature, discussions on termination focus on the extent to which the client's issues have been resolved and termination is expected to occur naturally when evaluations suggest sufficient progress (Egan, 1990). In this

157

era of managed care, school psychologists are often better positioned than psychologists practicing in the private sector to postpone termination until adequate client progress has occurred.

On the other hand, it is common for children to change schools and thus move from one school psychologist to another before problems are adequately resolved. Rather than termination, this should be considered bridging from one treatment provider to another. Bridging occurs when the child moves from one school to another, particularly from elementary to junior high, or from the junior high to the high school. While sharing case process notes and treatment plans is essential, many students greatly benefit from bridging in which the "old" school psychologist personally introduces the student to the "new" school psychologist. A session in which both psychologists meet with the student and review progress and future goals and objectives is particularly helpful.

SUPERVISION OF DIRECT INTERVENTIONS

Counseling

Supervising counseling of children is impacted by the following unique factors:

- they usually do not seek help voluntarily;
- most do not have an understanding of the nature of the therapeutic experience;
- children's cognitive and verbal skills are still developing; and,
- children, in contrast to adults, are more influenced by and dependent upon the family and school environments (Clarizio & McCoy, 1983 cited in Tharinger & Stafford, 1995).

In addition, providing counseling in schools can be challenging due to limitations on the school psychologist's time, insufficient privacy, and the demands of the school day on the child.

On the other hand, school psychologists benefit from the unique aspects of counseling children in schools including immediate, easy access to teachers, peers, and the classroom. This access results in readily available feedback about progress, observable social relationships and comparison groups, and convenient long-term follow-up (Tharinger & Stafford, 1995).

Tharinger & Koranek (1990) define counseling as "ongoing interactions between a mental health professional and a child who has sought, or for whom someone serving as his or her representative has sought, help for a particular problem or set of problems" (p. 407). Counseling is provided to alleviate the distress of both the child and the referring adult, and to improve the child's functioning by facilitating change in child and their environments including the family and school systems.

No specific theoretical model appears to be singularly adopted by school psychologists since school psychologists emerge from various training programs with different theoretical orientations, have unique professional roles within their systems, practice in highly individualized ways, and hold different visions of the future of school psychology (Tharinger & Stafford, 1995). Consequently, school psychologists acquire generic knowledge and generic counseling skills and then attempt to integrate these models and skills into their particular work setting (Ronnestad & Skovholt, 1993).

A school psychologist's adopted counseling model usually reflects the practitioner's underlying theory of what factors support growth and change in the individual. In an extension of supervisors' developing awareness of their own underlying beliefs, as discussed previously, an important supervision task is to assist practitioners in developing an awareness of their own underlying beliefs and theories. Differences between supervisor and supervisee should be explored and discussed.

158

Individual Counseling. In today's schools, mental health needs are diverse and plentiful. With the many demands facing school psychologists, it can become difficult to provide individual services for all but a few children (e.g., seriously emotionally disturbed children who have counseling written into their Individualized Educational Plans). Hence, children who are seen individually often present with moderate to severe problems. To serve them well, it is important to have a "treatment plan" developed when the counseling begins and to monitor implementation throughout the period of service delivery.

One such model, proposed by Tharinger and Stafford (1995) is provided in Table 10-1.

Table 10-1
School Counseling Model

Stage 1: Assess appropriateness of referral for school-based counseling.

Stage 2: Plan for counseling and prepare goals.

Stage 3: Begin counseling and establish a working relationship.

Stage 4: Implement the plan for change.

Stage 5: Continue counseling and adjust the plan for change.

Stage 6: Plan for termination.

Stage 7: Evaluate effectiveness.

Psychological counseling is often provided students as part of the Individual Education Plan (IEP), particularly when the team has judged that the student is in need of and will benefit from special education services. As is the case throughout the IEP, counseling objectives must be clearly defined, exact, and measurable. A sample goal with objectives and evaluation techniques is included in Case Study 10-1.

Case study 10-1 Sample IEP Goal

Goal: Improve impulse inhibition and decrease talking out in class

Objectives:

1. In the individual counseling setting, Joey will demonstrate the ability to use positive self-talk to gain control over his talking out impulses.

2. In the group counseling setting, Joey will covertly use positive self-talk, and overtly use a cognitive behavioral strategy (visual cueing), to inhibit talking out.

3. Joey will decrease talking-out behaviors in class.

Schedule of direct services:

Weekly individual sessions with a school psychologist lasting 30 minutes. Weekly group counseling sessions with a school psychologist lasting 60 minutes.

Evaluation procedures:

Case process notes from individual sessions. Log of talking out incidents in group counseling. Weekly memo to his teachers, asking to note progress. Monthly observation to assess frequency of talking out.

Counseling techniques. A wide variety of different counseling techniques and interventions are available, far beyond the scope of this volume. According to surveys of research, the appropriate counseling technique varies with the referral problem. For example, anxiety and depression are often responsive to cognitive behavioral interventions, while schizophrenics are most in need of case management and problem solving strategies. As stated previously, summaries of strategies are readily available and all supervisors and supervisees should obtain and use resources such as Bear et al. (1997), Cormier and Cormier, (1985), Egan (1990), Mead (1990), and Stoner et al. (1991).

159

Supervisors should require that supervisees consider student, therapist, and external variables when conceptualizing and deciding interventions and techniques. Student variables include age, mental health needs, cultural and ethnicity factors, gender, and the presenting problem. For example, the development and cognitive level of the child affects choice of technique: play therapy may be appropriate for some youngsters but group counseling preferred for others. Therapist variables include experience, orientation, availability, and time. External variables include constraints of time, space availability, materials available, and expectations of the referring person. Good supervisors assist practitioners to achieve the optimal equilibrium among all variables.

Group Counseling. Group counseling is often an optimal, preferred means of providing mental health services in the schools. Given the time constraints and multiple job demands of contemporary school psychologists, groups provide an economical way to service many children concurrently. In addition to their efficiency, school-based counseling groups offer an effective way to address the presenting problems commonly found among school-aged children. Therefore, supervisors must develop specific skills and methods to support supervisees as they facilitate groups. Some of the group-related issues that must be addressed by practitioners and by supervisors of school psychologists are:

- What is the age/grade range of participants and how are they selected for inclusion in the group? (It is best to select group members who are close to one another in terms of both age and counseling concerns.)
- What size should the group be? (Experience suggests that more than eight members in a school-based group can be unwieldy, but the optimal size of the group will vary with the ages of members and the targeted therapeutic issues.)
- Who should facilitate the group? (A practicum student may be capable of inde-

pendently leading an elementary social skills group, but may not be sufficiently skilled to deal independently with seriously disturbed high school students. Training needs cannot supercede client needs.)
- What are the rules of the group regarding time, place, duration, confidentiality, attendance, goals, etc.? How does the supervisee ensure that these rules are followed?
- What theory underlies the group topics and activities? (As suggested by Claiborn, Kerr, and Strong (1990) the "counselor's theory of group work determines what the counselor attends to in the group, and what language he or she uses to describe it" (p. 713).
- How are goals determined and how is goal attainment measured? How will termination occur?

It is important to determine in advance which technique will be used to supervise group counseling. As Bernard and Goodyear (1998) state, the effective supervisor maintains a balance between challenging and supporting the supervisee. When appropriate, one obvious, effective, and efficient means of supervision is the observation of the group. When this is contraindicated, alternative methods must be agreed upon with both the supervisee and group members.

Ethical dilemma 10-4

After weeks of preparation and care in obtaining appropriate parental permission, your intern begins a fourth-grade boys' social-skills group. Although she maintains that the group is going well, you immediately sense that she is nervous about the group and dreads meeting with them. After a few weeks, a significant conflict between the intern and the group seems to have developed and one day it developed into a confrontation. You passed by the door and observed her in a shouting match with several of the boys about whether they have to stay in the group. *What are the ethical conflicts? What should be done?*

Crisis intervention. Supervising school psychologists must prepare for crisis situations from two perspectives. First, supervisors are responsible for the quality of the crisis intervention services provided by supervisees. Second, as administrative leaders in the district, it is likely that others will seek guidance from supervising school psychologists in developing effective crisis intervention plans.

Crisis teams have become a valuable part of schools' mental health response teams in an era of increasing violence (Poland & Pitcher, 1990). Moreover, crisis response teams incorporate community members and agencies as participants. School psychologists are natural liaisons to external agencies and other constituents. Effective supervisors should become familiar with the literature and ensure that the district is prepared for all eventualities. Since school psychologists are well-versed in consultation skills and models, they are especially well-suited to fulfill such positions.

Ethical dilemma 10-5

A school psychologist has obtained certification as an instructor in non-violent crisis intervention and thus provides ongoing professional development for district personnel. With school personnel who are unlikely to need to employ specific physical interventions, she limits the training to verbal and non-verbal de-escalation techniques. With school personnel who are likely to be witness to physical altercations, including assistant principals and paraprofessionals working in programs for students with behavior disorders, she recommends appropriate techniques for de-escalating physical aggression. As part of this training, she appropriately forewarns participants of physical activity and requires that they sign injury waivers and provide evidence of a recent physical exam before participating. One day when she arrives to conduct the training session, one of the attendees insists on participating but refuses to sign the waiver. *What are the legal and ethical issues? What steps should be taken?*

Functional behavioral intervention

Functional behavioral analysis is used to monitor students' progress in addition to serving as an assessment tool. It has emerged as a federally-sanctioned means to provide efficient, cost-effective, and purposeful interventions. In an era of increasing accountability, it is easy to see that methods that are scientifically based, quantifiable, and research-based have emerged to the forefront. After a functional behavior analysis has been conducted (see chapter 11), the school psychologist helps the child substitute a more acceptable behavior for the inappropriate behavior through the use of coaching, cognitive behavior therapy, behavior management plans, modification of the antecedents, or modification of the environment.

In this process, there are several stages with which supervisees are likely to have the most difficulty. First, beginning school psychologists tend to have difficulty generating multiple hypotheses, particularly regarding the antecedents and consequences of the behaviors. Another area that frequently poses difficulty is the collection of data during both the assessment and intervention stages. Meaningful data is collected in a rigorously scientific manner: such data collection requires that the supervisee have the ability to define behaviors discretely and commit the necessary time. Finally, supervisees need guidance in appropriately choosing and applying interventions. The supervisor must provide support during the inevitable intervention modification that occurs throughout the intervention process; supervisees often do not realize that the behavioral intervention as first designed is rarely the intervention that is finally effective.

Obviously, supervisees who have been previously trained in a behaviorist tradition need far less intense supervision than supervisees without such training. Group supervision and peer consultations are particularly effective methods to improve skills in functional behavioral interventions.

Specific skills training

School psychologists can provide specific skills training in a broad range of areas, such as relax-

161

ation training, social skills training, peer mediation, and study skills. Many appropriate strategies are summarized in Thomas and Grimes (1990) and Bear et al. (1997).

Supervision of school psychologists who are teaching children a specific skill follows the same procedure as supervision of counseling. Again, the supervisor considers the nature of the referral question and student characteristics; his own knowledge, experience, and theoretical orientation; supervisee knowledge, experience, and theoretical orientation; expectations of parents, teachers, and administration; ethical considerations; plan development; methods of evaluation; and termination. Often beginning school psychologists greatly benefit from observing their supervisor model the actual implementation of specific skills training, particularly if they have not had the opportunity to observe such implementation as practicum students or interns.

Parent training and support groups

Running parent training and support groups can be an interesting and gratifying activity for school psychologists. Successful parent groups provide support for beleaguered parents and facilitate positive relationships with parents that prevent future conflicts with school personnel. Parents are particularly appreciative of groups that supply them with information. For example, groups for parents of junior high school students appreciate a curriculum that focuses on parenting teenagers, and groups for parents of preschool special education students appreciate information about negotiating the special education system.

In addition to the general considerations discussed at the beginning of this chapter, the initiation of parent groups raises unique issues. Determining a meeting time for parent groups is often problematic. Parents are very busy and find it difficult to make time to attend sessions on an ongoing basis. To counteract this, it is helpful to advertise the group as time-limited, perhaps six to

eight sessions. It is best, when time permits, to offer both midday and evening sessions. When midday sessions are offered, it is helpful to have them at lunchtime and enlist the assistance of student babysitters for parents without access to childcare.

Another issue specific to running parent groups is the intimidation felt by school psychologists inexperienced in this activity. Consequently, considerable supervisor support is required. Co-leading a group is an effective method for dealing with the anxiety of the inexperienced supervisee, although care must be taken to encourage the supervisee to take an active leadership role. Young school psychologists who are not parents themselves often find their expertise challenged by parents. Before the group is begun, the supervisor should help the supervisee develop a ready response to such challenges.

A number of parent-training curriculum programs exist that school psychologists can use as a foundation for group session content. Some have videotapes of parent-child scenarios enacted in vivid role-plays to which the parents can respond. Many of them also provide a parent manual, which can be helpful. However, it is our experience that faithfully following a pre-published program is less effective than choosing particular components based upon the needs of the group participants. Therefore, it is helpful to survey group members at the beginning of the sessions to ascertain expectations and preferred content.

Prevention programs

Yet another manifestation of direct school psychological services is the development and implementation of prevention programs. Prevention programs "seek to change the incidence of new cases by intervening proactively before disorders occur" (Hightower, Johnson, & Haffey, 1995, p. 311). In brief, steps in implementing a prevention program include: identifying needs; reviewing extant prevention programs; introducing the program to the system by engaging in professional small talk and making the initial presentation; determining aspects of the program (size, participants, communication system, support structure, integration into the school structure); and conducting an evaluation of the program (Hightower et al., 1995).

In implementing a prevention program, a high quality needs assessment is critical. This ensures that the prevention program is responding to a reality-based need and is positioned to obtain administrative support. As described by Nagle (1995), a needs assessment involves a determination of a gap between a current condition and a desired state. The level of analysis can be as broad as the entire district or as narrow as a classroom.

Steps in conducting a needs assessment are the same as in assessing a child's needs: identifying the problem, establishing an evaluation team, collecting qualitative and quantitative data, and recommending program modifications. The difference lies in the level of analysis and the sources of data. Rather than individually presented psychometric instruments, a needs analysis employs survey questions, interviews, and group assessment tools. Brainstorming is often used to generate possible solutions to identified problems (Nagle, 1995).

Supervisors can assist supervisees regarding the development of an effective prevention program. In addition to supervising the needs assessment, supervisors will likely need to assist in presenting and obtaining administrative support for the program, particularly in negotiating administrative bureaucracy.

Supervisees implementing a prevention program will require substantial emotional and consultative support throughout the implementation. Hightower et al. (1995) recommend developing a support network, "defined as groups, the smallest group being two people, who are able to support, encourage, inspire, assist, reassure, and strengthen each other in the face of day-to-day operations and during occasional, and even formidable, complications" (p. 319).

Finally, supervisors will be invaluable in helping design and institute the evaluation of the prevention program. The reader is referred to Chapter 13 for a summary of this procedure.

Computer-assisted interventions

Computer-assisted interventions have been found to be effective in interviewing and in treating specific problems (Carr, 1991; Reynolds et al., 1985; Sturges, 1998, Wagman & Kerber, 1984). Some research studies have found computer assisted interviewing and therapy to be as or more effective than human interviewing or therapy (Kobak, Reynolds, & Griest, 1994; Lewis, 1994). For example, computer interviews successfully predicted 70% of inpatient suicide attempts, compared with the 35% accuracy rate of human clinicians (Gustafson et al., 1977). Computer-assisted counseling has been found to have outcomes equivalent to standard career counseling (Stevens & Lundberg, 1998), cognitive rehabilitation (Skillbeck, 1991), cognitive-behavioral group treatment (Dolezal-Wood, Belar, & Snibbe, 1998), depression (Selmi, Klein, Greist, Sorrell, & Erdman, 1990), parent training (Armstrong, Munneke, Sim, Purtan, & McGrath, 1995), phobias (Carr, Ghosh, & Marks, 1988), and weight loss (Burnett, Taylor, & Agras, 1985). It has also been used successfully as an intervention tool for children with physical disabilities, communication disorders, learning disabilities, attention deficit disorders, and social skill deficits (Douglas, 1991).

It should be noted, however, that a psychologist using software maintains professional and legal responsibility for all treatment effects, good and bad (Harvey & Carlson, 1999). In addition, there are the ever-present questions regarding confidentiality of information transmitted electronically when computer networking systems are used. Therefore, if school psychologists adopt these approaches, their supervisors should ensure that they use these applications with extreme care and only to augment face-to-face interactions.

SAMPLE INTERN PERMISSION STATEMENT

I, the undersigned (parent/legal guardian of a child under 18, or a person over 18) give _____ permission to provide psychological treatment to my child _____, date of birth _____. This treatment will occur (frequency and duration) _____ and include the following types of service.

The goals of treatment are to:

I understand that _____ is training as a school psychologist and is being supervised by _____ using observation, tapes of sessions, and discussion. I understand that all tapes will be destroyed immediately after the supervisor reviews them, and that all information will be kept strictly confidential. However, I also understand that confidentiality will be broken if legally mandated, such as if my child appears to be a danger to self or others.

_____   _____

Signature   Date

Treatment Plan Development Form

1. **VISION:** Problem definition
   - Write the desired outcome defined by child, parent, and teacher.
   - What behaviors would each person like increased?
   - What behaviors would each person like decreased?
   - Write down the values, attitudes, or automatic responses that link the current status to the desired outcome.
   - Check that everyone agrees on definitions.

2. **ASSESSMENT**
   - What are the data?
   - What tools (i.e. a journal) could be used to get additional data?
   - Are there patterns in the data?
   - Can the problem be solved by techniques already in the psychologist's repertoire?
   - If not, how could appropriate techniques be acquired?

3. **STRATEGY**
   - Have you seen the problem or a similar problem before?
   - Do you know of a tested treatment for this or a similar problem or a method from another program that has similar desired outcomes?
   - Can the problem be restated or redefined to be more general or more specific, leading to alternative treatment strategies?
   - Can the desired outcomes, or conditions, be modified?

4. **STRUCTURE**
   - Develop hypotheses.
     - What variables control the client's current behavior?
     - What variable may control the desired outcome behaviors?
     - How can the client change these variables?
     - How can teachers, parents, or peers change these variables?
     - Are there other contributing variables?
     - What new hypotheses might they suggest?
     - What conceptual framework are you using to tie the data together?
     - Are there other conceptual frameworks that fit?
     - What hypotheses do they suggest?
     - What theoretical principles are you using?
     - What other theories might be used?
     - What hypotheses do they suggest?
     - What hypotheses can you eliminate based on your current data?
     - What additional data do you need to eliminate other hypotheses?
     - Does this suggest an intervention or series of interventions?
   - Write all possible hypotheses.
     - Write a treatment plan
     - Write a proposed treatment plan with enough detail so that another psychologist could take over treatment in your absence.
     - Indicate criteria for success, criteria for failure, plans for gathering data and deciding treatment changes, and an estimate of time necessary to reach desired outcome.

5. **IMPLEMENTATION**
   - Check whether the client finds each step related to desired outcome. Check that the steps are appropriate in size.
   - Check that formative data does not suggest altering the treatment.

6. **EVALUATION**
   - Does the client think the desired outcome has been reached?
   - Do parents and teachers think the desired outcome has been reached?
   - Does data indicate that treatment made a difference?
   - Can you use the same result or method for some other problem?
   - Have the supervisee's skills improved?
   - Have the supervisor's skills improved?
   - (Adapted from Mead, 1990)

165

166

Throughout the history of school psychology, conducting psychoeducational assessments has constituted a major job function (Curtis, Hunley, Walker, & Baker, 1999; Fisher, Jenkins, & Crumbley, 1986; Reschly, Genshaft, & Binder, 1987; Reschly & Wilson, 1995). Despite the many critics of assessment (Ysseldyke & Christenson, 1989), assessment courses continue to dominate graduate training programs in psychology (Rupert, Kozlowski, Hoffman, Daniels, & Piette, 1999), and the role of assessment has been and remains strong (Martin, 1994; Smith 1984; Thomas, 1999). Assessment and diagnosis remain critical to the determination of disability, and subsequent receipt of special education services (Sabatino et al., 1993).

Despite the many controversial aspects of assessment, when properly conducted, interpreted, and utilized, good assessment practices not only diagnose disabilities but also substantially benefit children's educational programs. Assessment addresses academic, cognitive, and emotional/behavioral issues in guiding diagnoses and providing the foundation for remediation. Furthermore, ongoing, dynamic assessment (e.g., curriculum-based measurement) provides invaluable direction and feedback regarding the efficacy of chosen interventions.

Assessments in schools cross multiple domains. In the course of their work, school psychologists appraise a broad range of both student and programmatic variables. In the course of one day, a practitioner might assess math skills and functional behavior in the morning, social skills during lunch, and systemic issues in the afternoon. An assessment's subject can be an individual student, an entire classroom, a specific program, or the school system as a whole. Moreover, assessment can be of a traditional nature (i.e., individual cognitive and academic testing) or more contemporary (i.e., alternative assessment, portfolio assessment, and/or curriculum-based). In sum, it is likely that a major part of our professional identity as school psychologists will continue to remain solidly intertwined with the assessment role (Alfonso & Pratt, 1997; Fagan & Wise, 1994; Thomas, 1999).

Whereas assessment constitutes a major component of the school psychologist's role, effective supervision in this area is essential. Supervising assessment consists of much more than ensuring that tests are administered properly and reviewing psychological reports. The effective supervisor of school psychologists addresses all activities within the assessment process. As described by Knoff (1986), these include:

1. The ability to objectively use knowledge and skill to benefit the referred student;
2. Application of a working knowledge of the theoretical and psychometric concepts behind the assessment processes;
3. Choosing appropriate assessment tools and methodologies in response to a specific referral;
4. Responding to issues of test bias, multicultural issues, and prejudice;
5. Skill in the technical administration, scoring, and interpretation of the tools and procedures;
6. The synthesis of results with other ecological and systemic data and school resources to determine intervention programs and appropriate placements;
7. The ability to generate comprehensive yet clearly written reports;
8. Interpersonal skills to interact with the child, parents, and school personnel in assessment interpretation; and
9. The ability to appropriately reach assessment conclusions, determine program recommendations, and implement follow-up procedures.

167

GENERAL CONSIDERATIONS

Benefiting students

As is true in all aspects of school psychology, in assessment the child is the primary client and all activities must be conducted with the child's benefit in mind. To this end, supervisors have an obligation to teach and model an approach that helps supervisees become exemplary consumers and administrators of assessment tools and processes. Ethical issues most prominent in educational assessment are: (a) equal protection, (b) due process, (c) the right to privacy, and (d) competence. Each of these will be briefly discussed.

To meet the ethical mandate for due process, school psychologists assure that individuals are informed of any pending action that might deprive them of liberty and/or property. Furthermore, individuals have the right to participate in such decisions. In educational practice, this means that students (and their parents) have the right to know when/if testing will take place and the potential ramifications of such testing. Furthermore, parents have the right to request a fair hearing when test results may produce a change in services or in eligibility for such services.

Additionally, school psychologists are ethically bound to adhere to laws and legal statutes. A number of components in the IDEA, and state adoptions of the IDEA, address issues relative to assessment. For example, to protect student's rights to a timely evaluation, school districts are mandated to adhere to timelines in the completion of assessments and supervisors are expected to ensure that their supervisees adhere to these timelines.

Ethical dilemma 11-1

A parent known as "difficult" finally signed permission for an evaluation after many hours of meetings. On the day the psychologist has set aside to conduct the evaluation, she arrives at the school to find a telephone message from the parent "withdrawing" permission. School personnel want the psychologist to pretend she did not get the message and go ahead with the testing. The school psychologist calls you in a panic for advice. *What should the school psychologist do?*

Ethical guidelines, as well as state and federal laws, govern the protection of privacy. Children cannot be tested without parental permission and results can be shared only with individuals who have a "need to know." Controversial ethical and legal issues have arisen regarding the concepts of privilege and confidentiality. Much of the recent conflict in this area relates to public (i.e., parental) access to protocols. Because this issue was addressed in Chapter 1, it will not be repeated at this time. However, it is essential that supervisors establish departmental policy and practice regarding the conflict between the laws and ethical principles that protect the rights of the children and their parents and those that protect copyright and test security.

Theoretical and psychometric concepts

A supervisor of school psychologists must address theoretical and psychometric concepts on a number of levels. At the most basic level, the supervisor must be aware of the theoretical and psychometric concepts of the psychometric instruments and the assessment of cognition and processing (e.g., both theories behind the Gc-Gf theory and behind the particular tests). At a more sophisticated level, the supervisor must know and address the theoretical and psychometric concepts inherent in disability diagnoses, particularly as they apply to practice.

Supervisors must be sensitive both to the theories underlying their own assessment procedures and methodologies and to the theories and psychometric concepts underlying their supervisees' assessment procedures and methodologies. As discussed in Chapter 3, when school psychologists conduct assessments they adhere to particular theories regarding the nature of and interaction among academic achievement, intelligence, and behavior and personality.

Supervisors' models of assessment impact their expectations for those they supervise. If supervisor and supervisee adhere to the same model, complications are minimal. However, because of the last decade's many changes in recommended assessment practices and theories, students are currently receiving training in theoretical and psychometric concepts differing markedly from the training received by their supervisors. Thus supervisors are likely to be asked to supervise the administration and interpretation of instruments based on theoretical models they did not encounter during their own graduate training. Therefore, it is imperative that supervisors continually update their knowledge of current theory and their skills in current instruments through professional development programs and formal coursework.

Formative vs. diagnostic assessment. Recently there has been a movement encouraging school psychologists to be involved in the formative evaluations of students, in contrast to diagnostic assessments, as characterized by curriculum based assessment (Shapiro, 1989, 1990), authentic assessment (Henning-Stout, 1994), and functional behavior assessment. In a formative evaluation, the function of the evaluation is to provide the student and teacher feedback on student progress so that remedial instructional activities can be prescribed and student learning improved.

One major issue in regard to standardized tests is that they provide little information that can reasonably guide future educational remediation. In an era of diminishing fiscal resources, there is a growing national concern about student achievement and the general efficacy of current special educational practice and policy (Graden, Zins, Curtis, & Cobb, 1989; Stainback & Stainback, 1989; Will, 1986).

This concern is accompanied by increasing consumer demands for teacher accountability and improved methods with which to assess and enhance students' performance (Algozzine & Ysseldyke, 1986; Fuchs & Fuchs, 1986). At the same time, the educational needs of the students found in a typical classroom are likely to be more varied than ever. As classrooms become populated by increasingly heterogeneous pupils with different learning styles, emotional needs, and socioeconomic backgrounds, it becomes essential for the classroom teacher to develop more effective instructional skills and methods. Meeting the varied needs of diverse learners is critically important.

Models of assessing academic functioning. There are two traditional models of assessing academic functioning: *criterion referenced* and *standardized assessment*. In *criterion referenced* testing the child is tested against set criteria and expected to attain a given degree of accuracy, regardless of peer performance or of test difficulty. Criterion referenced tests are most commonly used in classrooms, where a teacher designs tests based on the curriculum and the child is expected to know a certain percentage of the answers. When not using "a curve," the grading system is predetermined (with passing traditionally set at 70% accuracy). Current popular manifestations of this approach are high stakes tests implemented by state departments of education, in which children are required to demonstrate predetermined levels of perform-

169

ance before they are allowed to pass on to the next grade or graduate. If the test content does not match the educational experiences of the test takers, every child could potentially fail these tests.

Standardized testing compares a child with peers. Nationally standardized achievement tests (e.g. the Iowa Test of Basic Skills, the SAT-II, or the Wechsler Individual Achievement Test) rank a child's performance relative to the performance of peers on a sample of items presumed to reflect the curriculum. While these tests can be helpful in a general sense, if they do not reflect the schools curricula they are of little use in educational planning.

In contrast, *formative academic evaluations* are based on the concept that children should be assessed relative to the skills which they are expected to master in their specific curriculum. The development of curriculum-based measurement represents a shift from traditional assessment practices. It de-emphasizes the importance of standardized scores in favor of more meaningful, curriculum-based information. Teachers profit far more from knowing which phonemes a student has not mastered than from knowing his or her specific grade equivalent (Sabatino et al., 1993). Curriculum-based measurement effectively and efficiently guides prescriptive practice in the classroom. It measures mastery of specific curriculum learning tasks, and can link assessment to intervention by quickly identifying insufficient progress. Tindal (1989) states that "the data-based decision making perspective is the most important feature" of curriculum-based measurement (p.111). It is concerned with the both the assessment of treatment integrity (the extent to which an intervention is carried out as planned) and measures of student outcome.

Evidence regarding the effectiveness of formative evaluations such as curriculum based measurement is extremely strong, to the point that some educators feel that not using forma-

tive evaluations is unethical. Despite this reported effectiveness, many school psychologists and supervisors of school psychologists were not taught methods of formative assessment in their graduate programs and it appears to be a greatly underutilized methodology. Supervisors are likely to need to take responsibility to develop their own skills in this approach, as well as to monitor the practice of their supervisees. Therefore, a brief overview of these procedures, described in a number of readily available sources (Gickling & Rosenfield, 1995; Shapiro, 1989; Shinn, 1995), will be provided.

In curriculum based measurement, several probes for each subject area from the entire year's curriculum are developed and used repeatedly. The school psychologist, general education teacher, or special education teacher asks the child to read aloud a selection from his reading text for one minute, to complete as many math problems as possible in two minutes, to write for three minutes after thinking about a story starter for one minute, and/or take two minutes to spell a list of words. The reading, math, written expression, and spelling probes are taken from the regular curricula for the entire year. The child's score for each probe might be the number of words read correctly per minute, the number of numerals correctly generated in two minutes, the ratio of correct to incorrect words written for the writing sample, and/or the number of correct letter pairs in spelling (a space is assumed before and after the word, and _bat_ has five correct letter pairs: _b, ba, at, and t_). The child's skills are assessed weekly, and his scores are graphed and compared with a desired rate of skill acquisition. If the child is making less than satisfactory progress, teaching approaches and strategies are modified (Shapiro, 1989). For example, the pace of instruction might be altered, the material might be re-taught, or the method of instruction and presentation might be modified.

Curriculum based assessment (CBA) (Gickling & Rosenfield, 1995) also uses curriculum materials as an assessment tool. The assessment is conducted by selecting a task (such as reading a passage), assessing the ability to complete the task, matching assignments to instructional level and learning strategies, and implementing the instructional strategies in the classroom. A great advantage to CBA is that it can be used for any subject, including reading, social studies, science, and math. Core questions to be addressed when using CBA might be:

1. What does the student need to do in order to be successful within the curriculum?

2. What discrepancies exist between the outcomes anticipated by the teacher and the student's performance?

3. What knowledge and skills are needed for success with this curriculum? Which of these does the student already possess, and which are yet to be acquired?

4. What steps are being taken currently, and can be taken in the future, to match learning activities to the student's skills and learning needs?

5. Is classroom instruction currently being presented in a manner that maximizes this student's learning efficiency? To benefit the student, what modifications can be made in the following:
   - the amount of curriculum taught;
   - presentation;
   - requirements for specified instructional approaches;
   - requirements for examinations;
   - student strategies, practice, or approaches;
   - group size; group structure; and/or
   - teaching strategies?

6. How can student progress be regularly assessed, graphed, monitored, and used to modify instructional practice? (Gickling & Rosenfield, 1995; Sabatino et al., 1993).

Models of assessing cognition. For many years, school psychologists used a model of cognition assessment based on the Stanford-Binet or Wechsler definitions of intelligence, and this traditional psychometric model has been challenged vigorously (Sabatino et al., 1993). Interestingly, it can be argued that many of the criticisms are directed at more antiquated tests and assessment practices. As eloquently stated by Thorndike (1997), "the application and interpretation of test scores have changed more in the last 15 years than they did in the preceding 50, and to condemn current testing practice, as some critics do, on the basis of 20-year old evidence is to do tests and test users a great injustice" (p. 14).

Recently, new and revised theories of intelligence have emerged, have received increased attention and favor, and have affected the assessment of cognition. Importantly, some models of assessment proceed as if intelligence as we currently define it is irrelevant, and focus on discrete acquisition of academic skills as measured by curriculum based measurement. These theories include, among others, the Gf-Gc theory (Horn, 1991), information processing (Naglieri, 1997), multiple intelligences (Gardner, 1991), and learning potential (Feuerstein, 1979). These and other current theories are summarized in Flanagan, Genshaft, and Harrison (1997).

These new constructs have been accompanied by concerted efforts to construct cognitive assessment instruments which are based on theoretically sound, integrated models of human cognition. This proliferation of new and revised tests requires appropriate administration and new and different interpretation skills (Alfonso & Pratt, 1997). Not only the theories, but also the models of cognitive assessment are changing. Currently trained school psychologists are often using a cross-battery, integrative approach to assess intelligence (Flanagan & McGrew, 1997; McGrew & Flanagan, 1996).

171

Research-based developments in cognitive theory have also affected developments in the assessment of learning disabilities. For example, broader paradigms are emerging that regard learning difficulties as multi-faceted and heterogeneous. New models view learning difficulties within the context of multiple variables rather than as discrete processing deficits present in the child. Hence, accurate assessment of learning difficulties must consider the interaction of the child with the academic curricula, the classroom, and the family and social environment. For example, incorrect teaching approaches may lead to a reading deficit, but this should not be diagnosed as a learning disability.

Supervisors and practitioners are constantly faced with a barrage of emerging theories of cognitive processing and the new instruments that purportedly operationalize and measure them. Therefore, the goal of supervision should not be to teach a particular test or theory, but rather, to teach a methodology which supports future learning.

Models of assessing behavior and personality. The assessment of behavior and personality is multi-faceted, and encompasses the use of adaptive behavior scales, behavior observations, parent rating scales, projective techniques, self-report inventories, structured and semi-structured interviews, teacher rating scales, the use of DSM-IV diagnostic criteria, behavioral diagnosis, and the assessment of school and family context. As the reader is aware, each of these is based upon different theories, ranging from psychoanalytic to behavioral. Like the assessment of academic skills and cognition, the assessment of behavior and personality has changed in the past few years (Kamphaus & Frick, 1996). Projective techniques are viewed with less favor, behavioral assessment has been strengthened through psychometric advances in self-report and parent/teacher rating scales,

structured and semi-structured interview techniques are increasingly employed, and greater emphasis has been placed on considering the function of the child's behavior in the context where it occurs.

Functional behavior analysis is an example of the contextual analysis of behavior. The 1997 IDEA requirements have placed an important emphasis on the provision of functional behavioral analysis (FBA) in the schools. Now explicitly mandated under specified circumstances, FBA constitutes an important assessment activity. Therefore, effective supervisors must be well acquainted with both the nature and intent of FBA.

In addition to its assessment function which addresses the underlying purposes (i.e., functions) of specific behaviors exhibited by students, FBA is also used to monitor students' progress. It is a technique which "looks beyond the overt topography of the behavior, and focuses, instead, upon identifying biological, social, affective, and environmental factors that initiate, sustain, or end the behavior in question" (Quinn, Gable, Rutherford, Nelson, & Howell, 1998. P. 3). Guided by the traditional, research-based techniques of applied behavioral analysis, FBA has emerged as a federally sanctioned means to provide efficient, cost-effective, and purposeful interventions in the schools. A plethora of recent books and articles have addressed the ways in which to conduct FBA. In contrast, supervision of the practice has not yet been addressed. The same questions that guide practice of FBA can guide its supervision.

According to Macklem (1999), in conducting a functional behavior assessment the following steps are taken:

1. Define the problem behavior in specific, measurable, and easily understood terms through interviews with the student and teachers. Also describe the circumstances that are thought to maintain the problem

172

behavior. Prioritize problem behaviors and focus on one at a time.

2. Develop testable hypotheses regarding the context, antecedents, and consequences that maintain the behavior. For example, hypotheses regarding incomplete school work could be that the student (a) does not want to do the work, (b) spends very little time doing the work, (c) does not have enough help to do work, (d) is resisting a change in work requirements, or (e) is being given work that is too hard.

3. Test the hypotheses through additional interviews, observing the child in natural settings, documenting occurrences, setting events, triggering antecedents, and consequences. Interventions are used in hypothesis testing. For example, if it is hypothesized that the work is too hard, easier work is given as a test.

4. Develop a behavioral support plan that has strategies for replacing the defined problem behavior with desired behavior. Write out the plan and obtain parental consent and student assent.

5. Implement the behavioral support plan for at least three weeks. If the plan is not effective, revisit the problem definition, regenerate hypotheses, and modify the behavioral support plan as appropriate.

At times, a functional behavioral analysis focuses on how and when the child uses behavior rather than words to make requests and communicate feelings and in situations where he does so in socially unacceptable ways. The most critical exhibited behavior is targeted in the behavioral support or modification plan, its function is determined, and socially acceptable words or behaviors are taught as substitutions. Questions that can be used in conducting such a functional behavioral assessment are included at the end of this chapter.

Many school psychologists were not explicitly trained in functional behavioral analysis in their graduate programs. Although analyzing the purposes of behavior is hardly a new psychological concept, the term "functional behavior" was until recently more common in special education than school psychology literature. Because FBA is rooted so strongly in applied behavioral analysis, supervisees who have been previously trained in a behaviorist tradition will have fewer training needs than supervisees who have no such training. If a preponderance of school psychologists in the district have little or no previous training in behavioral interventions, it is useful to begin with staff development workshops and group consultation.

Choosing appropriate assessment tools

To meet the ethical mandate for equal protection, tests must meet strict requirements for reliability and validity. The APA (1992) and NASP Ethical Guidelines in the *Professional Conduct Manual* (1997) offer specific criteria for practitioners. Briefly, any test must be valid for the purpose of its use. Ethical violations can result if instruments with poor reliability, such as projectives, are used to draw conclusions in isolation

Ethical dilemma 11-2

Your immediate supervisor insists that you, as Supervising School Psychologist, develop a "standard battery" for the school psychologists to use for all cases that are referred for formal assessments. *What are the ethical issues? What can be done?*

Multicultural issues and test bias

Tests that result in disproportionate placement of minorities in special education violate the principle of equal protection. Existing tools are undeniably inadequate for the assessment of children who are not proficient in English. It is disheartening that test companies have indicated that they do not intend to develop multicultural versions of some instruments, such as a Spanish version of the WISC-III (personal communication). This leaves even the bilingual school psychologist in the uncomfortable position of being left without appropriate instruments to determine special education eligibility for non-native English speakers.

Administration, scoring, and interpretation

Both NASP and APA have formulated standards for practice which extensively govern ethical behavior in assessment. Supervisors are advised to re-visit these as warranted. Obviously, it is essential that assessment instruments be administered, scored, and interpreted as designed. However, research has repeatedly shown that students, interns, and practicing school psychologist alike make multiple errors in the administration and scoring of standardized assessment tools. The summary of 13 studies by Alfonso and Pratt (1997) suggests that on the WISC-R, examiner scoring errors result in approximately a 3.5 point difference (5.5 on "difficult" protocols). Hence, "it is logical to suspect that inappropriate diagnostic, placement, and educational planning decisions may occur as a result of tests that have been incorrectly administered or scored" (Alfonso & Pratt, 1997, p. 331).

In addition, the proliferation of computer technology and electronic communication has altered testing practices and will continue to do so (Harvey & Carlson, 1999). Both the American Psychological Association (1992) and the National Association of School Psychologists (NASP, 1997) have developed standards and ethical principles pertaining to computer-based test scoring and interpretation. They caution against using computer-generated scoring or computer-based reports unless the user is qualified in the relevant instrument, retains ultimate responsi-

bility for the product, provides understandable explanations, and uses this technology only to improve the quality of services (Harvey & Carlson, 1999).

Disability diagnosis. A large part of the school psychologist's task is the assessment of learning difficulties in order to determine if the child is eligible for special education services. Unfortunately, the lack of clarity around diagnoses can render this aspect of school psychology extremely frustrating. Because every state (and in some states, every community) has latitude in the interpretation of disabilty eligibility, there is little consistency from one state, community, or school to another.

For example, in the diagnosis of "learning disability" the federal definition requires a "severe discrepancy" between achievement and ability. Some states require a discrepancy of one standard deviation, while others require discrepancies of 1.5 or 2 standard deviations in standard scores. Some school psychologists use only a WISC-III Full Scale Score to calculate ability, while others use the higher of the Verbal or Performance Scales on the same instrument. Some communities use grade equivalent scores in the calculation of achievement tests, while others use age equivalent scores. All of these factors, and more, result in students being eligible for services as learning disabled in some communities and not in others. The lack of consistency is phenomenal and places supervisors in a very difficult position.

Similarly, the assessment of behavior and personality highlights a difficulty in our field's intersection between education and psychology. As educators, we are under the auspices of the IDEA. As psychologists, we are trained in the DSM-IV, and these two sets of criteria do not always comfortably fit together. For example, in the IDEA, the definition of "severe emotional disturbance" excludes students who are "socially maladjusted" unless they also meet criteria for "severe emotional disturbance." This is frequently interpreted to mean that students with academic deficiencies who meet the DSM-IV definition for depressed, schizophrenic, or anxious, also meet eligibility for special education programming, yet those who meet the DSM-IV criteria for conduct disorder or oppositional defiant disorder do not, unless depression or anxiety is co-morbid (Kamphaus & Frick, 1996). Psychologists working outside of schools find these distinctions arbitrary and confusing, while psychologists working in schools are often frustrated in their quest for student eligibility for appropriate interventions. Similarly, the diagnosis of ADHD is highly controversial and students suffering from anxiety, PTSD, or learning disabilities are not infrequently diagnosed with ADHD and prescribed medication rather than being referred for appropriate educational or psychological services. Frequently supervisors are asked for guidance in the interpretation and application of these diagnostic criteria.

Another issue experienced by supervisors of school psychologists is the changing face of special education. Because current special education practices emphasize service delivery within the confines of the regular education classroom (with or without modifications), it has been suggested that the importance of diagnostic testing is far less significant than it was in the past (Sabatino et al., 1993). "There are now school systems that forbid school psychologists to write custom-tailored recommendations, in which the school psychologist's function has been reduced to determining if selected eligibility requirement have been met" (Sabatino et al., 1993, p. 4). In order to retain the important information that can be gained with appropriate assessment, it is most important that supervisors ensure that contemporary practitioners utilize tests and test scores optimally. Appropriate supervision includes the implementation of practices that

suppress trends which proverbially "throw the baby out with the bath water."

Finally, it is important to note that the identification of need is not synonymous with the provision of appropriate services. All too often, too little information to guide future practice in the classroom is produced as a result of a referral for special education testing. One way to alleviate this problem is to increase the use of behavioral observation and use informal assessment instruments before a formal special education referral is made.

Ethical dilemma 11-3

As a supervisor of three school psychologists, you are in a position to compare their conclusions as you read their reports. You have noticed that, over time, they have become increasingly divergent in their diagnoses of learning disabilities. Often, a child diagnosed as learning disabled by one of your supervisees would not be diagnosed as learning disabled by another. *What are the ethical concerns? What can be done?*

Report writing

Writing clear, concise, and relevant psychoeducational assessment reports is difficult. Because sharing assessment results is of inestimable importance, developing and maintaining good communication is a critically important. During the task of report writing, diverse pieces of data, observations, test scores, and hypotheses are transformed into useful descriptions, diagnoses, and relevant remediation. When writing, the school psychologist incorporates diverse information about a specific student meaningfully. Especially in the case of a novice intern, helping improve report writing often take a primary role in supervision.

175

Report writing has changed with the advent of computer technology. A number of software programs integrate test results and generate recommendations including curriculum modifications and special education diagnoses. However, programs that generate reports must be used with extreme caution (Harvey & Carlson, 1999). Serious questions have been raised regarding insufficient validation (Moreland, 1985; 1992), the illusion of absolute accuracy (Matarazzo, 1985), the neglect of ecological variables (Harvey, Bowser, Carlson, Grossman, & Kruger, 1998; Ownby, 1997), neglecting to examine and evaluate the model used to develop the computer program (Maddux & Johnson, 1993), and practicing beyond ones level of competence (Harvey & Carlson, 1999).

Interpersonal skills

The skills used in consultation, discussed in Chapter 9, are similarly used in interpreting assessment results to students and parents. In addition, psychologists interpreting assessment results to students and parents have the additional challenge of interpreting difficult constructs, reporting sometimes unpleasant conclusions, and ensuring that the student and parent truly understand the findings. This requires skillful, tactful, and resourceful approaches.

Conclusions, recommendations, and follow-up

As Conoley and Gutkin (1986) suggest, "technical expertise in giving a test is no more important than technical expertise is disseminating results, planning intervention, and providing follow-up evaluation" (p. 459). All too often, school psychologists have conducted assessments and made recommendations, but neglected to follow-up on the implementation of these recommendations.

Salvia and Ysseldyke (1998) note that "there has been a dramatic shift from a focus on the process of serving students with disabilities to a

focus on the outcomes or results of the services provided" (p. 740). It can be anticipated that this emphasis on outcomes and their measurement may have a marked effect on the practice of school psychology. School psychologists, with their specialized expertise in testing and measurement, must be full participants in guiding and establishing best practices in the assessment of both regular and special education students. This will necessitate that supervisors, and their supervisees, acquire and maintain a broad spectrum of assessment knowledge and activities and invite the participation of multiple stakeholders.

STRATEGIES SPECIFIC TO SUPERVISING ASSESSMENT

Use knowledge to benefit the students

Strategy: Develop a model of assessment supervision. To develop an unique supervision method for each of the assessment instruments and/or techniques utilized by practitioners would be insurmountably difficult. Instead, effective supervisors develop a model of assessment supervision that applies to multiple instruments and activities.

Strategy: Foster strategies to encourage adherence to ethical principles and legal mandates. Supervisors must structure departmental policies adhering to the principles of privacy, due process, competence, and equal protection. Obviously, permission forms and other implementations of legal statutes must be developed with these factors in mind.

In order to facilitate supervisee adherence to legal and ethical standards, it is helpful to frame compliance as a way to protect the rights of children rather than as a capricious and arbitrary mandate. It is also helpful to use ethical dilemmas for discussion points in group supervision sessions.

Consider theoretical and psychometric concepts

Strategy: Update your knowledge. To obtain an overview, of current practices, read *Best Practices in School Psychology-III* (Thomas & Grimes, 1995). For more detailed information, obtain and read copies of current assessment texts such as Flanagan et al. (1997), McGrew and Flanagan (1996), and Shapiro (1989). Read current journal articles and discuss them in group or peer supervision.

Strategy: Directly address complexities of diagnosing ambiguously defined disorders. While diagnosis of almost any disorder is problematic, the difficulties of diagnosing learning disabilities and attention deficit hyperactivity disorder are legendary. As previously mentioned, not only are there significant differences from one state to another regarding eligibility requirements, but there are also differences from one community to another. Supervisors must guide their departments in developing operational definitions that simultaneously result in departmental consensus, permit supervisees with appropriate professional autonomy, and comply with state and federal laws.

Case study 11-1

A supervisor of school psychologists became so frustrated with the lack of departmental consensus over the diagnosis of learning disabilities that he required that all five school psychologists meet weekly to discuss any student so designated. The school psychologists met every Thursday after school to present and argue their cases. The meetings were long and sometimes contentious but forced all participants to thoroughly examine their practices.

Choosing appropriate assessment tools

Strategy: Re-examine your own training. Both supervisors and staff school psychologists are well aware of the reliability, validity, and applicability criteria necessary in the selection of assessment tools. Nonetheless, it is frequently necessary to revisit these criteria when facilitating supervisees' selection of assessment tools. For example, many school psychologists received training in techniques of questionable validity during their graduate programs and continue to use these techniques throughout their careers without re-considering their appropriateness. Corporations publishing test materials certainly continue to develop and publish tests of questionable validity. It is up to the supervisor and practicing school psychologist to take the time to review and validate instrument appropriateness in general, determine appropriateness regarding specific referrals, and clearly state reliability and validity issues in psychological reports.

Strategy: Encourage moderation in tools. To safeguard privacy, practitioners and their supervisors must also consider how much testing and what kind of testing should be conducted. Sandoval and Irvin (1990) suggests that "a good rule of thumb may be that only the information actually needed for good decision making should be obtained in response to the referral concern or the presenting problem" (p. 99). This indicates that personality assessment might not be warranted when the referral questions only addresses reading deficits.

Strategy: Develop a departmental policy that every student assessment completed by a school psychologist includes consideration of academic skills. This can be an observation of the student completing work, a curriculum based assessment (Gickling & Rosenfield, 1995), or a curriculum based measurement (Shinn, 1995, Shapiro, 1989).

Respond to issues of test bias and multicultural issues

Strategy: Address the assessment of English as a Second Language (ESL) students. In consultation with staff school psychologists and ESL specialists, the supervisor of school psychological services needs to develop a policy regarding the assessment of non-native English speakers. A sample policy developed by a supervising school psychologist, used to guide supervisees as they perform assessments with non-native English speakers, is attached at the end of this chapter.

Develop administration, scoring, and interpretation skills

Strategy: Re-examine your own skills. Do not presume that because you have been administering the same instrument for a number of years that you are administering it correctly. Research has demonstrated that skills deteriorate when individuals are unsupervised (Franklin et al., 1982), and that many practicing school psychologists make errors in test administration and scoring (Alfonso & Pratt, 1997).

Furthermore, since the average supervisor of school psychology interns has 17 years experience (Ward, 1999), it is highly likely that a supervisor will supervise the administration and interpretation of tools that did not exist at the time of their graduate training.

Strategy: Periodically review the test administration skills of supervisees. This can be accomplished by direct observation, review of video or audio tapes, or role-playing.

Strategy: Help supervisees develop self-guided learning to learn new assessment tools. Considering the wealth of constantly emerging assessment instruments and tech-

niques, learning how to administer and interpret new instruments is an enduring, professional task. Therefore, a major goal in the supervision of assessment is the development of self-guided learning and self-monitoring. For example, supervisors can help supervisees develop standard procedures to learn a new assessment tool. Example 11-1 is a sample of such a procedure.

Example 11-1 Steps to learn a new assessment tool

1. Read the manual.
2. Administer the test to yourself.
3. Read reviews of the test.
4. Administer the test to a volunteer. Score and review your scoring with another school psychologist.
5. Administer the test to another school psychologist who requires non-routine administration (i.e. makes errors such as reversing an early Picture Arrangement item), and obtain an analysis of administration errors.
6. Administer the test until no administration errors are made: under observation is preferable, but taping yourself and reviewing the tapes for administration errors is a satisfactory substitution.
7. Administer the test to at least six children as a practice instrument, using other instruments for the actual assessment.
8. Practice interpretation of these practice tests and review them with a colleague.

Strategy: Develop methods to foster learning new tool interpretation. While learning appropriate administration of a new instrument can be challenging, learning appropriate interpretation is considerably more difficult. This difficulty occasionally results in school psychologists inappropriately clinging to outdated versions of instruments. Learning new instrument interpretation is clearly a highly appropriate topic for peer supervision sessions, not only so that appropriate interpretation strategies are learned, but also so that problems in the application of the tool are immediately discerned and addressed.

Ethical dilemma 11-4

You are a supervisor of a large urban school district employing 57 school psychologists. Several of your supervisees enthusiastically adopted a new instrument as soon as it was published, because it was colorful and highly attractive to the preschoolers with whom they worked. After a period of a year, the publisher announced that recent research has revealed that the new instrument misdiagnoses attention deficits as mental retardation. Thus it appears that a sizeable number of children in your district were mistakenly diagnosed as retarded and placed in special education classes on that basis. *What are the ethical issues? What should be done?*

Develop skills in the synthesis of results with all data

Strategy: Develop a departmental protocol regarding ecological assessment. School psychology training programs vary to the extent that they require students to exhibit skills in functional assessment, and school systems vary in the degree to which they have adopted an ecological perspective. However, supervisors of school psychologists can steadfastly assert the inappropriateness of administering tests in isolation. Even if other team members are officially designated as the individuals who perform classroom observations, achievement testing, and parent interviews, school psychologists can and should make it a practice to observe the student in a natural setting, interview the student, have the student complete some academic work in their presence, and meet with the student's parents.

If an administrator questions this practice, the supervising school psychologist can explain that a comprehensive evaluation is ethically mandated in professional standards. Usually, however, this practice is not questioned because the inclusion of data gathered in natural observations, student interviews, student completion of academic work, and parent interviews greatly enriches the school psychologists' evaluation, report, and recommendations.

Strategy: Develop a department protocol for the functional behavior assessments. There is no one tool for the assessment of functional behavior. It requires compilation of all available information, particularly information gleaned in behavioral observations and school psychologists' interviews with teachers and parents. One district's protocol for the functional behavior assessment interview is included at the end of this chapter.

Foster comprehensive yet clearly written reports

Strategy: Emphasize the importance of clear reports. Psychological reports describe students from a fresh perspective to parents and teachers; communicate information regarding academic, intellectual, and social skills; and provide recommendations. To accomplish these purposes, reports must be clearly written and easily understood, yet they are often written at a level too difficult for the average parent to understand (Harvey, 1997b). In order for psychologists to develop and maintain appropriate report writing skills, it is necessary for supervisors to monitor report writing and ask supervisees to rewrite reports at more readable levels when appropriate. Supervisors can remind supervisees to shorten sentence lengths, minimize the number

179

of difficult words, reduce the use of jargon, reduce the use of acronyms, omit passive verbs, and increase the use of sub-headings. In addition, supervisors can request that supervisees obtain information about the readability of their writing through peer review, solicitation of consumer feedback (Ownby, 1987), calculation of reading level by hand, or the use of computer grammar checking programs.

Strategy: Use a rubric to provide feedback on reports. An example of such a rubric to use with beginning school psychologists is included at the end of the chapter.

Strategy: Ensure the ethical use of computer-generated reports. Supervisors should ensure that when they use computer scoring and computer generated reports, supervisees:

1. Edit any computer generated report by deleting overstatements, inappropriate hypotheses, and inappropriate recommendations, and by integrating results with other information (Eyde et al., 1993).
2. Retain ethical and professional responsibility for the accuracy of the results.
3. Use computer scoring systems only for instruments in which they are trained (Harvey & Carlson, 1999).
4. Validate computerized scoring systems for appropriateness before using (Harvey & Carlson, 1999).
5. Critically examine and evaluate the models upon which computer programs are based (Maddux & Johnson, 1993).
6. Include computer generated narratives only with clear data support, unless designated as speculation (Ownby, 1997).
7. Conceptualize the software as stemming from a consultant, rather than from an infallible machine (Harvey & Carlson, 1999).

Strategy: Carefully select computer scoring and report writing software. Supervisors of school psychologists frequently supervise the selection of computer software. As described by Harvey and Carlson (1999), specific selection considerations include the following: cost, compatibility, validity, expert reviews, procedures used to develop the software, qualifications of the software user, assessment of the "virtual consultant" embodied in the interpretive software, credentials of the software author, basis of the interpretive statements used in the system, and treatment validity.

Ethical dilemma 11-5

You are a supervising psychologist in a large city. Some school psychologists in private practice have begun using computer generated reports when conducting "third party" assessments. They present the unedited reports as their own work and charge a full fee for the service. The reports seem to make universal recommendations for private school placement, and do not consider resources available within the district. *What are the ethical issues? What can be done?*

Foster interpersonal skills in assessment interpretation

Strategy: Consider interpersonal skills. As mentioned previously, interpreting assessment results to parents, students, and teachers requires tact, skill, and resourcefulness. To facilitate supervisee's skills in this arena it is essential that supervisors know their level of skill. Assessment of this domain can easily be conducted through direct observation. In addition, role plays and audio-tapes of conferences with students and parents can be very helpful in the development of this skill.

Foster appropriate conclusions, recommendations, and follow-up

Strategy: maintain current skills in indirect and direct interventions. This is addressed in detail in chapters 9 and 10.

Strategy: Ensure that supervisees do not conceptualize the writing of a report as closure on a case. One method to facilitate this approach, when the supervisee is not involved in a direct intervention program, is to have them routinely consult with referring parties at one, three, and six months after the completion of a report.

E.S.L. EVALUATION CHECKLIST

1. Assess the academic setting

a. with the teacher, define nature of child's difficulties

b. examine relationship between language and academics:

   i. are math skills better developed than social studies skills?

   ii. in what language does the child speak in the classroom? speak with friends? speak on playground? take tests? write? read?

   iii. how competent is the child in English? in the first language?

c determine context of problem (groups vs. individual; social; academic); assess learning environments; determine whether the curricula is effective with bilingual students via test scores, grades, research; determine whether the curriculum is effectively implemented by the teacher via performance of other bilinguals, the quality of English and the primary language, comprehensibility of the teaching, and the degree of student participation

d. determine suitability of present instruction to child's learning style

e. determine appropriateness of services to develop English skills

f. determine whether modifications to the program were tried, documented, and reasonably comprehensive

g. determine whether other teachers have the same concerns

h. determine whether the child has really failed to learn or does not demonstrate learning (i.e., does not complete assignments)

2. Observe in more than one setting

a. in class(es) in which child is experiencing difficulty

b. in unstructured setting, compared with others of same culture (with sociodramatic play)

c. at home, to learn about child's experiential world

3. Collaborate with parents

a. determine whether an interpreter is needed. (Ideal interpreter: knowledgeable re schools, familiar to family, not family member.)

b. obtain background information about the referred child:

   i. country of origin, mobility, age on arrival, years in the US; previous stresses: war, deprivation, etc.; current stresses: economic conditions, acculturation

   ii. extent of exposure to formal education and past academic experiences: age began school? grade in school before entering the US? any problems in school in the past? retained in the past? any special classes? schooled in rural or urban setting? regular school attendance? number of schools attended? years of instruction in native language? proficiency in reading and writing in native language? proficiency in math, social studies, science? reads and/or studies at home?

   iii. whether family perceives a problem

   iv. parents perceptions of child's: positive attributes, strengths, friends, level of independence, interests, other things the child finds reinforcing

   v. health background: serious illnesses including fevers, injuries, vision, hearing, ear infections, developmental milestones, physical problems, medication (past and current)

   vi. language used at home between parents, siblings, parents and children, others: language child uses to speak with father, mother, siblings, in which stories are read to him, reads, writes, prefers to use in school, prefers to take test, of TV programs watched. Has the child learned more than one language previously?

c. Obtain general family information
   i. family composition, past and current;
   ii. health of family members;
   iii. educational levels and occupations of family levels, here and in the country of origin;
   iv. family's culture & customs, including gender roles and methods of discipline;
   v. extent of the child's acculturation;
   vi. family attitude toward school, academic achievement, exceptionalities, emotional problems, special education, and mental health services;
   vii. neighborhood factors and use of community supports.

4. **Determine language in which assessment and instruction should be done**
   determine child's dominant language & English proficiency
   in four language domains: listening, speaking, reading, writing

5. **Child interview**
   a. determine child's preferred language: interpreter needed?
   b. child's perception of the problem?
   c. what likes and dislikes about school; favorite and most disliked subject; perceptions of teacher; attitude toward teacher; teacher's clarity and willingness to repeat;
   d. special abilities, talents, interests, favored activities;
   e. friends, who prefers to play with, closest friends, who prefers to work with in school;
   f. feelings about home, school, relationships; what makes happy, sad, angry; what child does that make others happy, sad, angry; previous loss of significant persons; conflicts with parental values and/or adjustment to new culture; summer activities (job/camp);
   g. future hopes, dreams, vocational aspirations

6. **Measures of achievement**
   a. curriculum based assessments of math, language, spelling, reading ability
   b. informal reading inventory with textbooks, analysis of writing samples
   c. skills surveys to determine curricular gaps, resulting in recommendations for instruction
   d. determine whether the student needs to be referred for more formal assessment to determine eligibility for Special Education Services
   e. given in student's dominant language and/or with an interpreter when possible.

7. **Measures of cognition**
   a. given in dominant language, when possible
   b. if not possible, use non-verbal instruments. Do not report verbal scores in non-dominant language!

8. **Measures of behavior and personality**
   a. administered with an interpreter when appropriate
   b. functional behavior analysis
   c. Vineland (Spanish version available)
   d. Woodcock Johnson-SIB (Spanish version available)
   e. Child Behavior Checklist, BASC
   f. nonverbal tools such as play, drawings

9. **Pulling data together**
   a. Determine language proficiency through surveys, tests, and observations.
   b. Determine strengths, reasoning ability, problem solving skills
   c. Contextualize all scores and behavioral indicators
   d. Consult with a person knowledgeable about the child's culture, before drawing conclusions or making recommendations.
   e. Use the student's culture to help develop remediation strategies.

183

DETERMINING THE FUNCTION OF BEHAVIOR

Observe the child for an extended period. Then interview the parent(s) and teacher(s) with the following questions.

1. Typically, how does the child ask for
   ...an object?
   ...attention?
   ...time with other kids?
   ...time alone?
   ...praise?
   ...information?
   ...something to stop?
   ...a break?
   ...an activity to continue?

2. How does he let you know he
   ...just doesn't want to do it?
   ...is bored?
   ...is confused?
   ...is sad?
   ...is angry?
   ...is anticipating something?
   ...is afraid?
   ...is happy?

3. When do you feel the child
   ...uses grabbing or pulling others to communicate?
   ...uses changes in volume of voice to communicate?
   ...uses running to communicate?
   ...uses aggression to communicate?
   ...uses temper tantrums to communicate?
   ...uses verbal threats to communicate?
   ...uses ritualistic behavior to communicate?
   ...uses self-stimulation to communicate?
   ...uses proximity to others to communicate?
   ...uses self-injurious behavior to communicate?
   ...uses motor agitation to communicate?
   ...uses withdrawing to communicate?
   ...uses crying to communicate?

4. In which situation does he use behavior rather than words to communicate?

5. In which of the above naturally occurring events does he communicate in ways that are not socially acceptable?

6. What is the most critical behavior being exhibited? (choose one target behavior at a time)

7. What is the function of this critical behavior?

8. What socially acceptable words or behaviors can we substitute?

Rubric for Rating Psychological Reports

Examiner _____ Date _____

Examinee _____ Tests _____

Identifying information
first/fake name, age, sex, grade of student

Reason for referral

Background information
medical, social, cultural, adaptive behavior, educational history,

Previous test results

Brief classroom description
classroom observation of child
behavioral observations during assessment(s)

Assessment results and clinical impressions including
results of parent interview; teacher interview; child interview; cognitive assessment; achievement data regarding reading, writing, and math skills; functional behavioral, emotional, and social data.

Recommendations, including goals and measurable objectives

Summary

Signature

Required accompanying documentation
all test protocols
signed permission form

1	Observations clear and relevant.	☐ Excellent ☐ Satisfactory ☐ Unsatisfactory
2	Results clearly explained and presented.	☐ Excellent ☐ Satisfactory ☐ Unsatisfactory
3	Interpretations reasonable and accurate, traced sources and development of problem, answered specific referral questions.	☐ Excellent ☐ Satisfactory ☐ Unsatisfactory
4	Recommendations clear and realistic.	☐ Excellent ☐ Satisfactory ☐ Unsatisfactory
5	Summary includes essential facts, interpretations, and recommendations.	☐ Excellent ☐ Satisfactory ☐ Unsatisfactory
6	Style and communication: readable, clichés or jargon absent, inconsistencies absent, test data clearly differentiated from other data.	☐ Excellent ☐ Satisfactory ☐ Unsatisfactory
7	Organization: logical, meaningful, length appropriate.	☐ Excellent ☐ Satisfactory ☐ Unsatisfactory
8	Spelling.	☐ Excellent ☐ Satisfactory ☐ Unsatisfactory
9	Grammar.	☐ Excellent ☐ Satisfactory ☐ Unsatisfactory
10	Overall rating.	☐ Excellent ☐ Satisfactory ☐ Unsatisfactory

186

This chapter reviews the supervisory issues relevant to school psychologists and research, ranging from helping supervisees develop skills as research consumers and research disseminators to the development of school psychologists as conductors of research in both single-subject studies and program evaluations. Despite specific inclusion in the *Professional Conduct Manual* of the National Association of School Psychologists (1997), many school psychologists and school psychology supervisors are uncertain about their roles in these activities. The following pages will clarify potential roles, methods, and supervisory responsibilities.

RESEARCH

There is a dire need for greater reliance on research to empower school administrators and policy makers to make decisions based on data. Unfortunately, often we do not have sound data to either support or refute adopted positions, resulting in decisions being made in reaction to political forces or educational fads. The current "crisis in education" is an example of political forces driving educational decisions. There is no clear evidence that a crisis actually exists. Indeed, there is evidence to the contrary, such as subgroup SAT scores steadily increasing and high school dropout rates decreasing from 50% to 25% over the past 40 years. Nonetheless, mandates for school reform are strident, and the assumption that schools are ineffectual is implicit in these mandates. These assumptions may be the result of politicians using education as a rallying point, or it may be that "failure" is the result of the increasing skills required by today's high technology society (Cobb, 1995).

Regardless of the source, many state legislatures have responded by requiring stringent testing of both students and teacher candidates. In some states, tests without established reliability or validity are used to decide whether children progress to the next grade or graduate from high school. As school psychologists watch students with disabilities face discrimination in such situations, they can become extremely frustrated and all too often feel helpless to affect legislation and policy.

However, in reality, school psychologists are far from helpless. As consumers, distributors, and/or conductors of research they can directly impact educational policy (Cobb, 1995; Keith, 1995). As consumers and distributors of research, school psychologists are in a ready position to help school districts make informed decisions based on data rather than political forces or fads. As conductors of research, school psychologists are strategically positioned to gather information about a school's strengths and weaknesses, student learning, and the effectiveness of individual and group programs. Furthermore, research such as program evaluations is easily conducted, feasible, effective, and can result in remarkable systemic changes. "With a slight reshaping of the knowledge and skill base, school psychologists can be some of the best-trained professionals in schools to help teachers, schools, and districts implement and evaluate new types of educational outcomes" (Cobb, 1995, p. 333). Through analyzing and conducting research, individual school psychologists can significantly affect district level policy and programming by encouraging administrators to make data based decisions, and consequently can profoundly affect the capacity of the system to address children's needs.

187

Ethical dilemma 12-1

You are a supervisor of a school psychologist assigned to two elementary schools. One of the schools has a highly intense literacy program in the kindergarten and first grade level, including monthly curriculum based measurements conducted by the school psychologist. The school psychologist conducts a program evaluation and finds that 90% of children in this program read above grade level by the end of second grade. She tries to convince the teachers in the second elementary school to implement the same program, to no avail, and turns to you for suggestions. *What are the ethical dilemmas? What can be done?*

Each of the roles regarding research requires specific supervisory behaviors and professional skill development for individual school psychologists. It is the responsibility of the supervisor of school psychologists to facilitate this process.

Consuming research

School psychologists should be, at the very least, competent consumers of research, able to determine whether a research study demonstrates "anything and is...applicable to (our) situation" (Keith, 1995, p. 135). The development of this skill is critical for two reasons. First, if school psychologists are not competent research consumers their skills quickly become outdated. Secondly, the popular press and the Internet are fond of psychology and education as topics and have become disseminators of research studies and conclusions, which in turn affects the expectations of teachers and parents. Members of the general public do not have the skill to identify a research study as poorly conducted. This limitation can lead them to unwarranted conclusions. An ongoing need exists, therefore, for every school psychologist to be aware of popularly disseminated research results.

Supervisors of school psychologists must encourage supervisees to become skillful research consumers in a deliberate and ongoing manner so that supervisees develop these skills to an advanced level. Most specialist level programs include a research course in the curriculum, resulting in graduates attaining "advanced beginner" status as research consumers. Hopefully, these courses will have focused on conceptual material (Houser, 1998; Keith, 1995), for in a conceptual course, school psychology trainees learn how to evaluate the appropriateness of a research design and the generalizability of the results. However, for practicing school psychologists to develop advanced skills as research consumers, they must continue to practice and hone these critical skills. Supervisors can foster these characteristics by:

1. Encouraging supervisees to schedule time to read, discuss, and critique research;
2. Providing access to journals and other forms of research dissemination in the areas of school psychology, general education, special education, educational psychology, child and adolescent development, clinical psychology, neuropsychology, counseling, the sociology of schools, and systems theory;
3. Encouraging attendance at conferences where sound research is presented, including those conducted by the National Association of School Psychologists (NASP), the American Psychological Association (APA), the Council for Exceptional Children (CEC), and the American Educational Research Association (AERA) and their regional and state affiliates;
4. Encouraging participation in group supervision or peer supervision groups that maintain a focus on research review;
5. Encouraging the establishment of a peer supervision and/or support network whose

members develop specific areas of expertise and share knowledge with others;

6. Establishing a departmental custom of sharing articles and journals;

7. Including maintenance of current research knowledge as an item in school psychologists' job descriptions and evaluation forms; and

8. Scheduling time for the above activities when allocating time, resources, and supervisory consultation.

Practicing school psychologists face critical obstacles in becoming proficient research consumers, particularly time constraints. An informal canvassing of some school psychologists disclosed methods to cope with this difficulty:

1. Subscribe to a few journals, or obtain journals in conjunction with organizational memberships to NASP, CEC, AAMD, APA, etc., and trade with a colleague;

2. Read abstracts of all journals as soon as they arrive and subscribe to journal abstracts;

3. Keep a journal or two handy in the car and read articles during odd moments (e.g., while waiting for children at soccer games and music lessons);

4. Keep a journal or two handy at work and read them whenever you have some unexpected free time, such as appointment cancellations;

5. Set aside two hours per week to read;

6. Choose one or two areas of interest and read about them regularly;

7. Participate in a professional list serve on the Internet; and

8. Subscribe to one journal or publication in each of a variety of fields, for example, *School Psychology Review, Learning Disabilities, Educational Week, Educational Psychology,* or persuade the local school librarian to purchase at least one subscription on the list.

Difficulty accessing journals is another obstacle to becoming a proficient research consumer. Reynolds and Gutkin (1982) suggested a list of the most essential journals. However, many school psychologists do not have easy geographical access to these particular journals unless they have personal subscriptions (Harvey, 1990). Fortunately, resources are becoming increasingly available through electronic library services on the Internet. Many university libraries permit access to limited electronic library services to non-students, and many state university libraries are accessible to state residents who apply for access.

Distributing research

Steps involved in distributing research include defining the central and secondary research topics, evaluating the research, integrating the findings, drawing one or two appropriate conclusions, and making recommendations based on the conclusions (Keith, 1995). Effective school psychology supervisors frequently take responsibility for distributing research findings to supervisees and other school personnel. They also provide supervision to other school psychologists as they take the steps necessary for distributing research to teachers, administrators, parents, and other school personnel.

Supervisors can best facilitate the development of skills in research distribution by:

1. Including this activity in job descriptions and personnel evaluations;

2. Encouraging supervisees to explore relevant areas of research interest, particularly areas about which the administration is unsure of an appropriate course of action ("Should we institute a time-out room at our high school?");

3. Facilitating access to research, including increasing availability of conferences, journals, and data bases, such as ERIC and PsychLit through the Internet;

189

4. Helping supervisees clearly formulate the central and secondary topics to review;

5. Regularly meeting with supervisees to facilitate the progress of the project and ensure that a thorough review is conducted, appropriate conclusions drawn, and appropriate and feasible recommendations made.

Ethical dilemma 12-2

A school psychologist conducts a research review of literature comparing inclusive and non-inclusive programs for disabled children and found that parents, teachers, and children were generally more satisfied with the more restrictive programs. However, this district's administration is firmly committed to inclusive programs as a cost-saving measure and has told the school psychologist not to divulge the results to parents. The school psychologist wants you, as his supervisor, to battle with the administration on his behalf. *What are the ethical dilemmas? What can be done?*

Conducting research

For a number of reasons, practicing school psychologists seldom conduct research. First, we are so often "up to our necks in alligators" that we don't find time to "clear the swamp." Another reason is that school administrators tend to regard conducting research as not only a low priority, but even with some suspicion (Bardon & Bennett, 1974; Payne, 1982). Conducting traditional research in naturalistic settings is complicated by the number of variables involved and by myriad difficulties attached to setting up control groups. Additional deterrents are lack of accessibility to university libraries and to computer software capable of conducting sophisticated data analysis. Finally, although school psychologists with doctorates have training in research methodology and application, those with specialist degrees

may not have had enough training to feel comfortable conducting research.

Nonetheless, school psychologists are in an ideal position to conduct effective research studies. "School psychologists are awash in data...much of which would be ideal for research purposes with a little prior planning" (Keith, 1995, p. 137). All school psychologists should be able to at least develop single-case research designs to assess the effectiveness of interventions (Keith, 1995). In addition, with some training or practice in research design, school psychologists and supervisors of school psychologists are qualified to conduct applied research, particularly program evaluations (Harvey, 1989).

Conducting single-case research studies and program evaluations has many similarities to conducting a student evaluation (Harvey, 1989; Henning-Stout & Conoley, 1988; Sarason, 1996). School psychologists' skills in evaluation, interviewing, data analysis, and group leadership are effectively used in all components. In both situations the school psychologist:

- Identifies a problem or question;
- Gathers historical information;
- Determines evaluation procedures;
- Gathers and analyzes data; and
- Develops, implements, and subsequently evaluates the decided plan of action.

Ethical concerns

In conducting research, school psychologists must adhere to certain standards. The American Psychological Association ethical principles (1982, 1992) regarding research are supported by the NASP ethical principles in the *Professional Conduct Manual* (1997) and mandate the following:

- obtaining informed consent;
- communicating potential risks to participants prior to obtaining consent;

190

- taking extra precautions necessary when conducting research with special populations, including minors and individuals with disabilities;
- providing participants with the opportunity to be informed of the results of the study;
- using deception rarely and only when no other methods are available;
- using minimally invasive methods of data collection;
- taking extra precautions necessary when conducting research with socially sensitive repercussions; and,
- providing participants with non-punitive avenues for withdrawing from the study.

In addition, the Office of Protection from Research Risks (1993) provides ethical guidelines that specifically address research with human subjects. These guidelines require the review of proposed research by an Institutional Review Board that carefully scrutinizes proposals for evidence of informed consent, an assessment of risks and benefits to research participants, and methods to ensure confidentiality (Houser, 1998). This scrutiny is mandated for any institution receiving federal monies, which clearly includes school districts. In school districts, the upper level administration acts as the review board to ensure that all research adheres to the guidelines.

In conducting research, school psychologists must adhere to a number of ethical guidelines. These include:

- practicing within the realm of professional competence and responsibility;
- considering the welfare of clients;
- guaranteeing informed consent and maintenance of confidentiality;
- providing freedom from coercion and minimal risk;
- avoiding concealment and deception; and

- providing post-data collection debriefing and desensitization.

School psychologists will recognize most of these points as identical to the protections afforded children regarding testing and special education programming.

For research and program evaluation, permission must be obtained when procedures are out of the ordinary realm of educational practice. For example, if a child were to take part in an individualized, experimental reading program, permission would be needed for both participation and evaluation. On the other hand, individual permission is not required if a program evaluation is conducted on the effectiveness of a broadly applied reading program. Additionally, evaluations are often part of routine and required personnel actions.

Training and supervision in conducting research

If a school psychologist is a skillful research consumer and disseminator, moving toward becoming an effective researcher is best accomplished through collaboration with an experienced researcher. Many school psychologists have had some experience conducting research at the graduate level, whether as graduate assistants or in completing a master's research project or dissertation. Nonetheless, even with experience and coursework in research design, school psychologists will function at only the advanced beginner level unless they receive additional supervision. Even experienced researchers consult with others as they design projects. In addition to serving as a research consultant, supervisors are responsible for ensuring compliance with ethical issues as they supervise school psychologists conducting research.

Single-subject study supervision. School psychologists conducting a single-sample research study to determine whether a particular

191

intervention is successful will require ongoing supervisory consultation in which the supervisor carefully addresses the following:

1. The formulation of clearly defined, testable research questions;
2. The appropriateness of the literature search;
3. The appropriateness of the chosen intervention;
4. The ethical attainments of informed consent and assent from all relevant persons and the appropriateness of the consent and assent forms used;
5. The choice of an appropriate design, generally either a multiple-baseline design (across intervention implementation or across time), or a time series analysis in which three points of data are gathered prior to and after intervention implementation;
6. The integrity of the intervention implementation; and,
7. The appropriateness of the interpretation and results application.

Program evaluation supervision. As in all activities conducted by school psychologists, individuals conducting program evaluations progress through developmental stages of novice, advanced beginner, proficient, and expert as they become more skilled. Supervision is again necessary, particularly in the beginning stages. However, program evaluation is unique in that the supervision is not necessarily provided by a certified school psychologist. Often other individuals in the district, particularly administrators, have training and experience conducting program evaluations and are able to provide guidance. In addition, well-conducted program evaluations usually have a Steering Committee that serves in a supervisory role as the members provide feedback to the chief program evaluator throughout the evaluation. Finally, designing a research study is an ideal opportunity to utilize

peer supervision and obtain invaluable feedback from colleagues at each stage of the process.

Courses in program evaluation are readily available at most colleges and universities, although often they are housed in administration programs or other programs emphasizing applied research. Normally program evaluations do not require sophisticated statistical analysis, and simple calculations of means, standard deviations, and percentages are sufficient. Most school systems have basic spreadsheet software (such as Lotus 1-2-3 or Microsoft Excel) capable of calculating fundamental statistics. If school psychologists conduct evaluations requiring more complicated analysis they can consult with a person knowledgeable about statistics. For more sophisticated analyses, advanced statistical programs such as SPSS, SAS, and Statview are available at a reasonable cost (Canter, 1993). Funds are often available from state associations to support research and program evaluation, for example, to underwrite costs of postage or statistical software.

When school psychologists conduct program evaluations, their supervisors should ensure that this activity is seen as part of their job by both immediate supervisors and the general administration. Integration into the role description is essential for two reasons. First, official sanction is necessary so that appropriate resources (such as school psychologist, clerical, and faculty time) are allotted. Second, official sanction is necessary to lend authority to the findings and for recommendations to be implemented.

PROGRAM EVALUATIONS

As does a single-subject research study, a comprehensive program evaluation requires preparation, information collection, data analysis, presentation of results, recommendation development, intervention implementation, and evaluation (Bennett, 1988; Maher, 1984; Patton,

1982; and Tuckman, 1985). Schools and programs have several areas that benefit from data based decisions (Ulman, 1987):

1. *Goal development*. An appropriate needs assessment can identify new service delivery areas, leading to goal development and program development and implementation.
2. *Goal modification*. A formative program evaluation focused on process can determine whether goals or service delivery should be modified.
3. *Goal attainment*. A summative program evaluation focused on outcome measures can determine whether the goals have been achieved.
4. *Accountability*. A program evaluation that combines both summative and formative procedures can be used to evaluate the effectiveness of services, to justify their cost, and to communicate that effectiveness to consumers including administrators, school board members, and the community.
5. *Public relations*. When results of evaluations are disseminated through newspapers, parent groups, school board meetings, and other consumer information services, large groups become more aware of programs.

Preparation

Preparation includes discussing the evaluation, developing a Steering Committee, planning the evaluation components, determining procedures, preparing a proposal for approval by upper administration, and designing procedures. While planning the evaluation, it is important to keep in mind utility, feasibility, propriety, and accuracy.

The first step in conducting a program evaluation is to discuss the evaluation with program staff and program supervisors, obtain consensus that a program evaluation is desired, and formulate clearly defined, testable research questions.

The school psychologist can help individuals reach consensus concerning the value of conducting an evaluation by making the process as participatory as possible.

The next step, developing a Steering Committee, requires the recruitment of six to ten persons. These should include program staff, supervisors, and representatives of other relevant constituent groups who are "stakeholders" in the outcome of the evaluation. The more groups represented in the Steering Committee, the more likely the findings will result in meaningful change. Persons invited to be Steering Committee members should believe that the evaluation is worthwhile, have an interest in and concern for the appropriate use of the results, and have the authority and capability to implement the findings.

Persons asked to be members of the Steering Committee are most likely to agree to serve if they are notified of the time commitment when invited. Usually this time commitment can be limited to a few meetings to plan, monitor, and analyze the evaluation. The chair of the Steering Committee, often very appropriately a school psychologist, supervises the evaluation process and facilitates the meetings.

The Steering Committee decides on the purpose(s) of the evaluation and chooses one or two questions to be addressed. After the testable questions are clearly formulated, the Steering Committee chooses the evaluation components, which can include but are not limited to questionnaires, interviews, document analysis, file reviews, and outcome data. Appropriate methods and procedures of data collection are determined after the questions have been planned and the sources of data identified. The approximate costs of conducting the evaluation, including time, supplies, and projected methods of data analysis, are roughly calculated.

While it is possible to conduct an "inside" evaluation without the sanction of

193

upper level administration, the resulting recommendations are much more likely to be implemented if upper level administration is actively involved and has approved the project. Furthermore, the administration is responsible for acting as the equivalent of an Institutional Review Board and giving official approval for the study. Therefore, before conducting the evaluation, a proposal is presented to key decision makers in the school district. The proposal need only be a few pages to include the following:

1. The purpose of the evaluation and the questions posed;
2. A brief summary of the model to be employed and a plan for data analysis;
3. A discussion of the planned dissemination of results;
4. The estimated cost in terms of time and resources;
5. A description of methods to obtain informed consent and assent, and sample consent and assent forms; and,
6. A request for a letter indicating administrative sanctions and support.

Designing procedures

After obtaining permission to proceed with the evaluation, the Steering Committee designs the procedures more fully, establishes timelines, and designates persons responsible for each step. If questionnaires are used, the committee may choose to send one set of questions to parents, another to administrators, and yet another to teachers. They may also choose to send the same questions to each group. Cover letters are helpful; they should explain the project enough that any consent given is fully informed, suggest the possibility of non-participation, indicate upper administration approval, and urge completion of the questionnaire in a timely fashion. To increase response rate, it is helpful for questionnaires to be returned anonymously. When professional staff are involved,

it is helpful to employ a technique (such as a secretary receiving and recording the names of respondents) that enables school personnel to obtain professional development credit for participating.

If interviews are to be conducted, the questions to be included are determined at this point. Techniques for choosing individuals to interview and for sending questionnaires are established. Individuals who will actually conduct the interviews are chosen, and methods of training them are detailed. The Steering Committee decides who will conduct interviews, what format the interviews will take, and what questions will be asked. It is particularly helpful to field test the interview questions on a few persons to make sure the questions elicit the information you are seeking. After this field testing, the questions can be refined accordingly. Additional helpful suggestions about conducting program evaluation interviews are contained in Patton (1982).

If document analysis, file reviews, or outcome data collection are to be conducted, forms with relevant spaces for each item of data are developed. Then a computer program or spreadsheet for the data bank is developed.

Examining the ultimate effectiveness of services requires outcome data collection. As there generally will be no control groups, differences would probably be evidenced by a repeated time series design (Campbell & Stanley, 1966) which requires (three) data points prior to intervention and (three) data points following the intervention. Common student outcome measures include: achievement test scores, attendance, behavior, discipline reports, drop-out rates, emotional status, grades, graduation rates, hours per week assigned to special education services, peer relationships, suspensions, and tardiness.

Before deciding on particular outcome variables, the committee should determine how easily the data could be collected. Some data can be disconcertingly difficult to gather in schools. Examination of student files can provide a great deal of demographic or historical information that may be significant in a program evaluation. For example, evaluating whether or not a junior high program in study skills is effective may be illuminated by information about the elementary schools attended by participants, as the program may be more essential for students who graduated from an elementary school with little emphasis on study skills.

Ethical dilemma 12-3

A school psychologist is evaluating the outcome of a conflict resolution program she implemented in a high school. An essential question is whether disciplinary actions were less frequent after the program's implementation. Unfortunately, the school administrators have a practice of deleting all records of disciplinary actions every June, stating that keeping them would violate the students' right to privacy. The school psychologist understands the need for confidentiality, but feels firmly that being denied access the results of interventions is also an ethical violation. *What are the ethical issues? What can be done?*

Information collection

The Steering Committee monitors the timeliness of data collection, and compiles and stores collected information in a manner that maintains confidentiality and also expedites analysis. It is important to avoid modifying the instruments in the middle of the evaluation, and to monitor the accuracy of the information gathered. An important concern relative to the use of data from student files is that confidentiality must be scrupulously maintained. Therefore, data must be stored so that any person other than the principle researcher, such as a computer operator, is not able to attach student names to information. This may be facilitated by the use of stand-alone computers.

Data analysis

Often, only medians, means, and standard deviations are needed for meaningful interpretation of results. If data have been collected through file reviews, it is possible to contrast existing timelines with district policies, state standards, and federal guidelines. Interview responses and responses to open-ended questions can be compiled into a manageable and readable narrative format by grouping comments by topic. The data are then examined for patterns, consistencies, and inconsistencies, and a summary of strengths and weakness generated. This is not difficult to do on a word processor, although there are computer programs (NUD*IST, N-VIVO) that do this analysis as well.

Presentation of results and development of recommendations

There are many reasons to share the results of a program evaluation. When results are shared internally they can be used to improve the program. When results are shared externally, they can provide guidance to others who are attempting to deal with the same problems. Results are also useful in promoting programs and in demonstrating the need for additional support.

Sharing internally can be done at follow-up meetings with administrators. These meetings are essential. To gather data and fail to conduct follow-up meetings is as indefensible as conducting a student evaluation, identifying areas of weakness, and neglecting to develop a remedial plan. Some of the needs identified will result in complex and possibly costly program changes. These will require formalized program development, implementation, and evaluation. Henning-Stout and Conoley (1988) and Knoff (1995) provide detailed analyses of these steps. However, it is equally possible that a program evaluation will result in recommendations that are cost saving to the district. In taking steps to implement changes recommended as a result of program evaluations, school psychologists need

195

"courage, assertiveness, patience, persistence, vision, flexibility, and tact" (Henning-Stout & Conoley, 1988, p. 487), and a "strong self-concept, high tolerance for ambiguity, and the patience of a UN arbitrator" (Payne, 1982, p. 895).

Internally, results are presented initially to the Steering Committee. The Steering Committee designs a plan of action to remedy areas of weakness and within this plan, specific and measurable goals are developed and prioritized. Persons responsible for action items, timelines, and methods of goal measurement are designated. This plan of action is presented to all "stakeholders," and their feedback is taken into consideration in the development of the final evaluation report and plan of action.

The final report is presented to the upper administration for endorsement of the plan of action. After the plan of action is implemented and monitored, services should be re-evaluated at a future date.

Ethical dilemma 12-4

A group of teachers and school psychologists conduct a formative, standards-based program evaluation to determine effectiveness of in-district programs for children with emotional or behavioral disorders. The evaluation results in several intra-program recommendations that could be easily implemented by staff. The recommendations requiring school-wide or district-wide changes are less easily implemented. For example, recommendations include developing standardized referral methods, increasing vocational curricula, institutionalizing planning time, and increasing staff. The administration is resistant to a standardized referral method (preferring the option of "emergency placement"), and, despite acknowledging the need, indicates that it does not have the resources to institutionalize planning time or increase staff. *What are the ethical issues? What can be done?*

When sharing results externally, one must prepare a research report that describes, explains, and contextualizes the program evaluation. While this final step appears to be straightforward, it is complicated by the report's multifaceted purposes. The report must fully explain the rationale for the study, communicate the extent to which the design was appropriate, evaluate critical issues and recognize shortcomings, hypothesize about the meaning of the findings relative to the original hypotheses, and address how the results fit into the context of the general knowledge base (Kazdin, 1995).

Final reports can be published in professional newsletters, journals, or ERIC. The first two reach the largest immediate audience. Newsletters, including the *Communiqué*, prefer items of immediate and timely interest to readers. Journals consider themselves archival, and publishing usually involves blind submission to a jury of professors. Completed articles published in ERIC have a wide circulation among universities. ERIC is open to publishing final grant reports and is not juried. However, while the listings are readily available, the complete articles are often not accessible to practitioners.

To evaluate your final report, it is useful to compare it with the evaluation of research in Houser (1998) and Kazdin (1995), and in the *Publication Manual of the American Psycho-logical Association* (1994). An outline of the components is included in Table 12-1.

Table 12-1

Report Components

A. Introduction
Background and context
Relevant current theory, research, and practice
Unique aspects about this study
Purposes or predictions

B. Method

Participants

Selection method

Demographics: age, gender, and socioeconomic status

Percent selected who actually participated

Method of obtaining informed consent

Design

Relation of design to the study goals

Grouping of participants

Treatment of participants

Assessment

Constructs evaluated

Methods and tools of evaluation

Reliability and validity of these methods

C. Procedures

Setting

Material and equipment used

Sequence of events

Procedural checks

D. Results

Scores for different groups and sample as whole

Means

Measures of central tendency

Comparison of scores

Other studies or samples

Analyses used

Methods used to control error rates

Methods of dealing with incomplete data

E. Discussion

Major findings

Discussion of findings with regard to current theory

Alternative explanations

Limitations of the study

Suggestions for further research

(American Psychological Association, 1994 and Kazdin, 1995)

Case study 12-1

A system-wide program evaluation of special and general education services, focusing on program improvement rather than compliance, was conducted (Harvey, 1989). The procedure, sponsored by the state Department of Education and designed and supervised by the Center for Resource Management (1988), was an extremely effective evaluation that resulted in profound, systemic changes in the district.

Initially, a steering committee composed of special and regular educators met to determine the evaluation process. The process was presented to and approved by the administration, including the school board, central administration, and principals. Secretarial staff tabulated outcome data for all special education students and a sample of non-special education students at the elementary, junior high, and senior high levels on grades, attendance, suspension rate, and drop out rates.

Questionnaires were distributed to all teachers, administrators, and one third of the parents of special education students. The questionnaires asked respondents to indicate on a Likert scale whether or not positively worded indicators of effective education were adhered to "almost always," "frequently," "sometimes," "seldom," or "never." For example, a positively worded indicator was that "special and general education staff communicate and plan together." A selected sample of parents and staff were also interviewed.

The results of the outcome data, questionnaires, and interviews were tabulated and distributed in paper copy to administrators, school board members, and teachers. The results were also presented orally at administration, faculty, and school board meetings. Subsequently, a team of special education teachers, administrators, parents, and school board members analyzed the data, determined areas of strength and weakness, and developed recommended courses of action in a series of goals and objectives much like a student's IEP.

Because the indicators were worded positively, the results positively reframed even areas of weakness, and the use of both outcome and process data lent substantial credence to the results. As might be expected, there were instances of distress and anxiety when particular persons or schools were rated less positively than others. However, the positive nature of the questions and the positive focus of the program planning meetings minimized this effect. The evaluation results demonstrated that concerns were expressed repeatedly. Consensus on goals and objectives were reached easily and subsequently implemented.

CONCLUSION

198

There are substantial similarities between assessing and developing intervention plans for individual children and conducting research and program evaluations. School psychologists' training in consultation, assessment, the development of intervention plans, and knowledge of research methodology, render them adept at applying the necessary skills. Supervisors of school psychologists are often in an ideal position to observe programmatic needs and to encourage the school psychologists working under their supervision to plan and conduct such activities. Conducting research and program evaluations are excellent methods by which supervisors of school psychologists can increase the effectiveness of both school psychological services and school services in general.

Ethical dilemma 12-5

You and a school principal are co-supervisors of a school psychologist who initiated and directs an after-school program in a community center. An outcomes-based program evaluation, conducted by the school psychologist, found that the program was highly successful. Grades of participants improved, the referrals for psycho-educational evaluations decreased, and neighborhood vandalism decreased. The school now has a new principal, who believes that the after-school program should be taken over by paraprofessionals and that the school psychologist should not be spending time on this program. *What is the ethical dilemma? What can be done?*

This chapter reviews the skills and supervisory issues relevant to school psychologists and grant writing. Obtaining grant monies is a highly effective method for school psychologists to develop, implement, and evaluate innovative and exciting programs. Although writing and supervising grants is not always in a school psychologist's job description, most school districts are happy to have school psychologists become involved. There are innumerable benefits to a supervisor of school psychologists bringing money into the school district through grant writing. For example, grants increase services for children and families, make the grant-writing school psychologists invaluable to administrators, encourage the expansion of the school psychologists' roles, increase local prestige, and enlarge the group with whom school psychologists work.

Books and articles on writing grant proposals are extensive, and credit and non-credit courses on grant writing are available at many state universities. Co-authoring a grant with an individual accustomed to successful grant writing, such as a director of special education or a university affiliate, is an invaluable method for learning grant writing strategies. The first author had the good fortune to co-author a grant with her supervising during her internship. This experience removed the mystery from writing a grant at an early point in her career and paved the way for writing successful grant applications in the future.

Substantial amounts of money, both in the public and private sector, are available for programs in education and the social sciences. A comparison of private and public sector grants is found in Table 13-1.

Table 13-1

Comparison of private and public sector grants

	Private sector	Public Sector
Funding sources	Foundations, corporations	State and federal agencies (i.e., Department of Education)
Typical length	2 to 4 pages	25+ page narrative, plus appendix
Usual duration	One year	One to three years
Monies available	$5,000 to $30,000	At the federal level, often $80,000+ per year
Applicant status	Proactive: applicant initiates the application, sending it to foundations with that interest area	Reactive: Proposals with clearly specified mandates and guidelines are solicited through publicly announced Request for Proposals (RFP)
Deadlines	Usually open	Typically short (60 day) and inflexible
Competitors	The majority (70%) is awarded locally, in employee communities. The remaining 30% are national	State or nationwide, depending on funding source. State grants can be non-competitive, while federal grants are highly competitive, particularly if the competition is open to universities.

It is important to match your project with an appropriate funding source. As mentioned in Table 13-1, private sector corporations and foundations fund projects supporting particular areas of interest (such as children and youth), while state and federal agencies fund programs they are currently fostering, such as inclusion or violence prevention. Both public and private sectors are interested in funding innovative projects, rather than those they see as the responsibility of the school district. For example, a grant to replace outdated social studies books would be unlikely to be funded, while a grant to train teachers and obtain materials in order to implement an innovative literacy program in social studies would have a greater chance of being funded. Grant applications for projects that increase collaboration between public schools and community agencies, or public schools and universities, also have higher success rates.

Grants have five stages: planning, finding appropriate funding sources, writing, implementing, and evaluating. The actual writing process is the smallest portion: at least five days of planning are needed for each day of writing.

PLANNING

When planning, grant writers clearly define the intent and scope of the project on several levels. These include determining the agency and principal investigator; documenting the need and support; targeting the field, function, and populations; and finding appropriate funding sources.

Determine the agency and principal investigator

Grants must be administered by a tax-exempt agency. The director of the agency (such as a school district superintendent) signs off on grant applications, acts as the fiscal agent, and receives the grant monies. Since the agency and its director play critical roles, it is essential to meet with individuals at the agency who act as decision-makers, discuss the grant, and obtain their full support as soon as possible in the planning stage. When two agencies are involved (such as a school district and a university), often one agency signs off and is the recipient of the funds, including the indirect funds (those funds not specific to grant activities that support administrative costs, clerical personnel, and other indirect costs such as the physical plant). However, in a true collaboration, both agencies sign off and indirect funds are divided proportionately.

Although the head of the agency, such as the superintendent, signs off as the responsible person, an individual designated as the "Principal Investigator" or "Project Director" writes the proposal, oversees the implementation of the project, hires individuals funded by the grant, and writes the final report. It is important that the individual who formulated the idea for the project and who is most personally invested in the project is designated as Principal Investigator or Project Director.

Document need and support

The grant application must include the theoretical framework for the project and examples of earlier attempts to address the issue. A brief literature search that supports the underlying concepts of the project must be included.

The current need for the project, from the perspective of the target population, should be assessed and documented. It should be clear that the project was designed in response to a need and that the target population believes in and is interested in participating in the project.

Additional support for the project should be assessed and documented. Grant applications must have evidence, including letters of support, indicating that other professionals and community members perceive the need for the project and are willing to become involved in its implementation.

Target field, function, and populations

Planners must describe field, function, and target populations in grant proposals. Fields are areas such as "special education," "general education," "mental health," or "social services." Many projects have more than one field of application, which increases potential funding sources. Planners must also determine the function of a project, whether it is primarily construction, demonstration, direct service, support for ongoing services, or research.

Many projects have more than one target population, or persons expected to directly benefit from the program. In addition, programs indirectly benefit additional populations.

The geographical impact of the project must also be determined. Because funders desire maximum impact, the smaller the target population, indirect beneficiaries, or geographical area, the fewer the potential sources of funding. However, model projects can be implemented on a local level but considered to be regional, state, or national if the results are disseminated to a broader audience.

Finding appropriate funding sources

As mentioned previously, public sector grants generally originate from city, state, or federal agencies, particularly departments of education. Foundations generally fund private sector grants.

Public sector funders solicit projects by publishing Requests for Proposals (RFPs). At the federal level, these are published in the *Federal Register* at the time of fund allocation. RFPs designate absolute priorities that determine the appropriateness of the project. The following criteria should be carefully considered in deciding whether to respond to an RFP:

- eligibility;
- compatibility between the priorities and your function, field, target population, and need;

- time constraints imposed by the deadline (a minimum of 60 days is needed to develop a grant proposal);
- feasibility given your current infrastructure; and,
- competitiveness.

The competitiveness increases when there are fewer than 100 grants to be awarded throughout the nation, when universities are eligible to apply, and when several others in your state are responding to proposals that will have only one award per state. The Department of Education can often indicate who is applying for particular grants.

Private sector monies can originate from an independent foundation, a corporate foundation, an operating foundation, or a community foundation. These organizations are listed in Table 13-2. In selecting a foundation, first look at its areas of interest to see whether your field and target population match. It is also helpful to look at the list of trustees to see whether you know them or whether they have an area of interest that matches your need. After identifying several potential foundations, grant writers should call the foundations, identify themselves, and request a copy of the current application guidelines and the annual report. They should determine any relevant deadlines and obtain a list of current trustees. The greater the interpersonal contact with the foundation the greater the likelihood of funding.

As stated above, there are many grants available to those seeking funding for educational research. Websites are a good place to start seeking funds; many of those listed in Table 13-2 also contain information regarding other organizations.

201

Table 13-2

Sources of information on grants

Organization and Address	Information
Academic Research Information System, Inc. (ARIS) http://arisnet.com/links.html	Provides grants for basic and applied education research projects. Investigators generate topics and methods. Recent projects: Low Income Effects of School Readiness, Evaluations of HeadStart Programs. Includes the National Institute on Early Childhood Development and Education, National Institute on Postsecondary Education, Libraries and Lifelong learning, and National Institute on Education of At-Risk Students
American Psychological Association Guide to Research Support http://www.apa.org	Lists sources for psychological research from both federal and private resources.
Carnegie Corporation of New York http://www.carnegie.org/submit.htm	Provides grants for educational research. Recent grants have been: Assistance for School Districts in Implementing Comprehensive School Reform to Improve the Academic Performance of Disadvantaged Children; Support for the Evaluation of In-school and After-school Programs.
Catalog of Federal Domestic Assistance http://www.gas.gov/fdac/queryfdac.htm	Information on 51 federal agency grants including objectives and application and review processes.1,000+ assistance programs described.
Children's Defense Fund http://www.childrensdefense.org	Funds projects for at-risk children, particularly poor, minority, and disabled children.
Chronicle of Higher Education http://www.sura.net/gsa.html	Contains the National Institute of Child Health and Human Development and The Office of Education Research and Improvement. Accepts grant applications to teach English literacy to Spanish-speaking children.
Federal Register Superintendent of Documents U.S. Government Printing Office, Washington, DC 20401-9371 http://ocfo.ed.gov/fedreg/announce.htm	Lists funded projects. Helps identify funding priorities.

Foundation Directory of the Foundation Center http://fdncenter.org	Wide range of funding in all fields. Lists 4,400 foundations with assets of at least $1 million.
Guide to Educational Programs, U.S. Dept. of Education http://www.ed.gov	Describes federally funded projects in education.
Links to Online Funding Opportunities Services: FEDIX, MOLIS, Opportunities Alert http://www.fie.com/online/index.htm	Awarded $3.9 million for 24 grants in June of 1999. Grants awarded to institutes of secondary education, usually awarded to programs focused on strengthening the teaching skills of new and experienced teachers in grades 9-12.
National Endowment for the Humanities, (NEH) http://neh.fed.us/html/applying.html	Funds projects associated with the humanities including art and literature.
National Institutes of Health, (NIH) http://www.nih.gov/grants	Funds initiatives in health and health education.
National Science Foundation, (NSF) http://www.nsf/gov	Funds science programs.
The Grantsmanship Center Whole Non-Profit Catalog P. O. Box 6210 Los Angeles, CA 90014 http://www.tgci.com	Describes training and funding available to non-profit agencies seeking grantsmanship information.

WRITING

Whether the application is to be submitted to private or public sector funding agencies, the primary rule in writing a successful application is to meticulously follow guidelines provided by the funding agency. The proposal must be clearly related to the purpose and priorities of the funding agency.

Reading a successful application before beginning the writing process is extremely helpful. Funded grants are available for review at the federal Department of Education. If the potential applicant is not in the proximity of Washington, the Department of Education can provide the name of past local recipients (such as local universities) who may permit others to read their grant proposals.

It is also helpful to write one or two proposal drafts and have them read and reviewed prior to submission to eliminate confusing terms, logical inconsistencies, weak arguments, and spelling and grammatical errors. Often funding agencies have proposals reviewed by faculty at universities, so faculty reviews can be particularly helpful. Writing should be clear, concise, and direct. Avoid jargon, rambling, vague terms, and poor grammar and spelling (Office of Graduate Studies and Research, 1990).

Both public and private sector proposals have the same basic components. These include: the abstract; background and problem statement; the assessment of need; goals, objectives, and plan of operation; the capacity of the institution and staffing; the evaluation plan; the dissemination plan; the budget plan and description of cost effectiveness; references; signature; and the appendix.

Abstract

The information in the abstract of a public sector grant is included in the cover letter of a private sector grant. It is often separated from the proposal and judged on its own, and thus must be both concise and comprehensive. The abstract should be double-spaced, limited to one page, and contain the following:

1. Description of the problem and general goals;
2. Identification of the applicant agency and credentials of the applicant;
3. An explanation of the goals, objectives, and key activities of the project;
4. The total projected cost of the project;
5. Anticipated outcomes of the project and a brief evaluation plan; and
6. Description of the funding's relevance to the previously stated problem.

The body of the proposal follows the abstract. The body of a private sector grant is relatively short, often only seven to ten pages. Public sector grants are much longer, about 25 double-spaced pages, with at least that many additional pages in the appendix.

Background/Problem statement

This statement should clearly and succinctly state the fundamental problem you are targeting.

Assessment of need

In this portion, present the evidence of local need and reasons for requested project funding. Local statistics are compared with state and national trends. A sufficient literature review is included so that other projects that have attempted to address the same problem are discussed and related to your proposed project. The relevant component numbers from the RFP are cited in a public sector grant. This section should be written clearly and should not assume the reader knows educational or psychological jargon.

Goals, objectives, and plan of operation

This section describes what you expect the project to accomplish. Like a child's IEP, it includes long-range goals, short-term objectives for each goal, activities necessary for the accomplishment of each objective, a timeframe, and an evaluation plan.

The general goals, which indicate the broad purpose of the proposed project, are fairly nebulous. An example of a general goal is to "Promote the use of conflict resolution strategies in school." The objectives are specific, measurable outcomes regarding a specific population with a timeframe and percentage change expected. An example of an objective is "The number of inter-student conflicts resulting in disciplinary actions will decrease by 25% by the end of the four-year project." A list of actions accompanies each objective. This includes activities that "establish," "train," "design," and "implement." It must be easily apparent to the reader that the activities will achieve the objectives and the general goals within the designated timeframe. Examples of activities for a four-year grant in conflict resolution might be:

1. Training the school psychologist as an instructor in non-violent crisis intervention.

2. Holding monthly training sessions, by the school psychologists, so that all teachers, paraprofessionals, counselors, administrators, bus drivers, custodial staff, nurses, counselors, and peer mediators are trained in non-violent crisis intervention.

3. Establishing a conflict resolution room adjacent to the counseling suite.

4. Designing and implementing a peer conflict resolution program.

5. Training peer mediators and counselors in peer mediation techniques.

6. Designing and implementing a conflict resolution curriculum to include in all 9th grade health classes.

The goals, objectives, activities, timeframe, and outcome indicators are often presented in both a narrative and a chart. The narrative includes justifications and explanations (for example, reasons for the selection of a given approach, plans for obtaining participants, and methods for collaborating with other agencies or universities). The chart is more succinct and is included for clarity.

Capacity of the institution and staffing

This section describes the applicant, the agency, and the community well enough so that the funding agency considers the project worthy of funding. It should include the mission statement of the applicant agency, as well as participation in previous projects and any awards or citations received.

In public sector grants, a detailed project management plan is often required. This includes an "Organizational Chart" that shows administrative responsibilities and describes how the new project will be integrated into the administrative structure.

The relationship of the staff to the goals and objectives is shown in a "Person-loading Chart." This chart delineates the responsibilities of each person working on the project and the amount of time he or she will devote to the grant (".2" being equal to one day per week). Specific personnel connected with the project are indicated, including those whose positions will be funded by the grant and are not yet hired.

Public sector grants also require a narrative description of personnel quality. Relevant variables include degrees, professional experience, and awards and publications of each individual. If a position will be filled as part of the grant, the reader is referred to a proposed job description contained in the appendix.

Evaluation plan

This section describes the steps that will be taken to demonstrate the success or failure of the project. It should describe your plans to evaluate the project, what data you will collect, and how you will collect the data.

Evaluation plans should include both summative and formative evaluation components; that is, both process and outcome measures. The process measures are used throughout the course of the project to assess whether the project is being implemented in accordance with the plan of operation and to make appropriate adjustments. The outcome measures assess whether the objectives have been met. The names of any tools to be used are included in the evaluation plan, and copies of the tools are included in the appendix.

The evaluation plan in a public sector grant is quite extensive and often requires both internal and external (non-agency employee) evaluators, who must be included in the budget. An "Evaluation Chart" that has all goals and objectives listed, along with the assessment tools for each objective, the assessment date(s) for each tool, and the person responsible for each action is included. Generally, the evaluation plan should use both quantitative and qualitative measures, and should ultimately focus on the

205

purpose of the project (Office of Sponsored Projects, 1990).

Dissemination

The dissemination plan describes in detail methods to be used to disseminate descriptions of the project and its results. Methods of dissemination may include videotapes, journal articles, manuals, and conference presentations. The plan also indicates anticipated audiences. For example, results may be shared with project staff and school administrators, presented at regional or national conferences, or published in national journals or abstracts. Federal public sector grants will expect national dissemination, minimally at the national conference for grant recipients in Washington, D.C., which also must be included in the budget.

Budget plan and cost effectiveness

This section is a narrative explanation of the budget sheet included in the Appendix. All funds requested are placed in categories such as personnel, fringe benefits, space costs, equipment, consumable supplies, travel, telephone, contractual services, indirect charges, and other costs, such as postage and insurance. It also should include other sources of funds, such as state funds, and expenses such as fringe benefits, travel to conferences to disseminate the results, postage, insurance, travel expenses, and indirect costs mandated by schools to cover overhead. In addition to delineating fund uses, the budget plan should include all resources that the applicant agency will be "donating in kind" to the project. These should have a listed value of at least 25% of the requested grant allocation. This is essential, as funding agencies want to know that both the community and the agency are willing to contribute resources to the project.

Funding agencies look carefully at the cost effectiveness per user and prefer projects that will impact hundreds of children to those that impact only a dozen or fewer. In addition, funding agencies carefully consider the future funding plan, which describes funds available to continue the project after grant funding has been terminated. Some projects, such as model demonstration and capital improvement projects, are not expected to be continued by the agency. Projects that create new programs or hire staff, however, cause funding sources to ask for plans for agency project cost assumption.

References

The reference list contains references included in the earlier sections and sufficient references to support the approach taken in each component of the project. Often this section can be placed in the Appendix.

Signature

Every grant needs to bear, usually on forms, the official signatory of the applicant agency head. In school systems, this is the superintendent or designee.

Appendix

Appendix contents are dictated by the funding source, but generally include:

1. A copy of the tax exempt status;
2. A copy of the agency operating budget;
3. Resumés of the Principal Investigator(s), resumés of individuals listed in the person-loading chart, and job descriptions of persons yet to be hired;
4. Budget sheet;
5. Any evaluation instruments, especially those that are not standardized;
6. Other relevant documentation, such as syllabi for courses; and
7. Letters of support from any schools, community agencies, state agencies, non-profit agencies, and universities listed as potential project participants. These letters should

specify what part they are expecting to have in the project, acknowledge the need for the project, and confirm their professional endorsement of the applicant and applicant agency.

Public sector grant proposals must follow very specific guidelines delineated in the RFP. Following directions is imperative, as they are vigorously maintained. For example, a proposal mailed seconds after the postmark deadline will not be considered. An excessively long proposal will be read only up to the designated page limit. Grants must be written in the exact order specified in the RFP, with the same headings. If the RFP designates that all copies should have original signatures, follow that directive.

Public sector grants have more levels of review than private sector grants, and must go through an "Intergovernmental Review" at the state level. Usually this means that a copy of the abstract, cover sheet, and budget are sent to the state office.

If the grant is not funded, comments by reviewers are often available. These comments can be used to revise the proposal before resubmission.

IMPLEMENTING

Implementing a grant requires considerable time and energy. The time and energy required is often compensated by student improvement and increased staff morale. Participation is enthusiastic when grants are well planned, meet a high need, and include meaningful activities and objectives. At times, this can take surprising turns. For example, although staff training was definitely a goal in the project *Facilitating interagency services for children with emotional or behavioral disorders* (Harvey, 1994), it was surprising that one school district had sufficient demand to require 31 training workshops. By the

end of a one-year period, 875 different individuals had participated in workshops on non-violent crisis intervention, working with children with severe emotional disturbance through teamwork and interagency collaboration. Participants included public school administrators, alderman, school bus drivers, child welfare workers, city politicians, college trainers, school counselors, curriculum coordinators, developmental disability staff, juvenile workers, mental health workers, school nurses, paraprofessionals, parents, police, school principals, private providers, psychologists, reading teachers, recreation staff, regular class teachers, school board members, special education teachers, state department heads, and state senators.

The biggest challenge in implementing a grant involves time, as it is very easy to underestimate the time it takes to initiate a project, hire personnel, and implement activities. Furthermore, at times even the most carefully researched project will not be implemented as planned.

Ethical dilemma 13-1

You co-wrote a federal grant with an intern you are supervising. Although the needs assessment conducted prior to writing the grant indicated a high interest in school-based family therapy, very few families attend the therapy sessions. Therefore, a large sum of money from the grant remains to be spent. The internship, however, is soon to be concluded and the intern is looking for a job. You would like to hire her but do not have money in the general fund to do so. Someone suggests that you spend the unused "family therapy" grant money for hiring the intern. *What are the ethical dilemmas? What steps can be taken?*

EVALUATING

Evaluating a grant project is another example of a program evaluation and follows the same process described in the previous chapter.

CONCLUSION

Writing grants to support program development and evaluations is an excellent method for supervisors of school psychologists to increase the effectiveness of both school psychological services and school services in general. Supervisors of school psychologists are often in an ideal position to observe programmatic needs and to encourage the school psychologists working under their supervision to plan and conduct such activities. The analytical, consultative, communication, and evaluative skills needed for grant writing and implementation are often well within the province and expertise of school psychologists.

208

PROMOTING SCHOOL PSYCHOLOGICAL SERVICES

Promotion of school psychological services is necessary because the services are often neither understood nor widely publicized. This can result in necessary resources, such as personnel or equipment, being reduced or removed from district budgets. It also can cause individuals who are not knowledgeable about the effectiveness and efficiency of school psychological services to question whether the district should be underwriting the services, rather than hiring hourly consultants or test administrators. Supervisors of school psychologists should be careful not to interpret such questions as personal attacks. Both school board members and taxpayers believe the mission of the school board is to provide quality education for a reasonable cost. Questioning the efficacy of various budget items is not only reasonable but also necessary.

"Listening and responding to the consumer" is the fundamental and most important principle underlying promotion of any service. Therefore, several methods to promote school psychological services have already been discussed in earlier chapters. When supervisors consult with administrators, teachers, parents, and students in developing the vision for school psychology services, writing job descriptions, selecting staff, and evaluating services, they are listening and responding to the "consumers" of school psychological services.

The second principle underlying the promotion of a service is clear communication. All school board members, superintendents, principals, and other administrators should have a clear understanding of what their district school

psychologists do and how well they do it. With such an understanding, they can respond appropriately when (not "if") asked at a party, "Why does the district have school psychologists?"

Furthermore, they should be able to respond in a positive manner that fits the departmental vision. That is, we would prefer that they say something other than, "We have them because the Feds say we must for special ed testing." For this to be the case, the supervisor of school psychologists must communicate the activities and successes of supervisees to administrators on a regular basis.

Communication can and should take many forms. As Franklin (1995) indicates, it is important for supervisors of school psychologists to "report the accomplishments of the school psychology department to the teachers, administrators, governing board members, and constituents of the district" (p. 76). Vignettes of success stories, such as a reduction of playground aggression and violence through a peer mediation program, are very helpful. In addition, many administrators are particularly responsive to data generated in an evaluation of services. For example, enumeration of the number of students with whom the district's school psychologists have worked in conducting a comprehensive evaluation of school psychological services is an invaluable method for gathering information about departmental accomplishments.

The complexities of working as a school psychologist will not be understood or appreciated by administrators unless communicated in an honest and forthright manner. For example, it is not uncommon for administrators to believe that conducting a psychological assessment takes only the amount of time it takes to administer the tests. To correct such misunderstandings, accurate data can be gathered by documenting the "start to finish" time per case, finding an average, and presenting the information to administrators.

Furthermore, upper level administrators are often unaware of the conditions under which school psychologists work. They are surprised to learn of common problems such as the extra duties, the lack of confidential space and telephones to call parents, and insufficient materials and equipment. The following vignette, shared on the NASP Listserve in June 1999, illustrates the method Elizabeth Hage used to correct a resource deficit.

Case study 14-1

We convinced our boss to order laptops for each of us by demonstrating the efficiency of having one to tote with us to our various schools—expediting report writing and spending less time and mileage running back to our base office, etc. We also were able to get scoring software for various programs, again through demonstrating efficiency. Now that many of our schools are wired, we are also able to access the network, providing "on-line" consultation with teachers and professional support with each other. Even our colleagues that were computer/keyboard "illiterate" are finding them more useful than they imagined.

We researched needs and presented a proposal outlining system requirements, software requirements and costs, prioritizing so that we could at least get the essentials first, as well as the justifications. The boss was so sold that she even got herself a laptop!

(Printed with permission of author)

To place the administrators in a better position to advocate for resources for school psychology services, Forman and Cecil (1985) suggest that school psychologists meet annually with administrators to clarify the client population, goals, and their role. In addition, school psychologists should:

- keep administrators updated on activities throughout the year;
- provide them with a written summary of activities and accomplishments at the end of every year;
- invite them to local school psychology conferences;
- provide them with brief articles related to school psychology that may be of interest;
- increase visibility by volunteering to be on committees and by attending faculty meetings and open house night; and
- include administrators in school psychology program planning and professional development activities.

Supervisors of school psychologists have a responsibility to regularly communicate about, and to promote, school psychological services to all consumers, including district personnel and the community at large. Appropriate vehicles of communication are local newspapers, the school Website, school newsletters, and state and national education newsletters.

EVALUATING SCHOOL PSYCHOLOGICAL SERVICES

In addition to the individual performance evaluations of school psychologists described in Chapter 6, supervisors of school psychologists are also responsible for the program evaluation of services provided by the entire school psychology department. Evaluation of a department's services improves performance, guides professional development, and provides the opportunities for professional recognition. In addition, it identifies and leads to the improvement of programmatic and procedural weakness. Furthermore, it documents and promotes the effectiveness of psychological services as a whole.

The evaluation of school psychological services has the same basic components of any program evaluation, delineated in Chapter 12. These components will not be duplicated at this time. The evaluation of school psychological services does have some unique characteristics and considerations, however, which will be addressed in the following pages.

An evaluation of school psychological services can have a profound impact on both practice and employment, since the results of formal or informal assessments of services affects the employment and roles of school psychologists. When school psychologists assess their functioning by documenting professional activities, fund allocation can be justified and a need for change can be demonstrated (Zins, 1985a). However, documentation of professional activities is often narrowly defined and inappropriately applied, as when only the number of completed test administrations are calculated.

As described previously, the first steps in planning an evaluation are to (a) develop a Steering Committee to guide the process, and (b) determine questions to be answered. In developing a Steering Committee, the supervising school psychologist should be careful to include upper level administrators and school board members.

The underlying question in assessing school psychological services is whether the services provided are of high quality. However, quality can be defined from many different perspectives. A supervisor of school psychologists may be interested in exploring one or more of the following definitions of quality, or may be interested in altogether different definitions of quality. The following discussion considers the evalua-

tion of school psychological services from five different perspectives:

- Do they comply with local, state, and federal guidelines?
- Do they meet professional standards?
- Do they have an impact on students and staff?
- Do consumers consider them adequate?
- Are they are cost effective?

1. *Do school psychological service procedures comply with local, state, and federal guidelines?*

Answering this question requires conducting file reviews. Examination of files can illuminate many variables, such as:

- Average number of days from initial referral to initial contact;
- Average number of days from initial referral to implementation of counseling and/or behavior management consultation;
- Average number of days from parent permission for assessment to parental receipt of written results;
- The appropriateness of assessment techniques including:
  a. Use of multifaceted assessments;
  b. Use of valid and reliable instruments;
  c. Appropriateness to the handicapping condition;
  d. Use of the student's dominant language.
- Whether the data gathered justify the recommendations;
- Whether reports are jargon-free, readable, and professional in appearance.

2. *How do our school psychological services compare with professional standards?*

This question can be addressed by using questions based on the standard of practice developed by the National Association of School Psychologists, such as the questionnaires in the *Guidelines For Evaluating School Psychological Services* (Revised) (Harvey, 1997a), contained at the end of this chapter. These questions were adapted from standards in the *Professional Conduct Manual* (NASP, 1997) and are presented on a computer disk as well as in hard copy, so the program evaluators can choose particular items and delete others. Individuals within the school district who might be chosen to complete questionnaires are classroom teachers, school nurses, occupational therapists, paraprofessionals, principals, remedial teachers, school counselors, school psychologists, social workers, special education teachers, speech/language therapists, special education administrators, upper level administrators, and students. Others who might be asked to complete questionnaires include parents, physical therapists, physicians, and private practice psychologists.

The Steering Committee determines the method to distribute the questionnaires, the office or person to whom they are to be returned, whether a self-addressed, stamped envelope will be included, and what techniques would be used to ensure a high rate of return. Examples of processes that increase return rates are:

- Telephoning or sending letters explaining the purpose of the evaluation prior to mailing surveys;
- Ensuring anonymity of respondents;
- Sending follow-up postcards or memos a week after the original mailing;
- Re-mailing surveys with a different cover letter two weeks after the original mailing;
- Releasing press notices; and
- Giving school personnel staff development credits for questionnaire completion.

After the questionnaires are returned, the median response for each item is tallied and a summary is report presented to school psychologists and administrators.

3. *Do our school psychology services have an impact on students and staff?*

To answer this question school psychologists will need to gather relevant outcome data. The collection of outcome data as it relates to school psychological services is complicated by various obstacles such as time, varied definitions of success, and short-term versus long-term gains. Furthermore, school psychologists have multiple clients (administrators, parents, students, and teachers), increasing the likelihood that a particular outcome may be seen as a success by one person but as a failure by another (Fagan & Wise, 1994).

If the overriding goal of school psychological services is to improve the functioning of children, the ultimate outcome of school psychological services should be that referral problems are alleviated and student functioning improved. As mentioned previously, student outcome measures include, but are not limited to, achievement test scores, attendance, behavior, discipline reports, dropout rates, emotional status, grades, graduation rates, hours per week assigned to special education services, peer relationships, suspensions, and tardiness.

Additionally, school psychologists might select psychologically based measures, as described in Ogles, Lambert, and Masters (1996). For example, behavior could be assessed before and after the intervention using behavior rating scales such as the Behavior Assessment System for Children (BASC) (Reynolds & Kamphaus, 1992) or the Achenbach Child Behavior Checklist (Achenbach, 1991). Internal status of adolescents can be measured by the child report versions of the above, or by individual scales such as the Beck Depression Inventory (Beck, Steer, & Garbin, 1988) or the

212

Revised Children's Manifest Anxiety Scale (Reynolds & Richmond, 1985). Obviously, any scale must be carefully assessed regarding reliability and validity, particularly the validity relative to the chosen interventions.

4. *Do administrators, parents, and teachers consider school psychological services adequate?*

This question can be addressed by gathering information from administrators, parents, and teachers via questionnaires, as described previously. Interviews with administrators, parents, teachers, and students can also address this question. Interview questions will need to be field tested, and might include the following:

- In an ideal world, what impact would school psychological services have on students, teachers, parents, the school, the school system, and the community?
- Do you find the wide spectrum of school psychology services, including program evaluation and research, desirable?
- Are school psychologists sufficiently accessible to students, teachers, administrators, and parents? What would help make the psychologists be more accessible?
- Do school psychologists help you better analyze, understand, and solve problems?
- Are school psychologists' recommendations appropriate?
- What psychological services would you like increased? Decreased?

5. *Are our school psychology services cost effective? What would be the cost of these services if externally contracted psychologists provided them?*

This question is best answered by document analysis, the enumeration of the school psychologists' activities, and a comparison with the fees charged by consultants for the same amount of time. District school psychologists can submit monthly enumeration of their activities to the supervisor, who can then compile the information and submit it to the administration and school board in an easily digested format. In conducting such an analysis, it is important to look at the full range of the school psychologists' activities.

Activities that can be enumerated can be classified as indirect interventions, direct interventions, assessment activities, or activities relevant to program development and evaluation. Examples of indirect intervention activities that can be enumerated are:

- number of referrals for pre-referral intervention strategies,
- contacts with outside agencies and/or professionals,
- classroom observations conducted,
- school records reviewed,
- teacher interviews and contacts,
- parent interviews and telephone calls, and
- teacher assistance team meetings attended.

Direct interventions that can be tallied include:

- the number of intervention referrals received,
- the number of children counseled individually,
- the number of children counseled in groups,
- time per week spent providing direct services,
- parent conferences held,
- parent-training workshops held,
- staff development/in-service workshops conducted,
- parent information sessions held, and
- newsletters and other information distributed.

Assessment activities that can be enumerated include:

- the number of referrals received for assessment,

213

- assessments completed,
- the number of completed assessments during which children were identified as disabled,
- the number of assessments after which children were placed in more restrictive settings, and
- post-assessment meetings attended.

Finally, program development and evaluation activities can be enumerated. Possible sources of information include:

- the programs implemented, modified, or evaluated,
- grants written, awarded, and implemented,
- yearly goals attained,
- the number of children in these programs, and
- the number of staff trained by school psychologists at in-service workshops.

After the evaluation question is defined and procedures have been determined, the evaluation of school psychological services follows the same stages as those of general program evaluations described previously. After the evaluation is complete and strengths and weaknesses have been determined, the results should be shared first with all school psychologists and the Steering Committee to develop a list of potential recommendations. The strengths, weaknesses, and recommendations are then shared with the larger community.

The following pages include questionnaires based on the *NASP Professional Conduct Manual* (1997). One questionnaire is designed to be completed by school psychologists themselves. The others are designed to be completed by parents, school personnel such as teachers or counselors, and administrators. Finally, there are questionnaires that address issues applicable to school systems that contract psychological services, and for school psychologists in private

practice. Questions are keyed to facilitate comparison across surveys. For example, questions appearing in the Administrators Survey are numbered A1, A2, etc., while questions in the School Psychologist's Survey are numbered S1 and S2. When the same questions reappear in the School Personnel or Parent Surveys, they are keyed with a cross-reference.

214

SCHOOL PSYCHOLOGICAL SERVICES EVALUATION

To find ways to improve our services, we are evaluating our school psychology programs. As someone who has used our services, you can provide very valuable information. Your participation is voluntary, and your responses will be kept confidential. Please take a few minutes to complete the following questionnaire. Thank you!

a. Circle the school psychology services you feel are most important:

A. Academic interventions for the classroom.

B. Behavioral interventions for the classroom.

C. Case management for interagency wraparound services.

D. Consulting for pre-referral programming.

E. Coordinating services with outside agencies and therapists.

F. Crisis intervention.

G. Early intervention/prevention (before special education).

H. Evaluations for special education services.

I. Family therapy.

J. Group counseling.

K. Individual counseling.

L. In-service training.

M. Parent skills training.

N. Program evaluations.

O. Social skills training.

P. Study skills training.

Q. Substance abuse prevention/intervention.

b. How many times have you worked with one of our school psychologists?

   A. once   B. two to four times   C. five or more times

c. Do you have any comments about our school psychology services?

d. Do you have any suggestions for improving school psychology services?

SCHOOL PSYCHOLOGISTS' QUESTIONNAIRE

Organization of school psychological services

S1. School psychological services are planned, organized, directed, and reviewed by school psychologists.

5 Almost Always	4	3	2	1 Almost Never

S2. School psychologists participate in determining the recipients and type of psychological services offered.

5 Almost Always	4	3	2	1 Almost Never

S3. The goals and objectives of school psychological services are available in written form.

5 Almost Always	4	3	2	1 Almost Never

S4. A written set of procedural guidelines for the delivery of school psychological services is followed and made available upon request.

5 Almost Always	4	3	2	1 Almost Never

S5. A clearly stated referral system is in writing and is communicated to parents, staff members, students, and other referral agencies.

5 Almost Always	4	3	2	1 Almost Never

S6. The organization of school psychological services is in written form and includes lines of responsibility, supervisory, and administrative relationships.

5 Almost Always	4	3	2	1 Almost Never

S7. Where two or more school psychologists are employed, a coordinated system of school psychological services is in effect within that unit.

5 Almost Always	4	3	2	1 Almost Never

S8. Units providing school psychological services include sufficient professional and support personnel to achieve their goals and objectives.

5 Almost Always	4	3	2	1 Almost Never

Relationships to other professionals

S9. The school psychological services unit is responsive to the needs of the population that it serves. Psychological services are reviewed to ensure their conformity with the needs of the population served.

5 Almost Always	4	3	2	1 Almost Never

S10. School psychologists establish and maintain relationships with other professionals (e.g., bilingual specialists, audiologists, and parent advocates) who provide services, and collaborate with these professionals in prevention, assessment, and intervention efforts.

5 Almost Always	4	3	2	1 Almost Never

S11. School psychologists maintain a cooperative relationship with colleagues and co-workers in the best mutual interests of clients, in a manner consistent with the goals of the employing agency.

5 Almost Always	4	3	2	1 Almost Never

S12. School psychologists develop plans for the delivery of services in accordance with best professional practices.

5 Almost Always	4	3	2	1 Almost Never

S13. School psychologists employed within a school setting help coordinate with the services of mental health providers for other agencies (such as community mental health centers, guidance clinics, or private practitioners) to ensure a continuum of services.

5 Almost Always	4	3	2	1 Almost Never

S14. School psychologists are knowledgeable about community agencies and resources.

5 Almost Always	4	3	2	1 Almost Never

S15. School psychologists provide liaison and consulting services to the community and agencies regarding psychological, mental health, and educational issues.

5 Almost Always	4	3	2	1 Almost Never

S16. As needed, school psychologists communicate with, and refer clients to, state and community agencies and professionals.

5 Almost Always	4	3	2	1 Almost Never

217

S17. School psychologists are informed of and have the opportunity to participate in community agency meetings regarding their their clients.

5 Almost Always	4	3	2	1 Almost Never

S18. Community agency personnel are invited to participate in school system conferences concerning their clients, with written parent permission.

5 Almost Always	4	3	2	1 Almost Never

Consultation

S19. School psychologists consult and collaborate with parents, school, and outside personnel regarding mental health, behavioral, and educational concerns.

5 Almost Always	4	3	2	1 Almost Never

S20. School psychologists design and develop procedures for preventing disorders, promoting mental health and learning, and improving educational systems.

5 Almost Always	4	3	2	1 Almost Never

S21. School psychologists provide skill enhancement activities (such as in-service training, organizational development, parent counseling, program planning and evaluation, vocational development, and parent education programs) to school personnel, parents, and others in the community regarding issues of learning, development, and behavior.

5 Almost Always	4	3	2	1 Almost Never

S22. School psychologists facilitate the delivery of services by assisting those who play major roles in the educational system (parents, school personnel, community agency)

5 Almost Always	4	3	2	1 Almost Never

Psychological and Psychoeducational Assessment

S23. School psychologists conduct psychological and psycho-educational assessments which include consideration of:

a. personality

5 Almost Always	4	3	2	1 Almost Never

b. emotional status

5 Almost Always	4	3	2	1 Almost Never

c. social skills and adjustment

5 Almost Always	4	3	2	1 Almost Never

d. intelligence and cognitive functioning

5 Almost Always	4	3	2	1 Almost Never

e. scholastic aptitude

5 Almost Always	4	3	2	1 Almost Never

f. adaptive behavior

5 Almost Always	4	3	2	1 Almost Never

g. language and communication skills,

5 Almost Always	4	3	2	1 Almost Never

h. academic knowledge and achievement,

5 Almost Always	4	3	2	1 Almost Never

i. sensory & perceptual-motor functioning,

5 Almost Always	4	3	2	1 Almost Never

j. educational setting,

5 Almost Always	4	3	2	1 Almost Never

k. family/environmental-cultural influences,

5 Almost Always	4	3	2	1 Almost Never

l. career and vocational development, aptitude, and interests.

5 Almost Always	4	3	2	1 Almost Never

S24. School psychologists use a variety of instruments, procedures, and techniques. Interviews, observations, and behavioral evaluations are included in these procedures.

5 Almost Always	4	3	2	1 Almost Never

S25. When conducting psychological and psycho-educational assessments, school psychologists have explicit regard for the context and setting in which their assessments take place and are used.

5 Almost Always	4	3	2	1 Almost Never

S26. School psychologists adhere to professional resolutions and ethical guidelines regarding non-biased assessment and programming for all students.

5 Almost Always	4	3	2	1 Almost Never

Direct Service

S27. School psychologists provide direct service to facilitate the functioning of individuals, groups, and/or organizations.

5 Almost Always	4	3	2	1 Almost Never

S28. School psychologists design direct service programs to enhance cognitive, affective, social, and vocational development.

5 Almost Always	4	3	2	1 Almost Never

S29. School psychologists develop collaborative relationships with their clients and involve them in the assessment, direct services, and program evaluation procedures.

5 Almost Always	4	3	2	1 Almost Never

219

Supervision

S30. School psychologists provide and/or engage in supervision, peer review and Continuing Professional Development.

5 Almost Always	4	3	2	1 Almost Never

Research

S31. School psychologists report, utilize, design, and/or conduct research of a psychological and educational nature.

5 Almost Always	4	3	2	1 Almost Never

S32. School psychologists' research is in accordance with relevant ethical guidelines of the professional, with particular concern for obtaining informed consent, notifying subjects of the expected length of participation, and protecting subjects from breach of confidentiality, coercion, harm, or danger.

5 Almost Always	4	3	2	1 Almost Never

Program planning and evaluation

S33. School psychologists provide program planning and evaluation services to assist in decision-making activities.

5 Almost Always	4	3	2	1 Almost Never

S34. School psychologists serve on committees responsible for developing and planning educational and educationally related activities.	5 Almost Always	4	3	2	1 Almost Never

Autonomous functioning

S35. School psychologists have professional autonomy in determining the nature, scope, and extent of their specific services.	5 Almost Always	4	3	2	1 Almost Never
S36. School psychologists restrict their practice to those areas in which they have received formal training and supervised experience.	5 Almost Always	4	3	2	1 Almost Never
S37. The school psychologists adhere to the best available and most appropriate standards of practice.	5 Almost Always	4	3	2	1 Almost Never
S38. School psychologists keep abreast of new intervention techniques, assessment procedures, computerized assistance, and other advances in the field.	5 Almost Always	4	3	2	1 Almost Never
S39. School psychologists actively participate and engage in activities designed to continue, enhance, and upgrade professional training and skills, and to help ensure quality service provision.	5 Almost Always	4	3	2	1 Almost Never
S41. School psychologists receive at least one hour weekly of individual, face-to-face supervision for the first three years of full-time employment as a school psychologist.	5 Almost Always	4	3	2	1 Almost Never
S42. All school psychologists, even after three years of supervision, continue to engage in supervision and/or peer review on a regular basis to discuss cases or professional issues designed to assist with problem solving, decision making, and appropriate practice, and further their professional development by active participation in CPD activities.	5 Almost Always	4	3	2	1 Almost Never
S43. All school psychologists readily seek additional assistance from supervisors, peers, or colleagues with particularly difficult or complex cases, or when expanding their services into areas in which they infrequently practice.	5 Almost Always	4	3	2	1 Almost Never

Accountability

S44. School psychologists perform their duties in an accountable manner by keeping records of their efforts, evaluating effectiveness, and modifying practices and/or expanding services as needed.	5 Almost Always	4	3	2	1 Almost Never

220

S45. School psychologists devise systems of accountability and outcome evaluation, which aid in documenting the effectiveness of intervention efforts and other services they provide.	5 Almost Always	4	3	2	1 Almost Never
S46. School psychologists regularly evaluate their progress in achieving goals with consideration of the cost effectiveness of school psychological services in terms of time, money, and resources.	5 Almost Always	4	3	2	1 Almost Never
S47. School psychological services are evaluated internally and externally through state educational agency review or peer reviews.	5 Almost Always	4	3	2	1 Almost Never
S48. School psychologists are accountable for their services and make information about their services available to consumers so that the consumers can participate in decision-making concerning initiation, termination, continuation, modification, and evaluation of psychological services.	5 Almost Always	4	3	2	1 Almost Never

Professional Ethics and Guidelines

S49. Each school psychologist practices in full accord with the NASP *Principles for Professional Ethics* and the *Professional Conduct Manual*.	5 Almost Always	4	3	2	1 Almost Never

TEACHER AND SCHOOL PERSONNEL QUESTIONNAIRE
ON SCHOOL PSYCHOLOGICAL SERVICES

1.	The psychologist has genuine concern for students.	5 Almost Always	4	3	2 1 Almost Never
2.	The psychologist listens well and encourages others to ask questions.	5 Almost Always	4	3	2 1 Almost Never
3.	The psychologist comments on students' abilities, strengths, and talents.	5 Almost Always	4	3	2 1 Almost Never
4.	The psychologist helps others understand the student's functioning.	5 Almost Always	4	3	2 1 Almost Never
5.	The psychologist gives practical recommendations.	5 Almost Always	4	3	2 1 Almost Never
6.	The psychologist recommends programs that give the best chance for student success.	5 Almost Always	4	3	2 1 Almost Never
7.	The psychologist's reports are easy to understand.	5 Almost Always	4	3	2 1 Almost Never
8.	School psychological services are provided in a coordinated, organized fashion. (A1)	5 Almost Always	4	3	2 1 Almost Never
9.	Psychological services are available to all students served by the agency. (A3)	5 Almost Always	4	3	2 1 Almost Never
10.	Psychological services are available to an extent sufficient to meet the needs of the students. (A4)	5 Almost Always	4	3	2 1 Almost Never
11.	School psychologists use assessment techniques to provide information, which is helpful in maximizing student achievement and adjustment. (A20)	5 Almost Always	4	3	2 1 Almost Never
12.	School psychologists use assessment practices that help develop effective education programs. (A24)	5 Almost Always	4	3	2 1 Almost Never

13.	The multi-disciplinary team includes a fully trained and certified school psychologist. (A25)	5 Almost Always	4	3	2	1 Almost Never
14.	Assessment procedures and program recommendations are chosen to maximize the student's opportunities to be successful in the general culture, while respecting the student's ethnic background. (A27)	5 Almost Always	4	3	2	1 Almost Never
15.	Multifaceted assessment batteries are used which include a focus on the student's strengths. (A28)	5 Almost Always	4	3	2	1 Almost Never
16.	Communications are held in the client's dominant spoken language or alternative communication system. (A29)	5 Almost Always	4	3	2	1 Almost Never
17.	Records of meetings regarding test results and program recommendations are available to all concerned, on a need-to-know basis. (A37)	5 Almost Always	4	3	2	1 Almost Never
18.	School psychologists are involved in determining options and revisions of educational programs. (A38)	5 Almost Always	4	3	2	1 Almost Never
19.	School psychologists follow up on the effect of their recommendations. (A40)	5 Almost Always	4	3	2	1 Almost Never
20.	Student needs are given priority in determining educational programs. (A41)	5 Almost Always	4	3	2	1 Almost Never
21.	Regular systematic review of the student's program is conducted and includes program modifications as necessary. (A44)	5 Almost Always	4	3	2	1 Almost Never
22.	School psychologists clearly interpret school psychological records to non-psychologists. (A49)	5 Almost Always	4	3	2	1 Almost Never
23.	School psychologists help determine the recipients and the type of school psychological services offered. (S2)	5 Almost Always	4	3	2	1 Almost Never
24.	A clearly stated referral system is in writing and is communicated to parents, staff members, students, and other referral agencies. (S5)	5 Almost Always	4	3	2	1 Almost Never

25. School psychological services are responsive to the needs of the students. (S9)

   | 5 Almost Always | 4 | 3 | 2 | 1 Almost Never |

26. School psychologists collaborate with other professionals (e.g. therapists, bilingual specialists, parent advocates). (S10)

   | 5 Almost Always | 4 | 3 | 2 | 1 Almost Never |

27. School psychologists maintain a cooperative relationship with colleagues and co-workers. (S11)

   | 5 Almost Always | 4 | 3 | 2 | 1 Almost Never |

28. School psychologists employed within a school setting help coordinate with the services of mental health providers for other agencies. (S13)

   | 5 Almost Always | 4 | 3 | 2 | 1 Almost Never |

29. School psychologists are knowledgeable about community agencies and resources. (S14)

   | 5 Almost Always | 4 | 3 | 2 | 1 Almost Never |

30. School psychologists communicate with, and refer clients to, state and community agencies and professionals. (S16)

   | 5 Almost Always | 4 | 3 | 2 | 1 Almost Never |

31. School psychologists design and develop procedures for preventing disorders, promoting mental health and learning, and improving educational systems. (S20)

   | 5 Almost Always | 4 | 3 | 2 | 1 Almost Never |

32. School psychologists provide skill enhancement activities (such as in-service training, organizational development, parent counseling, program planning and evaluation, vocational development, and parent education programs) to school personnel, parents, and others in the community regarding issues of human learning, human development, and behavior. (S21)

   | 5 Almost Always | 4 | 3 | 2 | 1 Almost Never |

33. School psychologists facilitate the delivery of services by assisting those who play major roles in the educational system (i.e., parents, school personnel, community agencies). (S22)

   | 5 Almost Always | 4 | 3 | 2 | 1 Almost Never |

34. School psychologists conduct assessments which include consideration of all relevant aspects of students' functioning including personality, emotional status, social skills and adjustment, intelligence and cognitive functioning, scholastic aptitude, adaptive behavior, language and communication skills, academic knowledge and achievement, sensory and perceptual-motor functioning, educational setting, family/ environmental-cultural influences, career and vocational development, aptitude, and interests. (S23)

   | 5 Almost Always | 4 | 3 | 2 | 1 Almost Never |

		5	4	3	2	1
35.	School psychologists use a variety of instruments, procedures, and techniques. Interviews, observations, and behavioral evaluations are included. (S24)	Almost Always				Almost Never
36.	When conducting psychological and psycho-educational assessments, school psychologists have explicit regard for the context and setting in which their assessments take place and are used. (S25)	Almost Always				Almost Never
37.	School psychologists *provide* direct service (such as counseling) to facilitate the functioning of individuals, groups, and /or organizations. (S27)	Almost Always				Almost Never
38.	School psychologists *design* direct service programs to enhance cognitive, affective, social, and vocational development. (S28)	Almost Always				Almost Never
39.	School psychologists involve clients in the assessment, direct services, and program evaluation procedures. (S29)	Almost Always				Almost Never
40.	School psychologists develop their skills in new intervention techniques, assessment procedures, computerized assistance, and other advances in the field. (S38)	Almost Always				Almost Never
41.	School psychologists perform their duties in an accountable manner by keeping records of their efforts, evaluating effectiveness, and modifying practices and/or expanding services as needed. (S44)	Almost Always				Almost Never

225

PARENT QUESTIONNAIRE ON SCHOOL PSYCHOLOGICAL SERVICES

1. The psychologist has genuine concern for students.

   5 — 4 — 3 — 2 — 1
   Almost Always   Almost Never

2. The psychologist listens well and encourages others to ask questions.

   5 — 4 — 3 — 2 — 1
   Almost Always   Almost Never

3. The psychologist comments on students' abilities, strengths, and talents.

   5 — 4 — 3 — 2 — 1
   Almost Always   Almost Never

4. The psychologist helps others understand the student's functioning.

   5 — 4 — 3 — 2 — 1
   Almost Always   Almost Never

5. The psychologist gives practical recommendations.

   5 — 4 — 3 — 2 — 1
   Almost Always   Almost Never

6. The psychologist recommends programs that give the best chance for student success.

   5 — 4 — 3 — 2 — 1
   Almost Always   Almost Never

7. The psychologist's reports are easy to understand.

   5 — 4 — 3 — 2 — 1
   Almost Always   Almost Never

8. School psychological services are provided in a coordinated, organized fashion. (A1)

   5 — 4 — 3 — 2 — 1
   Almost Always   Almost Never

9. Psychological services are available enough to meet the needs of the students. (A4)

   5 — 4 — 3 — 2 — 1
   Almost Always   Almost Never

10. The psychologist provides information that helps student achievement and adjustment. (A20)

    5 — 4 — 3 — 2 — 1
    Almost Always   Almost Never

11. The school team includes a school psychologist. (A25)

    5 — 4 — 3 — 2 — 1
    Almost Always   Almost Never

12. School psychologist's assessments and program recommendations respect the student's ethnic background. (A27)

    5 — 4 — 3 — 2 — 1
    Almost Always   Almost Never

		5	4	3	2	1	
13.	School psychologist's assessment procedures include a focus on the student's strengths. (A28)	Almost Always				Almost Never	
14.	Communications are held in the client's language. (A29)	Almost Always				Almost Never	
15.	Parents gave written consent before school psychologists test or provide special programs. (A33)	Almost Always				Almost Never	
16.	Parents are given all important information and told how it relates to decision making. (A34)	Almost Always				Almost Never	
17.	Parents are invited to participate in decision-making meetings. (A35)	Almost Always				Almost Never	
18.	Records of meetings regarding test results and program recommendations are available to all who need to know. (A37)	Almost Always				Almost Never	
19.	School psychologists follow up on the effect of their recommendations. (A40)	Almost Always				Almost Never	
20.	Student needs are given priority in determining educational programs. (A41)	Almost Always				Almost Never	
21.	Student's program are regularly reviewed and modified. (A44)	Almost Always				Almost Never	
22.	Parents may inspect and review any personally identifiable data relating to their child which were collected, maintained, or used in an evaluation. (A46)	Almost Always				Almost Never	
23.	The school psychologist clearly interprets school psychological records to non-psychologists. (A49)	Almost Always				Almost Never	
24.	A clearly stated referral system is communicated to parents. (S5)	Almost Always				Almost Never	

25. School psychological services are responsive to the needs of the students. (S9)

| 5 Almost Always | 4 | 3 | 2 | 1 Almost Never |

26. The school psychologist collaborates with other professionals (e.g. bilingual specialists, therapists, and parent advocates). (S10)

| 5 Almost Always | 4 | 3 | 2 | 1 Almost Never |

27. The school psychologists coordinate with the services of mental health providers for other agencies. (S13)

| 5 Almost Always | 4 | 3 | 2 | 1 Almost Never |

28. The school psychologist is knowledgeable about community agencies and resources. (S14)

| 5 Almost Always | 4 | 3 | 2 | 1 Almost Never |

29. The school psychologist refers clients to state and community agencies and professionals. (S16)

| 5 Almost Always | 4 | 3 | 2 | 1 Almost Never |

30. The school psychologist consults and collaborates with parents regarding mental health, behavioral, and educational concerns. (S19)

| 5 Almost Always | 4 | 3 | 2 | 1 Almost Never |

31. The school psychologist develops procedures for preventing disorders, promoting mental health and learning, and improving educational systems. (S20)

| 5 Almost Always | 4 | 3 | 2 | 1 Almost Never |

32. The school psychologist provides skill enhancement activities (such as parent counseling and parent education programs) for parents regarding issues of learning, development, and behavior. (S21)

| 5 Almost Always | 4 | 3 | 2 | 1 Almost Never |

33. The school psychologist helps parents. (S22)

| 5 Almost Always | 4 | 3 | 2 | 1 Almost Never |

34. The school psychologist conducts comprehensive assessments. These include consideration of all aspects of students' functioning. (S23)

| 5 Almost Always | 4 | 3 | 2 | 1 Almost Never |

35. The school psychologist provides direct service (such as counseling) to individuals and /or groups. (S27)

| 5 Almost Always | 4 | 3 | 2 | 1 Almost Never |

ADMINISTRATOR QUESTIONNAIRE ON SCHOOL PSYCHOLOGICAL SERVICES

Comprehensive services

A1. School psychological services are provided in a coordinated, organized fashion.

| 5 Almost Always | 4 | 3 | 2 | 1 Almost Never |

A2. School psychological services include a comprehensive continuum of services including, but not limited to, consultation, assessment, research, program planning/evaluation, and direct service for individuals, groups, and systems.

| 5 Almost Always | 4 | 3 | 2 | 1 Almost Never |

A3. Psychological services are available to all students served by the agency.

| 5 Almost Always | 4 | 3 | 2 | 1 Almost Never |

A4. Psychological services are available to an extent sufficient to meet the needs of the population served. Usually at least one full-time school psychologist for each 1,000 children serviced by the LEA with a maximum of four schools served by one school psychologist.

| 5 Almost Always | 4 | 3 | 2 | 1 Almost Never |

A5. The breadth or availability of services is not dictated by the funding source (i.e., not limited to special education students because the school psychology budget came from special education sources).

| 5 Almost Always | 4 | 3 | 2 | 1 Almost Never |

Professional evaluation, supervision, and development

A6. An effective program of supervision and evaluation of school psychological services exists.

| 5 Almost Always | 4 | 3 | 2 | 1 Almost Never |

A7. School psychologists, in cooperation with their employing agencies, are responsible for the overall development, implementation, articulation, and professional supervision of school psychological service programs.

| 5 Almost Always | 4 | 3 | 2 | 1 Almost Never |

A8. Psychological services are supervised by a school psychologist who meets the criterion for supervising school psychologist and who demonstrates competencies needed for effective supervision.

| 5 Almost Always | 4 | 3 | 2 | 1 Almost Never |

229

A9. Sufficient supervision is available to all school psychologists to ensure the provision of effective and accountable services, usually one supervising school psychologist for every ten school psychologists.

5 Almost Always	4	3	2	1 Almost Never

A10. School psychology interns are supervised by a school psychologist with at least one year experience at the employing agency and who supervise no more than two interns at a time (up to six interns if the supervising psychologist has no other assigned duties).

5 Almost Always	4	3	2	1 Almost Never

A11. School psychologists receive supervision by a supervising school psychologist for the first three years as a school psychologist.

5 Almost Always	4	3	2	1 Almost Never

A12. School psychologists who have worked more than three years, including independent practitioners, continue to receive appropriate supervision, including peer review with other school psychologists.

5 Almost Always	4	3	2	1 Almost Never

A13. School psychologists are given appropriate time and support for peer review activities by employing agencies.

5 Almost Always	4	3	2	1 Almost Never

A14. Employing agencies ensure that school psychologists develop a coordinated plan for accountability and evaluation of all services provided in order to maintain and improve the effectiveness of services and that the plan includes specific, measurable objectives.

5 Almost Always	4	3	2	1 Almost Never

A15. Employing agencies provide release time and financial support for CPD activities for all school psychologists.

5 Almost Always	4	3	2	1 Almost Never

Conditions for effective service delivery

A16. School psychologists are not subjected to administrative constraints that prevent them from providing comprehensive services in accord with professional standards and guidelines for professional ethics. When conflict does occur, the principles of the *Ethics* and *Standards* take precedence.

5 Almost Always	4	3	2	1 Almost Never

A17. School psychologists have appropriate input into the general policy-making of the employing agency and the development of programs affecting the staff, students, and families they serve.

5 Almost Always	4	3	2	1 Almost Never

A18. School psychologists have appropriate professional autonomy in determining the nature, extent, and duration of services they provide. Legal, ethical and professional standards and guidelines are considered by the practitioner in making decisions regarding practice.

5 Almost Always	4	3	2	1 Almost Never

230

A19. School psychologists have access to adequate clerical assistance, appropriate professional work material, sufficient office and workspace, and general working conditions that enhance the delivery of effective services. Included are test materials, access to private telephone and office, secretarial services, therapeutic aids, profession books and journals, computers and related technology, and others.

5 Almost Always	4	3	2	1 Almost Never

Non-biased assessment

A20. School psychologists use assessment techniques to provide information that is helpful in maximizing student achievement, educational success, psychological adjustment, and behavioral adaptation.

5 Almost Always	4	3	2	1 Almost Never

A21. School psychologists have autonomous decision making responsibility to determine the type, nature, and extent of assessment techniques used in student evaluations

5 Almost Always	4	3	2	1 Almost Never

A22. School psychologists have autonomy in determining the content and nature of reports.

5 Almost Always	4	3	2	1 Almost Never

A23. Whenever possible, school psychologists use assessment techniques which have established validity and reliability for the purposes and populations for which the procedures are intended. If clinical procedures at the "research" stage of development are used, the reliability and validity of the procedures are clearly distinguished from those techniques that meet standards.

5 Almost Always	4	3	2	1 Almost Never

231

A24. School psychologists use, develop, and encourage assessment practices that increase the likelihood of the development of effective educational interventions and follow-up.

5 Almost Always	4	3	2	1 Almost Never

A25. The multi-disciplinary team involved in assessment, program decision-making, and evaluation includes a fully trained and certified school psychologist.

5 Almost Always	4	3	2	1 Almost Never

A26. The school psychologist communicates a written minority position to all involved when in disagreement with the multi-disciplinary team position.

5 Almost Always	4	3	2	1 Almost Never

A27. Assessment procedures and program recommendations are chosen to maximize the student's opportunities to be successful in the general culture, while respecting the student's ethnic background.

5 Almost Always	4	3	2	1 Almost Never

A28. Multifaceted assessment batteries are used which include a focus on the student's strengths.

| 5 Almost Always | 4 | 3 | 2 | 1 Almost Never |

A29. Communications are held in the client's dominant spoken language or alternative communication system. All student information is interpreted in the context of the student's socio-cultural background and setting in which they are functioning.

| 5 Almost Always | 4 | 3 | 2 | 1 Almost Never |

A30. Only personnel professionally trained use assessment techniques, including computerized techniques.

| 5 Almost Always | 4 | 3 | 2 | 1 Almost Never |

A31. School psychologists promote the development of objective, valid, and reliable assessment techniques.

| 5 Almost Always | 4 | 3 | 2 | 1 Almost Never |

A32. Interpretation of assessment results is based upon empirically validated research.

| 5 Almost Always | 4 | 3 | 2 | 1 Almost Never |

A33. Parents give written consent before school psychologists test or special programs are provided.

| 5 Almost Always | 4 | 3 | 2 | 1 Almost Never |

A34. Parents are fully informed of all important information, how it relates to decision-making, who has access, and where records are kept.

| 5 Almost Always | 4 | 3 | 2 | 1 Almost Never |

A35. Parents are invited to participate in decision-making meetings.

| 5 Almost Always | 4 | 3 | 2 | 1 Almost Never |

A36. Parents are routinely told that an advocate or friend can come to conferences about testing results and program changes.

| 5 Almost Always | 4 | 3 | 2 | 1 Almost Never |

A37. Records of meetings regarding test results and program recommendations are available to all concerned.

| 5 Almost Always | 4 | 3 | 2 | 1 Almost Never |

Program planning

A38. School psychologists are involved in determining options and revisions of educational programs to ensure that they are adaptive to the needs of students.

| 5 Almost Always | 4 | 3 | 2 | 1 Almost Never |

A39. The contributions of diverse cultural backgrounds are emphasized in educational programs.

| 5 Almost Always | 4 | 3 | 2 | 1 Almost Never |

A40. School psychologists follow-up on the efficacy of their recommendations.

5 Almost Always	4	3	2	1 Almost Never

A41. Student needs are given priority in determining educational programs.

5 Almost Always	4	3	2	1 Almost Never

A42. Specific educational prescriptions result from the assessment team's actions.

5 Almost Always	4	3	2	1 Almost Never

A43. Where a clear determination of the student's needs does not result from initial assessment, a diagnostic intervention or teaching program is offered as a part of additional assessment procedures.

5 Almost Always	4	3	2	1 Almost Never

A44. Regular systematic review of the student's program is conducted and includes program modifications as necessary.

5 Almost Always	4	3	2	1 Almost Never

Records

A45. The employing agency has an explicit policy on student records which is consistent with state and federal rules and laws. This ensures the protection of the confidentiality of the student and family, and specifies the type of data generated by the school psychologist that are classified as school records.

5 Almost Always	4	3	2	1 Almost Never

233

A46. Parents may inspect and review any personally identifiable data relating to their child which were collected, maintained, or used in an evaluation.

5 Almost Always	4	3	2	1 Almost Never

A47. School psychologists protect test security and observe copyright restrictions.

5 Almost Always	4	3	2	1 Almost Never

A48. Access to psychological records is restricted to those permitted by law who have legitimate educational interest in the records.

5 Almost Always	4	3	2	1 Almost Never

A49. School psychologists interpret school psychological records to non-psychologists who qualify for access.

5 Almost Always	4	3	2	1 Almost Never

A50. School psychological records are only created when parent(s) have given informed consent for the creation of such a record. Informed consent is defined as full knowledge of the purposes for which the information is sought and personnel who will have access.

5 Almost Always	4	3	2	1 Almost Never

A51. School psychological records are only created and maintained when the information is necessary and relevant for legitimate educational program needs.

| 5 Almost Always | 4 | 3 | 2 | 1 Almost Never |

A52. School psychologists assume responsibility for assuring the accuracy and relevance of material in the school psychology portions of students' records.

| 5 Almost Always | 4 | 3 | 2 | 1 Almost Never |

A53. School psychological records, including those on computer, are systematically reviewed, and when necessary, purged, in keeping with state and federal laws to protect students from decisions based on incorrect, misleading, or out-of-date information.

| 5 Almost Always | 4 | 3 | 2 | 1 Almost Never |

CONTRACTED SCHOOL PSYCHOLOGY SERVICES QUESTIONNAIRE

C1. Independently contracted school psychological services encompass the same comprehensive continuum of services as provided by regularly employed school psychologists and include opportunities for follow-up and continuing consultation.

5 Almost Always	4	3	2	1 Almost Never

C2. Independently contracted psychological services are provided by fully credentialed school psychologists or by clinical or industrial/organizational psychologists to supplement school psychological services in a coordinated manner.

5 Almost Always	4	3	2	1 Almost Never

C3. Independently contracted school psychological services are not used as a means to decrease the amount or quality of, nor supplant, school psychological services.

5 Almost Always	4	3	2	1 Almost Never

C4. School psychologists providing contractual services are given appropriate access and information, and are familiar with instructional resources of the employing agency,

5 Almost Always	4	3	2	1 Almost Never

C5. Independently contracted school psychological services are provided in a manner that protects the due process rights of students and their parents as defined by law.

5 Almost Always	4	3	2	1 Almost Never

235

C6. Independently contracted school psychological services are not used as a means to avoid legitimate employee rights, wages, or fringe benefits.

5 Almost Always	4	3	2	1 Almost Never

C7. Persons providing contractual school psychological services provide these services in a manner consistent with these professional standards, principles for professional ethics, and other relevant standards.

5 Almost Always	4	3	2	1 Almost Never

C8. Persons providing contractual school psychological services will encourage regular evaluation of the continued need for the service as well as the quality of the service.

5 Almost Always	4	3	2	1 Almost Never

PRIVATE PRACTICE QUESTIONNAIRE ON SCHOOL PSYCHOLOGISTS

P1. School psychologists practicing in the private sector adhere to the same standards and guidelines as those providing services in the public sector.

| 5 Almost Always | 4 | 3 | 2 | 1 Almost Never |

P2. School psychologists practicing in the private sector document that they have formal training, supervised experience, licensure and/or certification, demonstrated competence, and continued professional development in any areas of service they intend to deliver to clients within the private sector.

| 5 Almost Always | 4 | 3 | 2 | 1 Almost Never |

P3. School psychologists practicing in the private sector adhere to the NASP *Principles for Professional Ethics* and practice only within their areas of competence. If the services needed by the clients fall outside the school psychologist's area of competence, the clients are referred elsewhere for assistance.

| 5 Almost Always | 4 | 3 | 2 | 1 Almost Never |

P4. School psychologists practicing in the private sector inform clients that school psychological services are available without charge from the local school district.

| 5 Almost Always | 4 | 3 | 2 | 1 Almost Never |

P5. School psychologists practicing in the private sector do not provide services on a private basis to students who attend schools where the school psychologist is assigned, including students attending non-public schools.

| 5 Almost Always | 4 | 3 | 2 | 1 Almost Never |

P6. School psychologists practicing in the private sector ensure that, prior to the commencement of treatment, the client fully understands any and all fees associated with the services and any potential financial assistance that may be available (i. e., third party reimbursement).

| 5 Almost Always | 4 | 3 | 2 | 1 Almost Never |

P7. School psychologists inform parents that if a private school psychological evaluation is completed it constitutes only one portion of a multi-disciplinary team evaluation.

| 5 Almost Always | 4 | 3 | 2 | 1 Almost Never |

P8. School psychologists practicing in private practice conduct comprehensive evaluations.

| 5 Almost Always | 4 | 3 | 2 | 1 Almost Never |

236

Just as practitioners must acquire and develop requisite professional skills to practice competently, supervisors must learn and develop requisite professional skills to supervise competently. As Bernard and Goodyear (1998) astutely note, good athletes do not necessarily make good coaches, and good practitioners do not automatically make good supervisors. Supervisory skills must be carefully cultivated and monitored.

Supervisors follow developmental stages just as school psychologists do: their thinking and need for support change as they progress through the novice, advanced beginner, competent, proficient, and expert levels (Stoltenberg & Delworth, 1987). According to Mead (1990), beginning supervisors need three things: "help in developing technical skills so that they elicit better clinical thinking in therapists...help in learning not to counterattack therapists who make mistakes or...criticize the supervisor, and a model of supervision" (p 13).

As do beginning school psychologists, beginning supervisors need concrete rules and guidelines. Because this book was specifically designed to meet the needs of beginning supervisors of school psychologists, multiple guidelines have been provided. With successful practice, supervisors become less anxious and defensive, become more comfortable with a given model of supervision, perceive supervisory patterns, constantly assess their own and their supervisee's strengths and weaknesses, build professional development and supervisory strategies based on these assessments, and obtain regular feedback on their effectiveness. As is true for practitioners, supervisory growth is greatest when the practice of supervision itself is supervised.

Models of training

The concept of training and supervising supervisors is not new in counseling psychology (Bernard & Goodyear, 1998; Mead, 1990; Storm, 1997b; Storm, Todd, McDowell, & Sutherland, 1997). Unfortunately, it is quite recent and relatively unexplored in school psychology (Fischetti & Crespi, 1998, 1999). The almost universal lack of training and supervised practice in the supervision of school psychology is extremely unfortunate and verges on unethical practice, since practicing as a supervisor without adequate training can be construed as practicing outside the area of expertise (Stoltenberg & Delworth, 1987).

As described by Fischetti and Crespi (1998), training as a supervisor of school psychologists currently follows one of four models. Some school psychologists obtain generic clinical/counseling supervisory training that focuses on developing skills in counseling supervision. Some participate in a doctoral level course in school psychology supervisor training that focuses on the direct supervision of school psychologists in training. Some supervisors of school psychologists have acquired supervisory training through administrative coursework and credentials. Many, perhaps most, acquire supervisory training through direct experience and self-study.

These four models provide minimal opportunities for supervised supervision. This contrasts with supervisor training in marriage and family therapy, where trainees undergo coursework and also work a prescribed number of hours as a supervised supervisor before becoming credentialed (Storm, 1997b; Storm et al., 1997).

While each of the above models has strengths, none provides the complete training needed by supervisors of school psychologists. Complete

237

training covers clinical (professional) supervisory skills *and* administrative skills *and* supervised practice *and* self-study *and* extensive supervised practice as a supervisor. Hopefully, in the future, increasing numbers of school psychology programs will offer post-specialist level courses or certificates in supervision. These should include basic courses in supervision that address conceptual and interpersonal skills, and also include courses in current technical skills. Many supervisors would appreciate the opportunity to take advanced courses in current assessment practices, interventions, neuropsychology, and psychopharmacology.

Self-supervision of supervision. Focusing on the development of self-supervisory skills is an important method for addressing deficits in supervision training. When they self-supervise, supervisors protect the welfare of both clients and supervisees by monitoring and improving their own performance so it resembles the practice of experienced supervisors (Knoff, 1986; Mead, 1990; Todd, 1997b).

There are two primary tools in developing self-supervision. First, as self-supervisors, supervisors monitor their skills by self-applying supervisory techniques normally required with novices. These include taping and analyzing supervisory sessions; obtaining evaluative information from supervisees and administrators; and conducting evaluations of services.

Second, self-supervising supervisors seek consultation and collegial supervision. A self-supervising supervisor nurtures a network of supervisors with whom he or she can consult, usually both inside and outside the school district. The network within the school district probably includes principals or other administrators rather than other supervisors of school psychologists. A network of supervisors of school psychologists is more likely found outside the school district, perhaps through a group such as the NASP online support group.

Supervisors can use several methods to foster self-supervision. These can be conceptualized using the previously discussed model: developing a vision, assessing internal and external variables, developing a mission and goals, strategizing, implementing, and evaluating.

1. *Developing a vision:* develop a theoretical framework and a clear description of the behaviors shown by a competent supervisor. This process was described in detail in Chapter 4.

2. *Assessing internal and external variables:* assess external barriers and opportunities, ranging from relative strengths of staff school psychologists to the expectations of administrators and concerns of the state department of education. Questions relative to these variables are contained in Chapter 3.

   In assessing internal variables, supervisors assess their own professional skills in all areas relevant to the practice of school psychology (direct interventions, indirect intervention, assessment, program evaluation, etc.). They also assess their own interpersonal skills, including basic communication skills, identifying learning needs, goal writing, devising instructional strategies, presenting didactic material, developing experiential learning methods, evaluating the learning, taking a role of authority, and giving constructive feedback. Finally, supervisors assess their own conceptual skills, including the ability to view the broader environmental context and to identify supervisory models and theories, knowledge of the organizational structure and policies in education, knowledge of duties and responsibilities in the school systems, knowledge of ethical standards, ability to apply ethical principals, ability to foster the ethical development of supervisees, and ability to ensure the maintenance of non-exploitative relationships.

3. *Developing a mission and goals:* following the assessment, and in conjunction with the vision, self-supervising supervisors develop specific learning goals to improve areas of supervisory weakness. After determining areas of strength and weakness, they find ways to increase levels of proficiency in less developed areas and seek support from more proficient professionals when appropriate.

4. *Developing strategies:* self-supervising supervisors prioritize the development of an infrastructure that fosters effective supervision. For example, they schedule regular individual and group supervisory sessions with supervisees, and schedule time for consulting with other supervisors. They also develop contracts and supervision plans with each supervisee.

5. *Implementing strategies:* self-monitoring supervisors implement strategies that lead to a continual improvement of supervision. They keep meticulous notes of supervisory sessions to help remember to follow-up on previous issues. They consult with other supervisors regularly, using these sessions to generate alternative hypotheses and collaboratively brainstorm, rather than to obtain "correct" answers. They approach these consultative sessions with clearly defined goals and questions. They also regularly obtain structured feedback on the supervisory process; for example, by taking a few minutes at the end of each session to discuss what aspects of the supervisory session were particularly helpful.

6. *Conducting evaluations:* self-supervising supervisors obtain summative feedback from supervisees, administrators, and the clients of supervisees regarding the effectiveness of supervisory practices. They then use this feedback to modify their vision and assessment, and subsequently to improve performance as a supervisor.

The reader should recognize the above steps as the same as those that guide supervision itself and similarly guide effective practice of supervisees. The development of a supervisor overlays supervision itself, which in turn overlays the practice of school psychology. As Mead (1990) indicates, the development of the supervisor subsumes the system of the practitioner, and the system of the practitioner subsumes practice itself. This is graphically depicted in figure 15-1.

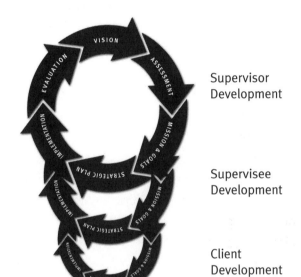

Supervisor Development

Supervisee Development

Client Development

Figure 15-1

SUPERVISION EVALUATION

As was stated at the beginning of this volume, children are our primary clients. The improved functioning of children treated by our supervisees is the most valid assessment of our supervision effectiveness. Consequently, assessment of supervisors must occur on all levels: the progress made by clients, the change in the supervisee's behavior, and the change in the supervisor's ability to supervise (Mead, 1990).

According to Bolton (1980), an evaluation of a supervisor serves to improve performance, focus professional development activities, identify and improve programs and procedures, provide professional recognition, and document effectiveness. Evaluations of school psychology supervisors are essential to the health of the school psychology department.

Sources of information

Typically, evaluations of supervisors of school psychologists are completed only by their direct administrative supervisor. This is unsatisfactory for two reasons: the information is limited, and the individuals supervising the supervisors of school psychologists are usually not trained as school psychologists and are unfamiliar with professional standards. Often these administrators are the district superintendents, assistant superintendents, directors of pupil personnel, or directors of special education (Hunley et al., in press).

To ameliorate these difficulties, several steps should be taken. First, it is critical that the supervisor of school psychologists help the administrator understand the principles of best practices in school psychology by sharing documents such as the professional standards, the ethical principles, and *Blueprint for Change* (Ysseldyke et al., 1997). Second, the supervisor of school psychologists should help develop an evaluation system that is comprehensive, meaningful, and adheres to professional standards. Third, this system should utilize sources of information other than the administrator: as described above, appropriate sources of information include supervisors, school psychologists and other personnel under their supervision, peers (i. e., principals), and other stakeholders. Finally, the system should use methods other than paper and pencil surveys completed by the administrator. Cherniss (1986) advocates the direct observation of a supervisor's method, style, and content communication with supervisees. Johnson (1998) recommends that portfolios be used to supplement the evaluation of supervisees.

Models of evaluating supervisors

The same principles, legal and ethical issues, and models discussed previously in Chapter 7 apply to the evaluation of supervisors of school psychologists. Again, supervisors may be rated on attributes, behaviors, or outcomes. An example of a scale based on desirable supervisor *attributes* is found in Example 15-1.

Example 15-1

Supervisor Attribute Scale

Please rate your supervisor on each attribute below.

1. Is resourceful.

    1_____2_____3_____4_____5
    excellent   poor

2. Thinks strategically and is a flexible problem solver.

    1_____2_____3_____4_____5
    excellent   poor

3. Has perseverance and focus in the face of obstacles.

    1_____2_____3_____4_____5
    excellent   poor

4. Quickly masters new knowledge.

    1_____2_____3_____4_____5
    excellent   poor

5. Builds and maintains positive and effective relation-ships.

    1_____2_____3_____4_____5
    excellent   poor

6. Leads subordinates effectively.

    1_____2_____3_____4_____5
    excellent   poor

7. Is compassionate, sensitive, and respectful.

    1_____2_____3_____4_____5
    excellent   poor

8. Is straightforward, honorable, and steadfast.

    1_____2_____3_____4_____5
    excellent   poor

9. Has a team orientation and accomplishes tasks through others.

    1_____2_____3_____4_____5
    excellent   poor

10. Is self-aware and is open to improvement.

    1_____2_____3_____4_____5
    excellent   poor

11. Hires talented individuals.

    1_____2_____3_____4_____5
    excellent   poor

12. Has warmth, sense of humor, and puts others at ease.

    1_____2_____3_____4_____5
    excellent   poor

13. Acts flexibly.

    1_____2_____3_____4_____5
    excellent   poor

(adapted from McCauley, Lombardo, & Usher, 1989)

When supervisor evaluations focus on behaviors, they typically include assessment of three areas (Johnson, 1998) (a) professional competencies including communication skills, ethical behavior, and relationships with supervisees; (b) task management; and (c) leadership skills. An adaptation of the Leadership Behavior Rating Scale, developed by Johnson (1998) and designed to elicit information about supervisor's leadership behaviors from supervisees, is found in Example 15-2.

Example 15-2

Leadership Behavior Rating Scale

The supervisor of school psychologists:

1.	Brings concerns to staff school psychologists and facilitates collaborative problem solving by participating in group discussions and sharing necessary information.	|____|____|____|____| constantly never
2.	Delegates tasks and authority effectively.	|____|____|____|____| constantly never
3.	Openly discusses his or her vision for the school psychological services.	|____|____|____|____| constantly never
4.	Encourages staff school psychologists to share expertise with others and function in leadership roles.	|____|____|____|____| constantly never
5.	Encourages staff to reflect on current practices and suggest improvements.	|____|____|____|____| constantly never
6.	Treats staff school psychologists as self-directed professionals who share professional standards.	|____|____|____|____| constantly never
7.	Meets frequently with staff, both formally and informally.	|____|____|____|____| constantly never
8.	Shares budget construction, resource management, and program evaluation with staff school psychologists.	|____|____|____|____| constantly never

(Adapted from Johnson, 1998)

242

Another example, based on the proposed *NASP Standards of Professional Practice* (under review), is found in Example 15-3.

Example 15-3

Supervisor Evaluation Form based on the Proposed (1999) NASP Standards

1.	The supervisor...	
1a.	Effectively supervises the overall development and implementation of district school psychological services.	|____|____|____|____| Almost Almost Always Never
1b.	Articulates school psychological service programs to others in the agency and constituent groups.	|____|____|____|____| Almost Almost Always Never
1c.	Provides leadership by promoting innovative service delivery systems that reflect best practices in the field of school psychology.	|____|____|____|____| Almost Almost Always Never
1d.	Leads the school psychology services unit in developing, implementing, and evaluating a coordinated plan for accountability and evaluation of all services.	|____|____|____|____| Almost Almost Always Never
1e.	Uses measurable objectives in both program and individual performance evaluations.	|____|____|____|____| Almost Almost Always Never
1f.	Conducts program and individual performance evaluations that are both formative and summative.	|____|____|____|____| Almost Almost Always Never
1g.	Evaluates and revises evaluation plans on a regular basis through the systematic collection, analysis and interpretation of process and performance data.	|____|____|____|____| Almost Almost Always Never
2.	**The supervisor provides supervision..**	
2a.	At a level adequate to ensure the provision of effective and accountable services.	|____|____|____|____| Almost Almost Always Never
2b.	Through an ongoing, positive, systematic, collaborative process.	|____|____|____|____| Almost Almost Always Never

243

2c.	That focuses on promoting professional growth and exemplary professional practice.	|____|____|____|____| Almost Almost Always Never
2d.	For at least 2 hours per week, in a face-to-face format, for interns and first year school psychologists.	|____|____|____|____| Almost Almost Always Never
2e.	Within the guidelines of the training institution and NASP *Standards for Training and Field Placement Programs in School Psychology*.	|____|____|____|____| Almost Almost Always Never
2f.	Or peer review for experienced school psychologists to ensure ongoing professional development.	|____|____|____|____| Almost Almost Always Never
3.	**The supervisor provides professional leadership...**	
3a.	Through participation in school psychology professional organizations	|____|____|____|____| Almost Almost Always Never
3b.	By coordinating the activities of the school psychological services unit with other professional service units.	|____|____|____|____| Almost Almost Always Never
3c.	Through active involvement in local, state, and federal public policy development and federal, state, and local educational organizations.	|____|____|____|____| Almost Almost Always Never
4.	**The supervisor's credentials include...**	
4a.	Certification as a Nationally Certified School Psychologist (NCSP).	|____|____|____|____| Almost Almost Always Never
4b.	Designation as a supervisor responsible for school psychology services.	|____|____|____|____| Almost Almost Always Never
4c.	A minimum of two years of experience as a practicing school psychologist.	|____|____|____|____| Almost Almost Always Never
4d.	A state school psychologist credential.	|____|____|____|____| Almost Almost Always Never
4e.	Training and/or experience in the supervision of school personnel.	|____|____|____|____| Almost Almost Always Never

Supervisory *outcomes* are often evaluated using the Management by Objective model. In this scenario, supervisors develop annual goals for themselves that reflect not only their job descriptions but also the goals of the school district and their professional development aspirations. These are approved by the administrator responsible for the supervisor's work and are used as the foundation for the end-of-the-year evaluation. An example of a supervisory goal and a few relevant objectives are found in Example 15-4.

Example 15-4

Goal: *Facilitate the professional development of supervisees.*
Objectives:

1. Collaboratively develops a professional development plan with each supervisee by September 15.
2. Collaboratively develops a group departmental professional development plan by September 15.
3. Sponsors attendance at relevant workshops through budgetary allocation.
4. Sponsors group department development by funding guest speakers at four department meetings per year.
5. Facilitates the dissemination of workshop information by devoting 50% of department meeting time to professional development conversations.
6. Encourages the acquisition of new skills through biannual supervision of individual psychologist's professional development plans.

Finally, supervisors can be evaluated with a *comprehensive* approach, such as the special education administrators evaluation model pro-

posed by Johnson (1998). This model, easily adaptable for use with supervisors of school psychologists, assesses professional behaviors, leadership behaviors, program management, and professional development using information from a variety of sources. To evaluate general professional behaviors, leadership behaviors, and program management, rating scales are completed by the supervisor, the administrator, and peers. Parents and supervisees complete abbreviated rating scales regarding general professional behaviors. The supervisor's professional development and program management are assessed through the use of a portfolio that provides evidence of technical skills, including personnel management, program leadership, program development, training and consultation, public relations, and program evaluation. Suggestions for the components of a supervisor of school psychologists' portfolio are contained in example 15-5.

Example 15-5
Supervision Portfolio Components

1. Items that demonstrate the supervisor's knowledge of standards and ethics of civil rights, special education, state reporting, and confidentiality laws. Examples: ethical dilemmas encountered by supervisees and the supervision supplied toward resolution, parental permission forms, parental rights handouts, and policies and procedures from the school psychologist's handbook.
2. Items that demonstrate the supervisor's knowledge and skill in communication and interpersonal skills. Examples: transcripts or tapes of supervisory sessions, evidence of implementation of conflict resolution techniques in resolving disputes, evidence of application of knowledge of team development processes in group department meetings, evidence of communication of program

information with stakeholder groups, and evidence of the implementation of collaborative consultation to improve staff effectiveness.

3. Items that demonstrate the supervisor's knowledge of models, theories, and strategies of supervision. Examples: formal and informal consideration of implications of supervisor's past training and supervision, personal statements that explain the supervisor's theoretical foundations in counseling, consultation, assessment, supervision, and similar personal statements by supervisees, and reconciling statements by the supervisor.

4. Items that demonstrate planning and decision making skills: departmental vision, goals, and objectives; departmental budget requests and justifications; and resource allocation plans and rationales.

5. Items that demonstrate skills in selecting staff, including job descriptions and ads, employment interview forms and grids, credential and reference checks, evidence of knowledge of the civil rights laws regarding staff recruitment and retention.

6. Items that demonstrate skill in conducting individual performance evaluations. Examples: appropriate tools developed to evaluate both staff school psychologists and the supervisor of school psychologists; samples of evaluative narratives; samples of staff observations and feedback provision.

7. Items that demonstrate skill in training and professional development: of school psychologists, such as collaboratively developed staff professional improvement plans; of other school personnel, such as the results of a needs assessment, information sources for current research in educational theory and methodology; staff development in-service work materials used in formal and informal settings; and results of effectiveness evaluations of training activities.

8. Items that reveal the ability to promote job satisfaction. Examples include evidence of provision of emotional support to supervisees, supervisee membership and participation in professional organizations, supervisee participation in research studies, evidence of consideration of physical environment, evidence of supervisee job enrichment, and evidence of strategies to facilitate supervisee adjustment.

9. Items that reveal skill in the supervision of indirect interventions, such as a series of process notes revealing (a) growth in supervisees over time and (b) growth in consultees over time.

10. Items that reveal skill in the supervision of direct interventions, such as a series of process notes and student outcomes revealing (a) growth in supervisees over time and (b) growth in the clients over time.

11. Items that reveal skill in the supervision of assessment, such as supervision notes tied to demonstrable growth in supervisees' evaluations.

12. Items that indicate skill in research and program evaluation, including a list of methods used to encourage supervisee participation in research consumption, reviews, studies, and program evaluations.

13. Items that indicate skill in grant writing, including lists of available funding sources and copies of grant applications submitted and awarded.

14. Items that indicate skill in evaluating and promoting school psychological services, such as a completed evaluation of service quality, and informational materials.

NEXT STEPS

As the reader may have predicted, the next step after the evaluation of the supervisor is to revisit the supervisory vision and redesign the goals, structure, and strategies of supervision. Hopefully, supervisors will engage in a never-ending process of assessment and improvement of both their own practices and those of their supervisees, leading to the improved functioning of the children served.

247

References

Achenbach, T. M. (1991). *Integrative guide for the 1991 CBCL/4-18, YSR, and TRF profiles*. Burlington: University of Vermont, Department of Psychiatry.

Ailes, R. (1988). *You are the message*. Homewood, IL: Dow Jones-Irwin.

Alessi, G. J., Lascurettes-Alessi, K. J., & Leyes, W. L. (1981). *Internships in school psychology: Supervision issues*. School Psychology Review, 10(4), 461-469.

Alfonso, V. C., & Pratt, S. I. (1997). Issues and suggestions for training professional in assessing intelligence. In D. P. Flanagan, J. L. Genshaft, & P. L. Harrison (Eds.), *Contemporary intellectual assessment: Theories, tests, and issues*. New York: Guilford.

Algozzine, B., & Ysseldyke, J. E. (1986). The future of the LD field: Screening and diagnosis. *Journal of Learning Disabilities*, 19(7), 394-398.

American Psychiatric Association. (1994). *Diagnostic and statistical manual of mental disorders* (4th ed.). Washington, DC: author.

American Psychological Association. (1981). Specialty guidelines for the delivery of services by school psychologists. *American Psychologist, 36*, 670-681.

American Psychological Association. (1982). *Ethical principles in the conduct of research with human participants*. Washington, DC: Author.

American Psychological Association. (1986). *Guidelines for computer based tests and interpretations*. Washington, DC: Author.

American Psychological Association. (1992). Ethical principles of psychologists and code of conduct. *American Psychologist, 47*, 1597-1611.

American Psychological Association. (1993a). Guidelines for providers of psychological services to ethnic, linguistic, and culturally diverse populations. *American Psychologist, 48*, 45-48.

American Psychological Association. (1993b). Record keeping guidelines. *American Psychologist, 48*, 984-986.

American Psychological Association. (1994). *Publication manual of the American Psychological Association* (4th ed.). Washington, DC: author.

American Psychological Association. (1996). Report of the ethics committee. *American Psychologist, 51*(12), 1279-1286.

Americans with Disabilities Act of 1990, (Pub. L. No. 101-336), 42 U.S.C. § 122101 (1991).

Anderson, W. T., Hohenshil, T. H., & Brown, D. T. (1984). Job satisfaction among practicing school psychologists: A national study. *School Psychology Review*. 13, 2, 225-230.

Armstrong, K. J., Munneke, D. M., Sim, K., Purtan, J., & McGrath, A. (1995, November). *Computerized interactive parent skills training and ADHD*. Poster session presented at the annual meeting of the Association of the Advancement of Behavior Therapy, Washington, DC.

Bardon, J. I. & Bennett, V. C. (1974). *School psychology*. Englewood Cliffs, NJ: Prentice-Hall.

Bardos, A. (Ed.), (1999). *Technological innovations and the school psychologist*. Unpublished manuscript.

Barona, A., & Garcia, E. E. (1990). *Children at risk: Poverty, minority status, and other issues in educational equity*. Washington, DC: National Association of School Psychologists.

Barth, R. S. (1990). A personal vision of a good school. *Phi Delta Kappan, 71*(8), 512-515.

Bartholeme, L. (1998). *The misteaching of academic discourses*. Boulder, CO: Westview Press.

Bass, B. M. (1990). *Bass and Stogdill's handbook of leadership* (3rd. ed.). New York: Free Press.

Batsche, G. M., & Knoff, H. M. (1995). Best practices in linking assessment to intervention. In A. Thomas & J. Grimes (Eds.), *Best practices in school psychology-III.* (pp. 569-585). Washington, DC: National Association of School Psychologists.

Bear, G. G., Minke, K. M., & Thomas, A. (Eds.),(1997). *Children's needs II: Development, problems, and alternatives.* Bethesda, MD: National Association of School Psychologists.

Beck, A. T. (1976). *Cognitive therapy and the emotional disorders.* NY: International Universities Press.

Beck, S. T., Steer, R. A., & Garbin, M. G. (1988). Psychometric properties of the Beck Depression Inventory: Twenty-five years of evaluation. *Clinical Psychology Review, 8,* 77-100

Beer, M. (1981, winter). Performance appraisal: Dilemmas and responsibilities. *Organizational Dynamics, 9,*(3), 24-36.

Beger, S. S. (1993). Group supervision of first-year doctoral students in social skills training: A lesson in integration. *Clinical Supervisor, 11,* 217-231.

Belar, C. D. (1998). Graduate education in clinical psychology: "We're not in Kansas anymore." *American Psychologist, 53,* 456-464.

Benner, P. (1984). *From novice to expert: Excellence and power in clinical nursing practice.* Menlo Park, CA: Addison Wesley.

Benner, P., Tanner, C., & Chesla, C. (1992). From beginning to expert: Gaining a differentiated clinical world in critical care nursing. *Advanced Nursing Science 14*(3), 13-28.

Benner, R. (1999). Online job search. *Communiqué, 28*(3), 28.

Bennett, R. C. (1988). Evaluating alternative delivery systems. In J. L. Graden, J. E. Zins, & M. J. Curtis (Eds.), *Alternative educational delivery systems: Enhancing instructional options for all students.* Washington, D. C.: National Association of School Psychologists.

Bergan, J. R. (1977). *Behavioral consultation.* Columbus, OH: Merrill.

Bergan, J. R., & Kratochwill, T. R. (1990). *Behavioral consultation and therapy.* New York: Plenum.

Bernard, J. M., & Goodyear, R. K. (1998). *Fundamentals of clinical supervision* (2nd ed.). Boston, MA: Allyn & Bacon.

Bersoff, D. N. (1995). *Ethical conflicts in psychology.* Washington, DC: American Psychological Association.

Block, P. (1987). *The empowered manager: Positive practical skills at work.* San Francisco: Jossey Bass.

Blumstein, P., & Schwartz, P. (1983). *American couples: Money, work, and sex.* New York: William Morrow.

Bolton, D. L. (1980). *Evaluating administrative personnel in school systems.* NY: Teacher's College Press.

Borden, B. L. (1992). School psychology interns' task time functioning as compared to literature samples of interns and practicing school psychologists. *Dissertation Abstracts International, 52* (9-A), 3220-3221.

Bordia, P. (1997). Face-to-face versus computer-mediated communication: A synthesis of the experimental literature. *The Journal of Business Communication, 34*(1), 99-121.

Boulding, K. (1956). General systems theory: skeleton of a science. *General Systems, 1,* 11-17.

Bowser, P. B. (1981). On school psychology supervision. *School Psychology Review, 10,* 452-454.

Bowser, P. B. (1995). Best practices in professional conduct: Meeting NASP's ethical standards. In A. Thomas & J. Grimes (Eds.), *Best practices in school psychology-III* (pp. 33-39). Silver Springs, MD: National Association of School Psychologists.

Boylan, J. C., Malley, P. B., & Scott, J. (1995). *Practicum and internship textbook for counseling and psychotherapy*. Washington, D. C.: Accelerated Development.

Brown, D. S. (1982). *Managing the large organization: Issues, ideas, precepts, innovations*. Mt. Airy, MD: Lomond Books.

Brown, D. T., & Minke, K. M. (1986). School psychology graduate training: A comprehensive analysis. *American Psychologist, 41*, 1328-1338.

Bryant, S., & Demian, (1994). Relationship characteristics of American gay and lesbian couples: Findings from a national survey. *Journal of Gay and Lesbian Social Services*, 1, 101-117.

Buehler, D. D. (1986). A survey of supervisory process in school psychology. *Dissertation Abstracts International, 46* (10-A), 2965.

Burnett, K. F., Taylor, C. B., & Agras, W. S. (1985). Ambulatory computer-assisted therapy for obesity: A new frontier for behavior therapy. *Journal of Consulting and Clinical Psychology, 53*, 698-703.

Burns, J. M. (1978). *Leadership*. New York: Harper & Row.

Cagnon, J., & Russell, R. K. (1995). Assessment of supervisee developmental level and supervision environment across supervisor experience. *Journal of Counseling and Development, 73*, 553-558.

Campbell, D. T., & Stanley, J. C. (1966). *Experimental and quasi-experimental designs for research*. Chicago: Rand McNally.

Canter, S. (1993). Statistical analysis: State of the art. *PC Magazine, 19*(3), 227-287.

Caplan, G. (1970). *The theory and practice of mental health consultation*. New York: Basic Books.

Caplan, G., & Caplan, R. B. (1993). *Mental health consultation and collaboration*. San Francisco: Jossey-Bass.

Caplan, G., Caplan, R. B. & Erchul, W. P. (1995). A contemporary view of mental health consultation: Comments on "types of mental health consultation" by Gerald Caplan (1963). *Journal of Educational and Psychological Consultation, 6*(1), 23-30.

Carr, A. C. (1991). Microcomputers and psychological treatment. In A. Ager & S. Bedall (Eds.). *Microcomputers and clinical psychology* (pp. 65-78). New York: Wiley.

Carr, A. C., Ghosh, A., & Marks, I. M. (1988). Computer-supervised exposure treatment for phobias. *Canadian Journal of Psychiatry, 33*, 112-117.

Center for Resource Management (1988). *Profiling effectiveness in special education: A profile of the Nashua Special Education Program based on indicators of effectiveness*. South Hampton, NH: author.

Chandler, A. D. (1962). *Strategy and structure: Chapters in the history of the industrial enterprise*. Cambridge, MA: M. I. T. Press.

Cherniss, C. (1986). Instrument for observing supervisor behavior in educational programs for mentally retarded children. *American Journal of Mental Deficiency, 91* (1), 18-21.

Civil Rights Act of 1871 or "Section 1983," 42 U.S.C. § 1983.

Civil Rights Act of 1964 (Pub. L. No. 92-318), 20 U. S. C. § 2000d.

Claiborn, C. D., Kerr, B. A., & Strong, S. R. (1990). Group interventions in the schools. In T. B. Gutkin & C. R. Reynolds (Eds.). *The handbook of school psychology* (2nd ed.), (pp. 703-732). New York: Wiley.

Cobb, C. T. (1995). Best practices in defining, implementing, and evaluating educational outcomes. In A. Thomas & J. Grimes (Eds.), *Best practices in school psychology-III* (pp. 325-336). Silver Spring, MD: National Association of School Psychologists.

Conoley, J. C., & Bahns, T. (1995). Best practices in supervision of interns. In A. Thomas & J. Grimes (Eds.), *Best practices in school psychology-III* (pp. 111-122). Washington, DC: National Association of School Psychologists.

251

Conoley, J. C., & Conoley, C. W. (1988). Useful theories in school-based consultation. *Remedial and Special Education, 9*(6), 14-20.

Conoley, J. C., & Gutkin, T. B. (1986). Educating school psychologists for the real world. *School Psychology Review, 15*(4), 457-465.

Constable, J. F., & Russell, D. (1986). The effect of social support and the work environment upon burnout among nurses. *Journal of Human Stress, 12*, 12-26.

Copyright Law of the United States of America, 1996, Title 17 of the United States Code.

Cormier, W. H., & Cormier, L. S. (1985). *Interviewing strategies for helpers: Fundamental skills and cognitive behavioral interventions* (2nd ed.). Monterey, CA: Brooks/Cole.

Correll, J. H., McElwain, R., and Iffert-Jacobson, M. (1986). *Peer review: A plan for intra-departmental evaluation*. Paper presented at the annual meting of the National association of School Psychologists, Hollywood, FL.

Crespi, T., & Fischetti, B. A. (1997). Clinical supervision for school psychologists: Bridging theory and practice. *School Psychology International, 18*, 41-48.

Curtis, M. J., Hunley, S. A., Walker, K. J., & Baker, A. C. (1999). Demographic characteristics and professional practices in school psychology. *School Psychology Review, (28)*1, 104-116.

Curtis, M. J., & Meyers, J. (1989). Consultation: A foundation for alternative services in the schools, In J. L. Graden, J. E. Zins, & M. J. Curtis (Eds.), *Alternative educational delivery systems: Enhancing instructional options for all students* (pp. 3-15). Washington, DC: The National Association of School Psychologists.

Curtis, M. J., & Yager, G. G. (1981). A systems model for the supervision of school psychologists. *School Psychology Review, 10*, 425-433.

Curtis, M. J., & Yager, G. G. (1987). A systems model for the supervision of school psychological services. In R. H. Dana & W. T. May (Eds.), *Internship training in professional psychology. Series in clinical and community psychology.* (pp. 340-352). Washington, DC: Hemisphere Publishing Corporation.

Curtis, M. J., & Zins, J. (1980). *The theory and practice of school consultation*. Springfield, IL: Thomas.

Dawson, M. (1999, February). *Strategic planning workshop*. Presented at the New Hampshire School Psychologists Winter Meeting, Concord, NH.

Delpit, L. (1995). *Other people's children: Cultural conflict in the classroom*. New York: New Press.

Dickens, F., & Dickens, J. B. (1991). *The black manager*. New York: American Management Association.

DiGilio, S. A. (1997). Integrative supervision: Approaches to tailoring the supervisory process. In T. C. Todd & C. L. Storm (Eds.), *The complete systemic supervisor: Context, philosophy, and pragmatics* (pp. 195-216). Boston: Allyn & Bacon.

Disenhouse, H. A. (1987). The supervisor as practitioner. In J. Grimes & D. Happe (Eds.), *Best practices in the supervision of school psychological services* (pp. 127-138). Des Moines, Iowa: Iowa State Dept. of Education. (ERIC Document Reproduction Service ED293037)

Disney, M. J., & Stephens, A. M. (1994). *Legal issues in clinical supervision*. Alexandria, VA: American Counseling Association Press.

Dolezal-Wood, S., Belar, C. D., & Snibbe, J. (1998). A comparison of computer-assisted psychotherapy and cognitive-behavioral therapy in groups. *Journal of Clinical Psychology in Medical Settings, 5*, 103-115.

Dougherty, A. M, (1995). *Consultation: Practice and perspectives in school and community settings*. Pacific Grove, CA: Brooks-Cole.

Douglas, J. (1991). Clinical applications of microcomputers with children. In A. Ager & S. Bedall (Eds.). *Microcomputers and clinical psychology* (pp. 119-138). New York: Wiley.

Dreyfus, H., & Dreyfus, S. (1991). Towards a phenomenology of ethical expertise. Human Studies, 14, 229-250.

Duffy, S., & Rusbult, C. (1986). Satisfaction and commitment in homosexual and heterosexual relationships. *Journal of Homosexuality, 12*, 1-24.

Dye, H. A., & Border, L. D. (1990). Counseling supervisors: Standards for preparation and practice. *Journal of Counseling and Development, 69*, 27-29.

Education of All Handicapped Children Act of 1975 (PL 94-142) 20 U. S. C. Sec. 401 (1975).

Egan, G. (1990). *The skilled helper: A systematic approach to effective helping* (4th ed.). Pacific Grove, CA: Brooks/Cole.

Ellis, M. V. (1991). Critical incidents in clinical supervision and in supervisor supervision: Assessing supervisory issues. *Journal of Counseling Psychology, 38*, 342-349.

Erchul, W. P., & Conoley, C. W. (February, 1991). Helpful theories to guide counselor's practice of school-based consultation. *Elementary School Guidance and Counseling*, 204-211.

Erchul, W. P., & Martens, B. K. (1997). *School Consultation: Conceptual and Empirical Bases of Practice.* New York: Plenum Press.

Eyde, L. D., Robertson, G. J., Krug, S. E., Moreland, K. L., Robertson, A. G., Shewan, C. M., Harrison, P. L., Porch, B. E., Hammer, A. L., & Primoff, E. S. (1993). *Responsible test use: Case studies for assessing human behavior.* Washington DC: American Psychological Association.

Fagan , T. K., & Wise, P. S. (1994). *School psychology: Past, present, and future.* New York: Longman.

Fairchild, T. N. (1985). Obtaining consumer feedback as a means of evaluating school psychology intern performance. *Psychology in the Schools, 22*, 419-428.

Family Education Rights and Privacy Act of 1974 (FERPA), Pub. Law 93-380, 20 U. S. C. A. § 1232g, 34 C. F. R. § Part 99 (1993).

Family Educational Rights and Privacy Act, Implementing Regulations, 34 C. F. R. Sec. 99.3 (1976).

Family and Medical Leave Act of 1993, 29 U.S.C. 2601.

Feuerstein, R. (1979). *The dynamic assessment of retarded performers: The learning potential assessment device, theory, instruments, and techniques.* Baltimore, MD: University Park Press.

Finkelhor, D., (1986). *A sourcebook on child abuse.* Newbury Park, CA: Sage.

Firth, G., & Pajak, E. (1994). *Handbook of research on school supervision.* New York: MacMillan Library Reference USA.

Fischer, L., & Sorenson, G. P. (1991). *School law for counselors, psychologists, and social workers.* New York: Longman.

Fischetti, B. A., & Crespi, T. (1998). Clinical supervision: Continuing education and training for school psychologists. *Communiqué, 27*(1), 30-31.

Fischetti, B. A., & Crespi, T. D. (1999). Clinical supervision for school psychologists: National practices, trends, and future implications. *School Psychology International, 20* (3), 278-288.

Fischetti, B. A., & Mortatti, A. L. (1998). Post-doctoral school based clinical supervision: A training model for credentialling as a licensed psychologist. *The School Psychologist, 52*, 105, 120-121.

Fisher, G. L., Jenkins, S. J., & Crumbley, J. D. (1986). A replication of a survey of school psychologists: Congruence between training, practice, preferred role, and competence. *Psychology in the Schools, 23*, 276-277.

Flaks, D., Ficher, I., Masterpasqua, F., & Joseph, G. (1995). Lesbians choosing motherhood: A comparative study of lesbian and heterosexual parents and their children. *Developmental Psychology, 31*, 105-114.

Flanagan, D. P., Genshaft, J. L., & Harrison, P. L. (Eds.), (1997). *Contemporary intellectual assessment: Theories, tests, and issues.* New York: Guilford.

Flanagan, D. P., & McGrew, K. S. (1997). A cross-battery approach to assessing and interpreting cognitive abilities: Narrowing the gap between practice and cognitive science. In D. P. Flanagan, J. L. Genshaft, & P. L. Harrison (Eds.). *Contemporary intellectual assessment: Theories, tests, and issues.* New York: Guilford, pp. 314-325.

Fleishman, E. A. (1967). The development of a behavior taxonomy for describing human tasks: A correlational-experimental approach. *Journal of Applied Psychology, 51*, 1-10.

Fleishman, E. A., & Harris, E. F. (1962). Patterns of leadership behavior related to employee grievances and turnover. *Personnel Psychology, 15*(1), 43-56.

Fleming, D. C., Fleming, E. R., Roach, K. S., & Oksman, P. F. (1985). Conflict management. In C. A. Maher (Ed.), *Professional self-management: Techniques for special services providers* (pp. 65-84). Paul H. Brookes: Baltimore.

Forman, S. G. (1981). Stress management training: Evaluation of effects on school psychological services. *Journal of School Psychology, 19*, 233-241.

Forman, S. G., & Cecil, M. A. (1985).Stress management. In C. A. Maher (Ed.), *Professional self-management: Techniques for special services providers* (45-63). Paul H. Brookes: Baltimore.

Fowler, E., & Harrison, P. L. (1995). Continuing professional development for school psychologists. In A. Thomas & J. Grimes (Eds.), *Best practices in school psychology-III* (pp. 81-90). Silver Springs, MD: National Association of School Psychologists.

Franklin, M. (1995). Best practices in planning school psychology service delivery programs. In A. Thomas & J. Grimes (Eds.), *Best practices in school psychology-III* (pp. 69-81). Silver Springs, MD: National Association of School Psychologists.

Franklin, M., Stillman, P., Burpeau, M., & Sabers, D. (1982). Examiner error in intelligence testing: Are you the source? *Psychology in the Schools, 19*(4), 563-569.

French, J. R. P., & Raven, B. (1960). The bases of social power. In D. Cartwright & A. F. Zanders (Eds.), *Group dynamics: Research and theory*, (2nd ed.). Evanston, IL: Row, Peterson.

Friedlander, M. L., Keller, K. E., Peca-Baker, T. A., & Olk, M. E. (1986). Effects of role conflict on counselor trainees' self-statement, anxiety level, and performance. *Journal of Counseling Psychology, 33*, 73-77.

Fuchs, D., & Fuchs, L. S. (1989). Mainstream assistance teams to accommodate difficult-to-teach students in general education. In J. L. Graden, J. E. Zins, & M. J. Curtis (Eds.), *Alternative educational delivery systems: Enhancing instructional options for all students* (pp. 49-70). Washington, DC: The National Association of School Psychologists.

Fuchs, D., Fuchs, L. S., Dulan, J., Roberts, H., & Fernstrom, P. (1992). Where is the research on consultation effectiveness? *Journal of Educational and Psychological Consultation, 3*, 151-174.

Fuchs, L. S., & Fuchs, D. (1986). Linking assessment to instructional interventions. *School Psychology Review, 15*(3).

Gardner, H. (1991). *The unschooled mind: How children think and how schools should teach.* New York: Basic Books.

254

Gickling, E. E., & Rosenfield, S. (1995). Best practices in curriculum based assessment. In A. Thomas & J. Grimes (Eds.), *Best practices in school psychology-III*. Washington, D. C.: National Association of School Psychologists, pp. 587-596.

Gile, L. (1987). Recruitment. In J. Grimes & D. Happe (Eds.), *Best practices in the supervision of school psychological services* (pp. 114-127). Des Moines, Iowa: Iowa State Dept. of Education. (ERIC Document Reproduction Service ED293037)

Goldberg, D. A. (1985). Process notes and videotape: Modes of presentation in psychotherapy training. *Clinical Supervisor, 3*(3), 3-13.

Goldberg, M. F. (1995, May). Portraits of educators: Reflections on 18 high achievers. *Educational leadership, 52*(8), 72-76.

Golumbok, S., Spencer, A., & Rutter, M. (1983). Children in lesbian and single parent households: Psychosexual and psychiatric appraisal. *Journal of Child Psychology and Psychiatry, 24*, 551.

Graden, J. L., Zins, J. E., Curtis, M. J., & Cobb, C. T. (1989). The need for alternatives in educational services. In J. L. Graden, J. E. Zins, & M. J. Curtis (Eds.), *Alternative educational delivery systems: Enhancing instructional options for all students* (pp. 3-15). The National Association of School Psychologists: Washington, D.C.

Greben, S. E., & Ruskin, R. (1994). *Clinical perspectives on psychotherapy supervision*. Washington, DC: American Psychiatric Press.

Green, R., (1982). The best interests of the child with a lesbian mother. *Bulletin of the American Academy of Psychiatry and the Law, 10*, 7-15.

Green, S. K. (1995). Implementing a staff development program. In A. Thomas & J. Grimes (Eds.), *Best practices in school psychology-III* (pp. 123-134). Silver Springs, MD: National Association of School Psychologists.

Gresham, F. M. (1989). Assessment of treatment integrity in school consultation and prereferral intervention. *School Psychology Review, 18*, 37-50.

Grimes, J., & Happe, D. (1987). *Best practices in the supervision of school psychological services*. Des Moines, Iowa: Iowa Department of Education.

Guidubaldi, J. (1981). On the way to Olympia, *Communiqué, 10*(3), 1-2.

Gustafson, D. H., Griest, J. H., Stauss, F. F., Erdman, J., & Laughren, T. (1977). A probabilistic system for identifying suicide attemptors. *Computers in Biomedical Research*, 10, 1-7.

Gutkin, T. B., & Curtis, M. J. (1982). School-based consultation: Theory and techniques. In C. R. Reynolds & T. B. Gutkin (Eds.), *The handbook of school psychology*, (pp. 796-828), New York: Wiley.

Gutkin, T. B., & Curtis, M. J. (1990). School-based consultation: Theory, techniques, and research. In T. B. Gutkin & C. R. Reynolds, (Eds.), *The handbook of school psychology* (pp. 577-611). New York: Wiley.

Gutkin, T. B., & Reynolds, C. R. (Eds.).(1990). *The handbook of school psychology* (2nd ed.). New York: Wiley.

Halloran, J. (1981). *Supervision: The art of management*. Englewood Cliffs, NJ: Prentice-Hall.

Harper, J., & Wild, S. (1989b). Stress and school psychological roles. In *School psychology in Wisconsin: Programs and practices* (Bulletin No. 9265) (pp. 89-91). Madison, Wisconsin: Wisconsin State Dept. of Public Instruction. (ERIC Document Reproduction Service ED307518)

Harris, M., & Turner, P. (1985-1986). Gay and lesbian parents. *Journal of Homosexuality, 12*, 101-113.

Harry, B., Allen, N., & McLaughlin, M. (1996). "Old-Fashioned, Good Teachers"; African American Parents' Views of Effective Early Instruction *Learning Disabilities Research and Practice, 11*(3), 193-201.

Harvey, V. S. (1989). System program evaluations: Feasible and effective. *Communiqué, 18* (4), 25.

255

Harvey, V. S. (1990, January). How available are psychology journals in New Hampshire? New Hampshire Association of School Psychologists, *The Protocol*, 3-5.

Harvey, V. S. (1994). *Final report: Facilitating interagency services for severely emotionally disturbed children in Nashua, NH*. Nashua, NH: Nashua Public Schools Special Education Department.

Harvey, V. S. (1997a).*Guidelines for evaluating school psychological services (Revised)*.Bethesda, MD: National Association of School Psychologists.

Harvey, V. S. (1997b). Improving readability of psychological reports. *Professional Psychology: Research and Practice, 28*(3), 271-274.

Harvey, V. S., Bowser, P., Carlson, J. F., Grossman, F., & Kruger, L. (1998, April). *School psychologists and high technology: Ethical dilemmas and considerations*. Symposium presented at the National Association of School Psychologists, Orlando, FL.

Harvey, V. S., & Carlson, J. F. (1999). Ethical and legal issues with computer related technology. In A. Bardos (Ed.), *Technological innovations and the school psychologist*. Unpublished manuscript.

Haynes, P. (1993). Effects of supervision on the practice of school psychology in public school settings: A comparison of collaborative problem-solving and peer problem-solving consultation. *Dissertation Abstracts International, 54* (12-A), 4259.

Henning-Stout, M. (1993). Theoretical and empirical bases of consultation. In J. E. Zins, T. R. Kratochwill, & S. N. Elliott, (Eds.), *Handbook of consultation services for children* (pp. 15-45). San Francisco: Jossey-Bass Publishers.

Henning-Stout, M. (1994). *Responsive assessment: A new way of thinking about learning*. San Francisco: Jossey-Bass.

Henning-Stout, M. (1996). ¿Que podemos hacer?: Roles for school psychologists with Mexican and Latino migrant children and families. *School Psychology Review, 25* (2), 152-164.

Henning-Stout, M. & Conoley, J. C. (1988). Influencing program change at the district level. In J. L. Graden, J. E. Zins, & M. C. Curtis (Eds.), *Alternative educational delivery systems: Enhancing instruction options for all students*. (pp. 471-490), Washington, DC: National Association of School Psychologists.

Henry, M. A., & Beasley, W. W. (1982). *Supervising student teaching the professional way: A guide for cooperating teachers (3rd ed.)*. Terre Haute, IN: Sycamore Press.

Heron, T. E., Martz, S. A., & Margolis, H. (1996). Ethical and legal issues in consultation. *Remedial and Special Education, 17*(6), 377-385.

Herzberg, F. (1964). The motivation-hygiene concepts and problems of manpower. *Personnel Administration, 27*, (1).

Hess, A. K. (Ed.), (1980). *Psychotherapy supervision: Theory, research, and practice*. New York: Wiley.

Hightower, A. D., Johnson, D., & Haffey, W. G. (1995). Best practices in adopting a prevention program. In A. Thomas & J. Grimes (Eds.), *Best practices in school psychology-III* (pp. 311-323). Silver Spring, MD: National Association of School Psychologists.

Hofstede, G. (1993). Cultural constraints in management theories, *Academy of Management Executive, 7*, 81-90.

Hogan, R., Curphy, G. J., & Hogan, J. (1994). What we know about leadership: Effectiveness and personality. *American Psychologist, 49*, 493-504.

Hopkins, W. S., & Moore, K. D. (1993). *Clinical supervision: A practical guide to student teacher supervision*. Dubuque, IA: Wm. C. Brown Communications.

256

Horn, J. L. (1991). Measurement of intellectual capabilities: A review of theory. In K. S. McGrew, J. K. Werder, & R. W. Woodcock, *The Woodcock-Johnson Revised technical manual.* Chicago: Riverside.

Houle, C. O. (1984). *Continuing learning in the professions.* San Francisco: Jossey-Bass.

House, J. S. (1981). *Work stress and social support.* Reading, MA: Addison-Wesley.

Houser, R. (1998). Counseling and educational research: Evaluation and application. Thousand Oaks, CA: Sage Publications.

Huberty, T. J., & Huebner, E. S. (1988). A national survey of burnout among school psychologists. *Psychology in the Schools, 25,* 54-61.

Hunley, S., Harvey, V. S., Curtis, M., Portnoy, L. A., Grier, E. C., & Helssrich, D. (in press). School psychology supervisors: A national study of demographics and professional practices. *Communiqué.*

Illback, R. J., & Morrissey, W. M. (1985). Personnel management. In C. A. Maher (Ed.), *Professional self-management: Techniques for special services providers* (pp. 149-162). Baltimore: Paul H. Brookes.

Individuals with Disabilities Education Act. (IDEA) (1991) 20 U. S. C. Chapter 33; Department of Education Regulations for IDEA at 34 CFR 300 and 301 (September 29, 1992).

Irvine, P. H. (1993). Effects of supervision on the practice of school psychology in public school settings: A comparison of collaborative problem-solving and peer problem solving. *Dissertation Abstracts International, 54*(1-A), 91.

Jacob-Timm, S., & Hartshorne, T. S. (1998). *Ethics and law for school psychologists* (3rd ed.). New York: Wiley.

Jamieson, D. W., & Thomas, K. W. (1974). Power and conflict in the student-teacher relationship. *Journal of Applied Behavioral Science, 10* (3), 321-336.

Jerrell, J. M. (1984). Boundary-spanning functions served by rural school psychologists. *Journal of School Psychology, 22,* 259-271.

Johnson, D. W., & Johnson, F. P. (1994). *Joining together: Group theory and group skills.* Boston: Allyn & Bacon.

Johnson, L. R. (1998). Performance evaluation of special education administrators: Considerations and recommendations *NASSP Bulletin, 82*(594), 24-32.

Jones, R. L. (1988). *Psychoeducational assessment of minority group children: A casebook.* Berkeley, CA: Cobb & Henry.

Jordan, R. (1987). Best practices in personnel evaluation. In J. Grimes & D. Happe (Eds.), *Best practices in the supervision of school psychological services* (pp. 86-95). Des Moines, Iowa: Iowa State Dept. of Education. (ERIC Document Reproduction Service ED293037)

Kadushin, A. (1985). *Supervision in social work* (2nd ed.). New York: Columbia University Press.

Kamphaus, R. W., & Frick, P. J. (1996). *Clinical assessment of child and adolescent personality and behavior.* Boston: Allyn & Bacon.

Katz, R. L. (1955). Skills of effective administrators. *Harvard Business Review,33*(1), 33-42.

Kaufman, R. A. (1972). *Educational systems planning.* Englewood Cliffs, NJ: Prentice-Hall.

Kazdin, A. E. (1995). Preparing and evaluating research reports. *Psychological Assessment, 7,* 228-237.

Keith, T. Z. (1995), Best practices in applied research. In A. Thomas & J. Grimes (Eds.), *Best practices in school psychology-III* (pp. 135-143). Silver Springs, MD: National Association of School Psychologists.

Kendall, P. C., & Braswell, L. (1985). *Cognitive-behavioral therapy for impulsive children.* New York: Guilford Press.

Kessler, M. (1998). Ethics in supervision. *APAGS Newsletter, 10* (2), 1-3.

Kirkpatrick, M., Smith, C., & Roy, R. (1981). Lesbian mothers and their children. *American Journal of Orthopsychiatry, 51*, 545-551.

Kirschenbaum, H., & Glaser, B. (1978). *Developing Support Groups.* LaJolla, CA: University Associates.

Kniskern, D. P., & Gurman, A. S. (1988). Research. In H. A. Liddle, D. C. Breunlin, & R. C. Schwartz (Eds.), *Handbook of family therapy training and supervision* (pp. 368-378). New York: Guilford Press.

Knoff, H. M. (1986). Supervision in school psychology: The forgotten or future path to effective services? *School Psychology Review, 15*, 529-545.

Knoff, H. M. (1995). Best practices in facilitating school-based organizational change and strategic planning. In A. Thomas & J. Grimes (Eds.), *Best practices in school psychology-III* (pp. 239-252). Washington, DC: National Association of School Psychologists.

Kobak, K. A., Reynolds, W. M., & Griest, J. H. (1994). Computerized and clinical assessment of depression and anxiety: Respondent evaluation and satisfaction. *Journal of Personality Assessment, 63*, 173-180.

Koocher, G. P., & Keith-Spiegel, P. (1998). *Ethics in psychology: Professional standards and cases* (2nd ed.). New York: Oxford University Press.

Kozol, J. (1991). *Savage inequalities: Children in America's schools.* New York: Harper.

Krajewski, R. (1996). Supervision 2015. *Wingspan, 11* (2), 15-17.

Kratochwill, T. R., & Gettinger, M. (1985). Intervention management. In C. A. Maher (Ed.), Professional self-management: Techniques for special services providers (pp. 163-200). Baltimore: Paul H. Brookes.

Kratochwill, T. R., Bergan, J. R., & Mace, F. C. (1981). Practitioner competencies needed for implementation of behavior psychology in the schools: Issues in supervision. *School Psychology Review, 10*(4), 434-444.

Kruger, L. J., Cohen, S., Marca, D., & Matthews, L. (1996). Using the Internet to extend training in team problem solving. *Behavior Research Methods, Instruments and Computers, 28*(2), 248-252.

Kruger, L. J., & Struzziero, J. A. (1997). Computer-mediated peer support of consultation: Case description and evaluation. *Journal of Educational and Psychological Consulting, 8*(1), 75-90.

Kruger, L. J., & Struzziero, J. A. (1999). Using the Internet for consultation, peer support, and supervision. In A. Bardos (Ed.), *Technological innovations and the school psychologist.* Unpublished manuscript.

Kruger, L. J., Wandle, C. H., & Watts, R. P. (1992). The recession and downsizing of school psychology in Massachusetts. *Communiqué, 20*(8).

Krumboltz, J. D., & Thorensen, C. E. (1969). *Behavioral counseling: Cases and techniques.* New York: Holt, Rinehart, & Winston.

Kurdek, L., & Schmitt, J. (1987). Relationship quality of partners in heterosexual married, heterosexual cohabiting, and gay and lesbian relationships. *Journal of Personality and Social Psychology, 14*, 57-68.

Lamb, D. H., Cochran, D. J., & Jackson, V. R. (1991). Training and organizational issues associated with identifying and responding to intern impairment. *Professional Psychology: Research and Practice, 22*, 291-296.

Lappin, J., & Hardy, K. V. (1997). Keeping context in view: the heart of supervision. In T. C. Todd & C. L. Storm (Eds.), *The complete systemic supervisor: Context, philosophy, and pragmatics* (pp. 41-58). Boston: Allyn & Bacon.

Lazarus, R. S. (1966). *Psychological stress and the coping process.* New York: McGraw-Hill.

Levinson, E. M. (1990). Actual/desired role functioning, perceived control over role functioning, and job satisfaction among school psychologists. *Psychology in the Schools, 27*, 64-74.

Levinson, E. M. (1991). Predictors of school psychologist satisfaction with school system policies/practices and advancement opportunities. *Psychology in the Schools, 28*, 256-266.

Levinson, E. M., Fetchkan, R., & Hohenshil, T. H. (1988). Job satisfaction among practicing school psychologists revisited. *School Psychology Review, 17*, 101-112.

Lewis, G. (1994). Assessing psychiatric disorder with a human interviewer or a computer. *Journal of Epidemology and Community Health, 48*, 207-210.

Likert, R. (1967). *The human organization: Its management and value*. New York: McGraw-Hill.

Littrell, P. C., Billingsley, B. S., & Cross, L. H. (1994). The effects of principal support on special and general educators' stress, job satisfaction, school commitment, health, and intent to stay in teaching. *Remedial and Special Education, 15*, 297-310.

Loen, R. O. (1994). *Superior supervision: The 10% solution*. New York: Lexington Books.

Loganbill, C., Hardy, E., & Delworth, U. (1982). Supervision: A conceptual model. Counseling Psychologist, 10, 3-42.

Long, J. K. (1997). Sexual orientation: Implications for the supervisory process. In T. C. Todd & C. L. Storm, *The complete systemic supervisor* (pp. 59-71). Boston: Allyn & Bacon.

Macklem, G. (1999). *Functional assessment*. Unpublished manuscript.

Maddux, C. D., & Johnson, L. (1993). Best practices in computer-assisted assessment. In H. B. Vance (Ed.), *Best practices in assessment for school and clinical settings* (pp. 177-200). Brandon, VT: Clinical Psychology Publishing.

Maher, C. A. (1984). *Planning and evaluating special education services*. Englewood Cliffs, NJ.: Prentice-Hall.

Maher, C. A., Brabrack, C. R. (1981). An approach to goal-based evaluation of school psychological service departments. *Psychology in the Schools, 18*, 309-315.

Maher, C. A., & Cook, S. A. (1985). Time management. In C. A. Maher (Ed.), *Professional self-management: Techniques for special services providers* (pp. 23-44). Baltimore: Paul H. Brookes.

Mann, F. C. (1965). Toward an understanding of leadership roles in formal organizations. In R. Dubin, G. Homans, & D. C. Miller (Eds.), *Leadership and productivity: Some facts of industrial life*. San Francisco: Chandler Publishing Co.

Martens, B. (1993). A behavioral approach to consultation. In J. E. Zins, T. R., Kratochwill, & S. N. Elliott (Eds.), *Handbook of consultation services to children* (pp. 65-86). San Francisco: Jossey Bass.

Martin, S. (1994). School psychologists: Little time for counseling. *APA Monitor, 27*(10), 46.

Maslow, A. (1954). *Motivation and personality*. New York: Harper and Row.

Matarazzo, J. D. (1985). Clinical psychology test interpretations by computer: Hardware outpaces software. *Computers in Human Behavior, 1*, 235-253.

McCarney, S. (1988). *The pre-referral intervention manual*. Columbus MO: Hawthorne Educational Services.

McCauley, Lombardo, & Usher, (1989). Diagnosing management development needs: An instrument based on how managers develop. *Journal of Management, 15*, 389-403.

McGrew, K. S., & Flanagan, D. P. (1996). *A Cross- training approach to intelligence test interpretation*. Workshop presented at the National Association of School Psychologists, Atlanta, GA.

McGrew, K. S., & Flanagan, D. P. (1998). *The intelligence test desk reference*. Needham Heights, MA: Allyn & Bacon.

McInerney, J. F. (1985). Authority management. In C. A. Maher (Ed.), *Professional self-management: Techniques for special services providers* (pp. 129-148). Baltimore: Paul H. Brookes.

259

McIntosh, P. (1989, July-August). White privilege: Unpacking the invisible knapsack. *Peace and freedom*, 10-12.

McWhirter, D., & Mattison, A. (1984). Stages in the development of gay relationships. In J. DeCecco (Ed.), *Gay relationships* (pp. 161-168). New York: Harrington Park.

Mead, D. (1990). *Effective supervision: A task-oriented model for the developing professions*. New York: Bruner/Mazel.

Meichenbaum, D. (1977). *Cognitive-behavior modification: An integrative approach*. New York: Plenum.

Miles, M. (1965). *Planned change and organizational health: Figure and ground. Change processes in the public schools*. Eugene, OR: The University of Oregon Center for the Advanced Study of Educational Administration.

Moreland, K. L. (1985). Validation of computer-based test interpretations: Problems and prospects. *Journal of Consulting and Clinical Psychology, 53*, 816-825.

Moreland, K. L. (1992). Computer-assisted psychological assessment. In M. Zeidner & R. Most (Eds.), *Psychological testing: An inside view* (pp. 343-376). Palo Alto, CA: Consulting Psychologists Press.

Mornell, P. (1998). *Hiring smart*. Berkeley, CA: Ten Speed Press.

Mosley-Howard, G. S. (1995). Best practices in considering the role of culture. In A. Thomas & J. Grimes (Eds.), *Best practices in school psychology-III* (pp.337-345). Washington, DC: National Association of School Psychologists.

Mowder, B. A., & Prasse, D. P. (1981). An evaluation model for school psychological services. *Evaluation and Program Planning, 4*, 377-383.

Munson, C. E. (1991). Duty to warn and the role of the supervisor. *Clinical Supervisor, 9* (2), 1-6.

Nagle, R. J. (1995). Best practices in conducting needs assessment. In A. Thomas & J. Grimes (Eds.), *Best practices in school psychology-III* (pp. 421-430). Silver Spring, MD: National Association of School Psychologists.

Naglieri, J. A. (1997). Planning, attention, simultaneous, and successive theory and the cognitive assessment system: A new theory-based measure of intelligence. In D. P. Flanagan, J. L. Genshaft, & P. L. Harrison (Eds.), *Contemporary intellectual assessment: Theories, tests, and issues* (pp. 247-267). New York: Guilford.

Nastasi, B. K., & DeZoll, D. M. (1994). *School interventions for children of alcoholics*. New York: Guilford Press.

National Association of School Psychologists (1994). *Standards: Training programs, field placement programs, credentialing standards*. Bethesda, MD: author.

National Association of School Psychologists (1997). *Professional conduct manual, 3rd edition*. Bethesda, MD: author.

National Association of School Psychologists' Supervision Work Group (1998). *Supervision in school psychology*. Unpublished manuscript.

Netherton, S. D., & Mullins, L. L. (1997). Working with Supervisors. In J. R. Matthews, & C. E. Walker (Eds.). *Basic skills and professional issues in clinical psychology* (pp. 39-58). Needham Heights, MA: Allyn & Bacon.

Neufeldt, S. A., Iversen, J. N., & Juntunen, C. L. (1995). *Supervision strategies for the first practicum*. Alexandria, VA: American Counseling Association.

Nieto, S. (1992). *Affirming diversity: The sociopolitical context of multicultural education*. New York: Longman.

Noe, R. A., Hollenbeck, J. R., Gerhart, B., & Wright, P. M. (1996). *Human resource management: Gaining a competitive advantage* (2nd ed.). Boston: McGraw-Hill.

Norcross, J. C., & Halgin, R. P. (1997). Integrative approaches to psychotherapy supervision. In J. C. E. Watkins (Ed.), *Handbook of psychotherapy supervision* (pp. 203-222). New York: Wiley.

Norton, M., & Perlin, R. (1989, August). Here's what to look for when evaluating school psychologists. *The Executive Educator, 11*(8),24-25.

Office of Graduate Studies and Research, University of Massachusetts at Boston (1990). *Faculty guide to sponsored projects*. Boston, MA: author.

Office of Protection from Research Risks (1993). *Protecting human research subjects: Institutional Review Board guidebook*. Washington, DC: U.S. Government Printing Office.

Ogles, B. M., Lambert, M. J., & Masters, K. S. (1996). *Assessing outcome in clinical practice*. Boston: Allyn & Bacon.

Okun, B., Fried, J., & Okun, M. L. (1999). *Understanding diversity*. Pacific Grove, CA: Brooks/Cole.

Ownby, R. L. (1997). *Psychological reports: A guide to report writing in professional psychology* (3rd ed.). New York: Wiley.

Ownby, R. L., & Wallbrown, F. (1986). Improving report writing in school psychology. In T. R. Kratochwill (Ed.), *Advances in school psychology, Volume V,* (pp. 7-50). Hillsdale, NJ: Lawrence Erlbaum.

Parsons, R., & Meyers, J. (1984). *Developing consultation skills: A guide to training, development, and assessment for human service providers*. San Francisco: Jossey-Bass.

Patterson, C. (1994). Children of the lesbian baby boom: Behavioral adjustment, self-concepts, and sex role identity. In B. Greene & G. Herek (Eds.), *Lesbian and gay psychology* (pp. 156-175). Thousand Oaks, CA: Sage.

Patton, M. Q. (1982). *Practical evaluation*. Beverly Hills, CA: Sage.

Payne, D. A. (1982). Portrait of the school psychologist as a program evaluator. In C. R. Reynolds & T. B. Gutkin (Eds.), *Handbook of school psychology*. New York: Wiley.

Pennington, L. (1989). Supervision of school psychologists. In *School psychology in Wisconsin: Programs and practices* (Bulletin No. 9265). Madison, Wisconsin: Wisconsin State Dept. of Public Instruction. (ERIC Document Reproduction Service ED307518)

Peplau, L., & Cochran, S. (1990). A relational perspective on homosexuality. In D. McWhirter, S. Sanders, & J. Reinisch (Eds.), *Homosexuality/heterosexuality: Concepts of sexual orientation* (pp. 321-349). New York: Oxford University Press.

Phillips, B. N. (1989). Education, training, and evaluation of practitioners today and in the future. *Professional School Psychology, 3,* 177-186.

Pinsoff, W. M. (1979). The family therapist behavior scale (FTBS): Development and evaluation of a coding system. *Family Process, 18,* 451-461.

Plas, J. M. (1986). *Systems psychology in the schools*. New York: Pergamon Press.

Poland, S. (1989). *Suicide intervention in the schools*. New York: Guilford Press.

Poland, S., & Pitcher, G. (1990). Best practices in crisis intervention. In A. Thomas & J. Grimes (Eds.), *Best practices in school psychology-II* (pp. 259-274). Washington, DC: National Association of School Psychologists.

Pope, K. S., & Vasquez, M. J. T. (1998). *Ethics in psychotherapy and counseling: A practical guide* (2nd ed.). San Francisco, CA: Jossey-Bass.

Pope , K. S., & Vetter, V. A. (1992). Ethical dilemmas encountered by members of the American Psychological Association: A national survey. *American Psychologist, 47*(3), 397-411.

261

Powers, B., & Ellis, A. (1995). *A manager's guide to sexual orientation in the workplace*. New York: Routledge.

Prasse, D. P. (1995). Best practices in school psychology and the law. In A. Thomas & J. Grimes, (Eds.), *Best practices in school psychology-III* (pp. 41-50). Washington, DC: National Association of School Psychologists.

Pruitt, D. B., McColgan, E. B., Pugh, R. L., & Kiser, L. J. (1986). Approaches to psychotherapy supervision. *Journal of Psychiatric Education, 10*(2), 129-147.

Pryzwansky, W. B. (1986). Indirect service delivery: Considerations for future research in consultation. *School Psychology Review, 15*(4), 479-488.

Putney, M. W., Worthington, E. L., & McColloughy, M. E.(1992). Effects of supervisor and supervisee theoretical orientation. *Journal of Counseling Psychology, 39* (2), 258-265.

Quinn, M. M., Gable, R. A., Rutherford, R. R., Nelson, C. M., & Howell, K. W. (January 16, 1998). *An IEP Team's introduction to functional behavioral assessment and behavior intervention plans*. Workshop presented at the Center for Effective Collaboration and Practice.

Rambo, A. H., & Shilts, L. (1997). Four supervisory practices that foster respect for difference. In T. C. Todd & C. L. Storm, *The complete systemic supervisor* (pp. 83-92). Boston: Allyn & Bacon. Rehabilitation Act of 1973, 20 U. S. C. Sec. 794.

Reiner, H. D., & Hartshorne, T. S. (1982). Job burnout and the school psychologist. *Psychology in the Schools, 19*, 508-512.

Reschly, D. J., Genshaft, J., & Binder, M. S. (1987). *The NASP survey: Comparisons of practitioners, NASP leadership, and university faculty on key issues*. Washington, DC: National Association of School Psychologists. (ERIC Document Reproduction Service No. 300 733)

Reschly, D. J., & Wilson, M. S. (1995). School psychology practitioners and faculty: 1986 to 1991-92. Trends in demographics, roles, satisfaction, and system reform. *School Psychology Review, 24*, 62-80.

Reschly, D. J., & Ysseldyke, J. E. (1995). School psychology paradigm shift. In A. Thomas & J. Grimes (Eds.), *Best practices in school psychology-III*. Washington, D. C.: National Association of School Psychologists, pp. 17-31.

Reynolds, C. R., & Gutkin, T. B. (Eds.), (1982). *The handbook of school psychology*. New York: Wiley.

Reynolds, C. R., & Kamphaus, R. W. (1992). *Behavior assessment system for children (BASC)*. Circle Pines, MN: American Guidance Services.

Reynolds, C. R., & Richmond, B. O. (1985). *Revised children's manifest anxiety scale (RCMAS)*. Los Angeles: Western Psychological Services.

Reynolds, R. V. C., McNamara, J. R., Marion, R., J., & Tobin, D. L. (1985). Computerized service delivery in clinical psychology. *Professional Psychology: Research and Practice, 16*(3), 339-353.

Rice, B. (1985, September). Performance review: The job nobody likes. *Psychology Today, 19*(9),30-36.

Rigazio-DiGilio, S. A. (1997). Integrative supervision: Approaches to tailoring the supervisory process. In T. C. Todd & C. L. Storm (Eds.), *The complete systemic supervisor: Context, philosophy, and pragmatics*. (pp. 195-216). Boston: Allyn & Bacon.

Riveria, R. (1987). Legal issues in gay and lesbian parenting. In F. Bozett (Ed.), *Gay and lesbian parents* (pp. 199-227). New York: Praeger.

Robiner, W. N., & Schofield, W. (1990). References on supervision in clinical and counseling psychology. *Professional Psychology: Research and Practice, 21*, 297-312.

Rogers, C. (1958). Characteristics of a helping relationship. *Personnel and Guidance Journal, 37*, 6-16.

Rogers, C. (1965). *Client-centered therapy*. Boston: Houghton Mifflin.

Romans, J. S. C., Boswell, D. L., Carlozzi, A. F., & Ferguson, D. B. (1995). Training and supervision practices in clinical, counseling, and school psychology programs. *Professional Psychology: Research and Practice, 26*, 407-412.

Ronnestad, M. H., & Skovholt, T. M. (1993). Supervision of beginning and advanced graduate students of counseling and psychotherapy. *Journal of Counseling and Development, 71*, 396-405.

Rosenfield, S. (1985). Professional development management. In C. A. Maher (Ed.), *Professional self-management: Techniques for special services providers* (pp. 85-104). Paul H. Brookes: Baltimore.

Ross, J. (1995). Social class tension within families. *The American Journal of Family Therapy, 23*, 329-341.

Ross, R. R., Altmaier, E. M., & Russell, D. W. (1989). Job stress, social support, and burnout among counseling center staff. *Journal of Counseling Psychology, 36*, 464-470.

Ross, R. P., & Goh, D. S. (1993). Participating in supervision in school psychology: A national survey of practices and training. *School Psychology Review, 22*, 63-80.

Ross, R. P., & Sisenwein, F. E. (1990). Best practices in internship supervision. In A. Thomas & J. Grimes (Eds.), *Best practices in school psychology-II* (pp. 441-454). Washington, DC: National Association of School Psychologists.

Rubenstein, B. R. (1993). University trainers' versus field supervisors' perceptions of training in school psychology: A comparative survey. *Dissertation Abstracts International, 53* (12-A), 4259.

Rue, L. W., & Byars, L. L. (1997). *Management: Skills and applications* (8th ed.). Chicago: Irwin.

Rupert, P. A., Kozlowski, N. F., Hoffman, L. A., Daniels, D. D., & Piette, J. M. (1999). Practical and Ethical Issues in Teaching Psychological Testing. *Professional Psychology: Research and Practice, 30*(2), 209-214.

Russell, D., Altmaier, E. M., & Van Velzen, D., (1987). Job-related stress, social support, and burnout among classroom teachers. *Journal of Applied Psychology, 72*, 269-274.

Sabatino, D. A., Vance, H. B., & Miller, T. L.(1993). Defining best diagnostic practices. In H. Booney Vance (Ed.), *Best practices in assessment for school and clinical settings* (pp. 1-27), Brandon, VT: Clinical Psychology Publishing, Co., Inc.

Salvia, J., & Ysseldyke, J. E. (1998). *Assessment* (7th ed.). New York: Houghton Mifflin Company.

Sandoval, J., & Irvin, M. G. (1990). Legal and ethical issues in the assessment of children. In C. R. Reynolds & R. W. Kamphaus (Eds.). *Handbook of psychological and educational assessment of children: Intelligence and achievement*. New York: Guilford.

Sandoval, J., & Lambert, N. M. (1977). Instruments for evaluating school psychologists' function and service. *Psychology in the Schools, 14*, 172-179.

Sarason, S. B. (1990). *The predictable failure of educational reform: Can we change course before it's too late?* San Francisco: Jossey-Bass.

Sarason, S. B. (1996). *Revisiting "The culture of school and the problem of change."* New York: Teachers College Press.

Schmuck, R., & Runkel, P. (1994). *The handbook of organizational development in schools* (4th ed.). Palo Alto, CA: Mayfield.

Scott, J. (1995). Definitions, phases, and standards. In J. C. Boylan, P. B. Malley, & J. Scott, *Practicum and internship* (2nd edition), (pp. 1-10). Washington, DC: Accelerated Development.

Selmi, P. M., Klein, M. H., Greist, J. H., Sorrell, S. P., & Erdman, H. P. (1990). Computer-administered cognitive-behavioral therapy for depression. *American Journal of Psychiatry, 147*, 51-56.

263

Sergiovanni, T. J. (1990). *Value-added leadership: How to get extraordinary performance in schools.* New York: Harcourt Brace.

Sergiovanni, T. J. (1995, May). Schools are special places. *Educational Leadership 48, 35.*

Sergiovanni, T. J., & Starratt, R. J. (1988). *Supervision: Human perspectives.* New York: McGraw-Hill.

Sergiovanni, T. J., & Starratt, R. J. (1998). *Supervision: A redefinition* (6th ed.). New York: McGraw-Hill.

Shapiro, E. S. (1989). *Academic skills problems: Direct assessment and intervention.* New York: Guilford.

Shapiro, E. S. (1990). An integrated model for curriculum-based assessment. *School Psychology Review, 19,* 331-349.

Sheridan, S. M., & Kratochwill, T. R. (1992). Behavioral parent-teacher consultation: Conceptual and research considerations. *Journal of School Psychology, 30,* 117-139.

Sheridan, S. M., Salmon, D., Kratochwill, T. R., & Carrington Rotto, P. J. (1992). A conceptual model for the expansion of behavioral consultation training. *Journal of Educational and Psychological Consultation, 3,* 193-218.

Sheridan, S. M., Welch, M., & Orme, S. F. (1996). Is consultation effective? A review of outcome research. *Remedial and Special Education, 17*(6), 341-354.

Sherry, P. (1991). Ethical issues in the conduct of supervision. *The Counseling Psychologist, 19,* 566-584.

Shinn, M. R. (1995). Curriculum base measurement and its use in a problem solving model. In A. Thomas & J. Grimes (Eds.), *Best practices in school psychology-III* (pp. 547-568). Washington, D. C.: National Association of School Psychologists.

Simon, H. A. (1960). *The new science of management decision.* New York: Harper & Row.

Sinclair, D. (1987). Designing and providing in service for school psychologists. In J. Grimes & D. Happe (Eds.), *Best practices in the supervision of school psychological services* (pp. 76-84). Des Moines, Iowa: Iowa State Dept. of Education. (ERIC Document Reproduction Service ED293037)

Skillbeck, C. (1991). Microcomputer-based cognitive rehabilitation. In A. Ager & S. Bedall (Eds.). *Microcomputers and clinical psychology* (pp. 95-118). New York: Wiley.

Skovholt, T. M., & Ronnestadt, M. H. (1992). *The evolving professional self: Stages and themes in therapist and counselor development.* Chichester, England: Wiley.

Smith, D. K. (1984). Practicing school psychologists: Their characteristics, activities, and populations served. *Professional Psychology: Research and Practice, 15,* 798-810.

Smith, E. (1987). Individualized growth of professionals. In J. Grimes & D. Happe (Eds.), *Best practices in the supervision of school psychological services* (pp. 37-46). Des Moines, Iowa: Iowa State Dept. of Education. (ERIC Document Reproduction Service ED293037)

Solly, D. C., & Hohenshil, T. H. (1986). Job satisfaction of school psychologists in a primarily rural state. *School Psychology Review, 15,* 119-126.

Sproull, L., & Kiesler, S. (1991). *Connections: New ways of working in the networked organization.* Cambridge, MA: The MIT Press.

Stainback, S., & Stainback, W. (1989). Changes needed to strengthen regular education. In J. L.. Graden, J. E. Zins & M. J. Curtis, (Eds.), *Alternative educational delivery systems: Enhancing instructional options for all students* (pp. 17-32). Washington, DC: The National Association of School Psychologists.

Stark, K. (1990). *Childhood depression: School based intervention.* New York: Guilford Press.

Stevens, D. T., & Lundberg, D. J. (1998). The Emergence of the Internet: Enhancing career counseling education and services. *Journal of Career Development, 24,* 195-208.

264

Stoltenberg, C. (1981). Approaching supervision from a developmental perspective: The counselor complexity model. *Journal of Counseling Psychology, 28,* 59-65.

Stoltenberg, C. D., & Delworth, U. (1987). *Supervising counselors and therapists: A developmental approach.* San Francisco, Jossey-Bass.

Stoltenberg, C. D., McNeill, B., & Delworth, U. (1998). *IDM supervision: An integrated developmental model for counselors and therapists.* San Francisco: Jossey-Bass.

Stoner, G., Shinn, M.R., & Walker, H.M. (1991). *Interventions for achievement and behavior problems.* Silver Spring, MD: National Association of School Psychologists.

Storm, C. L., & Haug, I. E. (1997). Ethical issues: Where do you draw the line? In T. C. Todd & C. L. Storm (Eds.), *The complete systemic supervisor: Context, philosophy, and pragmatics* (pp. 26-40). Boston: Allyn & Bacon.

Storm, C. L. (1997a). The blueprint for supervision relationships: Contracts. In T. C. Todd & C. L. Storm, *The complete systemic supervisor* (pp. 272-282). Boston: Allyn & Bacon.

Storm, C. L. (1997b). Teaching therapists to become supervisors. In T. C. Todd & C. L. Storm, *The complete systemic supervisor* (pp. 363-372). Boston: Allyn & Bacon.

Storm, C. L., Peterson, M., & Tomm, K. (1997). Multiple relationships in supervision. In T. C. Todd & C. L. Storm, *The complete systemic supervisor* (pp. 253-271). Boston: Allyn & Bacon.

Storm, C. L., Todd, T. C., McDowell, T., & Sutherland, T. (1997). Supervising supervisors. In T. C. Todd & C. L. Storm, *The complete systemic supervisor* (pp. 373-388). Boston: Allyn & Bacon.

Struzziero, J. A. (1998). *Computer-mediated consultation.* Unpublished doctoral dissertation. Northeastern University, Boston.

Sturges, J. W. (1998). Practical use of technology in professional practice. *Professional Psychology: Research and Practice, 29,* 183-188.

Supervision Interest Network (1990). Standards for counselor supervisors. *Journal of Counseling and Development, 69,* 30-32.

Sutherland, J. W. (1973). *A general systems philosophy for the social and behavioral sciences.* New York: George Braziller.

Talley, R. C. (1990). Best practices in the administration and supervision of school psychological services. In A. Thomas & J. Grimes (Eds.), *Best practices in school psychology-II* (pp. 43-62). Washington, DC: National Association of School Psychologists.

Talley, R. C., & Short, R. J. (1995).*Creating a new vision of school psychology: Emerging models of psychological practices in schools.* Washington, D.C.: The American Psychological Association.

Tarasoff v. Regents of California, 118 Cal. Rptr. 129, 529 P.2d 553 (Cal. 1974), (Tarasoff I) Tarasoff v. Regents of California, 131 Cal Rptr. 14, 551 P2d 334 (Cal. 1976). (Tarasoff II).

Tharinger, D. J. (1998). School psychologists: Promoting secure and autonomous attachment: A focus on supervision. *The School Psychologist, 52,* 106, 122-123.

Tharinger, D., & Koranek, M. (1990). Best practices in individual counseling with elementary students. In A. Thomas & J. Grimes (Eds.), *Best practices in school psychology-II* (pp. 407-424). Washington, DC: National Association of School Psychologists.

Tharinger, D., & Stafford, M. (1995). Individual counseling of elementary aged students. In A. Thomas & J. Grimes (Eds.), *Best practices in school psychology-III* (pp. 893-908). Silver Springs, MD: National Association of School Psychologists.

Thomas, A. (1995). Best practices in facilitating professional effectiveness and avoiding professional burnout. In A. Thomas & J. Grimes (Eds.), *Best practices in school psychology-III* (pp. 101-109). Silver Springs, MD: National Association of School Psychologists.

Thomas, A. (1999). School psychology 2000: A national database. *Communiqué, 28*(3), 12-13.

Thomas, A., & Grimes, J. (Eds.). (1990). *Best practices in school psychology-II.* Washington, DC: The National Association of School Psychologists.

Thomas, A., & Grimes, J. (Eds.).(1995), *Best Practices in school psychology-III.* Silver Springs, MD: National Association of School Psychologists.

Thomas, T. (1992). Psychoeducational adjustment of English-speaking Caribbean and Central American immigrant children in the United States. *School Psychology Review, 21,* 566-576.

Thorndike, R. M. (1997). The early history of intelligence testing. In D. P. Flanagan, J. L. Genshaft, & P. L. Harrison (Eds.). *Contemporary intellectual assessment: Theories, tests, and issues.* (pp. 3-16). New York: Guilford Press.

Tichy, N. M. (1997). *The Leadership engine: How winning companies build leaders at every level.* New York: Harper Collins.

Tindal, G. (1989). Curriculum-based measurement. In J. L.. Graden, J. E. Zins, & M. J. Curtis, (Eds.), *Alternative educational delivery systems: Enhancing instructional options for all students* (pp. 111-136). Washington, DC: The National Association of School Psychologists.

Todd, T. C. (1997a). Problems in supervision: Lessons from supervisees. In T. C. Todd & C. L. Storm, *The complete systemic supervisor* (pp. 241-252). Boston: Allyn & Bacon.

Todd, T. C. (1997b). Self-supervision as a universal supervisory goal. In T. C. Todd & C. L. Storm (Eds.), *The complete systemic supervisor: Context, philosophy, and pragmatics* (pp. 17-25). Boston: Allyn & Bacon.

Todd, T. C., & Storm, C. L. (1997). *The complete systemic supervisor.* Boston: Allyn & Bacon.

Tomm, K. (1991). The ethics of dual relationships. *The Calgary participator: A family therapy newsletter, 1,* 11-15.

Tuckman, B. W. (1985). *Evaluating instructional programs,* (2nd ed.). Needham Heights, MA: Allyn & Bacon.

Turner, J,, & Fine, M. (1997). Gender and supervision: Evolving debates. In T. C. Todd & C. L. Storm, *The complete systemic supervisor* (pp. 72-82). Boston: Allyn & Bacon.

Ulman, J. (1987). Program research, development and review in school psychology. In J. Grimes & D. Happe (Eds.), *Best practices in the supervision of school psychological services* (pp. 21-36). Des Moines, Iowa: Iowa State Dept. of Education. (ERIC Document Reproduction Service ED293037)

Urwick, L. F. (1938). Scientific principles and organizations. *Institute of Management Series No. 19.* (p. 8). New York: American Management Association.

Vargas, L. A., & Koss-Chioino (Eds.), (1992). *Working with culture: Psychotherapeutic interventions with ethnic minority children and adolescents.* San Francisco: Jossey-Bass.

Vasquez, M. T. (1992). Psychologist as clinical supervisor: Promoting ethical practice. *Professional Psychology: Research and Practice, 23,* 196-202.

Von Bertalanffy, L. (1956). General systems theory. *General Systems, 1,* 1-10.

Vroom, V. H., & Yetton, P. W. (1973). *Leadership and managerial decision making.* Pittsburgh, PA: University of Pittsburgh Press.

266

Wagman, M., & Kerber, K. W. (1984). Computer-assisted counseling: Problems and perspectives. *Counselor Education and Supervision, 24*, 142-153.

Wagner, R. B. (1989). *Accountability in education: A philosophical inquiry.* New York: Routledge.

Ward. S. (1999). Field-based intern supervision: A study of practices. *Communiqué, 28*(3), 32-33.

Wasik, B. H., & Fishbein, J. E. (1982). Problem solving: A model for supervision in professional psychology. *Professional Psychology, 13*, 559-564.

Weber, M. (1946). Bureaucracy. In H. Gerth & C. Wright Mills (Eds.), pp. 333-336. *From Max Weber.* New York: Oxford.

Welsh, J. S., & Stout, L. J. (1993). *Supervision in school psychology: A national survey of state departments of education policy and practice.* Paper presented at the annual convention of the National Association of School Psychologists, Washington, DC.

Wenger, R. D., & Pryzwansky, W. B. (1987). Implementation status of the APA guidelines for delivery of services by school psychologists. *Professional Psychology, Research and Practice, 18*, 461-467.

Whiston, S. C., & Emerson, S. (1989). Ethical implications for supervisors in counseling of trainees. *Counselor Education and Supervision, 28*, 318-325.

Wiley, M. O., & Ray, P. B. (1986). Counseling supervision by developmental level. *Journal of Counseling Psychology, 33*(4), 439-445.

Will, M. (1986). Educating children with learning problems: A shared responsibility, *Exceptional Children, 52*,411-415.

Wisconsin State Department of Public Instruction (1989). *School psychology in Wisconsin: Programs and practices* (Bulletin No. 9265). Madison, Wisconsin: author. (ERIC Document Reproduction Service ED307518).

Wise, A. E. (1994). The coming revolution in teacher licensure: Redefining teacher preparation. *Action in Teacher Education, 16*(2), 1-13.

Wise, A. E., & Leibbrand, J. (1996). Profession-based accreditation: A foundation for high-quality teaching. *Phi Delta Kappan, 78*(3), 202-206.

Wright, D., & Gutkin, T. G. (1981). School psychologists' job satisfaction and discrepancies between actual and desired work function. *Psychological Reports, 49*, 735-738.

Ysseldyke, J. E., & Christenson, S. L. (1989). Linking assessment to intervention. In J. L. Graden, J. E. Zins, & M. J. Curtis (Eds.), *Alternative educational delivery systems: Enhancing instructional options for all students* (pp. 91-110). Washington, DC: The National Association of School Psychologists.

Ysseldyke, J. E., Dawson, P., Lehr, C., Reschly, D., Reynolds, M., & Telzrow, C. (1997). *School psychology: A Blueprint for training and practice II.* Bethesda, MD: National Association of School Psychologists.

Yukl, G. A., Wall, S., & Lepsinger, R. (1990). Preliminary report on the validation of the management practices survey. In K. E. Clark & M. B. Clark (Eds.), *Measurement of leadership* (pp. 223-238). West Orange, NJ: Leadership Library of America.

Zins, J. E. (1984). Scientific problem-solving approach to developing accountability procedures for school psychologists. *Professional Psychology: Research and Practice, 1*, 56-66.

Zins, J. E. (1985). Best practices in improving psychological services through accountability. In A. Thomas & J. Grimes (Eds.), *Best practices in school psychology* (pp. 493-503), Kent, OH: National Association of School Psychologists.

Zins, J. E., & Erchul, W. P. (1995). Best practices in school consultation. In A. Thomas & J. Grimes (Eds.). *Best practices in school psychology-III* (pp. 609-624). Washington, DC: National Association of School Psychologists.

Zins, J. E., Maher, C. A., Murphy, J. J., Wess, B. P. (1988). The peer support group: A means to facilitate professional development. *School Psychology Review, 17*, 138-146.

Zins, J. E., Murphy, J. J., & Wess, B. P. (1989). Supervision in school psychology: Current practices and congruence with professional standards. *School Psychology Review, 18*, 56-63.

NATIONAL ASSOCIATION
OF SCHOOL PSYCHOLOGISTS

STANDARDS FOR TRAINING AND FIELD
PLACEMENT PROGRAMS IN SCHOOL PSYCHOLOGY

STANDARDS FOR THE CREDENTIALING
OF SCHOOL PSYCHOLOGISTS

1994

The contents of this booklet are standards documents that were approved by the Executive Board/Delegate Assembly of the Association on March 5, 1994.

This document was prepared by the Accreditation, Credentialing, and Training Committee and the Publications Board, National Association of School Psychologists.

269

Additional copies are available from:

NASP Publications
4340 East West Highway, Suite 402
Bethesda, MD 20814

270

Table of Contents

Standards for Training and Field Placement
Programs in School Psychology 1994

Standards for the Credentialing of School Psychologists 1994

PREFACE

The National Association of School Psychologists (NASP), founded in 1969 as a not-for-profit organization, is the world's largest association of school psychologists. NASP is dedicated to

- Promoting the rights, welfare, education and mental health of children and youth; and
- Advancing the profession of school psychology.

This is accomplished through education, service, research, and policy development. Consistent with its mission, NASP has adopted and promotes an integrated set of comprehensive standards for preparation, credentialing, and professional practice in school psychology.

- Standards for Training and Field Placement Programs in School Psychology

- Standards for the Credentialing of School Psychologists

- Principles for Professional Ethics

- Standards for the Provision of School Psychological Services

The standards for training and for credentialing are included in this publication. Standards for the provision of services and principles for professional ethics are included in the *Professional Conduct Manual* which is available through NASP Publications.

"Guidelines" for the training of school psychologists were adopted in 1972. *Standards for Training and Field Placement Programs* were first adopted in 1978. NASP standards were initially approved by the National Council for Accreditation of Teacher Education (NCATE) in 1982 for the review and accreditation of school psychology programs at the sixth-year/specialist and doctoral levels. In 1988, NCATE began to accredit education "units" (i.e., the administrative unit that houses professional education programs, typically the college of education), rather than programs. Concurrently, NCATE authorized the review of programs by professional member associations such as NASP for whom standards had been approved by NCATE. Consequently, only programs reviewed by NASP since 1988 can be identified as being "NASP approved."

Standards for the Credentialing of School Psychologists also were first adopted in 1978. The NASP credentialing standards serve as the foundation for the National School Psychology Certification System (NSPCS), established by NASP January 1, 1989.

Both the training standards and the credentialing standards have undergone review and revision several times since their initial adoption in 1978. The standards included in this document represent the most recent revision and were adopted by the Association in March, 1994.

It is worthy of note that these standards represent a conceptual shift from an almost exclusive emphasis on process requirements to the introduction of performance-based accountability for training programs, as well as for individuals who wish to be credentialed as school psychologists. It is anticipated that future revisions will reflect an increasing emphasis on performance-based criteria.

The importance and implications of training and credentialing standards for school psychology have been addressed in the professional literature. The reader is referred to the following references for a discussion of this topic.

Batsche, G. M. (1990). Best practices in credentialing and continuing professional development. In A. Thomas & J. Grimes (Eds.), *Best Practices in School Psychology II* (pp. 887-898). Washington, DC: National Association of School Psychologists.

Fagan, T. K. (1990). Best practices in the training of school psychologists: Considerations for trainers, prospective entry-level and advanced students. In A. Thomas & J. Grimes (Eds.), *Best Practices in School Psychology II* (pp. 723-741). Washington, DC: National Association of School Psychologists.

Pryzwansky, W. B. (1993). The regulation of school psychology: A historical perspective on certification, licensure, and accreditation. *Journal of School Psychology, 31*(1), 219-235.

The reader who is interested in a listing and description of graduate programs in school psychology or a state-by-state explanation of credentialing requirements for school psychologists is referred to the following documents. Both will be available through NASP publications beginning in the fall of 1995.

273

Directory of School Psychology Graduate Programs
    by Douglas K. Smith and Amy Henning

Handbook of Certification and Licensure Requirements for School Psychologists
by Michael Curtis, Sawyer Hunley, and Joseph Prus

PROCEDURES FOR REVISION AND ADOPTION OF STANDARDS FOR TRAINING AND CREDENTIALING IN SCHOOL PSYCHOLOGY

In accordance with Association policy, NASP standards for training and standards for credentialing are reviewed every five years under the direction of the Accreditation, Credentialing, and Training Committee. The most recent review and revision was initiated in January, 1992. Because of their interrelatedness, training standards and credentialing standards must be consistent. Therefore, to ensure consistency, as well as participation by a broad range of interested constituencies, both sets of standards were revised concurrently using a three-tiered structure. The individuals, groups, and organizations included are listed following the description of the structure and revision procedures.

Level I consisted of a 10-member Drafting Group that was responsible for soliciting and considering recommendations for revision of the standards, as well as reactions to drafts of revised standards. Five members were responsible for actually drafting revised training standards and five for revised credentialing standards. However, all 10 members were responsible for deciding what revisions were to be incorporated in each set of standards.

Level II was titled the Development Group and included 30 members who were asked to critically review each draft of the revised standards and to provide the Drafting Group with reactions and recommendations for further modification. The Development Group was carefully constituted to provide representation from a wide range of interested constituencies. The membership reflected gender and geographical balance, as well as representation for members of minority groups, university faculty, practicing school psychologists, state consultants, and students. Membership also included representation based on roles within NASP (state delegate, regional director, committee chair/editor, and National School Psychology Certification Board) and roles in other relevant organizations (e.g., Division of School Psychology of the American Psychological Association [APA], Council of Directors of School Psychology Programs [CDSPP], and state school psychology associations).

Level III was titled the Reaction Group and included the leadership of NASP and several other interested constituencies (Division of School Psychology of APA, CDSPP, and Trainers of School Psychologists [TSP]) from whom input, reactions, and recommendations were solicited. The faculty of every identifiable school psychology training program, all state school psychology association presidents, and all state school psychology consultants also were included in this group. The mailing list for dissemination of materials to the Reaction Group included approximately 500 individuals.

In January, 1992 all members of the NASP leadership and all members of the Development Group were invited to submit recommendations for revision of both sets of standards. Announcement of the revision of standards and an invitation to provide recommendations for revision was published in the NASP *Communiqué* which has a circulation of over 20,000. Open sessions were held at the NASP convention for the purpose of soliciting recommended revisions. In addition to announcement in the convention program, a letter was mailed to all university training program directors/coordinators notifying them of the revision of standards and inviting them and their faculty to the open session at the convention. A similar letter also was mailed to all state school psychology consultants. Recommendations for revision also were formally solicited from the National Council for Accreditation of Teacher Education (NCATE).

In July, 1992, an invitation for recommendations was again published in the NASP *Communiqué*. Requests that the invitation be published also were sent to *The School Psychologist* (newsletter of the Division of School Psychology of APA) and *The Forum* (newsletter of TSP). Letters inviting input were mailed to all members of the leadership of NASP, the Executive Board of the Division of School Psychology of APA, the Executive Committee of CDSPP, and the officers of TSP, as well as to all identifiable training programs, all state school psychology consultants, and all state school psychology association presidents. The invitation for input through direct mail went to approximately 500 individuals.

Based on input received, consideration of the school psychology literature, and a national demographic study conducted by NASP in 1992, the Drafting Group formulated a set of directions for the proposed revision. Those directions and potential revisions were presented to and discussed by the NASP Executive Board/Delegate Assembly in September, 1992. Following that discussion and approval to proceed as proposed, a draft of revised standards was completed and disseminated to all members of both the Development Group and the Reaction Group (i.e., the approximately 500 persons who received the July invitation for input). Reactions and implications for further revision were discussed with the NASP Executive Board in January, 1993.

Another draft of revised standards was disseminated to the Development Group. Reactions were used to further refine the revised standards. This draft was disseminated to the entire Reaction Group. Open sessions were again held in conjunction with the NASP convention (April, 1993) to discuss the proposed revisions. The proposed revisions also were discussed by the NASP Executive Board/Delegate Assembly.

Having received widespread support, the proposed standards were presented to the NASP Delegate Assembly in July, 1993 for the first formal reading prior to consideration of adoption. The proposed standards were again presented to the NASP Executive Board for discussion in January, 1994. In February, 1994, the proposed standards were disseminated for final review and approval by the Development Group. Having been formally approved by the Development Group through a written ballot, the proposed standards were presented to the NASP Delegate Assembly in March, 1994. Both the credentialing standards and the training standards were adopted by unanimous vote of the Delegate Assembly on March 5, 1994.

Three-Tiered Structure for Revision of Credentialing Standards and Training Standards

Level I: Drafting Group

Credentialing	Training
George Batsche	Cindy Carlson
Rhonda Broadwater	Michael Curtis
Joseph Prus	Peg Dawson
Ronald Reeve	Daniel Reschly
Nancy Waldron	Carole Robinson-Zanartu

Level II: Development Group

Randy Allison	Eric Andreassen
Mary Kay Braccio	Karen Carey
Ann Casey	Leslie Hale
Arlene Crandall	Debra Crockett
Ronald Edwards	Mary Fernandez
Paul Fernandez	Mel Franklin
Joseph French	Roland Good
Jeffrey Grimes	Howard Knoff
Susan Leahy	Joel Meyers
Antoinette Miranda	Sylvia Rosenfield
Susan Safranski	Jonathon Sandoval
Edward Schlossman	Frank Smith
Delores Spencer-Izegbu	Mark Swerdlik
Caroline Wandle	Connie Reyes
Markay Winston	Lamonte Wyche

275

Level III: Reaction Group

NASP Leadership: Officers, Directors, Delegates, Chairs

Div. of School Psychology (APA): Executive Committee

CDSPP: Executive Committee

TSP: Executive Committee

Presidents, State School Psychology Associations

State Consultants, School Psychological Services

School Psychology Training Programs: Directors/ Coordinators and Faculty

DATES OF IMPLEMENTATION

Standards for Training and Field Placement Programs in School Psychology (1994) shall be effective as of January 1, 1996 for all school psychology training programs. All program reviews conducted by NASP for which the date of approval would be January 1, 1996 or after shall be based on these standards.

All school psychology trainees who complete their programs of study on or after January 1, 1998 and all other new applicants for credentialing in school psychology on or after that date shall be trained and credentialed in accordance with *Standards for the Credentialing of School Psychologists* (1994).

ACKNOWLEDGEMENTS

The development, review, and revision of standards documents is one of the most important activities undertaken by a professional association. The most recent revision of the credentialing standards and the training standards of NASP took more than two years and involved the efforts of many individuals, some of whom invested countless hours in the process. In addition to those persons identified above who served in the Drafting Group, the Development Group, or among the leadership of the organiza-

tions included in the Reaction Group, the following individuals also contributed to the revision of these standards or to their printing and dissemination: Fran Floyd, Susan Granda, Sawyer Hunley, Karen Kinziger, Paul Mendez, Anne Rood, Nancy Suarez, and Hope Tunnicliffe. The National Association of School Psychologists expresses its appreciation to each of the individuals and organizations mentioned above, as well as to the practicing school psychologists, university faculty, state consultants, state association presidents, and students who contributed to the revision process.

STANDARDS FOR TRAINING AN FIELD PLACEMENT PROGRAMS IN SCHOOL PSYCHOLOGY 1994

The National Association of School Psychologists (NASP) is committed to the development of comprehensive and effective psychological services for all children and youth. The NASP *Standards for Training and Field Placement Programs in School Psychology* contribute to the development of services through the identification of critical content and training experiences needed by students preparing for careers in school psychology. These *Standards* serve to guide the design of school psychology graduate education, as a basis for program evaluation, and as the foundation for the recognition of strong programs through the program approval process.

I. VALUES AS A PROGRAM FOUNDATION

As a specialty within the profession of psychology, school psychology is founded in respect for the dignity and worth of each individual and in a commitment to furthered understanding of human behavior for the purpose of promoting human welfare. The values that serve as a foundation for this field should also provide a foundation for graduate education and professional practice in school psychology.

1.1 A commitment to understanding and responsiveness to human diversity is articulated and practiced throughout all aspects of the program, including admissions, faculty, coursework, practica, and internship experiences. Human diversity is recognized as a strength which is valued and respected. The program promotes recognition and valuing of the uniqueness of each individual, an affirmation of the inherent worth of all human beings, and a commitment to the enhancement of human development and capability through the application of school psychological services.

1.2 The program fosters a commitment to enhancing the strengths of critical socialization institutions such as families and schools through the delivery of school psychological services that are sensitive to the unique needs of systems and organizations, as well as effective in promoting mental health and the acquisition of competencies.

II. KNOWLEDGE BASE, TRAINING PHILOSOPHY, GOALS & OBJECTIVES

The essential knowledge base for the professional practice of school psychology encompasses psychological foundations, educational foundations, interventions and problem solving, statistics and research methodologies, and professional school psychology. That knowledge base should be delivered within a context of commonly held and publicly known values, and clearly articulated training philosophy, goals, and objectives for the preparation of future school psychologists. The same knowledge base standards apply to both specialist-level and doctoral programs. However, there shall be a clear distinction between the two levels and doctoral programs shall ensure greater breadth or depth in each of the areas.

2.1 An integrated and sequential program of study and supervised practice shall be provided to all trainees that reflects the values and training philosophy of the program and that ensures the preparation of all trainees in accordance with clearly articulated goals and objectives. There shall be a direct and obvious relationship between the components of the curriculum and the goals and objectives of the program.

NOTE: The specification of content areas in Standards 2.2-2.8 does not necessarily require that an entire graduate-level course be devoted to each of the areas. The criterion for program approval purposes will be "substantive" preparation in each of the areas. Substantive preparation, depending on the area and the organization of the program, may mean an entire course, portions of one or more courses, didactic components of practica or internship, or practica or internship experiences.

2.2 Psychological Foundations
The program employs a systematic process that ensures that all students have a foundation in the knowledge base for the discipline of psychology. That knowledge bases shall include:

- Biological Bases of Behavior (e.g., biological bases of development, neuropsychology, physiological psychology, psychopharmacology)
- Human Learning
- Social and Cultural Bases of Behavior (e.g., cross-cultural studies, social development, social and cultural diversity, social psychology)
- Child and Adolescent Development
- Individual Differences (e.g., Human Exceptionalities, Developmental Psychopathology)

2.3 Educational Foundations

The program employs a systematic process that ensures that all students have a foundation in the knowledge base for education. That knowledge base shall include:

- Instructional Design
- Organization and Operation of Schools (including but not limited to education of exceptional learners, school and community-based resources, alternative service delivery systems)

2.4 Interventions/Problem-Solving

The program employs a systematic process that ensures that all students possess the knowledge and professional expertise to collaborate with families and school- and community-based professionals in designing, implementing, and evaluating interventions that effectively respond to the educational and mental health needs of children and youth. Areas of knowledge and practice shall include:

- Assessment (diverse models and methods linked to direct and indirect interventions)
- Direct Interventions, both Individual and Group (including counseling and behavior management)
- Indirect Interventions (including consultation, systems and organizational change)

2.5 Statistics and Research Methodologies

The program employs a systematic process that ensures that all students are competent consumers of research and new knowledge, and are able to use diverse methodologies (e.g., ethnographic, single subject designs, quantitative methods) to evaluate professional practices (e.g., interventions) and/or programs. That knowledge base shall include:

- Research and Evaluation Methods
- Statistics
- Measurement

2.6 Professional School Psychology

The program employs a systematic process that ensures that all students have a knowledge base specific to the professional specialty of school psychology. That knowledge base shall include:

- History and Foundations of School Psychology
- Legal and Ethical Issues
- Professional Issues and Standards
- Alternative Models for the Delivery of School Psychological Services
- Emergent Technologies
- Roles and Functions of the School Psychologist

III. PRACTICA

Practica are an essential component in the professional preparation of school psychologists. They provide opportunities for students to practice, under supervision, the application of knowledge and specific skills in the resolution of individual, group, and system-level problems. Practica are consistent with the values and training model of the program. Laboratory or field-based practica are used to evaluate a trainee's mastery of distinct skills as one measure of preparedness to enter the internship.

3   The program provides a sequence of closely supervised practica experiences through which students practice and are evaluated regarding their mastery of distinct skills consistent with the goals and objectives of the program. Practica include, but are not

278

necessarily limited to, orientation to the educational process, assessment for intervention, direct intervention methods including counseling and behavior management, and indirect intervention methods including consultation.

Practica reflect the following characteristics:

a Practica experiences shall include: (1) orientation to the educational process; (2) assessment for intervention; (3) direct intervention (including counseling and behavior management); and (4) indirect intervention (including consultation). Student performance shall be systematically evaluated in each area.

b Practica experiences shall be distinct from and occur prior to the internship.

c Practica occur at time(s), are in settings, and are of sufficient length to be appropriate to the specific training objectives of the program.

d There is a direct and obvious relationship between practica experiences and the objectives for which the practica are intended.

e Practica experiences occur under conditions of supervision appropriate to the specific training objectives of the program.

f Practica experiences are provided appropriate recognition through the awarding of academic credit.

g Practica experiences occur with university involvement appropriate to the specific training objectives of the program.

h The quality of practica experiences are systematically evaluated in a manner consistent with the specific training objectives of the program.

i Practica experiences are conducted in accordance with current legal-ethical standards for the profession.

IV. INTERNSHIP

The internship is the culminating experience in school psychology graduate preparation. It is a comprehensive experience through which the student is required to integrate the knowledge base and applied skills of school psychology in promoting positive educational and mental health practices and in resolving individual, group, and system-level problems. The internship affords the student the opportunity to demonstrate knowledge and skills acquired through coursework and practica, as well as to acquire new knowledge and skills. Internship settings shall be appropriate for the goals and objectives of the training program; all students shall complete at least one-half of their internship in a school setting. (See Standard 6.10).

4 A comprehensive internship experience is provided through which all students are required to demonstrate, under supervision, their ability to integrate knowledge and skills in providing a broad range of school psychological services. The internship is conceptualized as the culminating component in school psychology graduate education. It affords the student the opportunity to work with diverse client populations, a range of problems, and different types of human service programs, using varied intervention methodologies.

The internship experience reflects the following characteristics:

a The internship experience is provided at or near the end of the formal training period.

b The internship experience occurs on a full-time basis over a period of one academic year, or on a half-time basis over a period of two consecutive academic years.

c The internship experience is designed according to a written plan that provides the student opportunities to gain experience in the delivery of a broad range of school psychological services. Services include, but are not limited to assessment for intervention, counseling, behavior management, and consultation.

d The internship experience occurs in a setting appropriate to the specific training objectives of the program.

e The internship experience is provided appropriate recognition through the awarding of academic credit.

f The internship experience occurs under conditions of appropriate supervision. Field-based internship supervisors hold a valid credential as a school psychologist for that portion of the internship that is in a school setting. That portion of the internship which appropriately may be in a non-school setting requires supervision by an appropriately credentialed psychologist.

g Field-based internship supervisors are responsible for no more than two interns at any given time. University internship supervisors are responsible for no more than twelve interns at any given time.

h Field-based internship supervisors provide, on average, at least two hours per week of direct supervision for each intern.

i The internship is based on a positive working relationship and represents a collaborative effort between the university program and field-based supervisors to provide an effective learning experience for the student. University internship supervisors provide at least one on-site contact per semester with each intern and supervisor.

j The internship placement agency provides appropriate support for the internship experience including: a) a written contractual agreement specifying the period of appointment and the terms of compensation, b) a schedule of appointment consistent with that of agency school psychologists (e.g., calendar, participation in in-service meetings, etc.), c) provision for participation in continuing professional development activities, d) expense reimbursement consistent with policies pertaining to agency school psychologists, e) an appropriate work environment including adequate supplies, materials, secretarial services, and office space, f) release time for internship supervisors, and g) a commitment to the internship as a training experience.

k The quality of the internship experience is systematically evaluated in a manner consistent with the specific training objectives of the program.

l The internship experience is conducted in a manner consistent with the current legal-ethical standards of the profession.

V. PERFORMANCE-BASED PROGRAM ACCOUNTABILITY

Systematic evaluation of coursework, practica, internship experiences, faculty, supervisors, and institutional resources is essential to monitoring and improving program quality. It is essential that programs also demonstrate accountability with regard to the overall effectiveness of the total curriculum. That accountability is demonstrated through the ability of the program's graduates to provide school psychological services that effectively respond to the educational and mental health needs of children and youth, their families, and the educational and mental health agencies that serve them.

5.1 Systematic evaluation procedures are used to ensure the integrity and quality of the program. Different sources of information (e.g., tests of knowledge, observations of skills, instructional evaluation, performance portfolios, perceptions of students or supervisors), are used, as appropriate, to evaluate components of the program.

5.2 The program employs a systematic process to ensure that all students, prior to the conclusion of the internship experience, are able to integrate domains of knowledge and applied professional skills in delivering a comprehensive range of services that result in measurable positive changes regarding the educational and mental health needs of children and youth.

5.3 The program systematically collects, analyzes, and interprets process and performance evaluation data; results are used to improve the program.

VI. PROGRAM LEVEL AND STRUCTURAL REQUIREMENTS

Standards 6.1-6.5 apply to both doctoral and specialist-level programs.

6.1 The program shall limit the number of credit hours acquired through courses, seminars, and other learning experiences not open exclusively to graduate students to no more than one-third of the student's program.

6.2 Program requirements exclude credit for undergraduate study, study which is remedial, or study which is designed to remove

deficiencies in meeting requirements for program admission.

6.3 A full-time continuous residency or an alternate planned experience is required for all students. Programs allowing alternate planned experiences as a substitute for full-time residency must demonstrate how those experiences are equivalent to experiences commonly associated with residency requirements.

6.4 The program shall provide an active continuing professional development program for practicing school psychologists.

6.5 The program shall meet established approval standards for the appropriate state credentialing body(ies).

REQUIREMENTS FOR SPECIALIST-LEVEL PROGRAMS (6.6-6.7)

6.6 Specialist-level programs shall consist of a minimum of three years of full-time study or the equivalent at the graduate level. The program shall include at least 60 graduate semester hours or the equivalent, at least 54 hours of which are exclusive of credit for the supervised internship experience. Institutional documentation of program completion shall be provided.

6.7 Specialist-level programs shall include at least one academic year of supervised internship experience, consisting of a minimum of 1200 clock hours, at least one-half of which must be in a school setting.

REQUIREMENTS FOR DOCTORAL PROGRAMS (6.8-6.10)

6.8 Doctoral programs shall provide greater breadth and depth in knowledge domains and applied competencies. NOTE: Doctoral programs are encouraged to provide opportunities for doctoral study for practicing school psychologists and to allow credit for prior training to the greatest extent possible.

6.9 Doctoral programs shall consist of a minimum of four years of full-time study or the equivalent at the graduate level. The program shall include a minimum of 90 graduate semester hours or the equivalent, at least 78 of which are exclusive of credit for the predoctoral supervised internship experience and any terminal doctoral project (e.g., dissertation) and shall culminate in institutional documentation.

6.10 Doctoral programs shall include at least one academic year of predoctoral supervised internship experience, consisting of a minimum of 1500 clock hours, at least one-half of which must be in a school setting.

Note: Doctoral students who have met the school-based internship requirement through a specialist-level internship or equivalent experience may complete the predoctoral internship in a non-school setting. Program policy shall specifically define equivalent experiences and explain their acceptance with regard to doctoral internship requirements. Demonstration of policy implementation in practice also shall be provided.

CRITERIA FOR PROGRAM FACULTY

7 Program Administrators

7.1 Both Doctoral and Sixth-Year/Specialist programs shall be directed/coordinated by persons who hold the doctorate with specialization in school psychology and are certified and/or licensed for the practice of school psychology in the state in which the program is located.

7.2 The director/coordinator of both Doctoral and Sixth-Year/Specialist programs shall possess at least two years of experience as a school psychologist in an appropriate setting.

8 Preparation of Full-time Faculty

8.1 Full-time faculty shall possess the doctoral degree in psychology, education, or a closely related discipline with a specialization supportive of their training responsibilities in school psychology.

8.2 Faculty with responsibilities for field supervision in school psychology and/or teaching professional courses in school psychology shall possess at least two years of experience as a school psychologist in a school setting.

8.3 Each full-time faculty member shall engage in ongoing learning relevant to his/her training responsibilities and shall provide evidence of continuing professional development in school psychology.

8.4 Each full-time faculty member shall provide evidence of ongoing contributions to the field of school psychology through professional service activities such as writing, research, consultation, involvement with professional organizations, and/or field experiences.

9 Preparation of Part-time Faculty

9.1 Part-time faculty shall meet the preparation requirements for appointment to the full-time faculty, (10.1, 10.2, 10.3, 10.4) and shall be selected based upon their ability to make special contributions to the school psychology program.

10 Composition of Faculty for Doctoral Degree Programs

10.1 The faculty for each doctoral program shall include at least three full-time positions. At least two of the positions must be filled by full-time faculty who hold the doctorate with specialization in school psychology and who possess at least two years of experience as a school psychologist in a school setting. At least one additional full-time position must be filled by a full-time faculty member who holds the doctorate in a field which directly supports the program.

10.2 The program shall provide a plan to recruit, maintain, and promote the professional development of faculty with minority characteristics in terms of sex, race, ethnic origin, and disabilities.

10.3 The faculty shall be sufficient to assure an average faculty-student ratio not in excess of 1:10.

11 Composition of Faculty for Sixth-Year/Specialist Degree Programs

11.1 The faculty for each Sixth-Year/Specialist program shall include at least three full-time equivalent positions. At least two of the positions must be filled by full-time faculty who hold the doctorate with specialization in school psychology and who possess at least two years of experience as a school psychologist in a school setting. At least one additional full-time equivalent position must be filled by faculty who hold doctorates in fields which directly support the program.

11.2 The program shall provide a plan to recruit, maintain, and promote the professional development of faculty with minority characteristics in terms of sex, race, ethnic origin, and disabilities.

11.3 The faculty shall be sufficient to assure an average faculty-student ratio not in excess of 1:10.

12 Conditions for Faculty Service

12.1 In addition to teaching, supervision, advising, professional involvement and research or scholarly activities, faculty responsibilities may also include community service and administrative functions.

12.2 Institutional policies shall provide for the allotment of sufficient time for faculty to engage in each area of responsibility.

12.3 Institutional policy shall limit teaching and supervision of practica and internship assignments to a maximum of 75% of the total faculty workload.

12.4 Institutional policy shall provide for at least 25% release time from other faculty responsibilities for the program administrator.

CRITERIA FOR STUDENTS

13 Admission to Program

13.1 The program shall apply specific published criteria, both objective and subjective, for the admission of students to the program at each level.

13.2 Program policy and actions shall reflect a commitment to multicultural education in the recruitment and retention of students with minority characteristics in terms of sex, race, ethnic origin and disabilities.

14 Evaluation of Students in the Program

14.1 The program shall apply a published selective retention process which includes clearly stated evaluative criteria and a time frame for the systematic review of the progress of all students.

14.2 The evaluation criteria included in the selective retention process shall address the academic and professional competencies as well as the personal characteristics appropriate for practice as a school psychologist.

INSTITUTIONAL RESOURCES AND FACILITIES

15   Physical Facilities

15.1   The program shall insure that adequate office, clinical and laboratory facilities, data and information processing facilities, supplies and equipment are available to and appropriate for the necessary demands of faculty and students in school psychology.

15.2   The program shall provide reasonable accommodation for the special needs of students and faculty with disabilities.

16   Library

16.1   The library shall provide resources that are adequate to support instruction, independent study,and research relevant to school psychology.

16.2   Through the library or a materials and instructional media center, pertinent films, videotapes, microfilms, and other media materials and equipment shall be accessible in support of the school psychology programs.

EVALUATION OF GRADUATES, PROGRAM AND PLANNING

17   Evaluation of Graduates

17.1   The program shall engage in systematic efforts to evaluate the quality of its graduates upon completion of their programs of study and after they enter their professional roles. The evaluation shall include evidence of graduate performance in relation to stated program objectives.

18   Evaluation of Program

18.1   The program shall engage in systematic efforts to evaluate the quality of its instructional offerings. Evaluation shall include consideration of student input.

18.2   The program shall insure representative student, faculty, and consumer participation in the evaluation of the school psychology program.

18.3   The results of the program evaluation shall be used in the modification and improvement of the school psychology program.

19   Program Development

19.1   The program shall have plans for its long-range development and the enhancement of its relationship to the profession of school psychology.

APPENDIX A

Practica Experiences
Suggested Practices

Practica are viewed as integral and essential components of professional training. They provide opportunities for trainees to gain knowledge and skills most appropriately learned in the field and to refine skills and clarify knowledge learned as a part of the university training program. Practica experiences are characterized in the following manner:

1   They may be offered through on-campus agencies (e.g., Child Study Center, Psychology Clinic), community agencies (e.g, public or private schools, mental health centers) or some combination of the two.
2   Supervision and principal responsibility for the student typically rest with the faculty of the university training program.
3   The experience is offered for academic credit.
4. The experience is completed prior to an internship.
5   The experience is a requirement for credential completion.
6   The experience is more limited than the internship with regard to the range of cases, situations, etc., to which the trainee is exposed.
7   On-campus instruction is often provided concurrently or as part of the experience.
8   The experience is a direct extension of specific training activities.
9   The experience is generally part-time.

Programs provide practica experiences as integral parts of the training sequence. This is typically accomplished through the provision of separate practicum courses or practical application components of courses specifically designed for skill acquisition.

Practica experiences are provided to students at times most appropriately related to the acquisition of specific skills. They also are of sufficient time to allow for desired skill acquisition. Courses designed to develop skills in diagnostic assessment, for example, have practicum components which allow students opportunities to become thoroughly familiar with procedures being taught.

Practica, or practical application course components, are provided under conditions appropriate to program objectives. The typically offered practicum experience in diagnostic assessment, for example, is offered in settings conducive to appropriate skill acquisition such as in schools, clinics or service agencies. Similarly, the tasks required of students are to be clearly related to the desired skill acquisition and the sample of subjects employed (or target population) is suitable.

Where practicum experiences and supervision are provided in the facilities of, and under the supervision of the program faculty, it may be assumed that adequate support is provided. Often, however, such experiences are provided in facilities which may be affiliated with the program in other administrative arrangements such as schools, clinics or service agencies outside the immediate administrative control of the program faculty. In such situations, attention is given to the provision of adequate support (e.g., equipment, facilities, resource personnel etc.).

As required by Standard 3 all practica supervision must be provided by program faculty or other supervisory personnel who possess background, training and credentials appropriate to the practicum experiences. Supervision is available to students in sufficient amounts of time (a minimum of two hours per week is recommended in courses designated specifically as practica) to assure the acquisition of desired skills. Program faculty and other supervisory personnel receive adequate release time from normal

285

duties to supervise practica students. Such assigned time is consistent with the academic credit assigned to the practicum and compatible with the full-time duties of the staff member. Thus program faculty members assigned to practicum supervision are credited with an hour load which is consistent with the credit hours assigned to the practicum when the practicum is provided as a separate course. When provided in the context of practical application to existing courses, the duties are reflected in the credit hour assignment for the course. Similarly, field-based supervisors are provided load recognition of their duties as field supervisors for university practica.

The program faculty are responsible for providing appropriate orientation to non-program supervisors. This facilitates the clarification of the role and function of all parties and assists the non-program supervisors in carrying out responsibilities in a manner consistent with the program objectives. The responsibility of program faculty and non-program supervisors are clearly understood and agreed upon by both parties when both are engaged in practicum supervision of the same students.

Support is also evidenced in the number of students considered reasonable to be supervised by either program faculty or field-based supervisors. A maximum of six students per practicum, when offered as a separate course, is advised for program faculty. Where field-based supervisors provide the major supervision as a part of their full-time duties, a maximum of three students is advised. The number of students to be supervised may vary as a function of the time allowed by the university or field agency.

There is a systematic means of evaluating the practicum experience which seeks to ensure the acquisition of desired skills by students. This evaluation is appropriate to the program objectives whether accomplished via on-campus or off-campus placements or through practical application components of separate courses. The evaluation also seeks to clarify the utility of the experience in terms of setting, supervision, etc. In this manner, the evaluation process is twofold, evaluating both the students' progress and the suitability of the various characteristics of the experience. This allows for future planning in terms of student needs and practicum placements. Where practical applications are incorporated into various courses in the training sequence, evaluation is appropriate to the total course evaluation conducted by the university department or program.

286

APPENDIX B

Internship Experiences
Suggested Practices

The internship has the basic characteristics of allowing the student to demonstrate skill proficiencies acquired during formal training on campus and to acquire additional knowledge and skills most appropriately gained through field placement settings. The internship experience is characterized in the following manner:

1 It is generally offered in school settings and in other agencies serving children from infancy to late adolescence.
2 Supervision and principal responsibility for the student typically rest directly with the local off-campus agency, although indirect supervision is provided by the university.
3 The experience is typically offered for academic credit.
4 The experience occurs after the successful completion of practica.
5 The experience is a requirement for credentialing.
6 The experience is far less limited than the practicum experience and allows the intern to be exposed to cases, situations, etc., that are considered representative of the role and function of the school psychologist.
7 The experience occurs on a full-time basis over a period of one academic year, or on a half-time basis over a period of two consecutive academic years.
8 The experience is primarily a training activity and provides a balance of training and service objectives and functions.
9 On-campus coursework is reduced in proportion to the demands of the internship experience.

The internship is an intense and diversified experience as compared to the practicum placement and requires the provision of close supervision.

Training programs have written guidelines which specify the academic and non-academic experiences prerequisite to the internship placement. Those guidelines are employed in determining whether or not students are adequately prepared for the internship experience.

A written plan for the internship experience is prepared and agreed upon by representatives of the local educational agency, the intern supervisor(s), training program supervisory staff and the intern, prior to the placement. Such plans identify internship objectives, describe appropriate experiences for the achievement of the objectives and outline an evaluation plan for determining the achievement of each objective. The plan also delineates the responsibilities for both the university and the local supervisory personnel.

The intern seeking credentialing as a school psychologist must have internship experiences in a school setting. Though other settings may be incorporated into the internship experience, the school setting shall constitute at least one-half of the internship experience. Where additional settings are employed, a rationale specifies its appropriate relationship to the practice of school psychology.

The school setting has the availability of:

a children of all school ages,
b pupil personnel services functioning within a team framework,
c full-range of services for children with both high and low incidence disabilities,
d regular and special education services at the preschool, elementary and secondary levels,
e at least one certificated school psychologist having at least two years of full-time school psychologist experience or the equivalent who serves as the internship supervisor.

It is not essential that the above all be provided within the context of the local educational agency to which the intern is assigned. However, it is essential that all elements be available and integrated into the internship experience. Thus rural districts participating in joint agreements, special education districts and other administrative arrangements for the provision of special services are considered equally appropriate as internship settings to larger educational agencies which provide all elements as part of their educational programs.

The required school-based internship experience is provided off-campus in a local educational agency. While the authority for providing internship credit and grades rests with the university faculty, primary responsibility for intern supervision usually rests with appropriately credentialed local educational agency personnel.

Local supervision is provided by a person(s) holding a valid credential as a school psychologist, who is employed full-time as a school psychologist in the local educational agency and who has held such employment in that agency for a minimum of one school year prior to undertaking supervisory responsibilities. In non-school settings, supervisory personnel hold an appropriate credential for that setting.

Program faculty are responsible for providing appropriate orientation to non-program supervisors. This facilitates the clarification of the role and function of all parties and assists the non-program supervisors in carrying out responsibilities in a manner consistent with the training objectives.

Both local and university supervisors demonstrate active involvement in the profession as evidenced through professional association memberships, scholarly pursuits, experience and professional competence, and continued professional development.

a **Contract and salary:**
A written contractual agreement is prepared and agreed to by both the local educational agency and the intern school psychologist. The contractual agreement specifies the time period and salary provided. When financially possible, the intern is provided a salary commensurate with his or her level of training, experience and period of appointment. Contractual agreements are not entered into which require the intern to remain in the employment of the local educational agency beyond employment during the internship. Moreover, such arrangements do not specify in advance that employment for the intern is guaranteed beyond the internship.

b **Schedule of appointment:**
The intern is assigned to the same schedule and calendar time as are other school psychology staff employed by the local educational agency. Experiences such as inservice meetings, conferences, etc., participated in by local educational agency school psychologists are also expected of interns. Like regularly employed psychological services personnel, the intern evidences a commitment to the provision of psychological services not necessarily reflected in hourly schedules.

c **Awareness of the need for continued professional development:**
It is important that continued professional development be recognized as a significant aspect of the internship. The intern is expected to participate in scheduled appropriate university, regional and state-wide meetings for school psychologists. The opportunity to participate in national level meetings is also encouraged. The appropriation of reimbursement monies is strongly encouraged. When reimbursement or other financial support is unavailable, released time for attendance at professional meetings

is provided. In instances where released time is judged to detract from the provision of the internship experiences as planned, an agreement may be reached in which the intern serves additional time beyond the contractual schedule or calendar.

d Travel expenses:

The provision of appropriate internship experiences often requires job-related travel. When such exists, the intern is provided reimbursement consistent with policies of the local educational agency.

e Work environment:

The provision of quality psychological services requires a supportive work environment. The local educational agency ensures that the intern is provided adequate supplies and materials to carry out the functions of the internship. In addition, adequate privacy of office facilities and access to secretarial assistance is maintained. The physical plant has available central office facilities for files, professional library, storage of supplies and material, and telephone services. Access to office equipment such as duplication devices and recording equipment is also provided. These provisions are consistent with the availability afforded regular staff members.

f Provision of supervision:

The local educational agency ensures that supervisory personnel meet the criteria specified in Standard 4. Release time for personal supervisory contact with each intern in the amount specified above and the maximum number of interns to be served is afforded the supervisor. In order to provide the quality of internship supervision required, local educational agency supervisors are granted the equivalent of one work day per week of assigned time for each intern supervised, with full-time assignment of duties granted to the supervision of six interns. In no instance shall more than six interns be assigned to one supervisor.

g Training commitment:

The local educational agency is committed to the internship as basically a training experience. The appointment of interns as a means of acquiring less expensive services is inappropriate. Interns are expected to engage in tasks appropriate to the completion of the plan of internship. The intern is not asked to serve in any capacity other than that for which he or she was appointed. Tasks requiring teaching assignment, playground or other supervision, etc., indigenous to the roles of other school personnel are included only when there is a specific rationale related to the completion of the internship objectives.

A specific plan of internship evaluation is provided. The plan includes provisions for the evaluation of all significant aspects of the internship experience, including:

a the experiences provided by the local educational agency,

b the quality of local supervision,

c the quality of university supervision,

d the competencies of the intern,

e the suitability of the setting for future internships,

f the suitability of the intern's preparation for internship.

Procedures are designated which recognize the importance of due process, respecting the rights and privileges of the parties involved. In most instances, the assignment of academic credit to the experience necessitates that the university personnel or specifically designated representatives have authority for the official specification of the grade. Significant input of local supervisory personnel to the internship must be indicated. Evaluation procedures indicate a process which allows for ongoing evaluation during the internship as opposed to any single evaluation occurring at the end of the experience. Evaluation is the combined responsibility of all parties involved, including local supervisors, interns and university faculty.

STANDARDS FOR CREDENTIALING OF SCHOOL PSYCHOLOGISTS 1994

Credentialing is the process which authorizes the use of the title School Psychologist, or related titles, by those professionals meeting accepted standards of training and experience who seek to provide school psychological services. The purpose of this document is to provide guidelines to state and national bodies for the establishment of, and procedural processes involved in, implementing credentialing standards. These guidelines were developed and approved by the National Association of School Psychologists (NASP) pursuant to its mission to further the mental health and educational development of children and youth and to advance the standards of the profession of school psychology.

The National School Psychology Certification System (NSPCS) was created by NASP to establish a nationally recognized standard for credentialing school psychologists. The title to be used by persons accepted into the NSPCS is Nationally Certified School Psychologist, or NCSP. Among the purposes of this national credentialing system are to promote uniform credentialing standards across states, agencies, and training institutions, and to facilitate credentialing of school psychologists across states through the use of reciprocity or equivalence. The NASP *Standards for the Credentialing of School Psychologists* are used by the NSPCS and are considered to be appropriate for states to use in executing their authority in credentialing school psychologists.

CREDENTIALING STRUCTURE

1   Legal Basis for Credentialing

1.1   Credentialing is the process whereby a state authorizes the provision of school psychological services and the use of the title School Psychologist (or related titles such as School Psychology Specialist) by professionals meeting acceptable standards of training and experience. The basis of a state's credentialing authority is found in its statutory laws, whereby all providers of school psychological services and all users of the title School Psychologist must hold a current credential, and legal sanctions and sanctioning procedures are provided for violators.

2   Credentialing Body

2.1   The state legislature shall empower one or more bodies to administer the credentialing (certification and/or licensure) process. Administrative codes and regulations adopted by such bodies shall comply with these *Standards for the Credentialing of School Psychologists*, and shall carry the weight of law.

3   Nature of the Credential

3.1   The credential shall be issued in writing and expressly authorize both the practice of school psychology and the exclusive use of the title School Psychologist in all settings, public and private.

3.2   The credential shall allow for the practice of school psychology as defined by NASP's *Standards for the Provision of School Psychological Services* (1992) in public and private settings (e.g., school, educational, mental health-related, or university-based child study clinics).

290

3.3 Where a state empowers more than one body to issue more than one type of credential, such as for the separate regulation of school psychological services in the public schools and in private practice, the lowest entry levels of all such credentials shall conform to these standards.

CREDENTIALING REQUIREMENTS

4 Criteria for Credential

4.1 The minimum requirement for credentialing shall be a sixth year/specialist program, with a 60 graduate semester hour minimum, consisting of coursework, practica, internship, and an appropriate graduate degree from an accredited institution of higher learning. Criteria for each area shall be consistent with NASP's *Standards for Training and Field Placement Programs in School Psychology* (1994).

4.2 The credentialing criteria shall require that competency be demonstrated in three areas: professional work characteristics, knowledge base, and applied professional practice. Each area is listed below and detailed in NASP's *Standards for Training and Field Placement Programs in School Psychology* (1994).

4.3 Professional Work Characteristics
The applicant's professional work characteristics shall be evaluated and verified by the applicant's school psychology training program through information collected during courses, practica, internship, and other appropriate means. Professional work characteristics shall include:

1 Communication Skills
2 Effective Interpersonal Relations
3 Ethical Responsibility
4 Flexibility
5 Initiative and Dependability
6 Personal Stability
7 Respect for Human Diversity

4.4 Knowledge Base
The applicant shall complete an integrated and sequential program of study that is explicitly designed to develop knowledge and competencies in the domains of psychological foundations, educational foundations, intervention and problem-solving, statistics and research methodologies, and professional school psychology.

Psychological Foundations
The applicant for the credential has a foundation in the knowledge base for the discipline of psychology, including:

Biological Bases of Behavior (e.g., biological bases of development, neuropsychology, psychopharmacology, physiological psychology)
Human Learning
Social And Cultural Bases of Behavior (e.g., social development, social and cultural diversity, social psychology, cross-cultural studies)
Child and Adolescent Development
Individual Differences (including human exceptionalities and developmental psychopathology)

Educational Foundations
The applicant for the credential has a foundation in the knowledge base for education, including:

Instructional Design

Organization and Operation of Schools (including, but not limited to, education of exceptional learners, school and community-based resources, alternative service delivery systems)

Intervention/Problem-Solving

The applicant for the credential has demonstrated knowledge and professional expertise to collaborate with families and school- and community-based professionals in designing, implementing, and evaluating interventions that effectively respond to the educational and mental health needs of children and youth.

Assessment (diverse models and methods linked to direct and indirect interventions)

Direct Interventions (individual and group, including counseling and behavior management)

Indirect Interventions (including consultation, systems and organizational change)

Statistics and Research Methodologies

The applicant for the credential is a competent consumer of research and new knowledge, and is able to use diverse methodologies (e.g., ethnographic, single-subject designs, quantitative methods) to evaluate professional practices (e.g., interventions) and/or programs.

Research and Evaluation Methods
Statistics
Measurement

Professional School Psychology

The applicant for the credential has a knowledge base specific to the professional specialty of school psychology and is able to demonstrate the application of that knowledge base to professional practice, including:

History and Foundations of School Psychology

Legal and Ethical Issues

Professional Issues and Standards

Alternative Models for Delivery of School Psychological Services

Emergent Technologies

Roles and Functions

4.5 Applied Professional Practice

The applicant shall provide written evidence of his\her ability to perform competently as a school psychologist. Such evidence shall consist minimally of successful completion and documentation of practicum experience and internship consistent with criteria outlined in NASP's *Standards for Training and Field Placement Programs in School Psychology* (1994).

A The practica shall consist of a sequence of supervised experiences that occur prior to internship, are conducted in laboratory or field-based settings, and provide for application of knowledge and mastery of distinct skills.

B The internship experience shall consist of a full-time experience over one year, or half-time over two years, with a minimum of 1200 clock hours, at least one-half of which must be in a school setting. Other acceptable internship experiences include private, state-approved educational programs, or other appropriate mental health-related programs or settings for the education of children and youth.

C Other practicum and internship criteria are outlined in NASP's *Standards for Training and Field Placement Programs in School Psychology* (1994).

IMPLEMENTATION OF CREDENTIALING PROCEDURES

Only graduates from NASP approved training programs, or programs consistent with NASP training standards, shall be eligible for credentialing. A complete listing of NASP approved programs, *Approved Programs in School Psychology*, is published annually. Each approved program shall be responsible for assessing a candidate's competency in the areas of professional work characteristics, knowledge base, and applied professional practice. The responsibility for the final determination of minimum professional competencies in all credentialing areas, however, rests with the credentialing body. All assessment methods by both the training program and the credentialing body shall rely on the most objective, quantifiable, and accountable procedures available.

5 **Type of Credential - State and National**

5.1 State Credential

The state credential shall be granted to individuals who meet the requirements described in Standard 4, including an appropriate graduate degree, professional work characteristics, knowledge base, and applied professional practice.

Upon initial granting of the credential, the individual shall arrange supervision and mentoring to assure that entry level qualifications are translated into ongoing competency in the provision of school psychological services. Supervision shall consist of a minimum of one face-to-face contact hour per week or two consecutive face-to-face contact hours once every two weeks for the initial academic year of full time practice, or the equivalent. Supervision and mentoring shall be provided by a school psychologist with a minimum of three years of experience. For any portion of the experience which is accumulated in a non-school setting, supervision and mentoring shall be provided by a psychologist or school psychologist appropriately credentialed for practice in that setting.

Subsequent to the completion of the supervision requirement, an individual holding the credential shall participate in an organized program of continuing professional development.

Upon completion of the initial year of post-degree supervision, the credential shall allow psychologists to have professional autonomy in determining the nature, scope, and extent of their specific services in all settings, public and private. These services shall be consistent with the NASP definitions of school psychological services and shall be delivered within the bounds of the school psychologist's training, supervised experience, and demonstrated expertise as specified in NASP's *Standards for the Provision of School Psychological Services* (1992) and *Principles for Professional Ethics* (1992).

Individual states may choose to grant a continuing credential to persons who have met the criteria for supervision and continuing professional development, and have a minimum of three years of experience.

293

5.2 Nationally Certified School Psychologist
The credential, Nationally Certified School Psychologist (NCSP), is granted to persons who have successfully met national training standards by:

A Completion of a sixth year/specialist level program or higher in school psychology, with a 60 graduate semester hour minimum, consisting of coursework, practica, internship, and an appropriate graduate degree from an accredited institution of higher education.

B Successful completion of a 1,200 clock hour supervised internship in school psychology, at least one-half of which must be in a school setting.

C Achieving a passing score on the National School Psychology Examination administered by the Educational Testing Service (ETS).

Persons who hold the credential Nationally Certified School Psychologist (NCSP) meet the criteria for an initial state credential. For renewal, all persons holding the NCSP must complete at least 75 contact hours of continuing professional development activities within a three year period.

6 Credential Renewal/Continuing Education

6.1 State Credential
The credential shall be issued for a period of three years. *Initial renewal* of the state credential shall be contingent upon the applicant providing verified evidence of one year of supervision as described in Standard 5.1 and continuing professional development activities. *Subsequent renewals* shall be granted to applicants meeting the following criteria:

A Evidence of public, private, or university-based practice for a minimum of one academic year of full-time equivalent (F.T.E.) experience during the previous three years.

B Evidence of continuing professional development for a minimum of 75 clock hours in the previous three year period during which the credential was in effect.

7 Withdrawal/Termination of the Credential

7.1 The credentialing body has the right to cancel, revoke, suspend, or refuse to renew the credential of any school psychologist, or to reprimand any school psychologist, upon proof that the school psychologist has engaged in unprofessional conduct as defined by NASP's *Principles for Professional Ethics* (1992) or *Standards for the Provision of School Psychological Services* (1992). Such action must be based on a formal finding of guilt by the appropriate adjudicating body after following a documented procedure ensuring that the due process rights of all parties involved have been fully observed.

8 New Application for Credentialing

8.1 All school psychology trainees completing an approved program on or after January 1, 1998 and all other new applicants, shall be trained and credentialed in accordance with these standards. All practitioners currently credentialed shall be recredentialed in an appropriate state or national renewal cycle.

APPENDIX A

Definition of Terms Included in
Standards for the Credentialing of School
Psychologists

STANDARD 3.2:

NASP Standards for the Provision of School Psychological Services (1992): The current standards document from the National Association of School Psychologists (NASP) describing the delivery of appropriate and comprehensive school psychological services for administrative and employing agencies.

Public Setting: Any setting (e.g., school, educational, mental health-related, or university-based) which is legislated, regulated, and/or supported by public funds and whose staff serve, without bias or special selection processes, individuals primarily from the public domain.

Private Setting: Any setting (e.g., school, educational, mental health-related, or university-based) which is supported in whole or in part by private funding sources, which may be for profit, and whose staff can specifically select the populations that it serves.

STANDARD 4.1:

NASP Standards for Training and Field Placement Programs in School Psychology (1994): The current standards document from the National Association of School Psychologists (NASP) describing procedural standards supporting the comprehensive training of school psychologists at the doctoral and sixth year/specialist levels.

STANDARD 4.5:

Practica Experiences, as defined in the NASP *Standards for Training and Field Placement Programs in School Psychology* (1994): Practica experiences include orientation to the educational process, assessment for intervention, and direct and indirect intervention methods; are distinct from and occur prior to internship; occur at times appropriate to the specific training objectives of the program; shall be of sufficient length and in settings that are appropriate to specific training objectives of the program; are provided appropriate recognition through the awarding of academic credit; are systematically evaluated in a manner consistent with the specific training objectives of the program; are conducted in accordance with current legal and ethical standards for the profession.

Internship experiences, as defined in the NASP *Standards for Training and Field Placement Programs in School Psychology* (1994): A comprehensive internship experience is required for students to demonstrate, under supervision, their ability to integrate knowledge and skills in providing a broad range of outcome-based school psychological services. Internship experiences are provided at or near the end of the formal training period; occur on a full-time basis over a period of one academic year, or on a half-time basis over a period of two consecutive academic years; are designed according to a written plan that provide a broad range of experiences; occur in a setting appropriate to the specific training objectives of the program; are provided appropriate recognition through the awarding of academic credit; occur under conditions of appropriate supervision; are systematically evaluated in a manner consistent with the specific training objectives of the program; are conducted in accordance with current legal and ethical standards for the profession.

School Setting (from Appendix B of the NASP *Standards for Training and Field Placement Programs in School Psychology,* 1994): Has the availability of (a) children of all school ages, (b) pupil personnel services functioning within a team framework, (c) regular and special education services at the preschool, elementary, and secondary levels, (d) full-range of services for children with high incidence and low incidence disabilities, (e) at least one credentialed school psychologist having a minimum of three years of full-time school psychology experience, or the equivalent who serves as internship supervisor. It is not essential that the above all be provided within the context of the local educational agency to which the intern is assigned. However, it is essential that all elements be available and integrated into the internship experience.

STANDARD 5:

Approved Programs in School Psychology: The National Association of School Psychologists (NASP) publishes annually a list of training programs in school psychology that have been determined to meet NASP *Standards for Training and Field Placement Programs in School Psychology* (1994). A copy of the Approved Program list can be obtained by contacting the National Association of School Psychologists, 4340 East West Highway, Suite 402, Bethesda, Maryland 20814.

Mentoring and Continuing Professional Development: In addition to the one year of post-degree supervision described in Standard 5.1, it is recommended that individuals enter an organized program of mentoring and continuing professional development. This recommendation is made in recognition of the complex problems in today's schools and the need to continue, enhance, and upgrade school psychologists' professional training and skills in an effort to ensure quality service delivery. Mentoring should be provided by a school psychologist with at least three years experience, and should involve, as is needed, elements of supervision, collegial discussion, and support regarding professional issues. Mentoring is often

one component of a continuing professional development plan, and should be arranged in an organized manner to enhance and develop an individual's professional skills and knowledge. Continuing professional development and mentoring may include, but are not limited to, discussions of professional issues with colleagues, readings of professional journals and books, memberships in professional organizations, and participation in formal continuing professional development programs.

STANDARD 7.1:

NASP Principles for Professional Ethics (1992): The current document of principles from the National Association of School Psychologists (NASP) describing guidelines for ethical behavior including professional competency, professional relationships and responsibilities, and professional practices in public and private settings.

National Association of School Psychologists

PRINCIPLES FOR PROFESSIONAL ETHICS

The contents of this booklet are standards documents that were approved by the Delegate Assembly of the Association on July 26, 1997, in Alexandria, Virginia.

This document was prepared by the Ethical and Professional Standards Committee in collaboration with the Publications Committee, National Association of School Psychologists.

Additional copies are available from:

NASP Publications
4340 East West Highway
Suite 402
Bethesda, Maryland 20814

298

Table of Contents

PREFACE TO THE 1997 EDITION

This is the third edition of the National Association of School Psychologists' *Professional Conduct Manual*, which contains the *Principles for Professional Ethics* and the *Standards for the Provision of School Psychological Services*. Every five years, the Association reviews the *Manual* to make sure that the principles continue to apply to changing conditions. In keeping with past practice, the Ethical and Professional Standards Committee solicited recommendations through a number of different channels.

The general membership received notice of the revision project from a series of announcements printed in the newsletter, *The Communiqué*, and from reports issued by their Regional Directors and State Delegates. State Affiliate Presidents and State Newsletter Editors received personal correspondence from the Committee asking them to encourage their members to comment. State Delegates and Committee Chairs received copies of the *Manual*, comment forms, and an invitation to participate in the revision process at the Minneapolis Delegate Assembly (1996). NASP leaders with e-mail received additional notices via the Internet. An open hearing gave all Anaheim convention participants one last chance to influence the final form of the document before it went before the Executive Council and Delegate Assembly. The document received a "first reading" in Anaheim and was eventually approved on July 26, 1997.

A project of this size is the result of many individuals collaborating, and the editor would like to thank them for their assistance. Bill Pfohl was President of NASP at the start of the revision process; Deborah Crockett was NASP President when the document received final approval. Fred Grossman was the chair and Jim Batts was the co-chair of the Ethical and Professional Conduct Committee, and they provided essential guidance throughout the project. Fred Provenzano and Lee Huff, convention co-chairs, helped to create the first public hearing for the purpose of obtaining member thoughts about the *Professional Conduct Manual*. (A particularly big **thank you** goes to the people who attended the hearing!) NASP office staff, especially Executive Director Susan Gorin, MIS Director Alex Hyman, Meetings Director Sheila Paige, Staff Services Director Rosemary O'Donnell, and Communications Director C. Paul Mendez contributed timely "behind the scenes" assistance. Special thanks go to Roseburg School District office manager, Debbie Ramey, for donating many hours of her own free time to the project. Individuals providing commentary included: Susan Attaway, Rhonda Broadwater, Nicole Colbert, Shelvie Cole, Jean Cronin, Michael Curtis, Carl DiMartino, Laura Stein-Douglas, Elyse Drossman, Vicki Dumois, Carolyn Meyer Durda, Bob Ellers, Barbara Fischetti, Kit Gerken, Patti Harrison, Wayne Holtzman, Stacy Horen, Lee Huff, Sawyer Hunley, Mary Johnson, Eric Mesmer, R. Moran, Rhonda Sawyer, Ed Schlossman, Rosalind Sharpe, Edward Stange, Hope Tunnicliffe, and Sue Vess.

Philip B. Bowser, NCSP
Editor

I.   INTRODUCTION

The formal principles that elucidate the proper conduct of a professional school psychologist are known as *Ethics*.   By virtue of joining the Association, each NASP member agrees to abide by the *Ethics*, acting in a manner that shows respect for human dignity and assuring a high quality of professional service. Although ethical behavior is an individual responsibility, it is in the interest of an association to adopt and enforce a code of ethics. If done properly, members will be guided towards appropriate behavior, and public confidence in the profession will be enhanced. Additionally, a code of ethics should provide due process procedures to protect members from potential abuse of the code.   The *Ethics* have been written to accomplish these goals.

The principles in this manual are based on the assumptions that: 1) school psychologists will act as advocates for their students/clients, and 2) at the very least, school psychologist will do no harm. These necessitate that school psychologists "speak up" for the needs and rights of their students/ clients even at times when it may be difficult to do so.   School psychologists are also constrained to provide only those services for which they have acquired an acknowledged level of experience, training, and competency.   Beyond these basic premises, judgment is required to apply the ethical principles to the fluid and expanding interactions between school and community.

There are many different sources of advice for the proper way to behave; local policies, state laws, federal laws, credentialing standards, professional association position statements, and books that recommend "Best Practices" are just a few. Given one's employment situation and the array of recommendations, events may develop in which the ethical course of action is unclear.

The Association will seek to enforce the *Ethical Principles* upon its members. The NASP

Standards for the Provision of School Psychological Services are typically not enforced, although all members should work toward achieving the hallmarks of quality services delivery that are described therein. Similarly, "position statements" and "best practices" documents are not adjudicated. The guidance of the *Ethical Principles* is intentionally broad , to make it more enduring than other documents that reflect short-term opinions about specific actions shaped by local events, popular trends, or recent developments in the field. The practitioner must use judgment to infer the situation-specific rule from the general principle. The lack of a specific reference to a particular action does not indicate permission or provide a defense against a charge of unethical practice. (For example, the document frequently refers to a school psychologist's relationships with a hypothetical "student/client." Since school psychologists work in a wide variety of settings, there is no single term that neatly identifies the "other" individual in the professional relationship. Therefore, one should apply these *Principles* in all professional situations, realizing that one is not released from responsibility simply because another individual is not strictly a "student" or a "client.")

The principles in this manual are organized into several sections as a result of editorial judgment.   Therefore, principles discussed in one section may also apply to other sections. Every school psychologist, regardless of position (e.g. practitioner, researcher, university trainer, supervisor, state or federal consultant, administrator of psychological services) or setting (e.g. public or private school, community agency, hospital, university, private practice) should reflect upon the theme represented in each ethical principle to determine its application to her/his individual situation. For example, although a given principle may specifically discuss responsibilities towards "clients", the intent is that the standards would also apply to supervisees, trainees, and research participants. At times, the *Ethics* may require a higher standard of behavior than the prevailing policies and pertinent laws. Under such conditions, members should adhere to the *Ethics*. Ethical behavior may occasionally be forbidden by policy or law, in which case members are expected to declare their dilemma and work to bring the discrepant regulations into compliance with the *Ethics*. To obtain additional assistance in applying these principles to your particular setting, consult with experienced school psychologists, and seek advice from the National Association of School Psychologists or your state school psychology association.

II. PROFESSIONAL COMPETENCY

A GENERAL

1 School psychologists recognize the strengths and limitations of their training and experience, engaging only in practices for which they are qualified. They must continually seek additional training with the welfare of children, families, the school community, and their trainees or supervisees in mind.

2 Competence levels, education, training and experience are accurately represented to clients in a professional manner.

3 School psychologists do not use affiliations with person, associations, or institutions to imply a level of professional competence which exceeds that which has actually been achieved.

4 School psychologists are aware of their limitations and enlist the assistance of other specialists in supervisory, consultative or referral roles as appropriate in providing services.

5 School psychologists engage in continuing professional development. They remain current regarding developments in research, training, and professional practices that benefit children, families, and schools.

6 School psychologists refrain from any activity in which their personal problems or conflicts may interfere with professional effectiveness. Competent assistance is sought to alleviate conflicts in professional relationships.

7 School psychologists know the *Principles for Professional Ethics* and thoughtfully apply them to situations within their employment setting. Ignorance or misapplication of an ethical principle is not a reasonable defense against a charge of unethical behavior.

III. PROFESSIONAL RELATIONSHIPS AND RESPONSIBILITIES

A GENERAL

1 School psychologists are committed to the application of their professional expertise for the purpose of promoting improvement in the quality of life for students, their families, and the school community. This objective is pursued in ways that protect the dignity and rights of those involved. School psychologists accept responsibility for the appropriateness of their treatments and professional practices.

2 School psychologists respect all persons and are sensitive to physical, mental, emotional, political, economic, social, cultural, ethnic, and racial characteristics, gender and sexual orientation, and religion.

3 School psychologists are responsible for the direction and nature of their personal loyalties or objectives. When these commitments may influence a professional relationship, the school psychologist informs all concerned persons of relevant issues in advance.

4 School psychologists in all settings maintain professional relationships with students, parents, the school and community.

Consequently, parents and students are to be fully informed about all relevant aspects of school psychological services in advance. The explanation should take into account language and cultural differences, cognitive capabilities, developmental level, and age so that the explanation may be understood by the student, parent, or guardian.

5 School psychologists shall attempt to resolve situations in which there are divided or conflicting interests in a manner which is mutually beneficial and protects the rights of all parties involved.

6 School psychologists do not exploit clients through professional relationships nor condone these actions in their colleagues. All individuals, including students, clients, employees, colleagues, and research participants, will not be exposed to deliberate comments, gestures, or physical contacts of a sexual nature. School psychologists do not harass or demean others based on personal characteristics. School psychologists do not engage in sexual relationships with their students, supervisees, trainees, or past or present clients.

7 Personal and business relations with students/clients or their parents may cloud one's judgment. School psychologists are aware of these situations and avoid them whenever possible.

8 School psychologists attempt to resolve suspected detrimental or unethical practices on an informal level. If informal efforts are not productive, the appropriate professional organization is contacted for assistance, and procedures established for questioning ethical practice are followed:

a The filing of an ethical complaint is a serious matter. It is intended to improve the behavior of a colleague that is harmful to the profession and/or the public. Therefore, school psychologists make every effort to discuss the ethical principles with other professionals who may be in violation.

b School psychologists enter into this process thoughtfully and with concern for the well-being of all parties involved. They do not file or encourage the filing of an ethics complaint that is frivolous or motivated by revenge.

c Some situations may be particularly difficult to analyze from an ethical perspective. School psychologists consult ethical standards from related fields and seek assistance from knowledgeable, experienced school psychologists, and relevant state/national associations to ascertain an appropriate course of action.

d School psychologists document specific instances of suspected ethical violations (date, time, relevant details) as well as attempts to resolve these violations.

9 School psychologists respect the confidentiality of information obtained during their professional work. Information is revealed only with the informed consent of the client, or the client's parent or legal guardian, except in those situations in which failure to release information would result in clear danger to the client or others. Obsolete information will be shredded or otherwise destroyed before placement in recycling bins or trash receptacles.

10 School psychologists discuss confidential information only for professional purposes and only with persons who have a legitimate need to know. Confidential materials should be shredded before disposal.

11 School psychologists inform their clients of the limits of confidentiality.

B STUDENTS

1 School psychologists understand the intimate nature of consultation, assessment,

303

and direct service. They engage only in professional practices which maintain the dignity and integrity of students and other clients.

2 School psychologists explain important aspects of their professional relationships with students and clients in a clear, understandable manner. The explanation includes the reason why services were requested, who will receive information about the services provided, and the possible outcomes.

3 When a child initiates services, school psychologists understand their obligation to respect the rights of a student or client to initiate, participate in, or discontinue services voluntarily. When another party initiates services, the school psychologist will make every effort to secure voluntary participation of the child/student.

4 Recommendations for program changes or additional service will be discussed, including any alternatives which may be available.

C PARENTS, LEGAL GUARDIANS, AND APPOINTED SURROGATES

1 School psychologists explain all services to parents in a clear, understandable manner. They strive to propose a set of options which takes into account the values and capabilities of each parent. Service provision by interns, practicum students, etc. should be explained and agreed to in advance.

2 School psychologists recognize the importance of parental support and seek to obtain this by assuring that there is direct parent contact prior to seeing the student/client on an on-going basis. (Emergencies and "drop-in" self-referrals will require parental notification as soon as possible. The age and circumstances under which students/clients may seek services without parental consent varies greatly; be certain to comply with III-E-5.) They secure continuing parental involvement by a frank and prompt reporting to the parent of findings and progress that conforms to the limits of previously determined confidentiality.

3 School psychologists encourage and promote parental participation in designing services provided to their children. When appropriate, this includes linking interventions between the school and the home, tailoring parental involvement to the skills of the family, and helping parents to gain the skills needed to help their children.

4 School psychologist respect the wishes of parents who object to school psychological services and attempt to guide parents to alternative community resources.

5 School psychologists discuss recommendations and plans for assisting the student/client with the parent. The discussion includes alternatives associated with each set of plans, showing respect for the ethnic/cultural values of the family. The parents are advised as to sources of help available at school and in the community.

6 School psychologists discuss the rights of parents and students regarding creation, modification, storage, and disposal of confidential materials that will result from the provision of school psychological services.

D SERVICE DELIVERY

1 School psychologists are knowledgeable of the organization, philosophy, goals, objective, and methodologies of the setting in which they are employed.

2 School psychologists recognize that an understanding of the goals, processes and legal requirements of their particular workplace is essential for effective functioning within that setting.

3 School psychologists attempt to become integral members of the client systems to

which they are assigned. They establish clear roles for themselves within that system and the local community

4 School psychologist who provide services to several different groups may encounter situations when loyalties are conflicted. As much as possible, the stance of the school psychologist is made known in advance to all parties to prevent misunderstandings.

5 School psychologist promote changes in their employing agencies that will benefit their clients.

E COMMUNITY

1 School psychologists are also citizens, thereby accepting the same responsibilities and duties as any member of society. They are free to pursue individual interests, except to the degree that these compromise professional responsibilities.

2 School psychologists may act as individual citizens to bring about social change in a lawful manner. Individual actions should not be presented as, nor suggestive of representing the field of school psychology or the Association.

3 As employees or employers, in public or private domains, school psychologist do not engage in or condone practices that discriminate against clients based on race, handicap, age, gender, sexual orientation, religion, national origin, economic status, or native language.

4 School psychologists avoid any action that could violate or diminish the civil and legal rights of clients.

5 School psychologist adhere to federal, state, and local laws and ordinances governing their practice. If regulations conflict with ethical guidelines, school psychologists seek to resolve such conflict through positive, respected, and legal channels.

F RELATED PROFESSIONS

1 To best meet the needs of students and clients, school psychologists cooperate with other professional disciplines in relationships based on mutual respect.

2 School psychologists recognize the competence of other professionals. They encourage and support the use of all resources to best serve the interests of students and clients.

3 School psychologists strive to explain their field and their professional competencies, including roles, assignments, and working relationships to other professionals.

4 School psychologists cooperate and coordinate with other professionals and agencies with the rights and needs of their client in mind. If a client is receiving similar services from another professional, school psychologists promote coordination of services.

5 The student or client is referred to another professional for services when a condition is identified which is outside the professional competencies or scope of the school psychologist.

6 When transferring the intervention responsibility for a student or client to another professional, school psychologist ensure that all relevant and appropriate individuals, including the student/client when appropriate, are notified of the change and reasons for the change.

7 When school psychologist suspect the existence of detrimental or unethical practices, the appropriate professional organization is contacted for assistance in determining the procedures established by that profession for examining the practices in question.

G OTHER SCHOOL PSYCHOLOGISTS

1 School psychologists who employ, supervise, or train other professionals accept the obligation to provide continuing professional development. They also provide appropri-

ate working conditions, fair and timely evaluation, and constructive consultation.

2 School psychologists who supervise interns are responsible for all professional practices of the supervises. They assure the students/clients and the profession that the intern is adequately supervised.

IV. PROFESSIONAL PRACTICES PUBLIC AND PRIVATE SETTINGS

A ADVOCACY

1 School psychologists consider the students or clients to be their primary responsibility, acting as advocates for their rights and welfare. When choosing a course of action, school psychologists take into account the rights of each individual involved and the duties of the school personnel.

2 School psychologists' concerns for protecting the rights and welfare of students are communicated to the school administration and staff as the top priority in determining services.

B ASSESSMENT AND INTERVENTION

1 School psychologists will maintain the highest standard for educational and psychological assessment.

   a In conducting psychological, educational, or behavioral evaluations, or in providing therapy, counseling, or consultation services, due consideration will be given to individual integrity and individual differences.

   b School psychologists respect differences in age, gender, sexual orientation, and socioeconomic, cultural, and ethnic backgrounds. They select and use appropriate assessment or treatment procedures, techniques, and strategies.

2 School psychologists are knowledgeable about the validity and reliability of their instruments and techniques, choosing those that have up-to-date standardization data and are applicable and appropriate for the benefit of the student/client.

3 School psychologists combine observations, background information, and information from other disciplines in order to reach comprehensive conclusions.

4 School psychologists use assessment techniques, counseling and therapy procedures, consultation techniques, and other direct service methods that the profession considers to be responsible, research-based practice.

5 School psychologists do not condone the use of psychological or educational assessment techniques, or the mis-use of the information these techniques provide, by unqualified persons in any way, including teaching, sponsorship, or supervision.

6 School psychologists develop interventions which are appropriate to the presenting problems and are consistent with data collected. They modify or terminate the treatment plan when the data indicate the plan is not achieving the desired goals.

C USE OF MATERIALS AND TECHNOLOGY

1 School psychologists maintain test security, preventing the release of underlying principles and specific content that would undermine the use of the device. School psychologists are responsible for the security requirements specific to each instrument they use.

2 School psychologist uphold copyright laws. Permission is obtained from authors to reproduce non-copyrighted published instruments.

3 School psychologists will obtain written prior consent or else remove identifying data presented in public lectures or publications.

4 When producing materials for consultation, intervention, teaching, public lectures, or publication, school psychologists acknowledge sources and assign credit to those whose ideas are reflected in the product. Recognition is given in proportion to the contribution. Plagiarism of ideas or product is a violation of professional ethics.

5 School psychologists do not promote or encourage inappropriate use of computer generated test analyses or reports. For example, a school psychologist would not offer an unedited computer report as one's own writing, nor use a computer scoring system for tests in which one has no training. They select scoring and interpretation services on the basis of accuracy and professional alignment with the underlying decision rules.

6 School psychologists maintain full responsibility for any technological services used. All ethical and legal principles regarding confidentiality, privacy, and responsibility for decisions apply to the school psychologist and cannot be transferred to equipment, software companies, or data processing departments.

7 Technological devices should be used to improve the quality of client services. School psychologists will resist applications of technology that ultimately reduce the quality of service.

8 To ensure confidentiality, student/client records are not transmitted electronically without a guarantee of privacy. (For example, a receiving FAX machine must be in a secure location and operated by employees cleared to work with confidential files; e-mail messages must be encrypted or else stripped of all information that identifies the student/client.)

D RESEARCH, PUBLICATION AND PRESENTATION

1 When designing and implementing research in schools, school psychologists choose topics, and employ research methodology, subject selection techniques, data gathering methods, and analysis and reporting techniques which are grounded in sound research practice.

2 Prior to initiating research, school psychologists working in agencies without review committees should have at least one other colleague, preferably a school psychologist, review the proposal.

3 In publishing reports of their research, school psychologists provide discussion of limitations of their data and acknowledge existence of disconfirming data, as well as alternate hypotheses and explanations of their findings.

4 School psychologists take particular care with information presented through various impersonal media (e.g. radio, television, public lectures, articles in the popular press, promotional materials.) Recipients should be informed that the information does not result from or substitute for a professional consultation. The information should be based on research and experience within the school psychologist's recognized sphere of competence. The statements should be consistent with these ethical principles, and should not mistakenly represent the field of school psychology or the Association.

E REPORTING DATA AND CONFERENCE RESULTS

1 School psychologists ascertain that student or client information reaches only authorized persons.

a The information is adequately interpreted so that the recipient can better help the student or client.

b The school psychologist assists agency recipients to establish procedures to properly safeguard the confidential material.

307

2 School psychologists communicate findings and recommendations in language readily understood by the intended recipient. These communications describe potential consequences associated with the proposals.

3 School psychologists prepare written reports in such form and style that the recipient of the report will be able to assist the student or client. Reports should emphasize recommendations and interpretations; unedited computer-generated reports, preprinted "check-off" or "fill-in-the-blank" reports, and reports which present only test scores or brief narratives describing a test are seldom useful. Reports should include an appraisal of the degree of confidence which could be assigned to the information. Alterations of reports previously released should be done only by the original author.

4 School psychologists review all of their written documents for accuracy, signing them only when correct. Interns and practicum students are clearly identified as such, and their work is co-signed by the supervising school psychologist.

5 School psychologists comply with all laws, regulations and policies pertaining to the adequate storage and disposal of records to maintain appropriate confidentiality of information.

V. PROFESSIONAL PRACTICES - PRIVATE SETTINGS

A RELATIONSHIP WITH SCHOOL DISTRICTS

1 Some school psychologists are employed in both the public and private sectors, and in so doing, may create a conflict of interest. School psychologists operating in both sectors recognize the importance of ethical standards, the separation of roles, and take full responsibility for protecting and completely informing the consumer of all potential concerns.

2 A school psychologist, while working in the private sector, may not accept any form of remuneration from clients who are entitled to the same service provided by the same school psychologist while working in the public sector. This includes students who attend the non-public schools within the school psychologist's public school assignment area.

3 School psychologists in private practice have an obligation to inform parents of any free school psychological services available from the public or private schools prior to delivering such services for remuneration.

4 School psychologists working in both public and private sectors will conduct all private practice outside of the hours of contracted public employment.

5 School psychologists engaged in private practice do not use tests, materials, equipment, facilities, secretarial assistance, or other services belonging to the public sector employer, unless approved in advance through a written agreement.

B SERVICE DELIVERY

1 School psychologists conclude a financial agreement in advance of service delivery.

   a School psychologists ensure to the best of their ability that the client clearly understands the agreement.

   b School psychologists neither give nor receive any remuneration for referring clients for professional services.

2 School psychologists in private practice adhere to the conditions of a contract until service thereunder has been performed, the contract has been terminated by mutual consent, or the contract has otherwise been legally terminated.

3 School psychologists in private practice prevent misunderstandings resulting from their recommendations, advice, or information.

Most often, direct consultation between the school psychologist in private practice and the school psychologist responsible for the student in the public sector will resolve minor differences of opinion without unnecessarily confusing the parents, yet keep the best interests of the student or client in mind.

4 Personal diagnosis and therapy are not given by means of public lectures, newspaper, columns, magazine articles, radio and television programs, or mail. Any information shared through mass media activities is general in nature and is openly declared to be so.

C ANNOUNCEMENTS/ADVERTISING

1 Appropriate announcement of services, advertising and public media statements may be necessary for school psychologists in private practice. Accurate representations of training, experience, services provided and affiliation are done in a restrained manner. Public statements must be made on sound and accepted theory, research, and practice.

2 Listings in telephone directories are limited to the following: name/names, highest relevant degree, state certification/licensure status, national certification status, address, telephone number, brief identification of major areas of practice, office hours, appropriate fee information, foreign languages spoken, policy regarding third party payments, and license number.

3 Announcements of services by school psychologist in private practice are made in a formal, professional manner, using the guidelines of section 2, above. Clear statements of purposes with unequivocal descriptions of the experiences to be provided are given. education, training, and experience of all staff members are appropriately specified.

4 School psychologists in private practice may use brochures in the announcement of services. The brochures may be sent to professional person, schools, business firms, governmental agencies and other similar organizations.

5 Announcements and advertisements of the availability of publications, products, and services for sale are professional and factual.

6 School psychologists in private practice do not directly solicit clients for individual diagnosis or therapy.

7 School psychologists do not compensate in any manner a representative of the press, radio or television in return for personal professional publicity in a news item.

PROCEDURAL GUIDELINES FOR THE ADJUDICATION OF ETHICAL COMPLAINTS

SECTION I. RESPONSIBILITY AND FUNCTION

The Ethical and Professional Standards Committee shall be responsible for developing and maintaining a clearly defined position for the Association regarding the ethical and professional conduct principles to be adhered to by its members and also the members of the National School Psychology Certification System (NSPCS). The major area of particular ethical concern to the Committee will be that of the protection and general well-being of individuals served by school psychologists, in schools and in private practice, and in institutions or agencies through which the service is rendered. The Committee is further charged to study and make recommendations to the Executive Council when it is alleged that a NASP or NSPCS member has failed to follow the ethical principles of the Association.

Members of the Ethical and Professional Standards Committee recognize that their role is an extremely important one, involving the rights of many people, the reputation of the profession and the careers of individual professionals. They

309

bear a heavy responsibility because their recommendations may alter the lives of others. Therefore, they must be alert to personal, social, organizational, financial or political situations or pressures that might lead to misuse of their influence. The Ethical and Professional Standards committee shall assure the responsible use of all information obtained in the course of an inquiry or investigation. The objective with regard to the individual shall, whenever possible, be constructive, rather than punitive in character.

The function of the Committee in investigating complaints of alleged ethical misconduct involves obtaining a thorough and impartial account of the behaviors or incidents in order to be able to evaluate the character of the behaviors in question. When responding to complaints, members of the Ethics and Professional Standards Committee have the responsibility to consider the competency of the complainant, to act in an unbiased manner, to work expeditiously, and to safeguard the confidentiality of the Committee's activities. Committee members and their designees have the added responsibility to follow procedures which safeguard the rights of all individuals involved in the complaint process.

SECTION II. **SCOPE AND AUTHORITY**

The Ethical and Professional Standards Committee shall address issues of ethical misconduct in an investigatory, advisory, educative and/or remedial role. What constitutes ethical misconduct shall be determined on the basis of the provisions of the NASP *Principles for Professional Ethics* and any published advisory opinions that from time to time are developed by the Ethical and Professional standards Committee. In applying the Principles, the authorized opinions of those charged by NASP with the administration and interpretation of the ethical principles shall be binding on all NASP members, individuals who hold a certificate issued by the National School Psychology Certification

Board (NSPCB), and on the members of state associations affiliated with NASP.

When investigating and/or responding to a complaint or inquiry, the Ethical and Professional Standards Committee shall conduct itself in a manner consistent with the Bylaws of the Association and the NASP *Principles for Professional Ethics* and shall also be bound by these procedures. The Ethical and Professional Standards Committee shall endeavor to settle cases informally, recommend disciplinary action when unethical conduct has occurred, report regularly to the Delegate Assembly on its activities and shall revise and amend (subject to ratification by the Delegate Assembly) the NASP Principles and these procedures in a timely manner. The Association may at the recommendation of the Ethical and Professional Standards Committee, and in accordance with the Bylaws of the Association, expel a NASP member. The Ethical and Professional Standards committee will also issue a recommendation to the NSPCB regarding charges filed against any nationally certified school psychologist.

When a complaint is received about a non-member, the Ethical and Professional Standards Committee shall respond only if the individual complained against is a member of the National School Psychology Certification System. Otherwise, the committee may act only in an advisory or educative fashion and shall have no authority to investigate the case or to discipline the individual in question.

Complaints that address concerns about professional standards, organizations, employers and the like, shall be referred to the Ethical and Professional Standards Committee. Never-the-less, it should be recognized that in situations where an individual school psychologist is being coerced to behave unethically, he/she bears certain ethical responsibilities and to fail to take appropriate action, e.g., refusing to behave unethically, could eventuate in charges of misconduct against the individual psychologist involved. However, as a rule such "standards" concerns would not fall under the purview of this complaint process.

Complaints received by the Ethical and Professional Standards Committee shall be reviewed and judged on the basis of the *Principles for Professional Ethics* in force at the time of the alleged misconduct. Investigation and adjudication of ethical complaints shall be on the basis of the "Procedural Guidelines for the Adjudication of Ethical Complaints" in force at the time the complaint is received by the Committee.

SECTION III. RECEIPT AND ACKNOWLEDGMENT OF COMPLAINTS AND INQUIRIES

A The Ethical and Professional Standards committee shall recognize and respond to all complaints and inquiries from any responsible individual or group of individuals in accordance with these procedures. The individual who petitions the Committee (hereinafter referred to as the complainant) need not be a member of NASP or the affiliated state association. Anonymous letters and phone calls will not be recognized. Complaints by members which are judged by the committee to be frivolous or revengeful may be cause for action against the complainant.

B An oral complaint or inquiry may be informally handled, referred elsewhere when appropriate, or an Ethical and Professional Standards Committee chairperson may request that the complaint be formally submitted in writing. Only written statements expressing the details of the alleged misconduct will be accepted for action. Such written statements shall be signed by the complainant and should state, in as much detail as practicable, the facts upon which the complaint is based. NASP will maintain appropri-

ate records regarding the number and nature of all written complaints filed against NASP members and members of the National School Psychology Certification System. All the correspondence, records and activities of the Ethical and Professional Standards Committee shall remain confidential.

C Within 15 days of receipt of a written statement outlining the details of the alleged misconduct, the chairpersons of the Ethical and Professional Standards Committee shall do the following:

1 Determine if the individual against whom the complaint is made (hereinafter referred to as the respondent), is a member of NASP or an NCSP. If the respondent is not a member of NASP or an NCSP, the complainant shall be so advised and when appropriate, referred to other agencies and/or associations who would have authority in the matter.

2 If the respondent is a member of NASP or an NCSP, the Ethical and Professional Standards Committee chairpersons, with any advisory opinions deemed necessary, shall review the complaint. If it is determined that the alleged misconduct, even if true, would not constitute an actual violation of the NASP Principles, a chairperson shall notify the complainant.

3 If the information obtained from the complainant is insufficient to make a determination regarding the alleged misconduct, the chairpersons may send a written request to the complainant, asking for clarification and/or additional information as would be needed to make such a determination.

4 If it is determined that the alleged misconduct, if substantiated, would constitute an actual violation of NASP Principles, the Ethical and Professional Standards Committee chairperson shall

311

direct a letter to and advise the complainant that the allegation will be investigated by the Committee. The complainant shall be asked to sign a release, authorizing that his/her name be revealed to the respondent.

5   If the complainant refuses to permit his/her identity to be made known to the respondent, such refusal will serve as a basis for forfeiting the complaint process. However, the Ethical and Professional Standards Committee may proceed on its own volition when a member appears to have engaged in ethical misconduct that tends to injure the Association or to adversely affect its reputation, or that is clearly inconsistent with or destructive of the goals and objectives of the Association.

SECTION IV.   CONDUCT OF AN INFORMAL INQUIRY

A   Within 15 days of receipt of the signed release, the Ethical and Professional Standards Committee shall inform the respondent, in writing, with the envelope marked "confidential," that a complaint has been filed against him/her. This letter shall describe the nature of the complaint, indicate the principle(s) which appear to have been violated, and request the respondent's cooperation in obtaining a full picture of the circumstances which led to the allegations. A copy of the NASP Principles for Professional Ethics, these procedures, and any pertinent advisory opinions of the Ethical and Professional Standards committee shall also be enclosed. Ordinarily the respondent shall be informed of the name of the complainant, when written permission to do so has been obtained. (See Section III, C-5 above, for exception.)

B   The respondent shall be asked to provide a written statement outlining his/her view of the situation in order that the Committee may be cognizant of all relevant aspects of the case.

C   Whenever, possible, the Ethical and Professional Standards Committee shall attempt to resolve differences privately and informally through further correspondence with all parties involved. An attempt shall be made to bring about an adjustment through meditative efforts in the interest of correcting a general situation or settling the particular issues between the parties involved.

D   If the respondent does not respond to the original inquiry within 30 days, a follow-up letter shall be sent to the respondent by registered or certified mail, marked "confidential," with a return receipt requested.

E   If the respondent refuses to reply to the Committee's inquiry or otherwise cooperate with the Committee, the Committee may continue its investigation, noting in the record the circumstances of the respondent's failure to cooperate. The Committee shall also inform the respondent that his/her lack of cooperation may result in action which could eventuate in his/her being dropped from membership in the Association.

F   As a rule, if the complainant wishes to withdraw the complaint, the inquiry is terminated, except in extreme cases where the Committee feels the issues in the case are of such importance as to warrant completing the investigation in its own right and in the interest of the public welfare or that of the Association. (See Section III, C-5.)

G   The Association will not recognize a respondent's resignation from membership while there is a complaint pending before the Ethical and Professional Standards Committee or before an ethics committee of a state association unless he/she submits an affidavit stating that:

1   The resignation is free and voluntary;

2   He/she is aware of a pending investigation into allegations of misconduct;

3 He/she acknowledges that the material facts upon which the complaint is based are true; and

4 He/she submits the resignation because he/she knows that if charges are predicated on the misconduct under investigation, he/she could not defend him/herself successfully against them.

H Within 30 days of receipt of the written statement from the respondent, or (in the event the respondent fails to reply or otherwise cooperate), within 30 days of receipt of the return receipt requested from the second notification by the Committee (Section IV, D, E), the chairpersons, through advice of the Committee, shall determine if a violation may have occurred, and if so, what principles have potentially been violated.

I If, in the opinion of the Committee, the complaint has a basis in fact but is considered likely to be corrected without further action, the chairpersons shall so indicate in the record and shall so inform all parties involved.

J If, in the opinion of the chairpersons, the issues raised by the complaint would, if true, constitute a violation of the principles, and if it appears that the complaint cannot be resolved by less formal means, the chairpersons, shall, in coordination with the appropriate State Delegate, appoint two impartial NASP members from the state in which the respondent practices to form an Ad Hoc Committee, together with the chairpersons of the Ethical and Professional Standards Committee. The purpose of this Ad Hoc Committee is to investigate the case, to evaluate the character of the behavior(s) in question and to make recommendations to the Ethics and Professional Standards Committee for final disposition of the case.

K The Ethical and Professional Standards Committee chairpersons shall transmit to the members of the Ad Hoc Committee, by registered or certified mail, in envelopes marked "confidential," copies of the following:

1 The original complaint or material;

2 The letter to the respondent apprising him/her of the nature of the alleged violation;

3 The response from the respondent; and

4 Any such further facts related to the case as the chairpersons can assemble from sources of evident reliability.

L The Ad Hoc Committee shall then determine whether:

1 The case shall be closed;

2 Further investigation by correspondence is indicated;

3 Future investigation by a Fact-Finding Committee is indicated (see Section V);

4 The respondent and/or complainant shall be asked to appear before the Ad Hoc Committee; or

5 Some other action or a combination thereof shall be taken.

313

SECTION V. **RECOMMENDATIONS OF THE AD HOC COMMITTEE**

A When the Ad Hoc Committee has obtained sufficient information with which to reach a decision, or in any event, in not more than 60 days from the formation of the Ad Hoc Committee, the Ethical and Professional Standards Committee chairpersons shall request that the Ad Hoc Committee vote on the disposition of the case.

B If, in the unanimous opinion of the Ad Hoc Committee members, a violation of the NASP Principles has occurred and if, in the opinion of the Ad Hoc Committee, the unethical behavior can be terminated by action of the Committee itself, one or more of the following recommendations shall be made:

1 The Ad Hoc Committee shall request, in writing, that the respondent take corrective measures to modify or stop certain activities or practices;

2   The Ad Hoc Committee shall, in writing, censure or reprimand the respondent;

3   The Ad Hoc Committee shall require that the respondent provide restitution to or apologize, in writing, to an individual, or organization harmed by the respondent's unethical conduct.;

4   The Ad Hoc Committee shall recommend that the respondent be placed under a period of probation of membership or surveillance under fixed terms agreed to by the respondent;

5   The Ad Hoc Committee may recommend a combination of the above four recommendations. (NOTE - In all cases, supervision of the member's behavior for a period of time will be required component of the corrective action.)

C   Within 5 days, the Ethical and Professional Standards Committee chairpersons shall inform the respondent of the Ad Hoc Committee's determination and recommendations. The respondent shall be notified that he/she may make a request for a hearing on the charges within 30 day from the receipt of a statement of the charges and the Committee's findings and recommendations. Such a request shall be in writing and directed to the President of the Association.

D   The Ethical and Professional Standards committee chairperson shall draft a report summarizing the findings and recommendations of the Ad Hoc Committee, copies of which shall be distributed to the two other Ad Hoc Committee members, the respondent and, at the Committee's discretion, the complainant. This report shall be transmitted in envelopes marked Aconfidential@ in the case of the respondent, by registered or certified mail with a return receipt requested.

E   A summary report shall then be edited by the Ethical and Professional Standards Committee

chairpersons, ensuring the confidentiality of all persons involved is strictly maintained, for purposes of reporting to the Delegate Assembly at the next regularly scheduled meeting on the activities and recommendations of the Ethical and Professional Standards Committee and its designees, e.g., any Ad Hoc Committee so convened in the interim.

F   The unanimous decision of the Ad Hoc Committee shall be binding on the Association unless overturned by the Hearing Committee, Executive Council or Delegate Assembly in accordance with the procedures outlined herein. (See Section VIII)

SECTION VI.   CONDUCT OF A FORMAL INVESTIGATION

A   A formal investigation shall be undertaken if any one of the following circumstances prevails:

1   The Ad Hoc Committee finds that it lacks sufficient data with which to proceed;

2   The Ad Hoc Committee is unable to reach consensus;

3   The recommendations of the Ad Hoc Committee do not lead to resolution of the problem; or

4   The facts alleged in the complaint, if substantiated, would likely require action leading to termination of the respondent's membership in the Association, or revocation of a National Certificate.

B   When a formal investigation is warranted under these procedures, the Ethical and Professional Standards Committee chairpersons, in coordination with the President of the Association, shall appoint a Fact-Finding Committee, which shall appoint its own chairperson, to consist of not less than three nor more than five members of the Association, for the specific purpose of more fully investigating the charges. No member previously involved in reviewing the case may serve on the Fact-Finding Committee. The Ethical and Professional Standards Committee chairpersons shall serve on the Fact-Finding Committee in ex-officio status in order to apprise the Fact-Finding Committee of the procedures by which they are bound and to serve in an advisory capacity.

C   The Fact-Finding Committee shall be bound by the same procedures and timelines as outlined in Sections III and IV of these procedures. In addition, the Fact-Finding Committee may, at the discretion of the Executive Council, retain a legal advisor as counsel to the committee while investigating its case.

D   The respondent may seek advice from any individual, including an attorney or another member of the Association, for assistance in preparing and presenting documentary evidence requested by the Fact-Finding Committee.

SECTION VII.   **RECOMMENDATIONS OF THE FACT-FINDING COMMITTEE**

A   If the formal investigation was convened following a decision by consensus of the Ad Hoc Committee, and if the Fact-Finding Committee unanimously concurs with the Ad Hoc Committee's findings and recommendations, all parties shall be so informed and this decision shall be binding on the Association unless overturned by the Hearing Committee, Executive Council or Delegate Assembly, in accordance with the procedures outlined herein.

B   If the case was not resolved at the Ad Hoc Committee level, the Fact-Finding Committee must announce its findings and recommendations within the prescribed timelines. The Fact-Finding Committee may exercise any of the recommendations open to the Ad Hoc Committee (Section V, B) and in addition may also recommend that the respondent's membership in the Association be terminated.

C   Should the Fact-Finding Committee so recommend, the chairpersons of the Ethical and Professional Standards Committee must present the findings and recommendations of the Fact-Finding Committee to the NASP Executive Council and Delegate Assembly. A summary report shall be prepared, such that the confidentiality of all parties involved, i.e., identifying information of the informer, is strictly maintained. The case shall be reviewed in sufficient detail so as to allow the Executive Council and the Delegate Assembly members to vote to concur or overrule the decision of the Fact-Finding Committee.

D   In accordance with NASP Bylaws, cases involving a recommendation for expulsion from the Association by the Ethical and Professional Standards Committee shall be confirmed by a 2/3 vote of the Executive Council, with a majority ratification by the Delegate Assembly. If the expelled NASP member is also a member of the NSPCS, the expulsion shall be reported to the NSPCB along with a recommendation for further action, if any, the NSPCB should take.

E   At the discretion of the Executive Council and Delegate Assembly, the respondent may be allowed to voluntarily resign his/her membership in the Association.

F   Within five days, the Ethical and Professional Standards Committee chairpersons shall inform the respondent of the decision of the Executive Council and Delegate Assembly in the same manner as provided in Section V-C of these procedures.

G   If the Executive Council and/or the Delegate Assembly do not concur with the Committee's recommendation for expulsion from membership, the case shall be remanded back to the Fact-Finding Committee for consideration of a lesser penalty.

315

SECTION VIII. **CONDUCT OF THE HEARING COMMITTEE**

A Within 30 days of receipt of a statement of the charges against him/her and a statement of the Committee's findings and recommendations, the respondent has the right to request from the President of the Association a hearing on the charges. This right shall be considered waived if such request is not made in writing within the 30 day period.

B If the respondent does request a hearing, the President shall select a panel of ten members of the Association, none of whom shall be members of the Ethical and Professional Standards Committee or have had any prior connection with the case. From the panel, the respondent shall have 30 days in which to choose a Hearing committee of five members. If he/she does not make a selection, the President shall choose the five members to comprise the Hearing Committee.

C The President shall select a chairperson of the Hearing Committee who shall conduct the hearing and assure that the procedures are properly observed. There shall be no communication between the members of the Hearing Committee and the Ethical and Professional Standards Committee or any of its representatives prior to the hearing itself.

D A date for the hearing shall be set by the President with the concurrence of the respondent. In no event shall the hearing take place later than 90 days from the date of the respondent's request for a hearing.

E At least 30 days prior to the hearing, the respondent and the Hearing Committee members shall be provided with copies of all documents to be presented and the names of all witnesses that will be offered by the Ethical and Professional standards Committee in support of the charges.

F Presentation of the case against the respondent shall be the responsibility of the Ethical and Professional Standards Committee, or such others as the Ethical and Professional Standards Committee has designated to investigate the complaint. Legal counsel for the Association may participate fully in the presentation of the case.

G All evidence that is relevant and reliable, as determined by the chairperson of the Hearing Committee, shall be admissible. Evidence of mitigating circumstances may be presented by the respondent.

H The respondent shall have the right to counsel, to present witnesses and documents and to cross-examine the witnesses offered by the Ethical and Professional Standards Committee.

I The hearing may be adjourned as necessary and the Ethical and Professional Standards Committee may introduce rebuttal evidence.

J In the interest of obtaining a full and accurate record of the hearing, a tape recorder or other transcription device may be used, at the discretion of the Hearing Committee and the respondent.

SECTION IX. **RECOMMENDATIONS OF THE HEARING COMMITTEE**

A At the conclusion of the hearing, the Hearing Committee shall have 30 days in which to issue its report and recommendations.

B If the Hearing Committee recommends that the respondent be dropped from membership or that the respondent be permitted to resign, the matter shall be referred to the Executive Council. A recommendation that the respondent be expelled or be allowed to resign must be made by 4 of the 5 committee members. Other disciplinary measures would be decided upon per individual case and would require a simple majority vote.

C Only the disciplinary measures specified by the Ethical and Professional Standard Committee in the formal statement of charges, or a lesser penalty, shall be recommended by the Hearing Committee. Although the Ethical and Professional Standards Committee recommendations may be modified by the Hearing Committee, it may not increase the penalty recommended.

D The Hearing Committee shall submit its report and recommendations simultaneously to the Executive Council and to the respondent.

E The respondent shall have 15 days from receipt of the Hearing Committee's report in which to file a written statement with the Executive Council. The Ethical and Professional standards Committee shall then have 15 days in which to file a response.

F After consideration of the record, the recommendation of the Hearing Committee and any statements that may be filed, the Executive Council shall adopt the recommendations of the Hearing Committee unless it determines that:

  1 The NASP Principles and/or the procedures herein stated have been incorrectly applied;

  2 The findings of fact of the Hearing Committee as stated in the report are not supported by the evidence; or

  3 The procedures followed were in violation of the Bylaws of the Association.

G The Ethical and Professional Standards Committee shall inform the respondent and, at its discretion, may inform the complainant of any final action taken by the Executive Council. The Ethical and Professional Standards Committee shall report to the Delegate Assembly at its next regularly scheduled meeting, in Executive Session, the names of those members who have been allowed to resign or who have been expelled from membership, and the ethical principle(s) involved. Actions involving individuals who hold a certificate issued by the NSPCB will be reported to the national certification board in a timely manner.

H The Ethical and Professional Standards Committee shall report annually and in confidence to the delegate Assembly and Executive Council, in Executive Session, the names of members who have been expelled from the Association and the ethical principle(s) involved.

I In severe cases and when the welfare of the public is at stake, and when the Ethical and Professional Standards Committee deems it necessary to maintain the principles of the Association and the profession, it may also notify affiliated state and regional associations and state and local licensing and certification boards of the final disposition of the case. Other interested parties, including the respondent's employer, may be notified of the final action when, in the opinion of the Ethical and Professional Standards Committee, notification is necessary for the protection of the public or the profession.

317

PROCEDURAL GUIDELINES FOR THE ADJUDICATION OF ETHICAL COMPLAINTS SUMMARIZED IN CHART FORM

A COMPLAINT IS RECEIVED BY THE COMMITTEE.	
Is the complaint anonymous?	If so, take no action
Is the complaint oral?	If so, advise only.
Is the complaint about Standards?	If so, advise only.
Is the complaint frivolous or vengeful?	If so, consider action against complainant.
Is the ethical complaint about a NASP member or a member of the National Certification system?	If not, advise complainant that the situation is out of NASP jurisdiction.
WITHIN 15 DAYS OF THE COMPLAINT:	
The committee reviews the written complaint.	
Is there a potential violation of NASP Ethics?	If not, notify complainant and get more information, or stop.
Complainant is advised that an informal investigation will occur, and is asked for a release so that respondent may know who issued the complaint.	
Is the release obtained?	If not, the committee must decide whether to proceed on its own volition.
WITHIN 15 DAYS OF SIGNED RELEASE:	
Inform the respondent, describe the complaint and the principles believed to be involved, request cooperation, and send a copy of the Ethics. Ask for a written response.	
Attempt to resolve the situation informally, if possible.	
IF NO ANSWER WITHIN 30 DAYS:	
Follow up with another request for a written response, using a certified letter with return receipt requested.	
If there is still no reply, or if the respondent refuses to cooperate, note this in the record and inform the respondent that a lack of cooperation could result in expulsion from NASP.	

WITHIN 30 DAYS OF THE WRITTEN STATEMENT:	
If the facts seem to suggest that a violation may have occurred, is the situation likely to correct itself without further action?	If so, inform all parties and monitor the situation.

WITHIN THE NEXT 60 DAYS:
Contact the state delegate, appoint two impartial NASP members in the respondent's state, and form an Ad Hoc committee.
Ad Hoc Committee receives copies of the original complaint materials, the committee's letter to the respondent, the respondent's written response, and other pertinent material.

Can the situation be settled at the informal level?	If so, contact parties and monitor the situation.
Can the needed information be obtained through correspondence?	If so, the Ad Hoc committee continues to gather the facts.
Does the Ad Hoc committee need for the complainant and the respondent to appear?	If so, arrange for them to appear before the committee.
Does the Ad Hoc Committee have enough information to decide the issues at hand?	If not, begin fact-finding procedures.
Is the Ad Hoc committee unanimous in its decision?	If not, begin formal investigation procedures.

THE COMMITTEE ISSUES A DECISION, WHICH IS BINDING UNLESS OVERTURNED BY A HEARING; SUPERVISION IS REQUIRED:				
Order corrective action.	Censure or reprimand.	Require an apology or restitution.	Require probation.	Determine no violation occurred.

WITHIN 5 DAYS:
Notify the respondent of the decision.

WAIT 30 DAYS FOR RESPONDENT TO REQUEST A HEARING:
If there is no request for a hearing, draft a report and advise the Delegate Assembly of the actions of the committee. Make recommendation to National Certification Board if respondent holds national certification.

FORMAL INVESTIGATION PROCEDURES

Follow these steps if:

- The Ad Hoc Committee lacks the data to proceed.

- The Ad Hoc Committee cannot reach a consensus.

- The solutions available to the Ad Hoc Committee are unlikely to resolve the problem.

- The facts, if substantiated, could lead to the expulsion of a NASP member or a member of the NSPCS.

The chairs of the Ethical and Professional Standards Committee, along with the NASP President, appoint members of a fact finding committee. This committee follows the same basic procedures as the Ad Hoc committee.

Does the fact finding committee concur unanimously with the Ad Hoc Committee?	If so, the Ad Hoc Committee decisions are binding unless overturned by a hearing, Executive Council, or Delegate Assembly.

The fact finding committee reaches its own conclusions. The recommendation may include expulsion.

If expulsion is advised, the Ethical and Professional Standards chairs will present the findings to the NASP Executive Council and the Delegate Assembly, with all due consideration for matters of confidentiality.

Is the expulsion recommendation confirmed by a two thirds vote of the Executive Council and ratified by a majority of the Delegates?	If not, have the fact finding committee review the situation and consider a lessor penalty.

WITHIN 5 DAYS:

Notify the respondent.

WAIT 30 DAYS FOR RESPONDENT TO REQUEST A HEARING:

If there is no request for a hearing, draft a report and advise the Delegate Assembly and the National Certification Board (if necessary) of the actions of the committee.

CONDUCT OF THE HEARING COMMITTEE

Upon receipt of a written decision by the Ad Hoc or the Fact Finding Committee, a respondent has thirty days in which to ask for a hearing. Should a hearing be requested within the 30 days.

The NASP President selects a panel of 10 impartial NASP members. From this group, the respondent selects 5 to serve on the committee. The President then selects the Chair.

NO LATER THAN 90 DAYS FROM THE DATE OF THE HEARING REQUEST:

The date for the hearing is set.

AT LEAST 30 DAYS BEFORE THE HEARING:

Hearing committee members and respondent receive copies of all relevant documents.

AT THE HEARING:

The Ethical and Professional Standards Committee chair, or designee, presents the facts in the complaint. The respondent has the right to counsel, to present witnesses and documents, and to cross-examine witnesses. The Ethical and Professional Standards Committee may offer rebuttal.

WITHIN 30 DAYS:

The hearing committee issues a report and recommendations to the respondent and the NASP Executive Council.

WITHIN 15 DAYS:

The Ethical and Professional Standards Committee and the respondent may file comments on the hearing committee report.

AT THE NEXT EXECUTIVE COUNCIL MEETING:

Does the NASP Executive Council believe that there is no evidence of ethical misconduct, or that there was a problem with the application of the principles or procedures for investigation?	Is yes, the matter is ended.

The Executive Council adopts the findings and recommendations of the Hearing Committee.

The Ethical and Professional Standards Committee informs the respondent, and has the discretion to inform the complainant or not. The EB/DA is notified of member expelled and the ethical principles involved. The National School Psychology Certification System will be notified if the proceedings involve an NSPCS member.

When the welfare of the public is at stake, NASP may notify other interested parties of the final disposition of the case.

321

NATIONAL ASSOCIATION OF SCHOOL PSYCHOLOGISTS

STANDARDS FOR THE PROVISION
OF SCHOOL PSYCHOLOGICAL SERVICES

Table of Contents

PREFACE

PURPOSE

The *Standards for the Provision of School Psychological Services* represent the position of the National Association of School Psychologists regarding the delivery of appropriate and comprehensive school psychological services. First written in 1978, revised in 1984, 1992, and 1997 the *Standards* serve as a guide to the organization and delivery of school psychological services at the federal, state, and local levels. The *Standards* provide direction to school psychologists, students and trainers in school psychology, administrators of school psychological services, and consumers of school psychological services regarding excellence in professional school psychology. They also delineate what services might reasonably be expected to be available from most school psychologists, and thus should help to further define the field. In addition, they are intended to educate the profession and the public regarding appropriate professional practices, and hopefully will stimulate the continued development of the profession.

A principal objective of the *Standards* is to inform policy and decision-makers of the major characteristics of comprehensive school psychological services. Thus, the first two sections of the document contain suggestions and recommendations for federal and state educational agencies regarding the school psychology profession. The third outlines responsibilities which should be assumed by organizations which employ school psychologists. The final section presents the resulting responsibilities of the individual school psychologist.

Not all school psychologists or school psychological service units will be able to meet every standard contained within this document. Nevertheless, it is anticipated that these guidelines will serve as a model of "good practice" for program development and professional practice on a federal, state, and local level.

School psychologists will perceive that it is in their own best interest -- and that of the agencies, parents, and children they serve -- to adhere to and support these *Standards*. NASP encourages state and federal legislators, local school boards, and the administrative leaders of federal, state, and local education agencies to support the concepts contained within these *Standards*.

NASP acknowledges that the *Standards* set requirements for services not presently mandated by federal law or regulation, and not always mandated in state laws and administrative rules.Future amendments of such statues and rules, and the state and local plans resulting from them, should incorporate the suggestions contained in this document. Furthermore, NASP understands that school psychological services are provided within the context of ethical and legal mandates. Nothing in these *Standards* should be construed as superseding such relevant rules and regulations.

The *Standards* provide flexibility,permitting agencies and professionals to develop procedures, polices, and administrative organizations which meet both the needs of the agency and the professional's desire to operate within recognized professional standards of practice. At the same time, the *Standards* have sufficient specificity to insure that services will be provided appropriately and adequately.

DEVELOPMENT OF THE STANDARDS

The *Standards* were officially adopted by the National Association of School Psychologists at the Executive Council/Delegate Assembly (EB/DA) meeting during the April, 1984, convention. Previously, they had been presented for a "first reading" at the October, 1983, EB/DA meeting.

In preparing the 1984 Standards, a number of relevant documents were carefully reviewed and may of the ideas contained in them were incorporated. These materials included NASP's *Standards for the Provision of School Psychological Services*

(1978), *Resolution on Non-Biased Assessment* (1976), *Standards for Field Placement and Training Programs* (1983), *Principles for Professional Ethics*, and other draft documents being developed by NASP committees. Ideas from the Specialty Guidelines for the Delivery of Services by School Psychologist (1981) published by the American Psychological Association, and from a number of position papers and standards developed by state school psychology organizations were also incorporated. Furthermore, numerous ideas and suggestions proposed by the NASP membership were included.

In order to insure the input of NASP members and leadership in the preparation of the Standards, a lengthy development and review process was conducted. These procedures included a random survey of NASP members and the opportunity for every NASP member to provide input. Three separate drafts were distributed to the NASP leadership, practitioners, trainers, and school psychology supervisors. Written comments on these drafts were received from numerous persons. Every comment was thoughtfully and carefully considered, and most of these ideas were incorporated into the final version.

The following revisions of the *Standards* were conducted in this tradition of lengthy development and review. Realizing the importance of this document, changes were carefully considered and subject to comments from NASP leaders and members alike. This edition was first presented to the Delegate Assembly in Anaheim on April X, 1997 and final approval was achieved at the Delegate Assembly in Alexandria, Virginia, on July 26, 1997.

The National Association of School Psychologists encourages thoughtful reactions and suggestions from its members, the public, other psychologists and educators, and the profession with regard to these *Standards*.

STANDARDS FOR THE PROVISION OF SCHOOL PSYCHOLOGICAL SERVICES

1.0 DEFINITIONS

1.1 A school Psychologist is a professional psychologist who has met all requirements for credentialing as stipulated in the appropriate NASP standards. The credential is based upon the completion of a school psychology training program which meets the criteria specified in the NASP *Standards for Training and Field Placement Programs in School Psychology*.

1.2 A Supervising School Psychologist is a professional psychologist who has met all NASP requirements for credentialing, and who has been designated by an employing agency as a supervisor responsible for school psychological services in the agency. Coursework or other training in the supervision of school personnel is desirable.

1.3 Parent(s), as used in these *Standards*, includes both biological parent(s) and legal guardian(s) or appointed surrogates.

2.0 STANDARDS FOR ADMINISTRATIVE AGENCIES

The purpose of this section of the standards is to provide guidance to federal and state administrative agencies in regard to administrative organization, laws, policies, and regulations as they pertain to the provision of school psychological services.

2.1 FEDERAL LEVEL ADMINISTRATIVE AGENCY

2.1.1 ORGANIZATION

The federal education agency should employ a supervising school psychologist in order to accomplish the following objectives:

325

2.1.1.1 To provide professional leadership and assistance to the federal education agency, state education agencies, and the school psychology profession in regard to standards, polices, and procedures for program delivery, and for utilization, funding, education and training, and inservice education of school psychological services personnel.

2.1.1.2 To participate in the administration of federal programs providing funding for school psychological services in state, intermediate, and local education agencies, and for the education and training of school psychologists.

2.1.1.3 To encourage and assist in evaluation, research, and dissemination activities; to determine the effectiveness of school psychological education, training, and service programs; to determine needed changes; and to identify and communicate exemplary practices to training and service units.

2.1.1.4 To assure that consistent communication is established and maintained among professional organizations, federal, state, and local education agencies, and university training programs involved in providing and developing school psychological services.

2.1.2 LAWS

2.1.2.1 The Congress of the United States should ensure that the rights of all parents and children are protected by the creation and modification of laws which provide for the services of school psychologists. These services, as related to students' need, include, but are not limited to, consultation, assessment, research, program planning/evaluation, and

direct service for individuals, groups, and systems. These services should be available to all children, their families, and school personnel.

2.1.2.2 The Congress should ensure that school psychological services, as related to students' needs, are provided in a free and appropriate manner to all children, their families, and school personnel in need of such services.

2.1.2.3 The Congress should ensure that federal laws recognize the appropriate involvement of school psychologists in educational programs and that adequate federal funding is made available for the education, training, services, and continuing professional development of school psychologist in order to guarantee appropriate and effective services.

2.1.2.4 The Congress should create no laws which effectively prohibit the credentialed school psychologist from the ethical and legal practice of his/her profession in the public or private sector, or which would be in violation of these standards.

2.1.3 REGULATIONS

2.1.3.1 All federal agencies should utilize the services of the federal educational agency school psychologist in developing and implementing regulations pursuant to all relevant federal laws.

2.1.3.2 All federal agencies should seek the advice and consultation of the National Association of School Psychologist prior to the adoption of regulations pursuant to any federal law which relates to the education or mental health of students and/or families, or which otherwise involves or should reasonably involve the profession of school psychology.

2.1.3.3 Federal agencies should promulgate regulations consistent with the principles set forth in these *Standards* and the NASP *Principles for Professional Ethics*.

2.2. STATE LEVEL ADMINISTRATIVE AGENCIES

2.2.1 ORGANIZATION

Each state educational agency (SEA) should employ at least one full-time supervising school psychologist, as defined in section 1, for each 500 (or fewer) school psychologists within the state. An equivalent ratio should be maintained if there are more than 500 school psychologists. It is recognized that this ratio may vary based upon administrative structures, available resources, and types of programs served, however the intention is to assign the individual(s) full-time (1.0 FTE) to the supervision of school psychology. Appropriate objectives to be accomplished by the SEA school psychologist(s) include the following:

2.2.1.1 To provide professional leadership assistance to the SEA, local educational agencies, and the profession with regard to standards, policies, and procedures for school psychology program delivery.

2.2.1.2 To support the utilization, funding, education, training, and in-service education of school psychologists.

2.2.1.3 To participate in the administration of state and federal programs providing funding for school psychological services in intermediate and local educational agencies, and for the education and training of school psychologists.

2.2.1.4 To encourage and assist in evaluation, research, and dissemination activities to determine the effectiveness of school psychological education, training, and service programs; to determine needed changes; and to identify and communicate exemplary practices to training and service units.

2.2.1.5 To maintain communication with and assure consultation with state school psychological associations and practicing school psychological personnel into the policy making of the SEA.

2.2.1.6 To communicate with the federal education agency school psychologist to ensure recognition of state issues and to facilitate consultation regarding federal policy.

2.2.2 LAWS

2.2.2.1 All state legislative bodies should ensure that the rights of all parents and children are protected by the creation and modification of laws which provide for the services of school psychologists. As related to students' needs, these services include, but are not limited to, consultation for individuals, groups, and systems, assessment, program planning/evaluation, research, and direct service. These services are available to all children, their families, and school personnel.

2.2.2.2 The state legislature should ensure that school psychological services, as related to students' needs, are provided in a free and appropriate way to all children, their families, and school personnel in need of such services.

2.2.2.3 The state legislature should ensure that state laws recognize the appropriate involvement of school psychologists in educational programs.

327

2.2.2.4 The state legislature should ensure that adequate funding is made available for the education, training, services, and continuing professional development of school psychologists in order to guarantee appropriate and effective services.

2.2.2.5 The state legislature should ensure that state laws provide for the credentialing of school psychologists consistent with NASP standards.

2.2.2.6 The state legislature should create no laws which prohibit the school psychologist from the ethical and legal practice of his/her profession in the public or private sector, or that prevent the school psychologist from practicing in a manner consistent with these *Standards*.

2.2.2.7 The state legislature should ensure that there are sufficient numbers of adequately prepared and credentialed school psychologists to provide services consistent with these Standards. In most settings, this will require at least one full-time school psychologist for each 1,000 children served by the LEA, and a maximum of four schools served by one school psychologist. It is recognized that this ratio may vary based upon the needs of children served, the type of program served, available resources, distance between schools, and other unique characteristics.

2.2.3 REGULATIONS

2.2.3.1 All state agencies should utilize the services of the SEA school psychologist(s) in developing and implementing administrative rules pursuant to all relevant state laws, federal laws, and regulations.

2.2.3.2 All state agencies should seek the advice and consultation of the state school psychologists' professional association prior to the adoption of rules pursuant to any state law, federal law, or regulation which involves or should reasonably involve the profession of school psychology.

2.2.3.3 All state education agencies should utilize the services of the SEA school psychologist(s) and the school psychologists' professional association in the SEA review and approval of school psychology training programs.

2.2.3.4 All state education agencies should utilize the services of the SEA school psychologist(s) and the school psychologists' professional association in developing and implementing administrative rules for credentialing school psychologists. Such rules shall be consistent with NASP *Standards for the Credentialing of School Psychologists*.

2.2.3.5 State education agencies should promulgate regulations consistent with the principles set forth in these *Standards* and the NASP *Principles for Professional Ethics*.

3.0 STANDARDS FOR EMPLOYING AGENCIES

The purpose of these standards is to provide employing agencies with specific guidance regarding the organization, policies, and practices needed to assure the provision of adequate school psychological services.

3.1 COMPREHENSIVE CONTINUUM OF SERVICES

Employing agencies assure that school psychological services are provided in a coordinated, organized fashion, and are deployed in a manner which ensures the provision of a comprehensive continuum of services as outlined in Section 4.0 of these *Standards*. Such services are available to all students served by the agency and are available to an extent sufficient to meet the needs of the population served. Breadth or availability of services should not be dictated by the funding source. (For example, some Districts have been known to limit services to special education students only because the school psychology budget came from special education sources. Similarly, other Districts provided assessment services only because funds were taken from State or Federal assessment grants. Both cases are considered to be mistakes in the attempt to provide comprehensive school psychological services to all students.)

3.2 PROFESSIONAL EVALUATION, SUPERVISION, AND DEVELOPMENT

3.2.1 SUPERVISION

Employing agencies assure that an effective program of supervision and evaluation of school psychological services exists. School psychologists, in cooperation with their employing agencies, are responsible for the overall development, implementation, and professional supervision of school psychological service programs, and are responsible for articulating those programs to others in the employing agency and to the agency's constituent groups.

3.2.2 SUPERVISOR(S)

The school psychological services program is supervised by a designated school psychologist who meets the requirements for a supervising school psychologist (Section 1.2) and who demonstrates competencies needed for effective supervision.

3.2.3 AVAILABILITY OF SUPERVISION

Supervision is available to all school psychologist to an extent sufficient to ensure

the provision of effective an accountable services (see Section 4.6 for specific requirements). In most cases, one supervising school psychologist should be employed for every ten school psychologists to be supervised (an equivalent ratio should be maintained for part-time supervisors). It is recognized that this ratio may vary based upon the type of program served, staff needs, and other unique characteristics.

3.2.4 INTERN SUPERVISION

A credentialed school psychologist meeting the requirements of a supervising school psychologist, with at least one year of experience at the employing agency, supervises no more than two school psychology interns at any given time (consistent with the NASP *Standards for Training and Field Placement Programs in School Psychology*), unless the supervising school psychologist has no other assigned duties. In such cases, a maximum of six school psychology interns may be supervised at any given time.

3.2.5 PEER REVIEW

After attaining independent practice status (see Section 4.5), school psychologists continue to receive appropriate supervision. The independent practitioner engages in peer review with other school psychologists. (Peer review involves mutual assistance with self-examination of services and the development of plans to continue professional growth and development.) Employing agencies assure that school psychologists are given appropriate time and support for peer review activities.

3.2.6 ACCOUNTABILITY AND PROGRAM EVALUATION

Employing agencies assure that school psychologists develop a coordinated plan

329

for accountability and evaluation of all services provided in order to maintain and improve the effectiveness of services. Such plans include specific, measurable objectives pertaining to the planned effects of services on all relevant elements of the system. Evaluation and revision of these plans occurs on a regular basis.

3.2.7 CONTINUING PROFESSIONAL DEVELOPMENT

Employing agencies recognize that all school psychologists, not just those holding national certification, are obligated to continue their professional training and development through participation in a recognized Continuing Professional Development (CPD) program (see Section 4.6). Employing agencies provide release time and financial support for such activities. They recognize documented continuing professional development activities in the evaluation and advancement of school psychologists. Private practitioners who contract to provide services are responsible for their own CPD program, and these activities should also be encouraged by employing agencies.

3.3 CONDITIONS FOR EFFECTIVE SERVICE DELIVERY

In order to assure that employment conditions enable school psychologists to provide effective services, employing agencies adopt policies and practices ensuring that Section 3.3.1 through 3.3.4 are met.

3.3.1 School psychologists are not subjected to administrative constraints which prevent them from providing services in full accordance with these *Standards* and NASP *Principles for Professional Ethics*. When administrative policies conflict with these *Standards* or the NASP *Ethics*, the princi-

ples outlined in the *Standards* or *Ethics* take precedence in determining appropriate practices of the school psychologist.

3.3.2 School psychologists have appropriate involvement with the general policy making of the employing agency and the development of programs affecting the staff, students, and families they serve.

3.3.3 School psychologists have appropriate professional autonomy in determining the nature, extent, and duration of services they provide. Specific activities are defined within the profession, although school psychologists frequently collaborate and seek advice from others in determining appropriate service delivery. Legal, ethical, and professional standards and guidelines are considered by the practitioner in making decisions regarding practice (see Section 4.4).

3.3.4 School psychologists have access to adequate clerical assistance, appropriate professional work materials, sufficient office and work space, and general working conditions that enhance the delivery of effective services. Included are test materials, access to private telephone and office, secretarial services, therapeutic aids, professional literature (book, journals), computers and related technology, and so forth.

3.4 CONTRACTUAL SERVICES

It is recognized that employing agencies may obtain school psychological services on a contractual basis in order to ensure the provision of adequate services to all children. However, each student within the educational system must be assured the full range of school psychological services necessary to maximize his/her success and adjustment in school. When an employing agency utilizes contractual services, the following standards are observed:

3.4.1 Contractual school psychological services encompass the same comprehensive continuum of services as that provided by regularly employed school psychologists. Overall, psychological services are not limited to any specific type of service and include opportunities for follow-up and continuing consultation appropriate to the needs of the student. Individual contracts for services may be limited as long as comprehensive services are provided overall.

3.4.2 Psychologists providing contractual school psychological services provide those services in a manner consistent with these *Standards*, NASP *Principles for Professional Ethics*, and other relevant professional guidelines and standards.

3.4.3 Persons providing contractual psychological services are fully credentialed school psychologists as defined by these *Standards*. In specific limited instances, however, services by psychologist in other specialty areas (e.g., clinical, industrial/organizational, neuropsychology, etc.) might be used to supplement school psychological services in a coordinated manner.

3.4.4 Contractual school psychological services are not to be utilized as a means to decrease the amount and quality of school psychological services provided by an employing agency. They may be used to augment programs but not to supplant them.

3.4.5 School psychologists providing contractual services are given appropriate access and information. They are familiar with the instructional resources of the employing agency to ensure that students they serve have the same opportunities as those served by regularly employed school psychologists.

3.4.6 Contractual school psychological services are provided in a manner which protects the due process rights of students and

their parents as defined by state and federal laws and regulations.

3.4.7 Contracting for services is not to be used as a means to avoid legitimate employee rights, wages, or fringe benefits.

3.4.8 Psychologists providing contractual school psychological services will encourage regular evaluation of the continued need for the service as well as the quality of the service.

3.5 NON-BIASED ASSESSMENT AND PROGRAM PLANNING

Employing agencies should adopt policies and practices in accordance with the following standards:

3.5.1 GENERAL PRINCIPLES

3.5.1.1 School psychologists use assessment techniques to provide information which is helpful in maximizing student achievement, educational success, psychological adjustment, and behavioral adaptation.

3.5.1.2 School psychologist have autonomous decision-making responsibility (as defined in Section 4.4) to determine the type, nature, and extent of assessment techniques they use in student evaluation.

3.5.1.3 School psychologists have autonomy (as defined in Section 4.4) in determining the content and nature of reports.

3.5.1.4 Whenever possible, school psychologists use assessment techniques and instruments which have established validity and reliability for the purposes and populations for which the procedures are intended. In addition, certain clinical procedures and measures at the "research" stage of development may be used by practitioners trained in their use

331

provided the reliability and validity of the procedures are reported and clearly distinguished from those techniques which meet standards.

3.5.1.5 School psychologists use, develop, and encourage assessment practices which increase the likelihood of the development of effective educational interventions and follow-up.

3.5.2 PROFESSIONAL INVOLVEMENT

3.5.2.1 A multi-disciplinary team is involved in assessment, program decision making, and evaluation. The team conducts periodic evaluations of its performance to ensure continued effectiveness.

3.5.2.2 The multi-disciplinary team includes a fully trained and certified school psychologist.

3.5.2.3 The school psychologist communicates a written minority position to all involved when in disagreement with the multi-disciplinary team position.

3.5.3 NON-BIASED ASSESSMENT TECHNIQUES

3.5.3.1 Assessment procedures and program recommendations are chosen to maximize the student's opportunities to be successful in the general culture, while respecting the student's ethnic background.

3.5.3.2 Multifaceted assessment batteries are used which include a focus on the student's strengths.

3.5.3.3 Communications are held and assessments are conducted in the client's dominant spoken language or alternative communication system. All student information is interpreted in the context of the student's socio-cultural background and the setting in which she/he is functioning.

3.5.3.4 Assessment techniques (including computerized techniques) are used only by personnel professionally trained in their use and in a manner consistent with these *Standards*.

3.5.3.5 School psychologists promote the development of objective, valid, and reliable assessment techniques.

3.5.3.6 Interpretation of assessment results is based upon empirically validated research.

3.5.4 PARENT/STUDENT INVOLVEMENT

3.5.4.1 Informed written consent of parent(s) and/or student (if the student has reached the age of majority) is obtained in the native language (or form of communication) of the parents/guardians before assessment and special program implementation.

3.5.4.2 The parent(s) and/or student is fully informed of all essential information considered and its relevancy to decision-making.

3.5.4.3 The parent(s) and/or student is encouraged to participate in decision-making meetings.

3.5.4.4 The parent(s) and/or student is routinely notified that an advocate can participate in conferences focusing on assessment results and program recommendations.

3.5.4.5 A record of meetings regarding assessment results and program recommendations is available to all directly concerned.

3.5.5 EDUCATIONAL PROGRAMMING AND FOLLOW-THROUGH

3.5.5.1 School psychologists are involved in determining options and revisions of educational programs to ensure that they are adaptive to the needs of students.

3.5.5.2 The contributions of diverse cultural backgrounds should be emphasized in educational programs.

3.5.5.3 School psychologists follow-up on the efficacy of their recommendations.

3.5.5.4 Student needs are given priority in determining educational programs.

3.5.5.5 Specific educational prescriptions result from the assessment team's actions.

3.5.5.6 Where a clear determination of the student's needs does not result from initial assessment, a diagnostic intervention or teaching program is offered as part of additional assessment procedures.

3.5.5.7 Regular, systematic review of the student's program is conducted and includes program modifications as necessary.

3.6 SCHOOL PSYCHOLOGICAL RECORDS

3.6.1 The employing agency's policy on student records is consistent with state and federal rules and laws, and ensures the protection of the confidentiality of the student and his/her family. The policy specifies the types of data developed by the school psychologist which are classified as school or pupil records. The policy gives clear guidance regarding which documents belong to the school and which are the personal property of the school psychologist.

3.6.2 Parents may inspect and review any personally identifiable data relating to their child which were collected, maintained, or used in his/her evaluation. Although test protocols are part of the student's record, school psychologists protect test security and observe copyright restrictions.

3.6.3 Access to psychological records is restricted to those permitted by law who have legitimate educational interest in the records.

3.6.4 School psychologists interpret school psychological records to non-psychologists who qualify for access.

3.6.5 School psychological records are only created and maintained when the information is necessary and relevant to legitimate educational program needs and when parents (or student if age of majority has been attained) have given their informed consent for the creation of such a record. This consent is based upon full knowledge of purposes for which information is sought, and the personnel who will have access to it. The school psychologist assumes responsibility for assuring the accuracy and relevancy of the information recorded.

3.6.6 School psychological records are systematically reviewed, and when necessary purged, in keeping with relevant federal and state laws in order to protect children from decisions based on incorrect, misleading, or out-of-date information.

4.0 STANDARDS FOR THE DELIVERY OF COMPREHENSIVE SCHOOL PSYCHOLOGICAL SERVICES

The purpose of these standards is to ensure the delivery of comprehensive services by school psychologists.

4.1 ORGANIZATION OF SCHOOL PSYCHOLOGICAL SERVICES

4.1.1 School psychological services are planned, organized, directed, and reviewed by school psychologists.

4.1.2 School psychologists participate in determining the recipients and the type of school psychological services offered.

4.1.3 The goals and objectives of school psychological services are consistent with these standards and are available in written form.

4.1.4 A written set of procedural guidelines for the delivery of school psychological services is followed and made available upon request.

4.1.5 A clearly stated referral system is in writing and is communicated to parents, staff members, students, and other referral agents.

4.1.6 The organization of school psychological services is in written form and includes lines of responsibility, supervisory, and administrative relationships.

4.1.7 Where two or more school psychologists are employed, a coordinated system of school psychological services is in effect within that unit.

4.1.8 Units providing school psychological services include sufficient professional and support personnel to achieve their goals and objectives.

4.2 RELATIONSHIP TO OTHER UNITS AND PROFESSIONALS

4.2.1 The school psychological services unit is responsive to the needs of the population that it serves. Psychological services are periodically and systematically reviewed to ensure their conformity with the needs of the population served.

4.2.2 School psychologists establish and maintain relationships with other professionals (e.g., pediatricians, bilingual specialists, audiologists) who provide services to children and families. They collaborate with these professionals in prevention, assessment, and intervention efforts as necessary. They also cooperate with advocates representing children and their families.

4.2.3 Providers of school psychological services maintain a cooperative relationship with colleagues and co-workers in the best mutual interests of clients, in a manner consistent with the goals of the employing agency. Conflicts should be resolved in a professional manner.

4.2.4 School psychologist develop plans for the delivery of services in accordance with best professional practices.

4.2.5 School psychologist employed within a school setting help coordinate the services of mental health providers from other agencies (such as community mental health centers, child guidance clinics, or private practitioners) to ensure a continuum of services.

4.2.6 School psychologists are knowledgeable about community agencies and resources. They provide liaison and consulting services to the community and agencies regarding psychological, mental health, and educational issues.

4.2.6.1 School psychologists communicate as needed with state and community agencies and professionals (e.g., child guidance clinics, community mental health center, private practitioners) regarding services for children, families, and school personnel. They refer clients to these agencies and professionals as appropriate.

4.2.6.2 School psychologists are informed of and have the opportunity to participate in community agency staffing of cases involving their clients.

4.2.6.3 Community agency personnel are invited to participate in school system conferences concerning their clients (with written parental permission).

4.3 COMPREHENSIVE SCHOOL PSYCHOLOGICAL SERVICES DELIVERY

School psychologists provide a range of services to their clients. These consist of direct and indirect services which require involvement with the entire educational system: (a) the students, teachers, administrators, and other school personnel; (b) the families, surrogate caretakers, and other community and regional agencies, and resources which support the educational process; (c) the organizational, physical, temporal, and curricular variables which play major roles within the system; and (d) a variety of other factors which may be important on an individual basis.

The intent of these services is to promote mental health and facilitate learning of students. Comprehensive school psychological services are comprised of diverse activities. These activities complement one another and therefore are most accurately viewed as being integrated and coordinated rather than discrete services. However, for descriptive purposes, they will be listed and described separately. The following are the services that comprise the delivery system:

4.3.1 CONSULTATION: the act of meeting to discuss, decide, or plan, typically regarding primary prevention or the reasons for an identified problem, and the resulting intervention(s). The school psychologist usually does not personally provide the intervention, but guides those who do. (See direct service for contrast.)

4.3.1.1 School psychologists consult and collaborate with parents, school, and outside personnel regarding mental health, behavioral, and educational concerns.

4.3.1.2 School psychologists design and develop procedures for preventing disorders, promoting mental health and learning, and improving educational systems.

4.3.1.3 School psychologists provide skill enhancement activities (such as inservice training, organizational development, parent counseling, program planning and evaluation, vocational development, and parent education

programs) to school personnel, parents, and others in the community, regarding issues of human learning, development, and behavior.

4.3.1.4 School psychologists facilitate the delivery of services by assisting those who play major roles in the educational system (i.e., parents, school personnel, community agencies.)

4.3.2 PSYCHOLOGICAL AND PSYCHOEDUCATIONAL ASSESSMENT: the process of obtaining data about human functioning according to the current practices of the fields of psychology and education for the purpose of identifying critical factors and evaluating their importance for answering referral questions.

4.3.2.1 School psychologists conduct mulifactored psychological and psychoeducational assessments of children and youth as appropriate.

4.3.2.2 Psychological and psychoeducational assessments include evaluation, as appropriate, of the areas of: personality, emotional status, social skills and adjustment, intelligence and cognitive functioning, scholastic aptitude, adaptive behavior, language and communication skills, academic knowledge and achievement, sensory and perceptual-motor functioning, educational setting, family/environmental/cultural influences, career and vocational development, aptitude, and interests.

4.3.2.3 School psychologists utilize a variety of instruments, procedures, and techniques. Interviews, observations, and behavioral evaluations are included in these procedures.

4.3.2.4 When conducting psychological and psychoeducational assessments,

335

school psychologist have explicit regard for the context and setting in which their assessments take place and will be used.

4.3.2.5 School psychologists adhere to the NASP resolutions non-biased assessment and programming for all students (see Section 3.5.3). They also are familiar with and consider the *Standards for Educational and Psychological Tests* (developed by APA, AERA, and NCME) and other related publications in the use of assessment techniques.

4.3.3 **DIRECT SERVICE:** techniques applied in a face-to-face situation (e.g. individual/group counseling, classroom-based interventions, etc.) designed to enhance the mental health, behavior, personality, social competency, academic or educational status of the student/client, or prevent difficulties in these areas. (*Contrast with consultation*).

4.3.3.1 School psychologists provide direct service to facilitate the functioning of individuals, groups, and/or organizations.

4.3.3.2 School psychologists design direct service programs to enhance cognitive, affective, social, and vocational development.

4.3.3.3 School psychologists develop collaborative relationships with their clients and involve them in the assessment, direct service, and program evaluation procedures.

4.3.4 **SUPERVISION:** the process of overseeing and managing the activities of a school psychologist for the purpose of quality assurance, assistance with difficult assignments, and the improvement of performance.

4.3.4.1 School psychologists provide and/or engage in supervision, peer review, and continuing professional development as specified in Section 3.2. and 4.6.

4.3.5 **RESEARCH:** the process of careful, systematic investigation to discover or establish facts.

4.3.5.1 School psychologists design, conduct, report, and utilize the results of research of a psychological and educational nature. All research conducted is in accordance with relevant ethical guidelines of the profession (e.g., *APA Ethical Principles in the Conduct of Research with Human Participants*), with particular concern for obtaining informed consent, notifying subjects of the expected length of participation, and protecting subjects from breach of confidentiality, coercion, harm, or danger. Applied and/or basic research should be pursued, focusing on:

a Psychological functioning of human beings;

b Psychoeducational assessment tools and procedures;

c Educational programs and techniques applied to individual cases and groups of various sizes;

d Educational processes;

e Social system interactions and organizational factors associated with school communities; and

f Psychological treatments and techniques applied to individual cases or groups.

4.3.5.2 School psychologists' involvement in research can range from support or advisory services to having direct responsibility for one or more major components of a research project. These components may include planning, data collecting, data analyzing, disseminating, and translating research into practical applications within the school community.

4.3.6 PROGRAM PLANNING AND EVALUATION: the process of designing and judging the effectiveness of educational structures at all levels.

4.3.6.1 School psychologists provide program planning and evaluation services to assist in decision-making activities.

4.3.6.2 School psychologists serve on committees responsible for developing and planning educational and educationally-related activities.

4.4 AUTONOMOUS FUNCTIONING

School psychologists have professional autonomy in determining the nature, scope, and extent of their specific services. These activities are defined within the profession, although school psychologists frequently collaborate with and seek advice from others in determining appropriate services delivery. Legal, ethical, and professional standards and guidelines are considered by the practitioner in making decisions regarding practice. All practice is restricted to those areas in which the school psychologist has received formal training and supervised experience.

4.4.1 PROFESSIONAL RESPONSIBILITY AND BEST PRACTICES

Professional autonomy is associated with professional responsibility. The ultimate responsibility for providing appropriate comprehensive school psychological services rests with the individual practitioner.

While being cognizant of the fact that there often are not explicit guidelines to follow in providing comprehensive school psychological services, the individual practitioner has a responsibility to adhere to the best available and most appropriate standards of practice. There is no substitute for sensitive, sound, professional judgment in the determination of what constitutes best practice. Active involvement in supervision and other continuing professional development activities will assist the practitioner in adhering to best professional practices.

4.5 INDEPENDENT PRACTICE

A credentialed school psychologist who has completed a school psychology training program which meets the criteria specified in the NASP *Standards for Training and Field Placement Programs in School Psychology* and three years of satisfactory, properly supervised experience is considered qualified for personally supervised, independent practice with peer review, regardless of work setting. (NOTE: "independent practice" as used in this paragraph refers to autonomous functioning within the employing agency. Contrast this with the licensure rules various states have for "private practice".)

4.6 CONTINUING PROFESSIONAL DEVELOPMENT

The practice of school psychology has and will continue to undergo significant changes as new knowledge and technological advances are introduced. The development of new intervention techniques, assessment procedures, computerized assistance, and so forth, will require that practitioners keep abreast of these innovations as well as obtain appropriate professional education and training in these areas. All school psychologists will actively participate in activities designed to continue, enhance, and upgrade their professional training and skills to help ensure quality service provision. These efforts are documented by participation in Continuing

337

Professional Development (CPD) programs, as sponsored by NASP and other organizations, although they are not limited to such activities. Memberships in professional organizations, reading of professional journals and books, discussions of professional issues with colleagues, and so forth, are also an integral component of a school psychologist's overall CPD activity.

4.6.1 Participation in CPD activities and the maintenance of high professional standards and practice are continuing obligations of the school psychologist. These obligations are assumed when one initially engages in the practice of school psychology and should be required for continued credentialing.

4.6.2 School psychologists receive supervision by a supervising school psychologist for the first three years of full-time employment (or the equivalent) as a school psychologist. The supervisor shares professional responsibility and accountability for the services provided. While the level and extent of supervision may vary, the supervisor maintains a sufficiently close relationship to meet this standard. Individual face-to-face supervision is engaged in for a minimum of one hour per week or the equivalent (e.g., two hours bi-weekly). Standards for intern supervision are contained in the NASP *Standards for Training and Field Placement Programs in School Psychology*.

4.6.3 After completion of the first three years of supervision, all school psychologists continue to engage in supervision and/or peer review on a regular basis, and further their professional development by actively participating in CPD activities. The level and extent of these activities may vary depending on the needs, interest, and goals of the school psychologist, with more comprehensive service delivery requiring more

extensive related professional exchanges. At a minimum, however, these activities are at the level required for successful participation in an appropriate CPD program.

4.6.4 School psychologists, who after three years no longer have required supervision, engage in peer review activities. These may include discussion of cases and professional issues designed to assist with problem solving, decision-making, and appropriate practice.

4.6.5 School psychologists readily seek additional assistance from supervisors, peers, or colleagues with particularly complex or difficult cases, and/or when expanding their services into new areas or those in which they infrequently practice (e.g., low incidence assessment).

4.6.6 Nationally Certified School Psychologists engage in continuing professional development as a requirement of certificate renewal.

4.7 ACCOUNTABILITY

4.7.1 School psychologists perform their duties in an accountable manner by keeping records of these efforts, evaluating their effectiveness, and modifying their practices and/or expanding their services as needed.

4.7.2 School psychologists devise systems of accountability and outcome evaluation which aid in documenting the effectiveness of intervention efforts and other services they provide.

4.7.3 Within their service delivery plan, school psychologist include a regular evaluation of their progress in achieving goals. This evaluation should include consideration of the cost effectiveness of school psychological services in terms of time, money, and resources, as well as the availability of professional and support personnel. Evaluation of the school psychological delivery system

338

is conducted internally, and when possible, externally as well (e.g., through state educational agency review, peer review). This evaluation includes an assessment of effectiveness, efficiency, continuity, availability, and adequacy of services.

4.7.4 School psychologists are accountable for their services. They should make information available about their services, and provide consumers with the opportunity to participate in decision-making concerning such issues as initiation, termination, continuation, modification, and evaluation of their services. Rights of the consumer should be taken into account when performing these activities.

4.8 PRIVATE PRACTICE

4.8.1 School psychologists practicing in the private sector provide comprehensive services and adhere to the same standards and guidelines as those providing services in the public sector.

4.8.2 School psychologists document that they have formal training, supervised experience, licensure and/or certification, and demonstrated competence, in any areas of service they intend to deliver to clients within the private sector. They also have a responsibility to actively engage in CPD activities.

4.8.3 School psychologists in private practice adhere to the NASP *Principles for Professional Ethics*, and practice only within their area of competence. If the services needed by clients fall outside the school psychologist's area of competence, they are referred elsewhere for assistance.

4.8.4 It is the responsibility of the school psychologist engaging in private practice to inform the client that school psychological services are available without charge from the client's local school district.

4.8.5 School psychologists do not provide services on a private basis to students who attend the school(s) to which the school psychologist is assigned, or would normally be expected to serve. This includes students who attend non-public schools served by the school psychologist.

4.8.6 School psychologists offering school psychological services in the private sector ensure that, prior to the commencement of treatment/services, the client fully understands any and all fees associated with the services, and any potential financial assistance that may be available (i.e., third-party reimbursement).

4.8.7 Parents must be informed by the school psychologist that if a private school psychological evaluation is to be completed, this evaluation constitutes only one portion of a multidisciplinary team evaluation. Private services must be equally comprehensive to those described in Section 4.3.

4.8.8 School psychologists in private practice provide and maintain written records in a manner consistent with Section 3.6.

4.9 PROFESSIONAL ETHICS AND GUIDELINES

Each school psychologist practices in full accordance with the NASP *Principles for Professional Ethics*, and these *Standards*.

5.0 STANDARDS FOR SCHOOL PSYCHOLOGY TRAINING PROGRAM

Each school psychology training pr~~~le should meet the criteria specifie~~ield NASP *Standards for Training* ~~ogy. *Placement Programs in School P*

339

REFERENCES

American Psychological Association. (1974). Rules and Procedures - Committee on Scientific and Professional Ethics and Conduct. *American Psychologist*, 703-710.

American Psychological Association. (1980, February 22-23). Amendments in CSPEC's Rules and Procedures. (As documented in the non-confidential minutes of CSPEC's Action Agenda). Washington, D.C.: Author.

American Psychological Association. (1995). *Ethical Principles of Psychologists and Code of Conduct*. Washington, D.C.: Author.

American Psychological Association. (1997). *Ethical Standards of Psychologists*. Washington, D.C.: Author.

Bersoff, D.N. (1980, February 6). Review of CSPEC Rules and Procedures. (American Psychological Association Memorandum). Washington, D.C.: American Psychological Association.

Bersoff, D.N. (1995) *Ethical Conflicts in Psychology*. Washington, D.C.: American Psychological Association

Bowser, P.B.(1995). Best Practices in Professional Conduct: Meeting NASP's Ethical Standards. In Thomas, A. & Grimes, J. (Eds.) *Best Practices in School Psychology - III*. Washington, D.C.: The National Association of School Psychologists.

Illinois Psychological Association. (1975). *Revised Procedural Guidelines for Ethics Committee. Illinois Psychologist*. 23-31.

Illinois School Psychologists Association. (1980). *Procedures for Handling Complaints of Alleged Violations of Ethical Principles*.

National Association of School Psychologists (1974). *Principles of Professional Ethics*. Washington, D.C.: Author.

ional Association of School Psychologists. (1974). Procedures for Handling of Complaints of Alleged ilations of Ethical Principles. Washington, D.C.: Author.

Natic
*NA*ssociation of School Psychologists. (1990). National School Psychology Certification System. *erations Handbook*. Washington, D.C.:Author.

National A
Professidion of School Psychologists. (1992). Professional Conduct Manual: Principles for
Maryland: ics and Standards for the Provision of School Psychological Services. Silver Springs,

ACKNOWLEDGEMENTS

Contributors to previous editions of the *Professional Conduct Manual* include: Carolyn Allen, William Allen, Russell Armour, David W. Barnett, Thomas Barry, George Batsche, David Bolocofsky, Philip Bowser, John Boyle, John Brandt, John C. Brandtley, Rhonda Broadwater, Andrea Canter, Karen Carey, Barbara Chaplik, M. Judy Claxton, Deborah Clemmensen, Kevin Coats, John H. Correll, W. Alan Coulter, Mike Curtis, Peg Dawson, John DeFrancesco, Caroline DeMar, Kristal Ehrhardt, Art Eichbauer, Ann Ertz, Mel Franklin, Sharon Goskoski, Janet Graden, Stuart N. Hart, Mary Anne Healy-Romanello, Larry Hilgert, Thomas Huberty, Mari Irvin, Reid Johnson, Nicola Jordan, Howard Knoff, Sue Leahy, Sophie Lovinger, Michael Martin, Liz McDaniel, Marcia McEvoy, Thomas McMahan, David Peterson, Bill Pfohl, Charlene R. Ponti, Karen Pritchard, John Reinhardt, Donna Reisbec, Connie Reyes, Wilma Rush, Owen Saunders, Ed Schlossman, Eleanor Smith, Mary Ann Sullivan, Peter Whelley, Markay Winston, Joseph E. Zins.